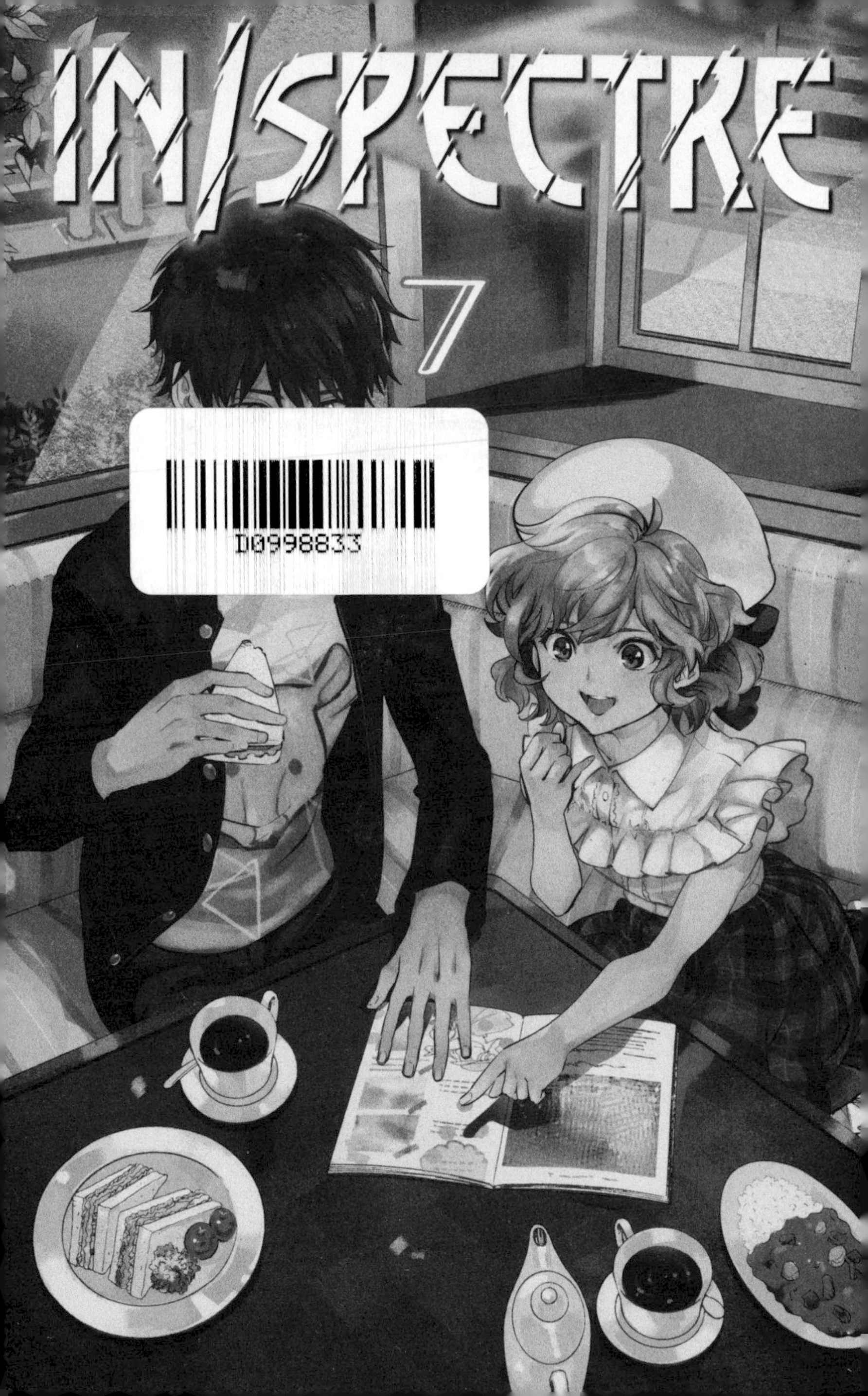
IN/SPECTRE
7

CONTENTS

CHAPTER 14: "A FAVORITE CAFÉ"   3

CHAPTER 15: "WHAT THE GUARDIAN SERPENT HEARD"   31

CHAPTER 16: "LUCKY DAY AT THE UNAGI RESTAURANT"   125

BONUS MANGA   198

CHAPTER 14: "A FAVORITE CAFÉ"

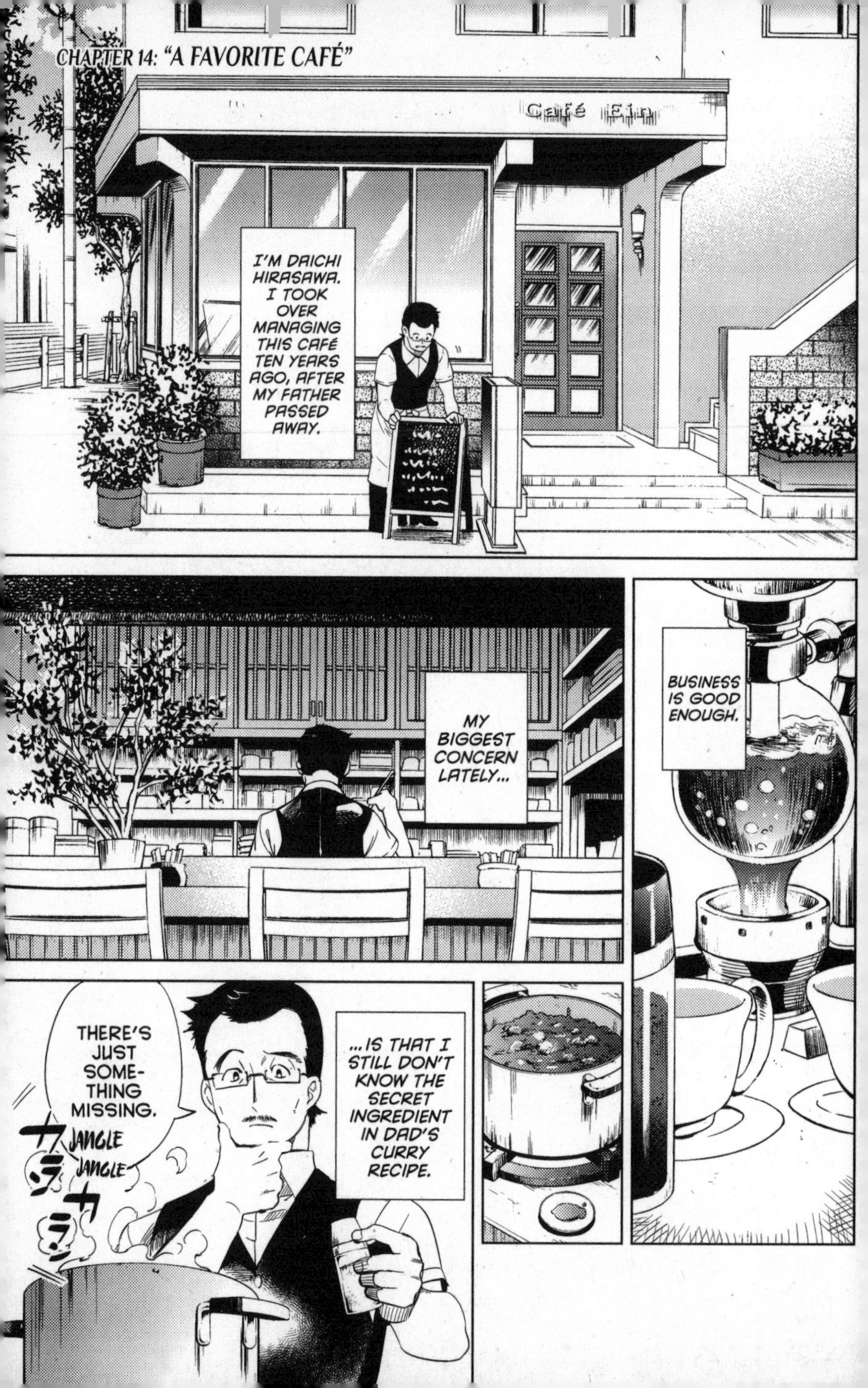
Café Ein
I'M DAICHI HIRASAWA. I TOOK OVER MANAGING THIS CAFÉ TEN YEARS AGO, AFTER MY FATHER PASSED AWAY.
BUSINESS IS GOOD ENOUGH.
MY BIGGEST CONCERN LATELY...
...IS THAT I STILL DON'T KNOW THE SECRET INGREDIENT IN DAD'S CURRY RECIPE.
THERE'S JUST SOME-THING MISSING.
JANGLE JANGLE

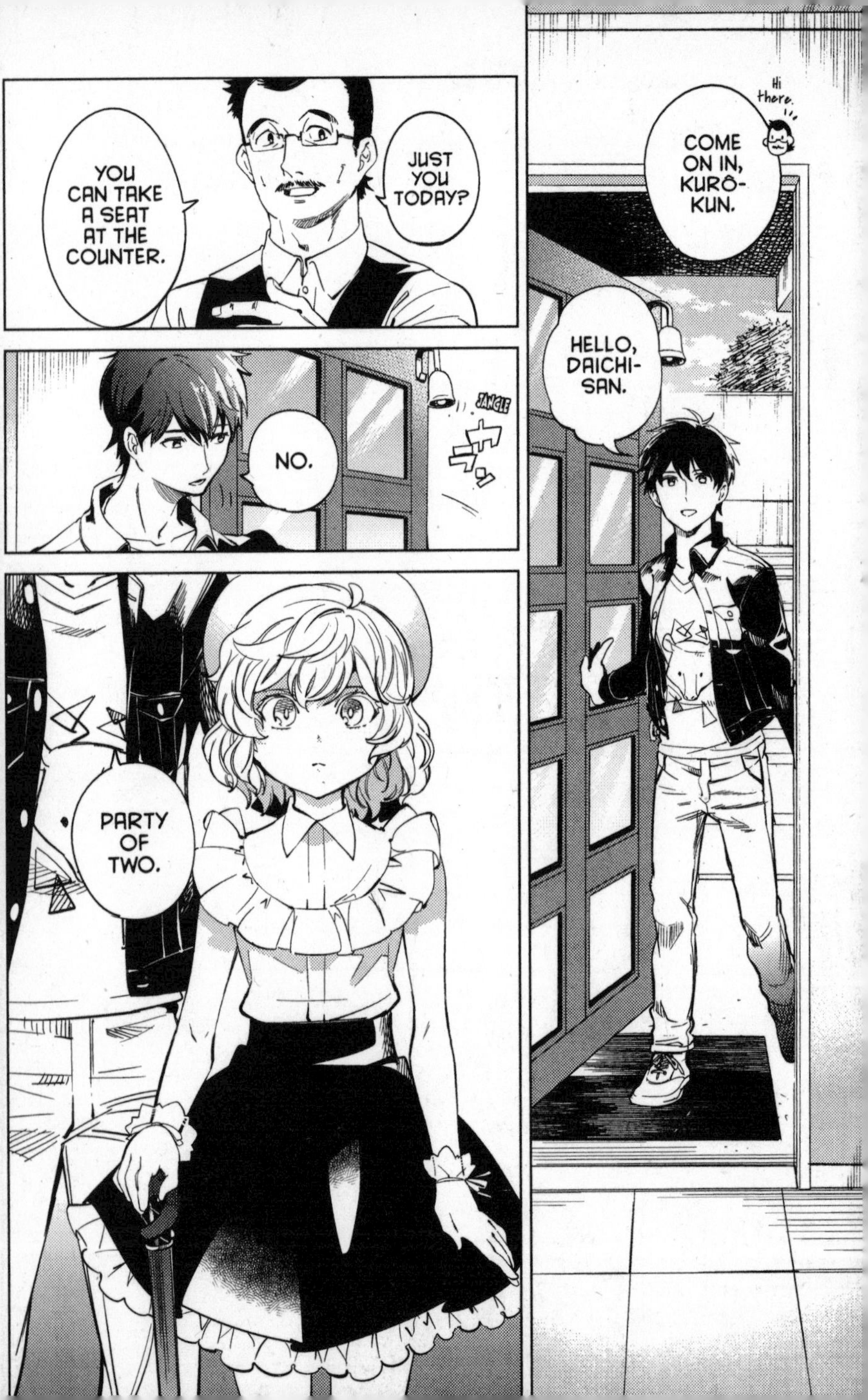

Hi there.
COME ON IN, KURÔ-KUN.
HELLO, DAICHI-SAN.
JUST YOU TODAY?
YOU CAN TAKE A SEAT AT THE COUNTER.
JANGLE
NO.
PARTY OF TWO.

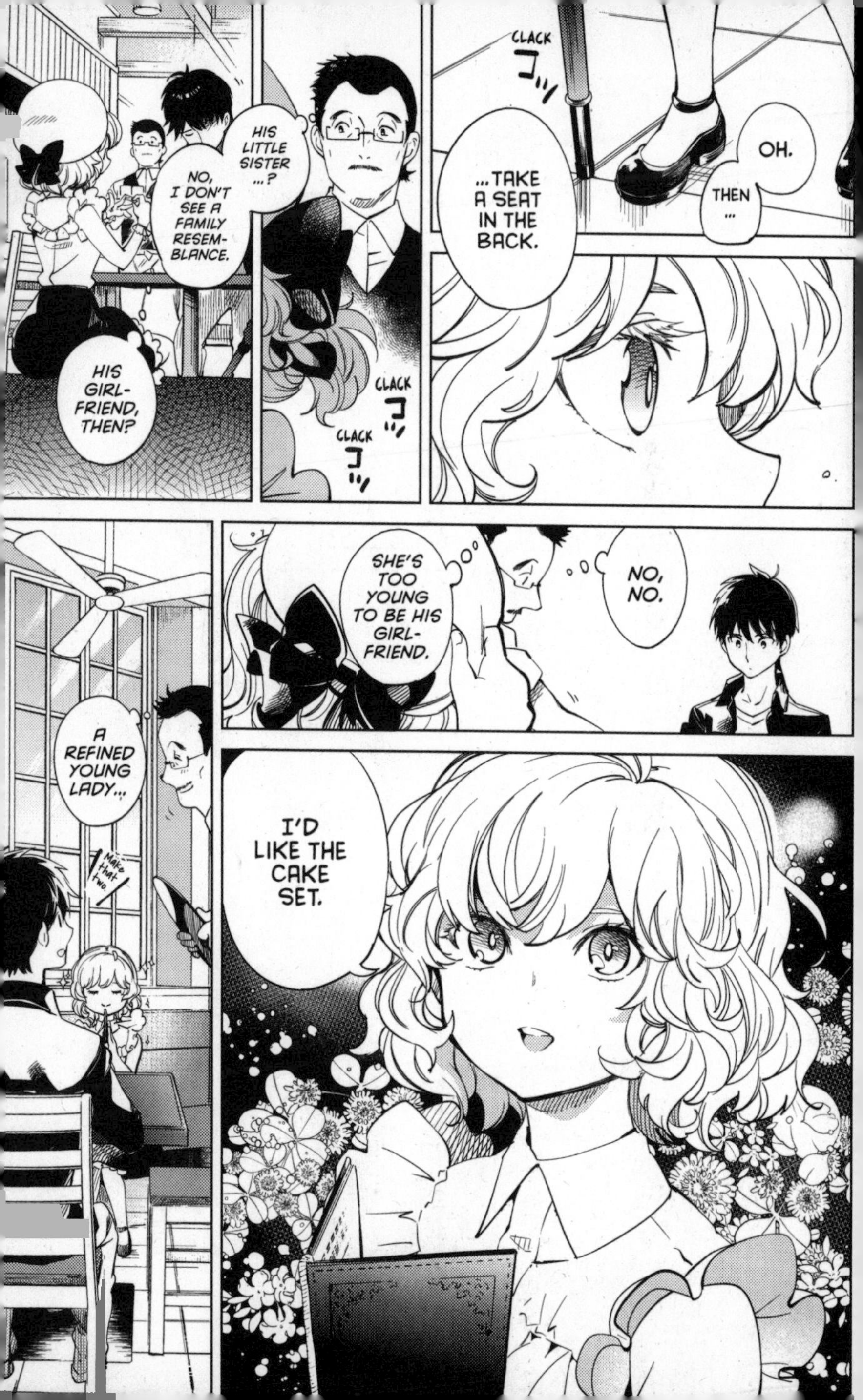
OH.
THEN ...
CLACK ゴッ
...TAKE A SEAT IN THE BACK.
HIS LITTLE SISTER ...?
CLACK ゴッ
CLACK ゴッ
NO, I DON'T SEE A FAMILY RESEMBLANCE.
HIS GIRLFRIEND, THEN?
NO, NO.
SHE'S TOO YOUNG TO BE HIS GIRLFRIEND.
I'D LIKE THE CAKE SET.
A REFINED YOUNG LADY...
Make that two.

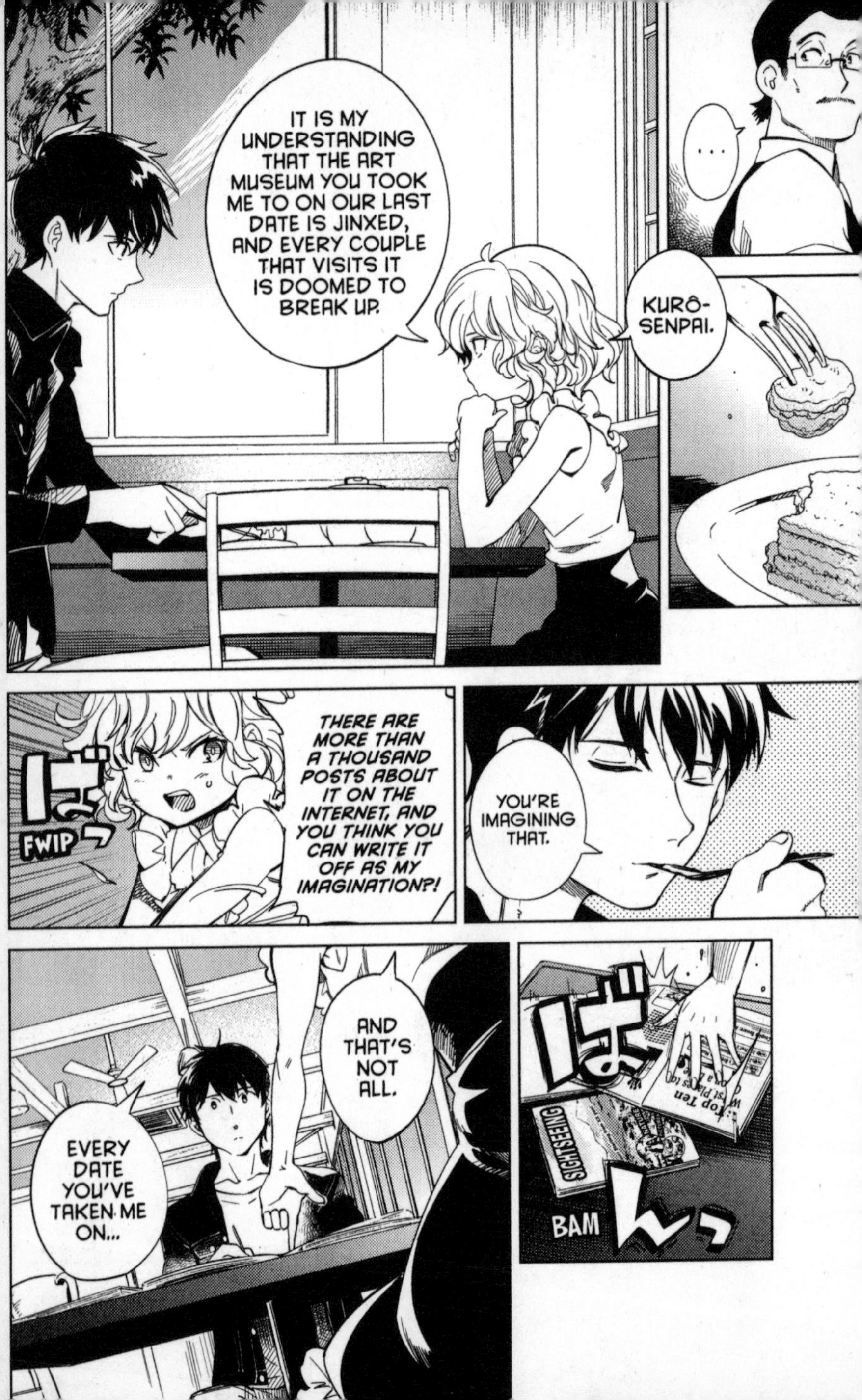

...
KURÔ-SENPAI.
IT IS MY UNDERSTANDING THAT THE ART MUSEUM YOU TOOK ME TO ON OUR LAST DATE IS JINXED, AND EVERY COUPLE THAT VISITS IT IS DOOMED TO BREAK UP.
YOU'RE IMAGINING THAT.
FWIP
THERE ARE MORE THAN A THOUSAND POSTS ABOUT IT ON THE INTERNET, AND YOU THINK YOU CAN WRITE IT OFF AS MY IMAGINATION?!
Top Ten
SIGHTSEEING
BAM
AND THAT'S NOT ALL.
EVERY DATE YOU'VE TAKEN ME ON...

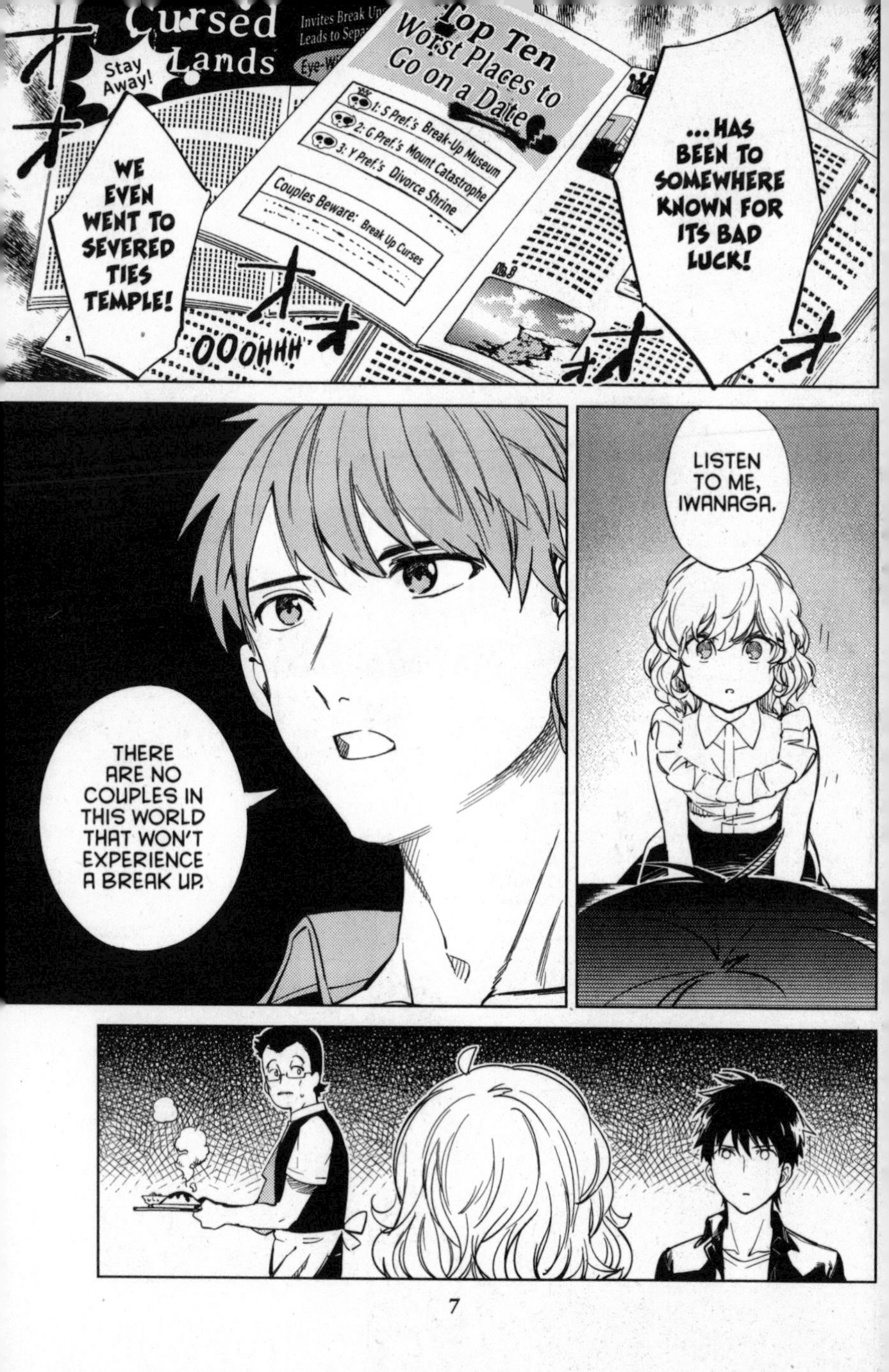
Top Ten Worst Places to Go on a Date
1: S Pref.'s Break-Up Museum
2: G Pref.'s Mount Catastrophe
3: Y Pref.'s Divorce Shrine
Couples Beware: Break Up Curses
No.8
Cursed Lands
Stay Away!
...HAS BEEN TO SOMEWHERE KNOWN FOR ITS BAD LUCK!
WE EVEN WENT TO SEVERED TIES TEMPLE!
OOOHHH
LISTEN TO ME, IWANAGA.
THERE ARE NO COUPLES IN THIS WORLD THAT WON'T EXPERIENCE A BREAK UP.

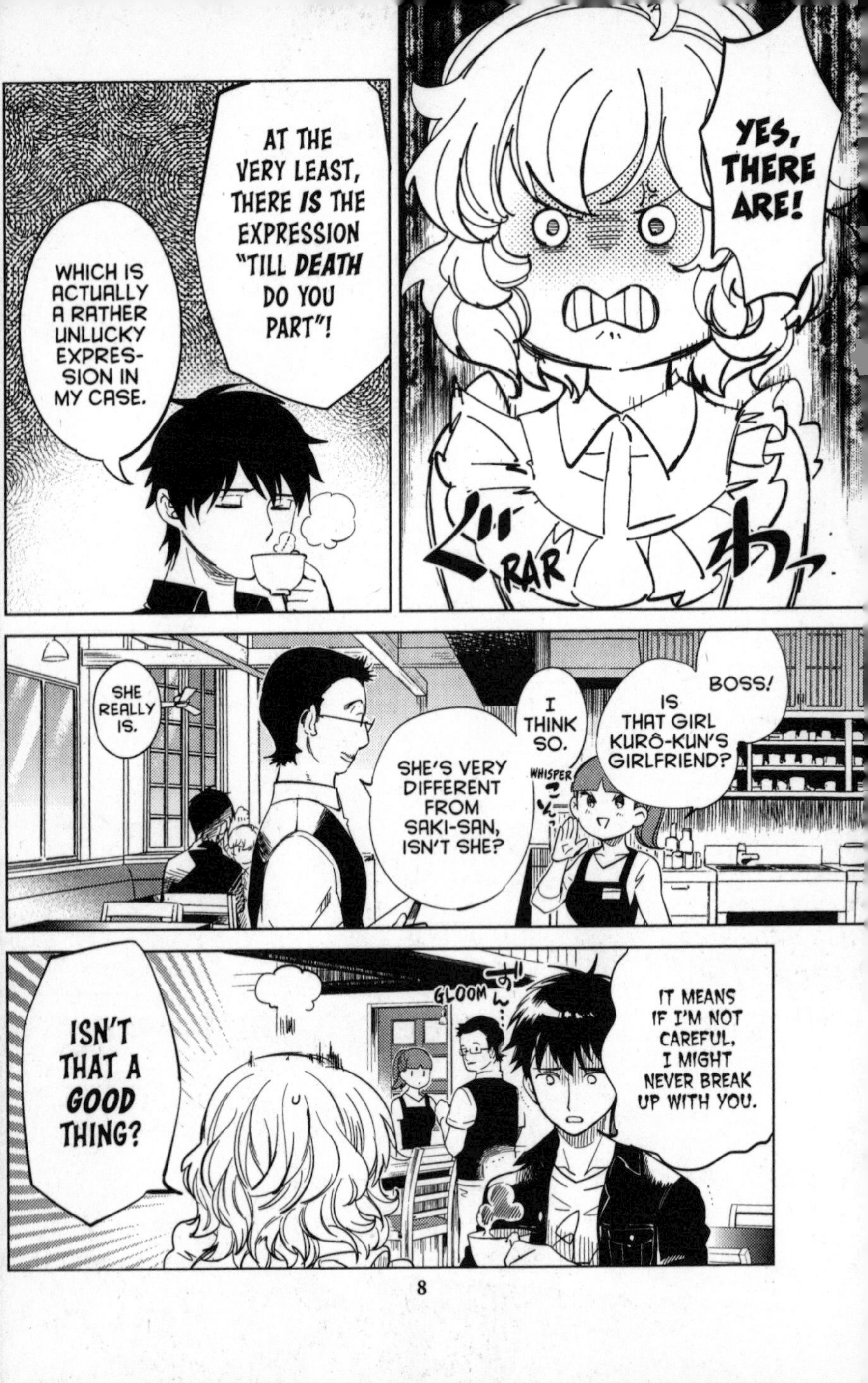
YES, THERE ARE!
RAR
AT THE VERY LEAST, THERE IS THE EXPRESSION "TILL DEATH DO YOU PART"!
WHICH IS ACTUALLY A RATHER UNLUCKY EXPRES-SION IN MY CASE.
BOSS!
IS THAT GIRL KURÔ-KUN'S GIRLFRIEND?
I THINK SO.
WHISPER
SHE'S VERY DIFFERENT FROM SAKI-SAN, ISN'T SHE?
SHE REALLY IS.
IT MEANS IF I'M NOT CAREFUL, I MIGHT NEVER BREAK UP WITH YOU.
GLOOM
ISN'T THAT A GOOD THING?

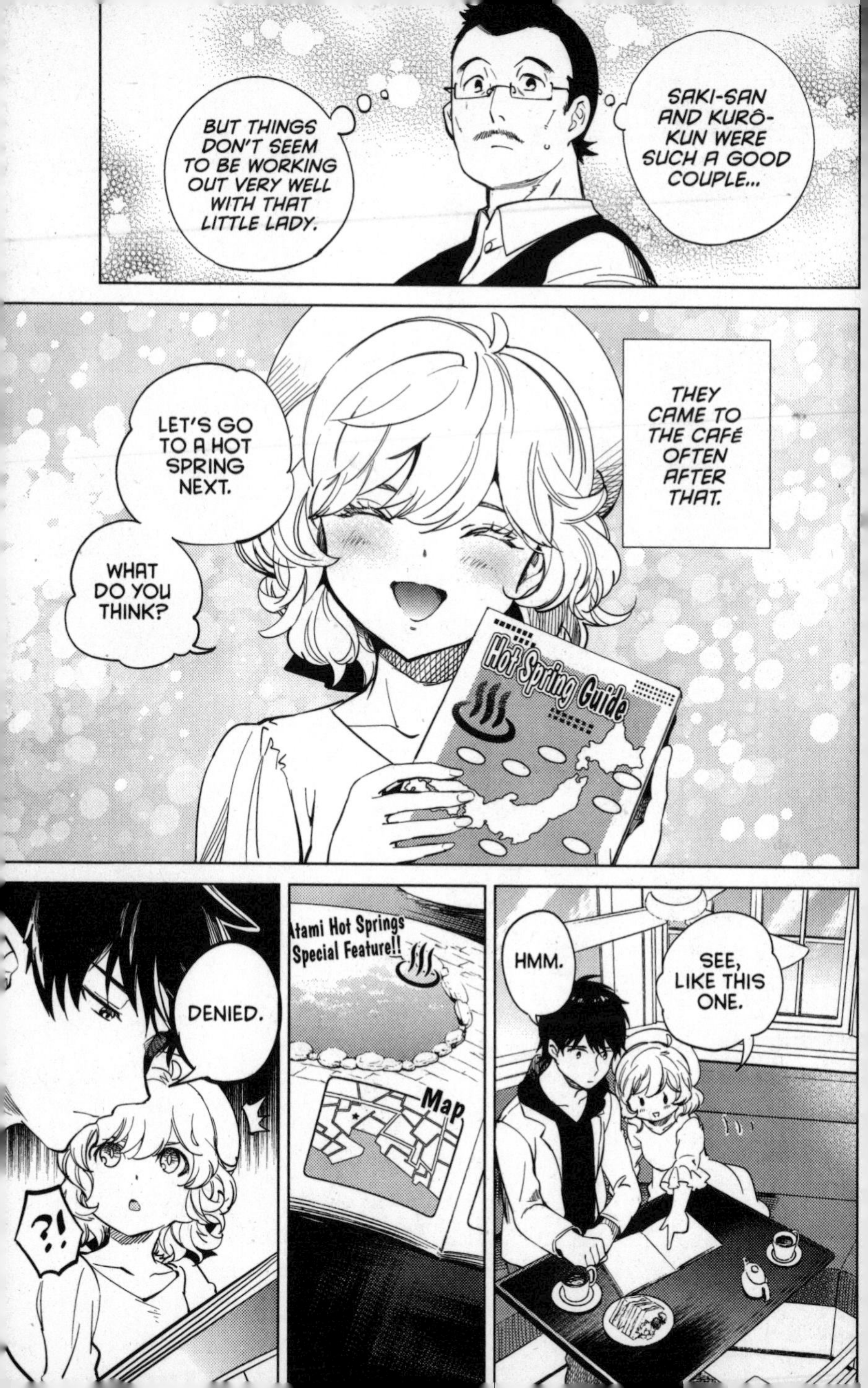
SAKI-SAN AND KURÔ-KUN WERE SUCH A GOOD COUPLE...
BUT THINGS DON'T SEEM TO BE WORKING OUT VERY WELL WITH THAT LITTLE LADY.
THEY CAME TO THE CAFÉ OFTEN AFTER THAT.
LET'S GO TO A HOT SPRING NEXT.
WHAT DO YOU THINK?
Hot Spring Guide
SEE, LIKE THIS ONE.
HMM.
Atami Hot Springs Special Feature!!
Map
DENIED.
?!

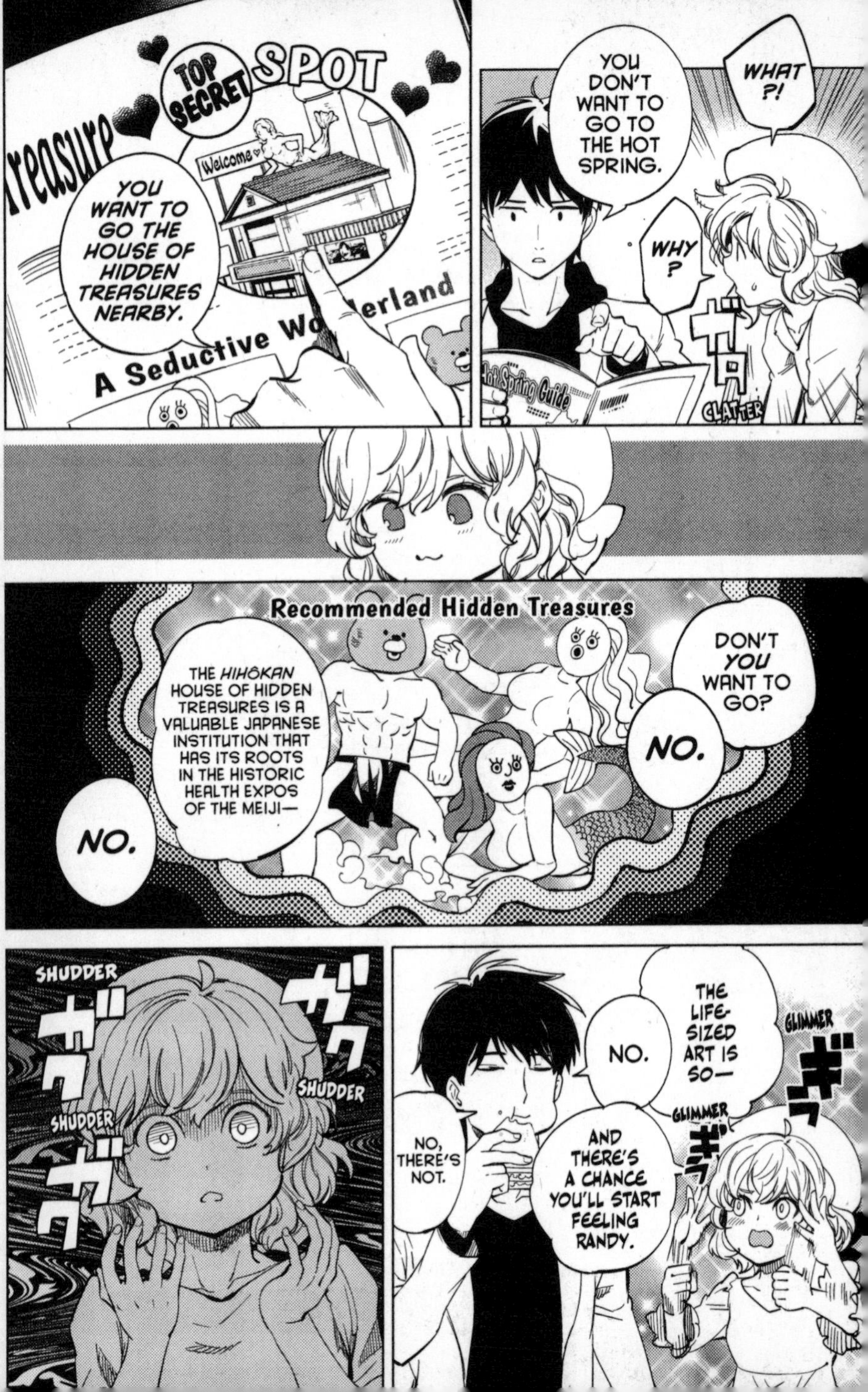

WHAT ?!
YOU DON'T WANT TO GO TO THE HOT SPRING.
WHY ?
CLATTER
Hot Spring Guide
TOP SECRET SPOT
Treasure
Welcome
YOU WANT TO GO THE HOUSE OF HIDDEN TREASURES NEARBY.
A Seductive Wo
erland
Recommended Hidden Treasures
DON'T *YOU* WANT TO GO?
NO.
THE *HIHÔKAN* HOUSE OF HIDDEN TREASURES IS A VALUABLE JAPANESE INSTITUTION THAT HAS ITS ROOTS IN THE HISTORIC HEALTH EXPOS OF THE MEIJI—
NO.
GLIMMER
THE LIFE-SIZED ART IS SO—
NO.
GLIMMER
AND THERE'S A CHANCE YOU'LL START FEELING RANDY.
NO, THERE'S NOT.
SHUDDER
SHUDDER
SHUDDER

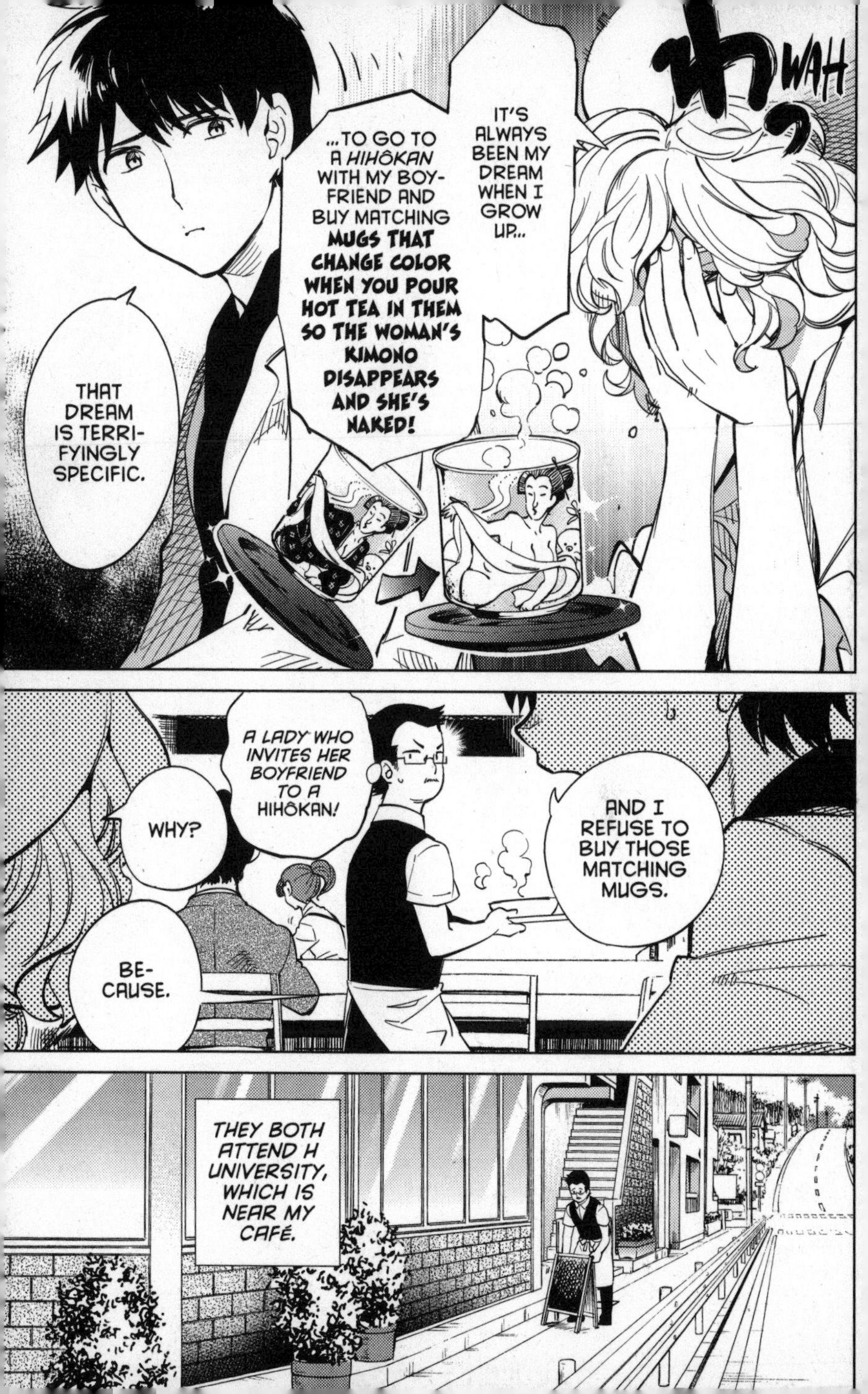
わ WAH
IT'S ALWAYS BEEN MY DREAM WHEN I GROW UP...
...TO GO TO A HIHÔKAN WITH MY BOYFRIEND AND BUY MATCHING MUGS THAT CHANGE COLOR WHEN YOU POUR HOT TEA IN THEM SO THE WOMAN'S KIMONO DISAPPEARS AND SHE'S NAKED!
THAT DREAM IS TERRIFYINGLY SPECIFIC.
AND I REFUSE TO BUY THOSE MATCHING MUGS.
A LADY WHO INVITES HER BOYFRIEND TO A HIHÔKAN!
WHY?
BECAUSE.
THEY BOTH ATTEND H UNIVERSITY, WHICH IS NEAR MY CAFÉ.

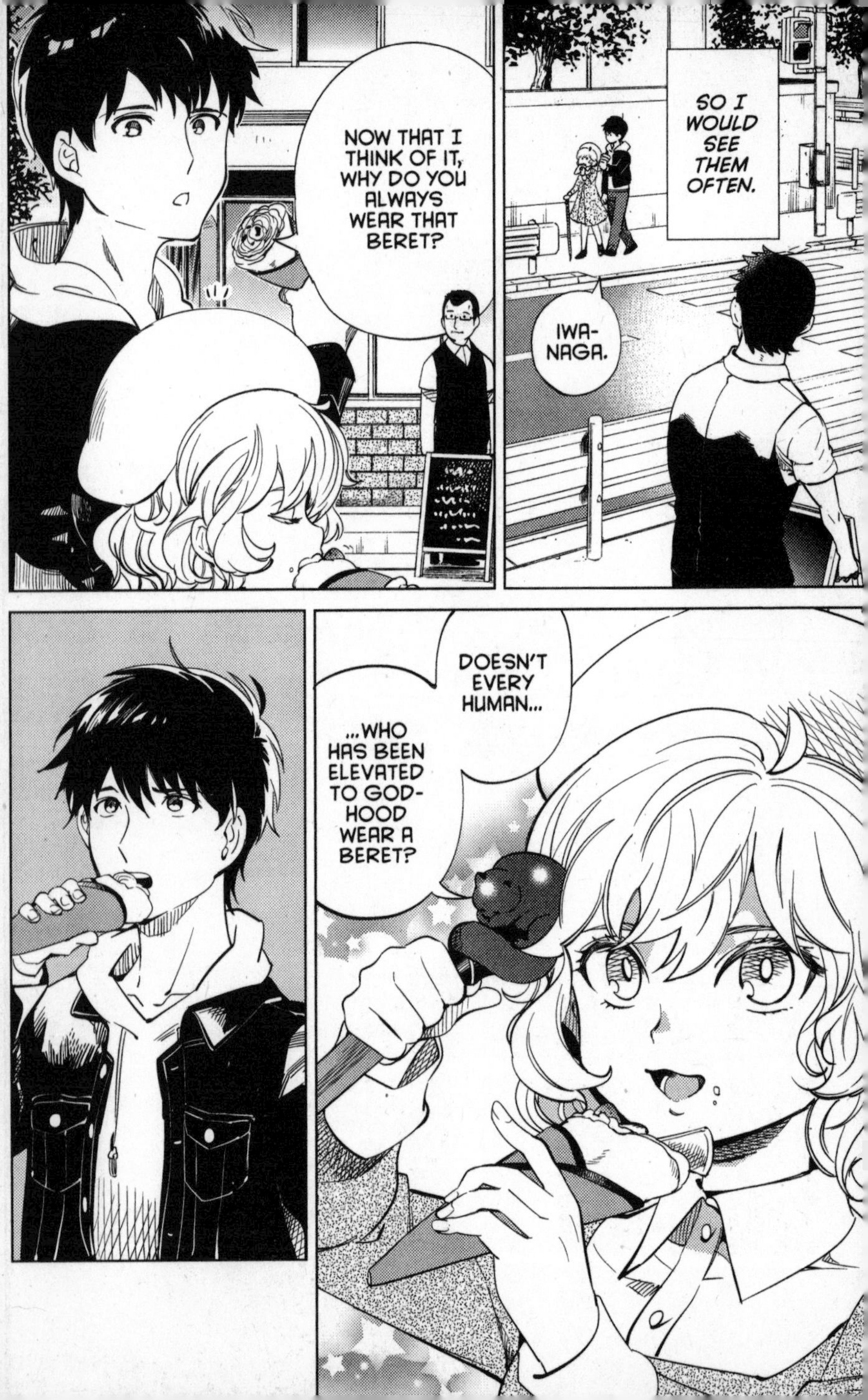
SO I WOULD SEE THEM OFTEN.
IWA-NAGA.
NOW THAT I THINK OF IT, WHY DO YOU ALWAYS WEAR THAT BERET?
DOESN'T EVERY HUMAN...
...WHO HAS BEEN ELEVATED TO GOD-HOOD WEAR A BERET?

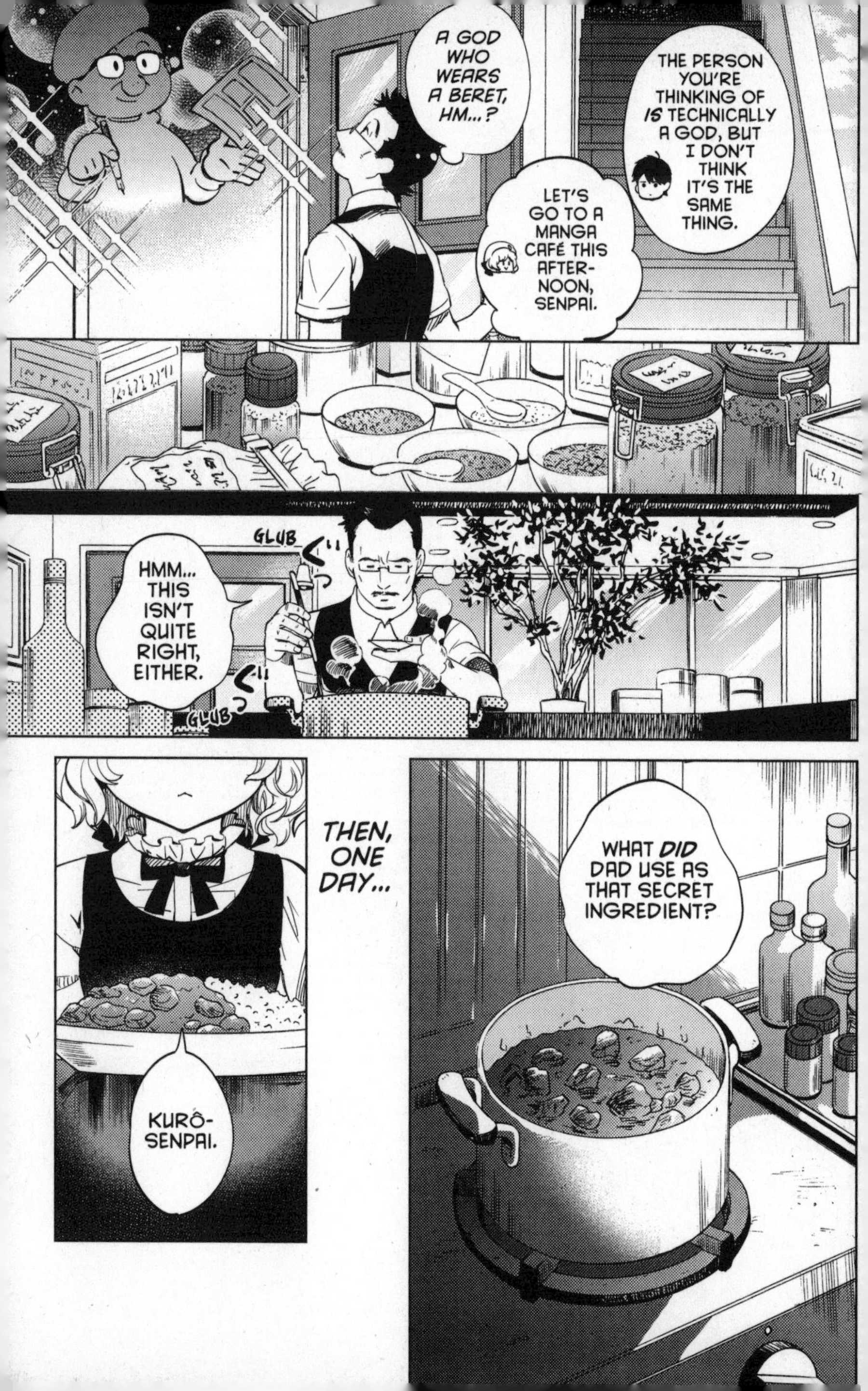
A GOD WHO WEARS A BERET, HM...?
THE PERSON YOU'RE THINKING OF *IS* TECHNICALLY A GOD, BUT I DON'T THINK IT'S THE SAME THING.
LET'S GO TO A MANGA CAFÉ THIS AFTERNOON, SENPAI.
GLUB
HMM... THIS ISN'T QUITE RIGHT, EITHER.
GLUB
WHAT *DID* DAD USE AS THAT SECRET INGREDIENT?
THEN, ONE DAY...
KURÔ-SENPAI.

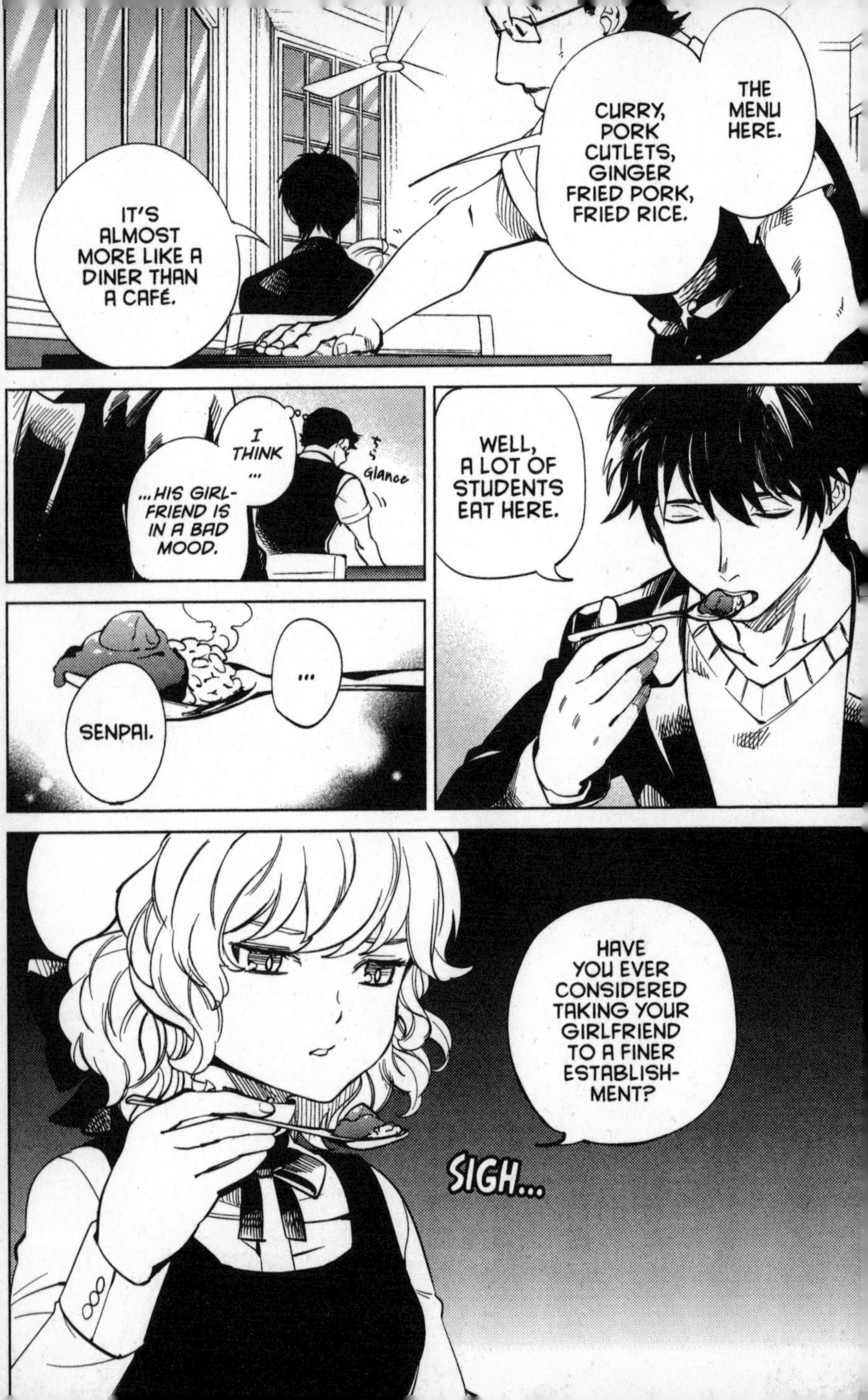
THE MENU HERE.
CURRY, PORK CUTLETS, GINGER FRIED PORK, FRIED RICE.
IT'S ALMOST MORE LIKE A DINER THAN A CAFÉ.
WELL, A LOT OF STUDENTS EAT HERE.
Glance
I THINK ...
...HIS GIRL-FRIEND IS IN A BAD MOOD.
...
SENPAI.
HAVE YOU EVER CONSIDERED TAKING YOUR GIRLFRIEND TO A FINER ESTABLISH-MENT?
SIGH...

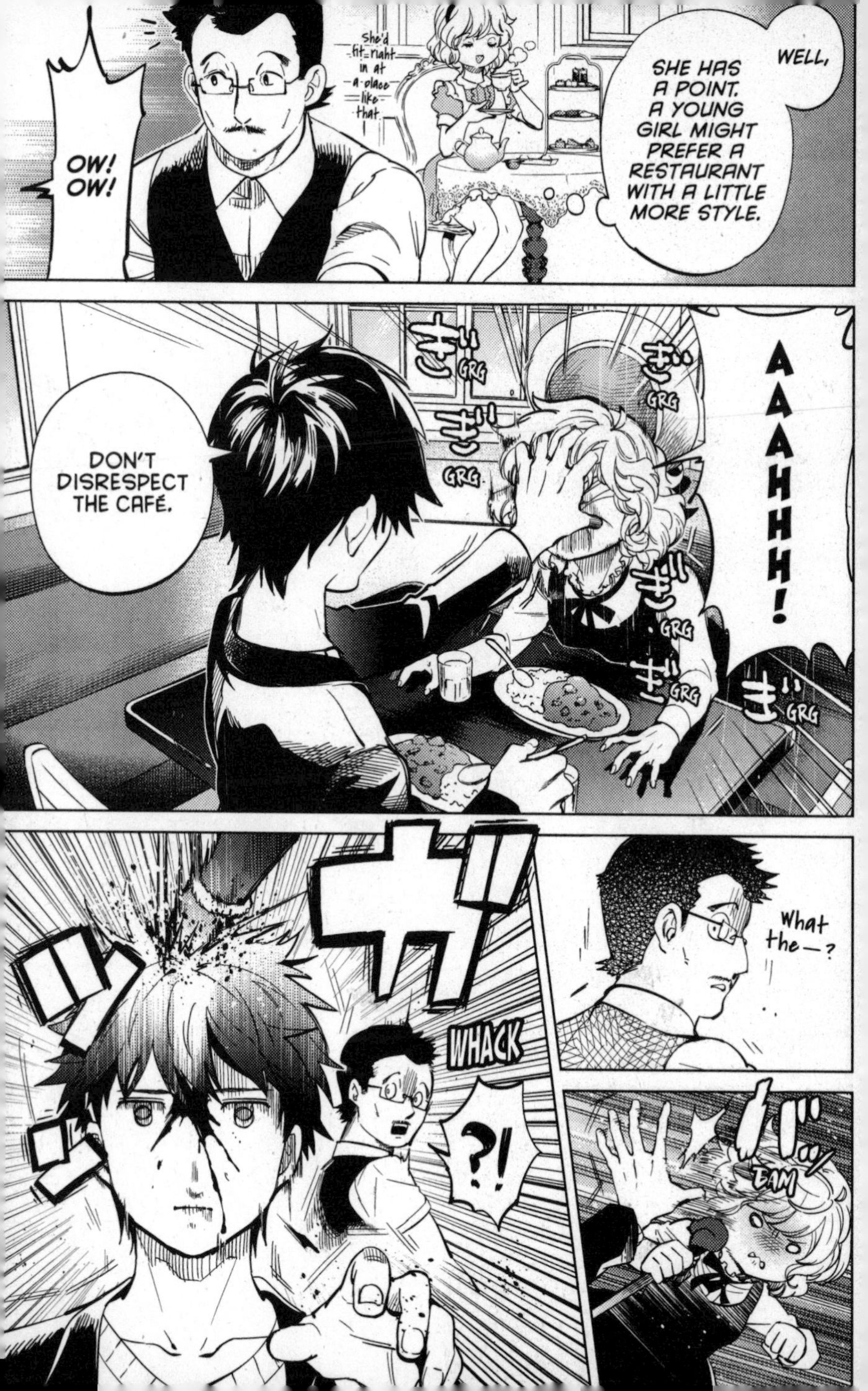
WELL, SHE HAS A POINT. A YOUNG GIRL MIGHT PREFER A RESTAURANT WITH A LITTLE MORE STYLE.
She'd fit right in at a place like that.
OW! OW!
AAAHHH!
GRG
GRG
GRG
GRG
GRG
GRG
DON'T DISRESPECT THE CAFÉ.
What the—?
BAM
WHACK
?!

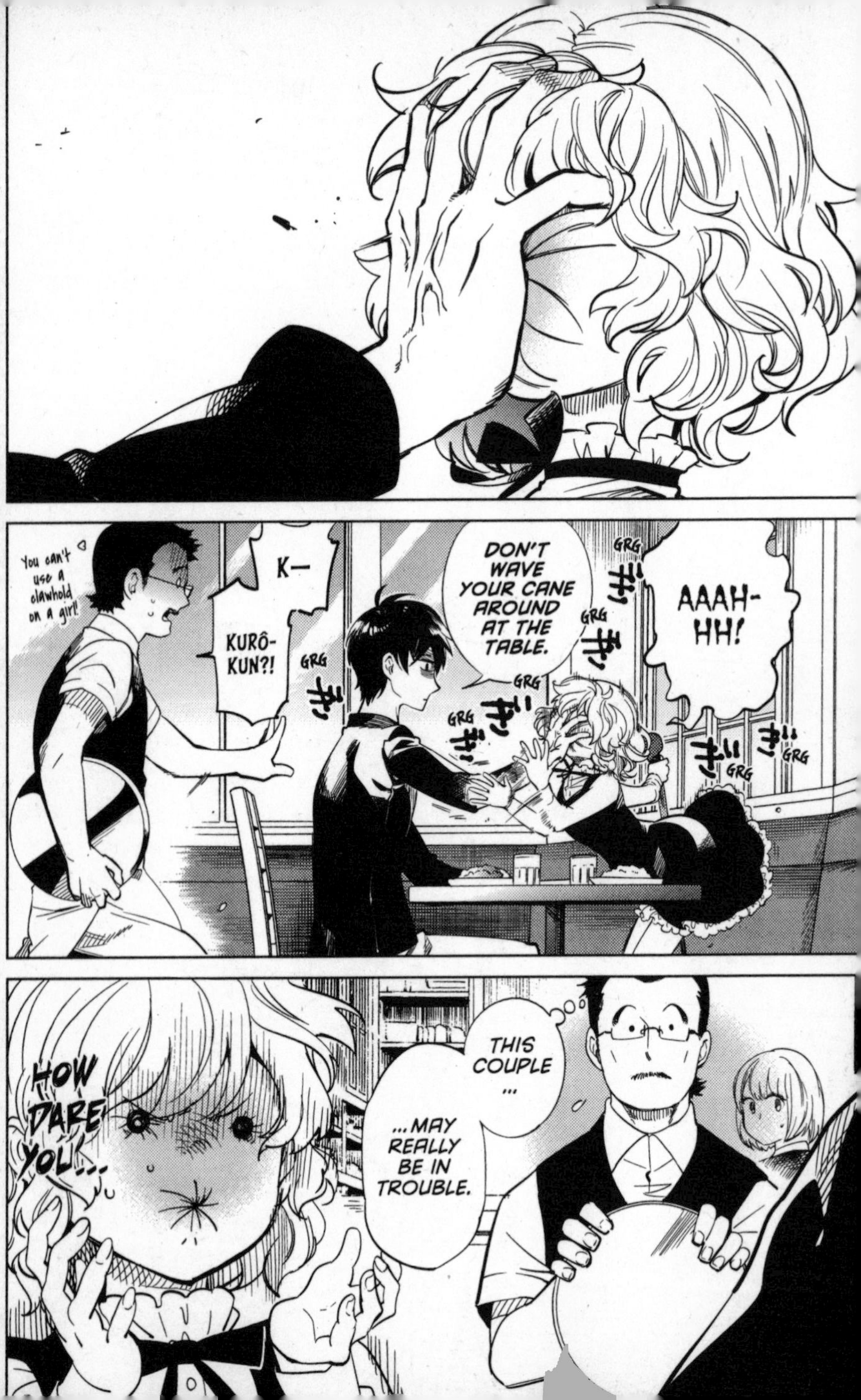
AAAH-HH!
GRG GRG GRG GRG
DON'T WAVE YOUR CANE AROUND AT THE TABLE.
GRG GRG GRG GRG
K—
KURÔ-KUN?!
You can't use a clawhold on a girl!
THIS COUPLE ...
...MAY REALLY BE IN TROUBLE.
HOW DARE YOU...

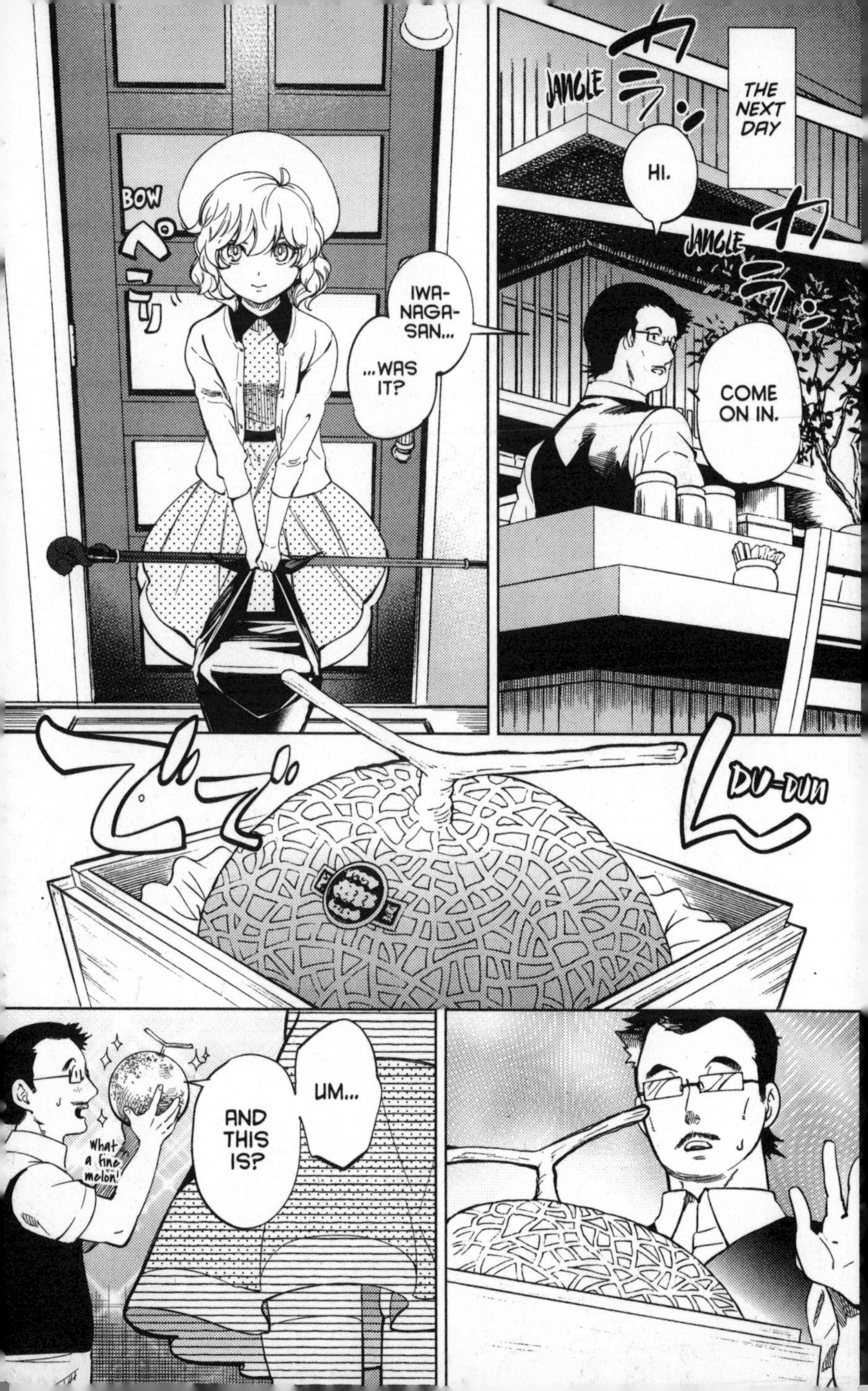
THE NEXT DAY
JANGLE
HI.
JANGLE
COME ON IN.
BOW
IWA-NAGA-SAN...
...WAS IT?
DU-DUN
UM...
AND THIS IS?
What a fine melon!

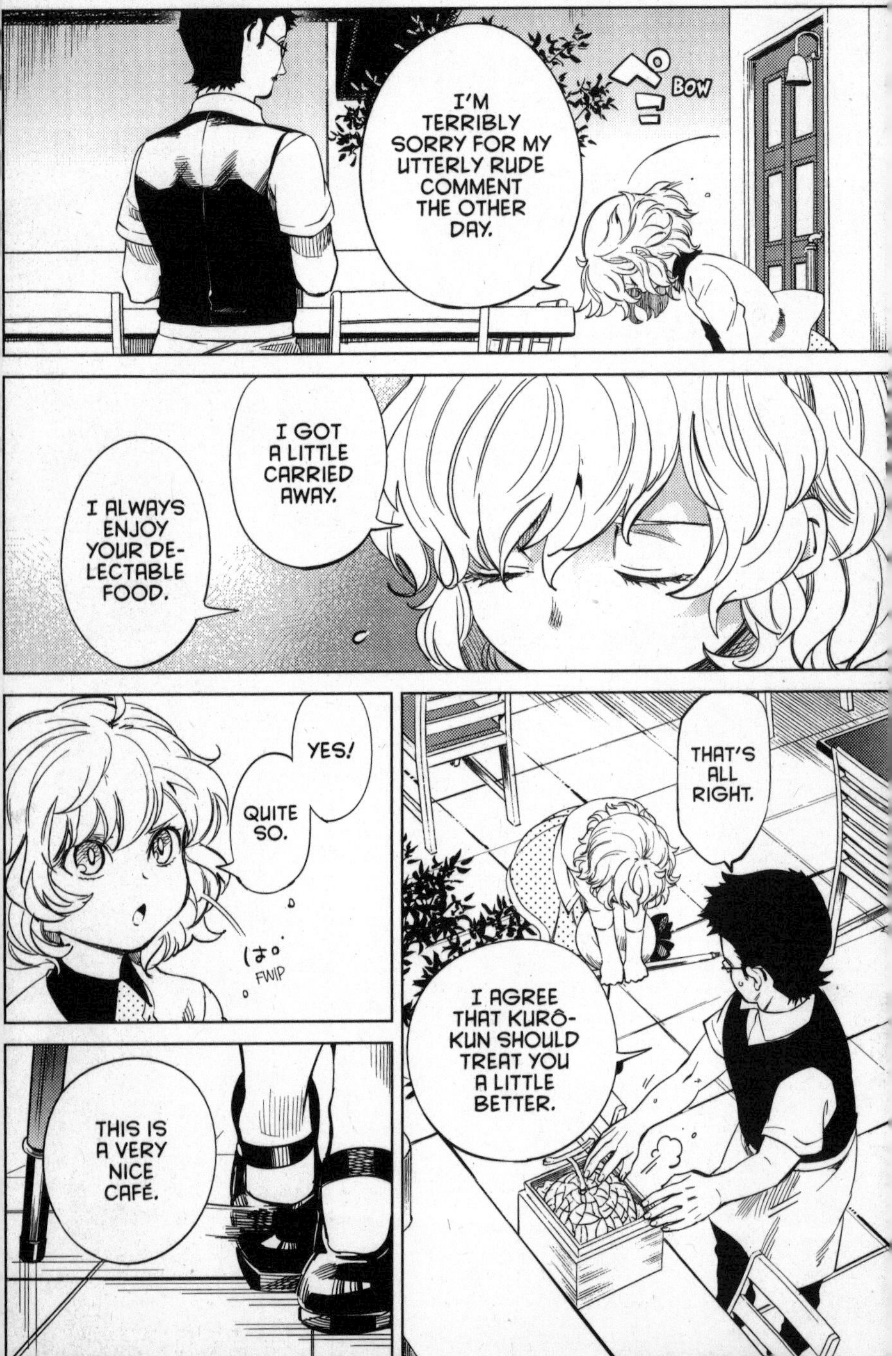
BOW
I'M TERRIBLY SORRY FOR MY UTTERLY RUDE COMMENT THE OTHER DAY.
I GOT A LITTLE CARRIED AWAY.
I ALWAYS ENJOY YOUR DE-LECTABLE FOOD.
THAT'S ALL RIGHT.
I AGREE THAT KURÔ-KUN SHOULD TREAT YOU A LITTLE BETTER.
YES!
QUITE SO.
FWIP
THIS IS A VERY NICE CAFÉ.

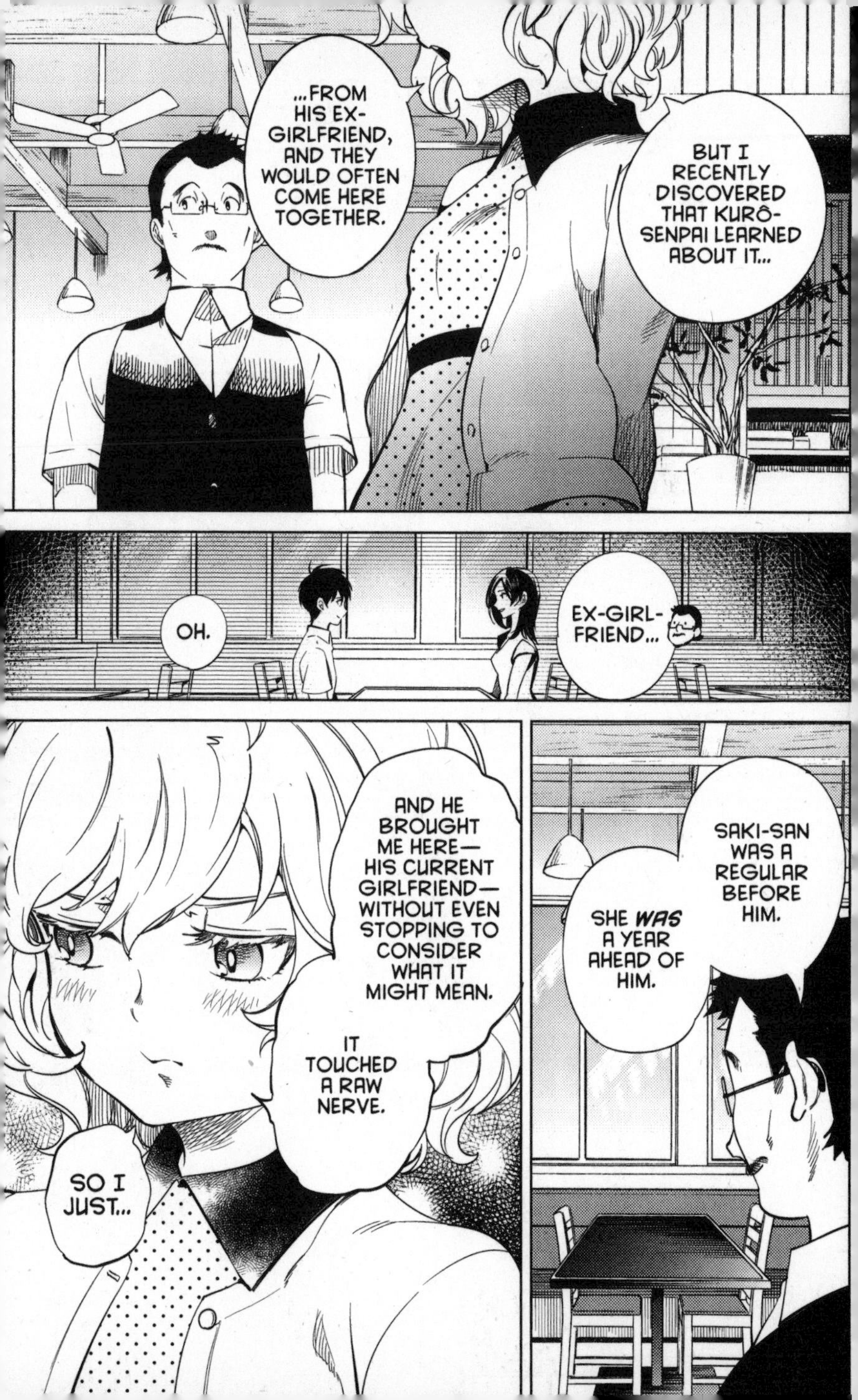
BUT I RECENTLY DISCOVERED THAT KURÔ-SENPAI LEARNED ABOUT IT...
...FROM HIS EX-GIRLFRIEND, AND THEY WOULD OFTEN COME HERE TOGETHER.
EX-GIRL-FRIEND...
OH.
SAKI-SAN WAS A REGULAR BEFORE HIM.
SHE *WAS* A YEAR AHEAD OF HIM.
AND HE BROUGHT ME HERE—HIS CURRENT GIRLFRIEND—WITHOUT EVEN STOPPING TO CONSIDER WHAT IT MIGHT MEAN.
IT TOUCHED A RAW NERVE.
SO I JUST...

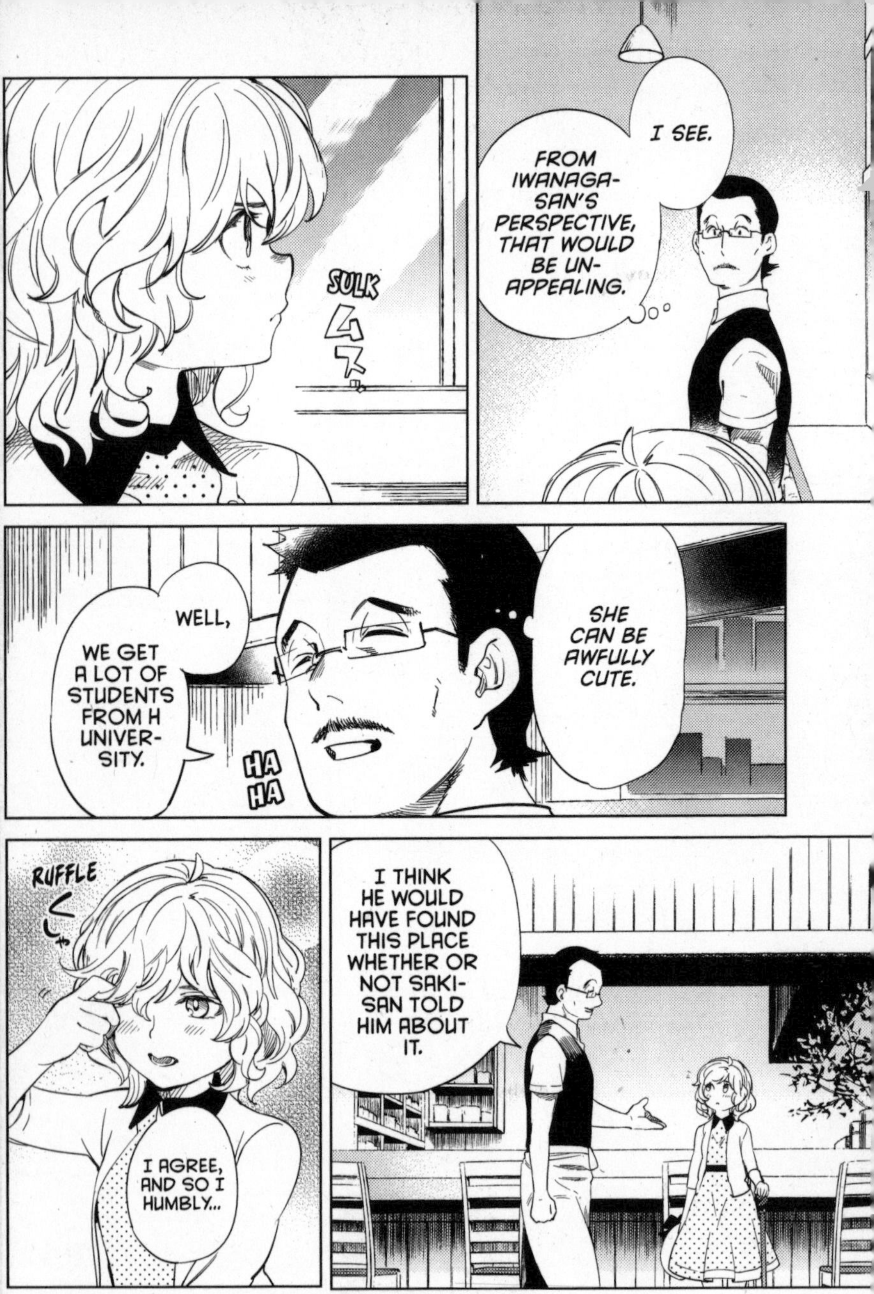
I SEE.
FROM IWANAGA-SAN'S PERSPECTIVE, THAT WOULD BE UN-APPEALING.
SULK
ムス
SHE CAN BE AWFULLY CUTE.
WELL,
WE GET A LOT OF STUDENTS FROM H UNIVERSITY.
HA HA
I THINK HE WOULD HAVE FOUND THIS PLACE WHETHER OR NOT SAKI-SAN TOLD HIM ABOUT IT.
RUFFLE
くしゃ
I AGREE, AND SO I HUMBLY...

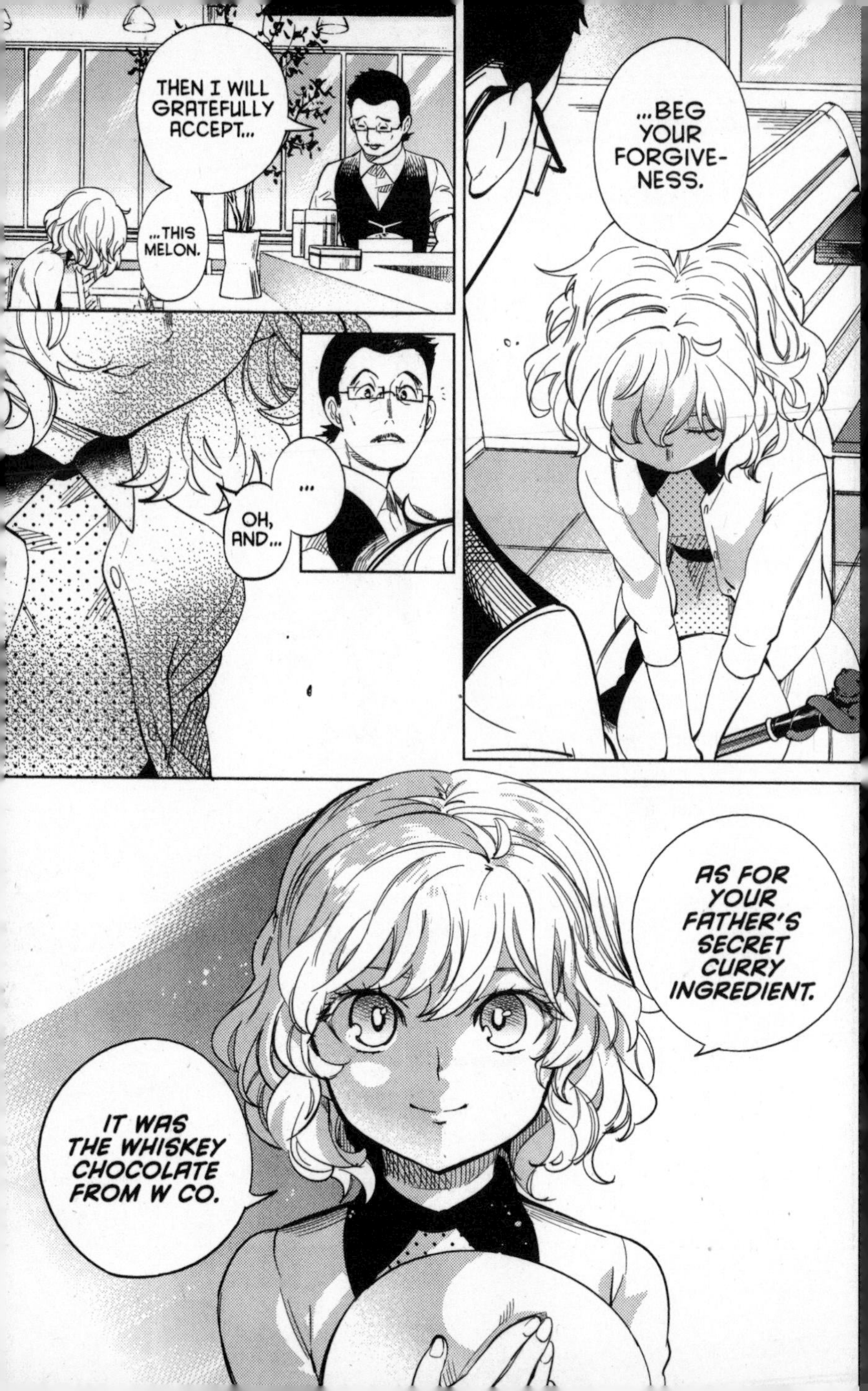
THEN I WILL GRATEFULLY ACCEPT...
...THIS MELON.
...
OH, AND...
...BEG YOUR FORGIVE-NESS.
AS FOR YOUR FATHER'S SECRET CURRY INGREDIENT.
IT WAS THE WHISKEY CHOCOLATE FROM W CO.

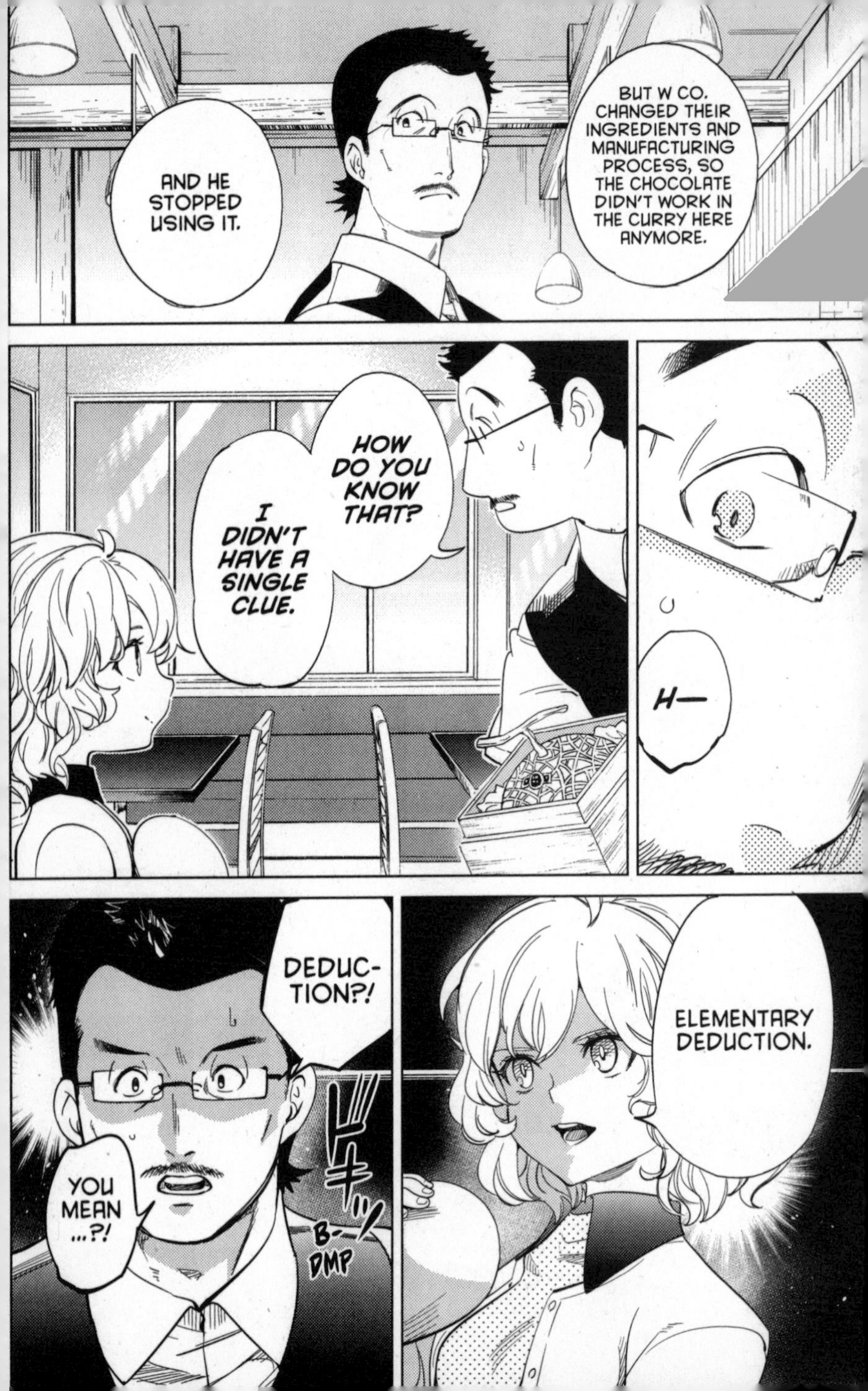
BUT W CO. CHANGED THEIR INGREDIENTS AND MANUFACTURING PROCESS, SO THE CHOCOLATE DIDN'T WORK IN THE CURRY HERE ANYMORE.
AND HE STOPPED USING IT.
H—
HOW DO YOU KNOW THAT?
I DIDN'T HAVE A SINGLE CLUE.
ELEMENTARY DEDUCTION.
DEDUC-TION?!
YOU MEAN ...?!
B-DMP

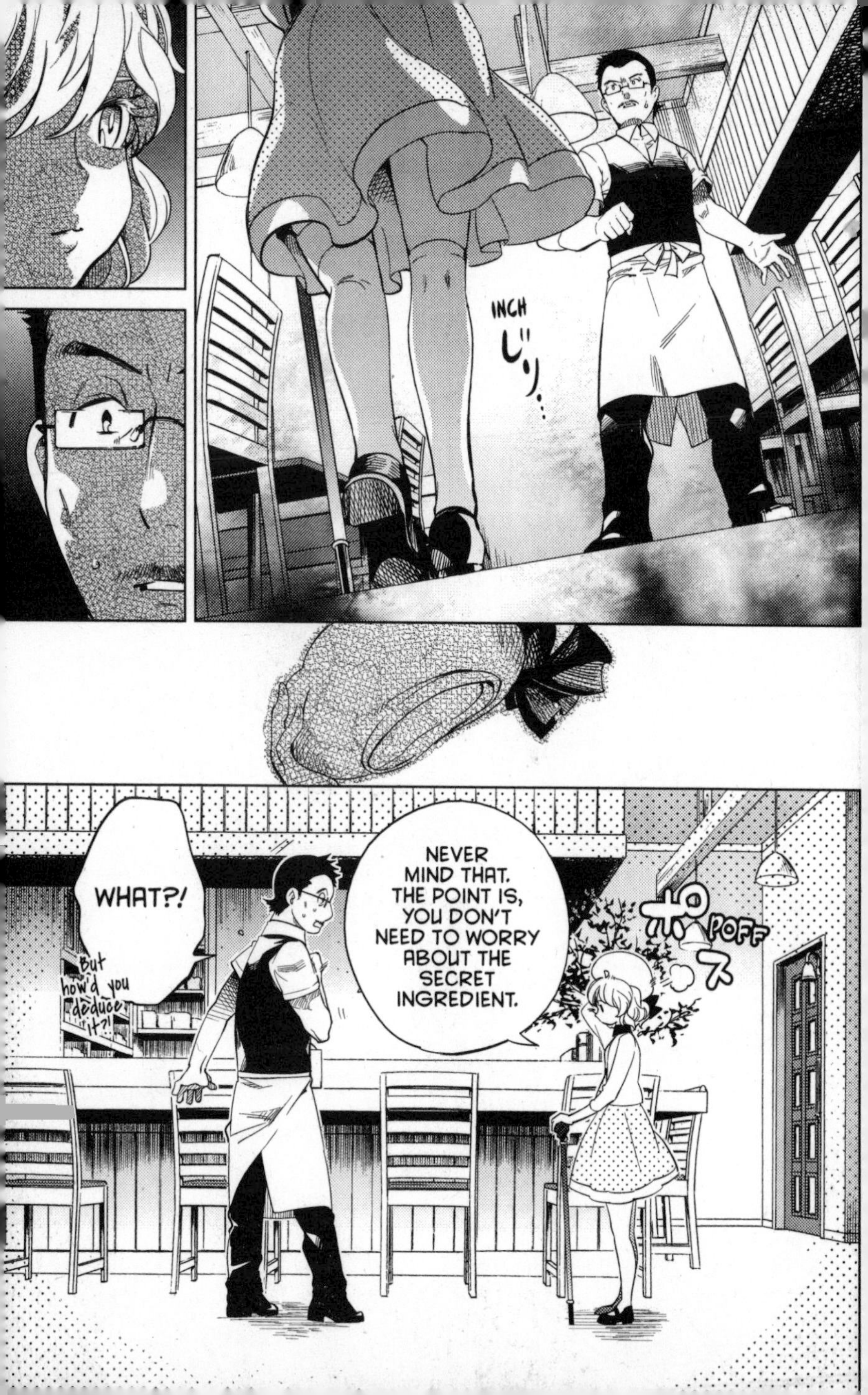

INCH
じり…
ポフ POFF
NEVER MIND THAT. THE POINT IS, YOU DON'T NEED TO WORRY ABOUT THE SECRET INGREDIENT.
WHAT?!
But how'd you deduce it?!

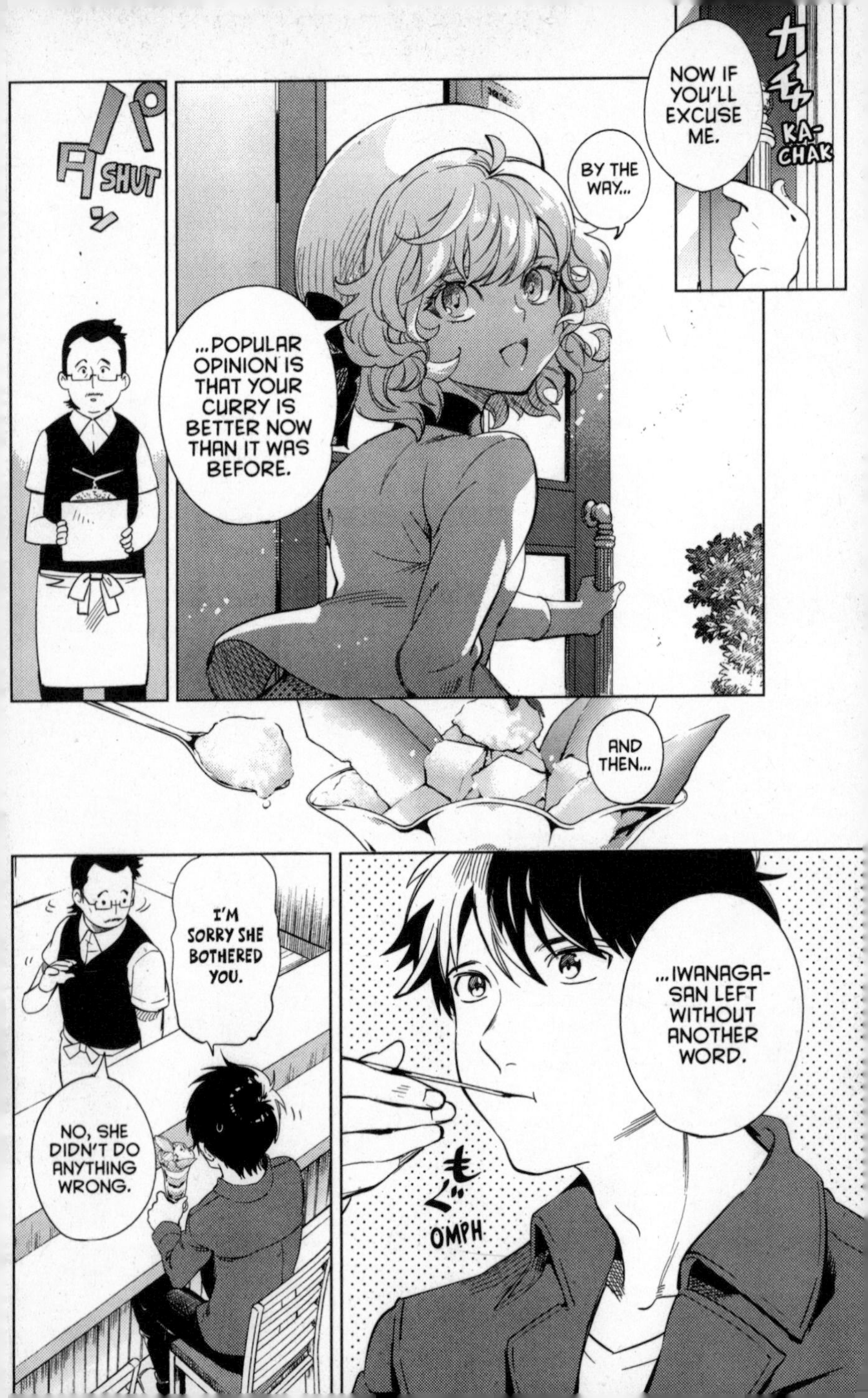
カチャ
KA-CHAK
NOW IF YOU'LL EXCUSE ME.
BY THE WAY...
...POPULAR OPINION IS THAT YOUR CURRY IS BETTER NOW THAN IT WAS BEFORE.
パタン
SHUT
AND THEN...
...IWANAGA-SAN LEFT WITHOUT ANOTHER WORD.
もぐ
OMPH
I'M SORRY SHE BOTHERED YOU.
NO, SHE DIDN'T DO ANYTHING WRONG.

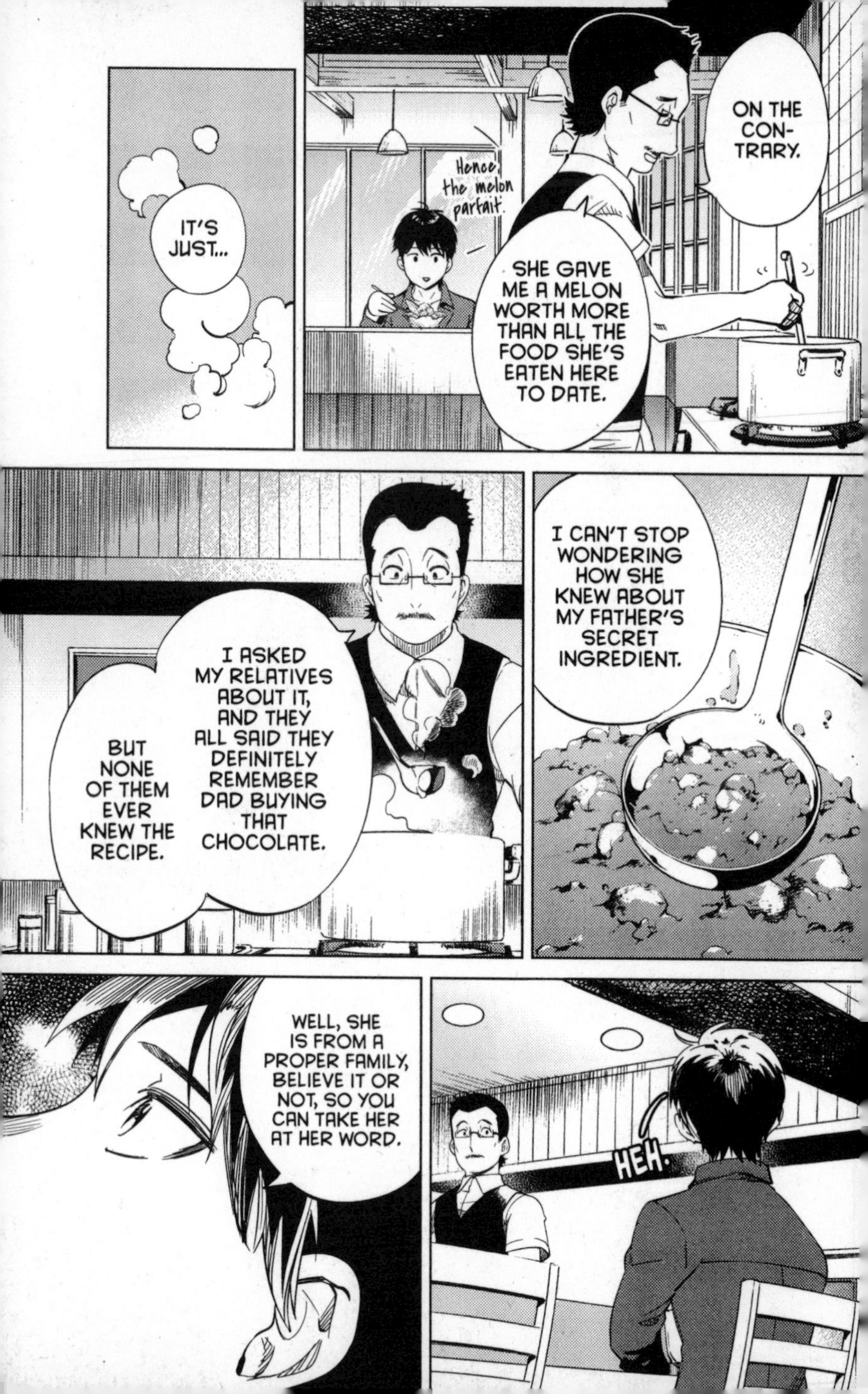
ON THE CON-TRARY.
Hence, the melon parfait.
SHE GAVE ME A MELON WORTH MORE THAN ALL THE FOOD SHE'S EATEN HERE TO DATE.
IT'S JUST...
I CAN'T STOP WONDERING HOW SHE KNEW ABOUT MY FATHER'S SECRET INGREDIENT.
I ASKED MY RELATIVES ABOUT IT, AND THEY ALL SAID THEY DEFINITELY REMEMBER DAD BUYING THAT CHOCOLATE.
BUT NONE OF THEM EVER KNEW THE RECIPE.
HEH.
WELL, SHE IS FROM A PROPER FAMILY, BELIEVE IT OR NOT, SO YOU CAN TAKE HER AT HER WORD.

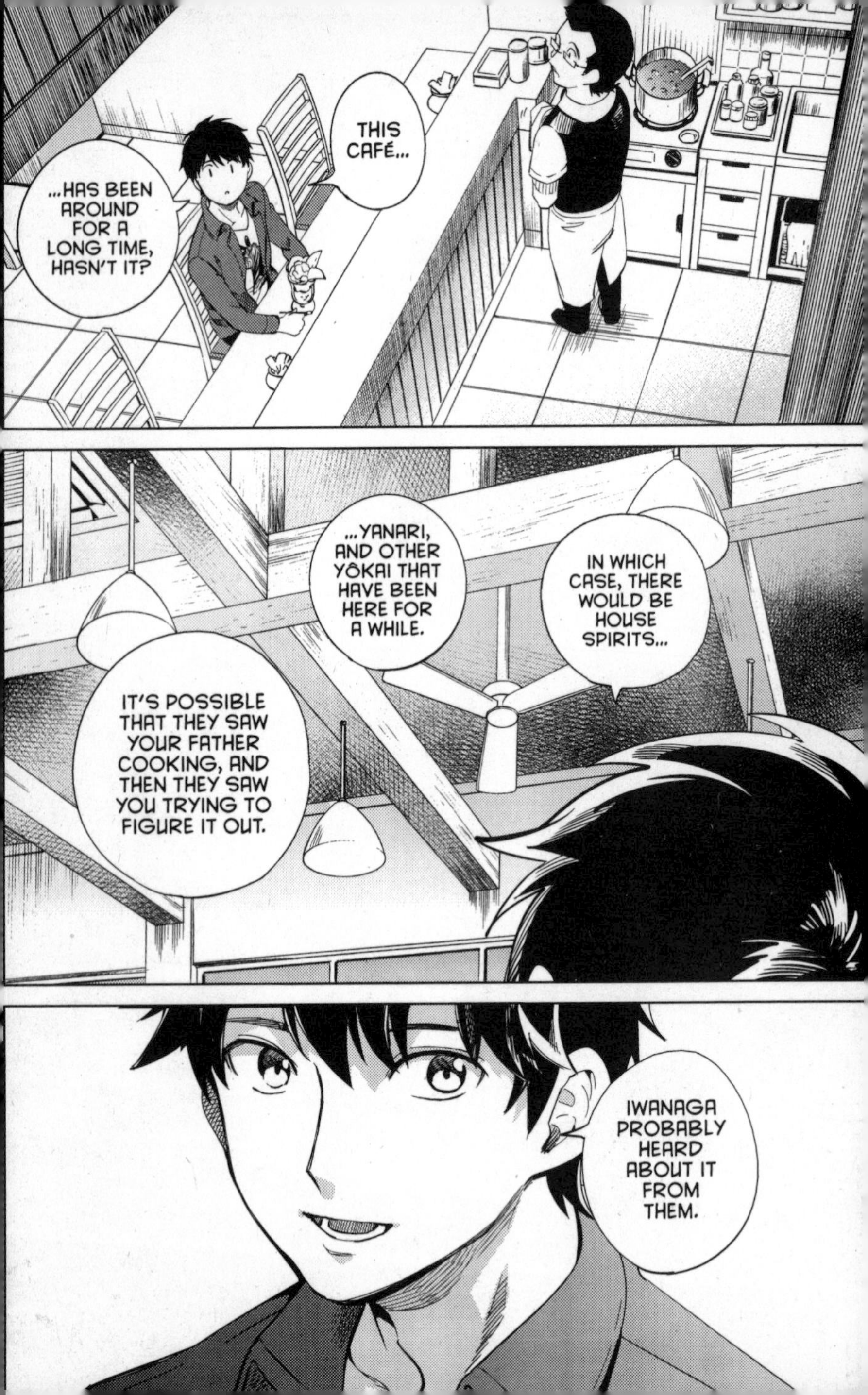
THIS CAFÉ...
...HAS BEEN AROUND FOR A LONG TIME, HASN'T IT?
IN WHICH CASE, THERE WOULD BE HOUSE SPIRITS...
...YANARI, AND OTHER YÔKAI THAT HAVE BEEN HERE FOR A WHILE.
IT'S POSSIBLE THAT THEY SAW YOUR FATHER COOKING, AND THEN THEY SAW YOU TRYING TO FIGURE IT OUT.
IWANAGA PROBABLY HEARD ABOUT IT FROM THEM.

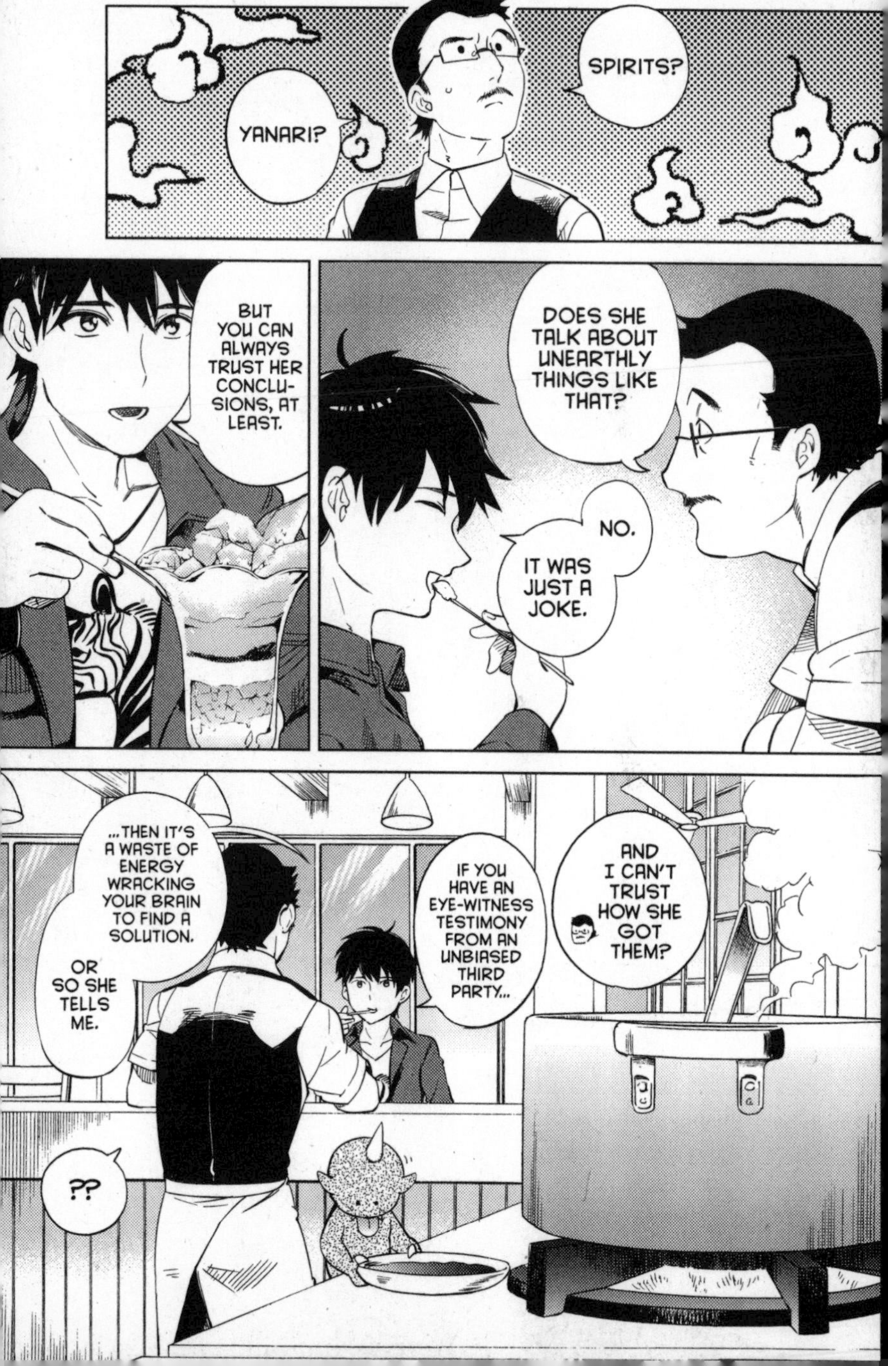
SPIRITS?
YANARI?
DOES SHE TALK ABOUT UNEARTHLY THINGS LIKE THAT?
NO.
IT WAS JUST A JOKE.
BUT YOU CAN ALWAYS TRUST HER CONCLUSIONS, AT LEAST.
AND I CAN'T TRUST HOW SHE GOT THEM?
IF YOU HAVE AN EYE-WITNESS TESTIMONY FROM AN UNBIASED THIRD PARTY...
...THEN IT'S A WASTE OF ENERGY WRACKING YOUR BRAIN TO FIND A SOLUTION.
OR SO SHE TELLS ME.
??

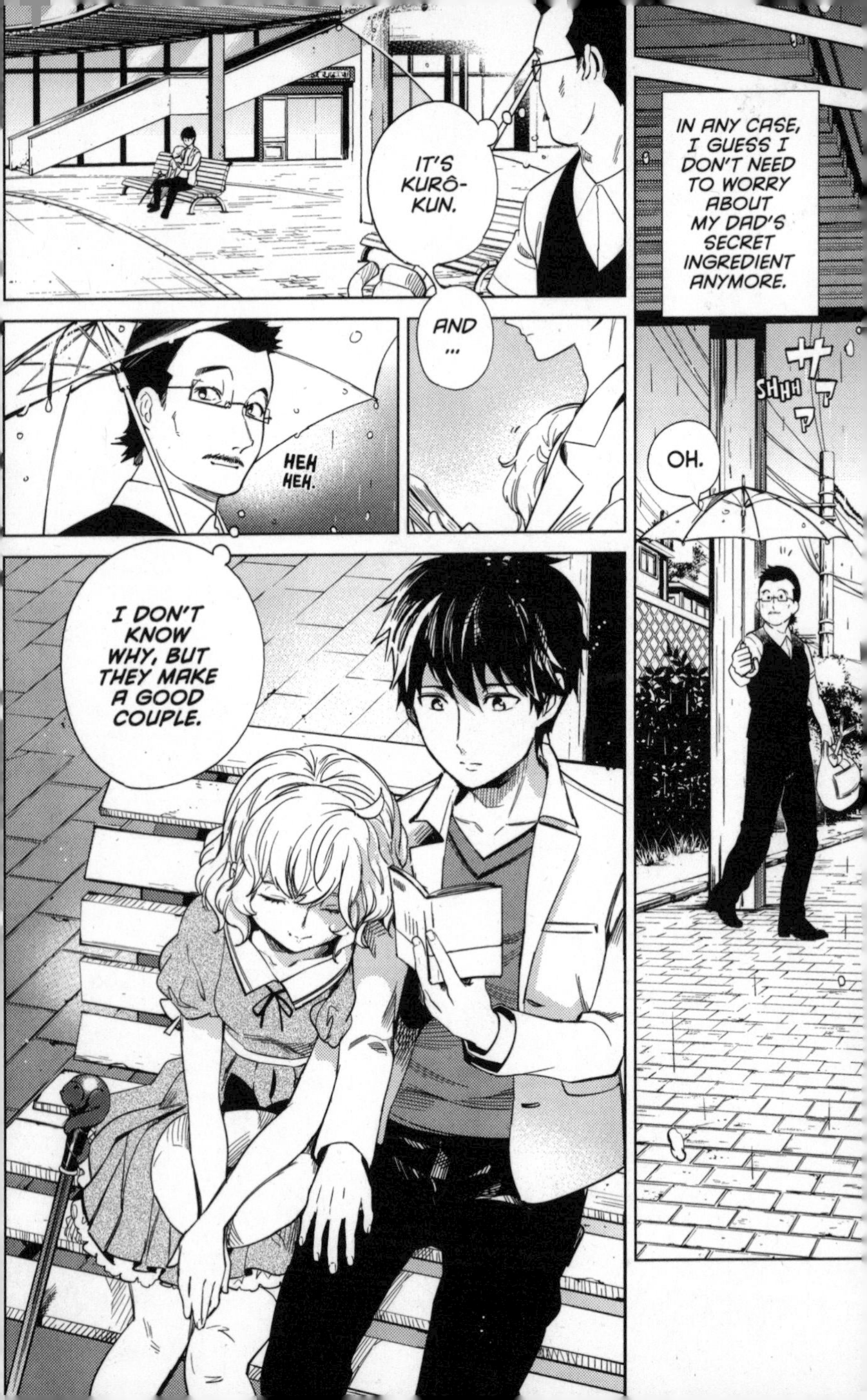
IN ANY CASE, I GUESS I DON'T NEED TO WORRY ABOUT MY DAD'S SECRET INGREDIENT ANYMORE.
SHHH
OH.
IT'S KURÔ-KUN.
AND ...
HEH HEH.
I DON'T KNOW WHY, BUT THEY MAKE A GOOD COUPLE.

IN/SPECTRE

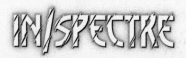

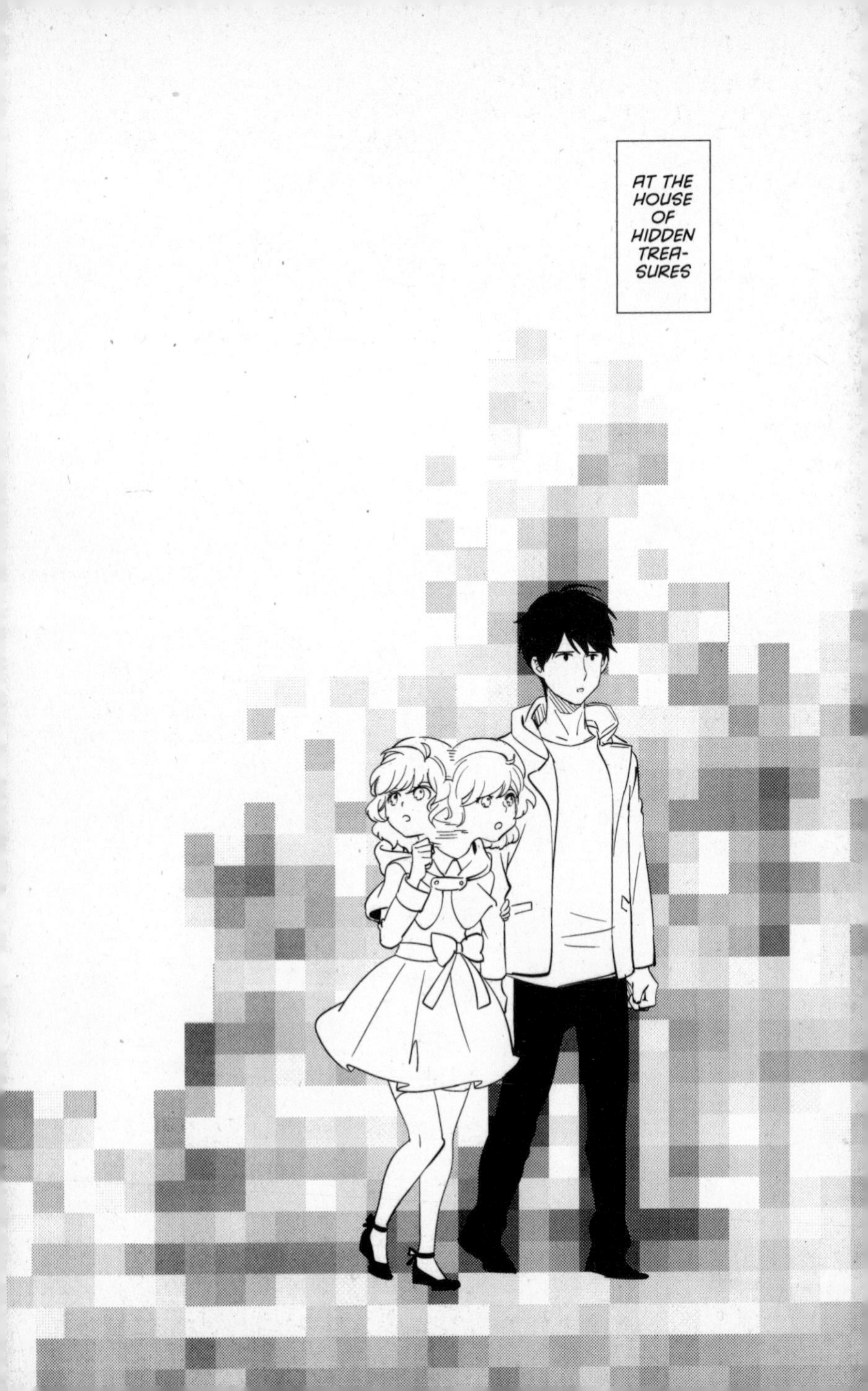
AT THE HOUSE OF HIDDEN TREA-SURES

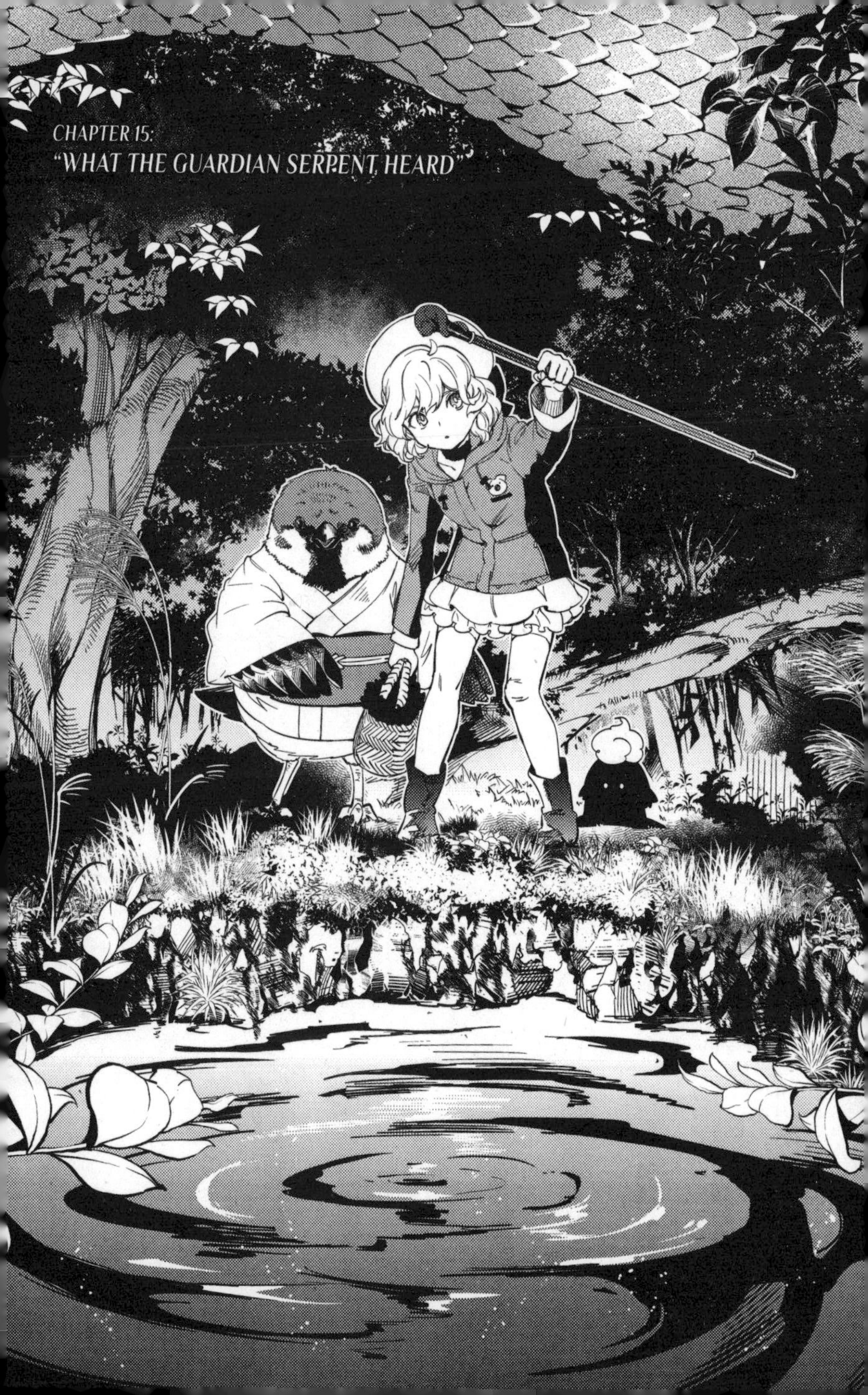
CHAPTER 15:
"WHAT THE GUARDIAN SERPENT HEARD"

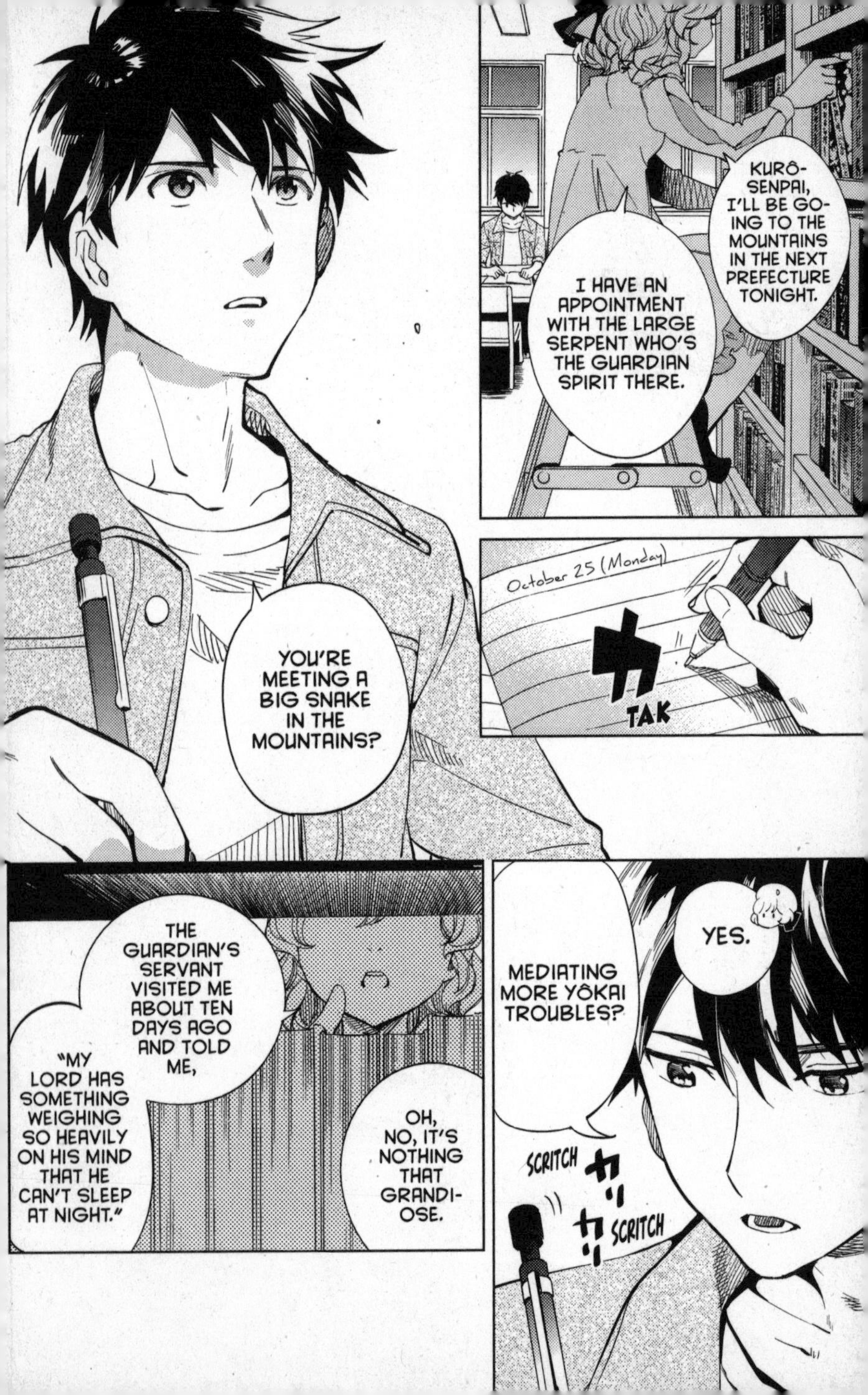
KURÔ-SENPAI, I'LL BE GOING TO THE MOUNTAINS IN THE NEXT PREFECTURE TONIGHT.
I HAVE AN APPOINTMENT WITH THE LARGE SERPENT WHO'S THE GUARDIAN SPIRIT THERE.
October 25 (Monday)
TAK
YOU'RE MEETING A BIG SNAKE IN THE MOUNTAINS?
YES.
MEDIATING MORE YÔKAI TROUBLES?
SCRITCH
SCRITCH
OH, NO, IT'S NOTHING THAT GRANDIOSE.
THE GUARDIAN'S SERVANT VISITED ME ABOUT TEN DAYS AGO AND TOLD ME,
"MY LORD HAS SOMETHING WEIGHING SO HEAVILY ON HIS MIND THAT HE CAN'T SLEEP AT NIGHT."

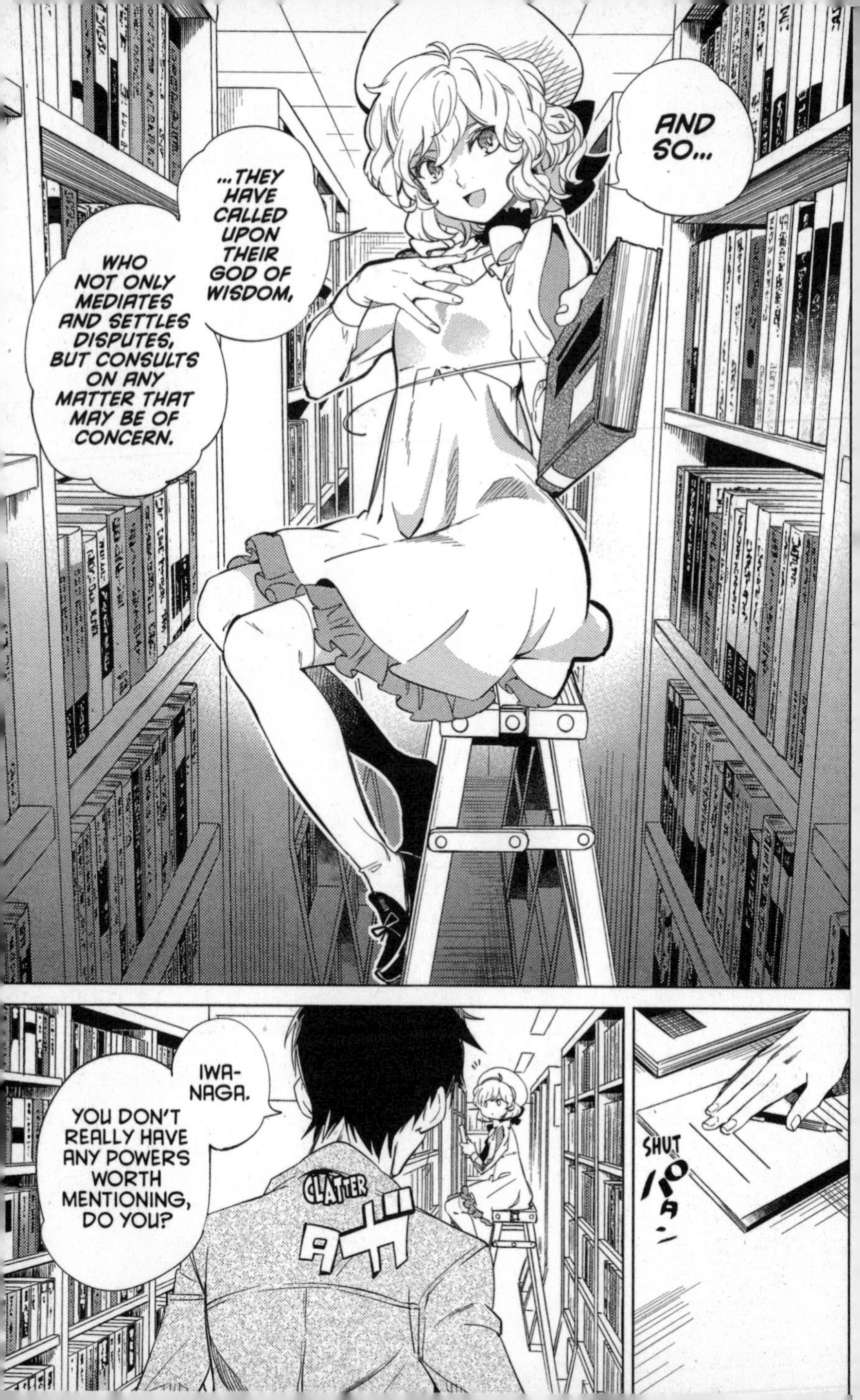
AND SO...
...THEY HAVE CALLED UPON THEIR GOD OF WISDOM,
WHO NOT ONLY MEDIATES AND SETTLES DISPUTES, BUT CONSULTS ON ANY MATTER THAT MAY BE OF CONCERN.
SHUT
IWA-NAGA.
YOU DON'T REALLY HAVE ANY POWERS WORTH MENTIONING, DO YOU?
CLATTER

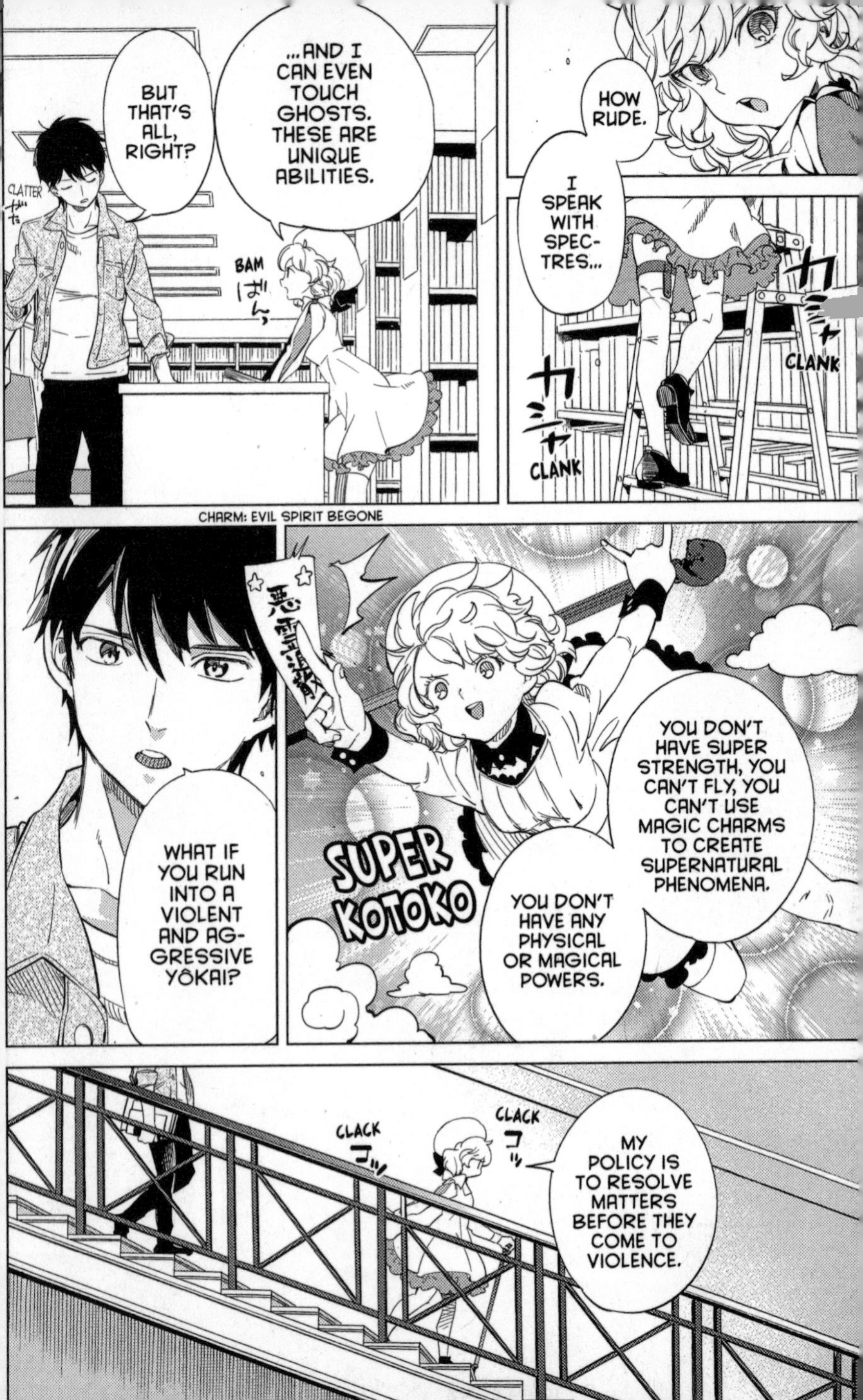
HOW RUDE.
I SPEAK WITH SPECTRES...
CLANK
CLANK
...AND I CAN EVEN TOUCH GHOSTS. THESE ARE UNIQUE ABILITIES.
BUT THAT'S ALL, RIGHT?
BAM
CLATTER
CHARM: EVIL SPIRIT BEGONE
YOU DON'T HAVE SUPER STRENGTH, YOU CAN'T FLY, YOU CAN'T USE MAGIC CHARMS TO CREATE SUPERNATURAL PHENOMENA.
YOU DON'T HAVE ANY PHYSICAL OR MAGICAL POWERS.
SUPER KOTOKO
WHAT IF YOU RUN INTO A VIOLENT AND AGGRESSIVE YÔKAI?
MY POLICY IS TO RESOLVE MATTERS BEFORE THEY COME TO VIOLENCE.
CLACK
CLACK

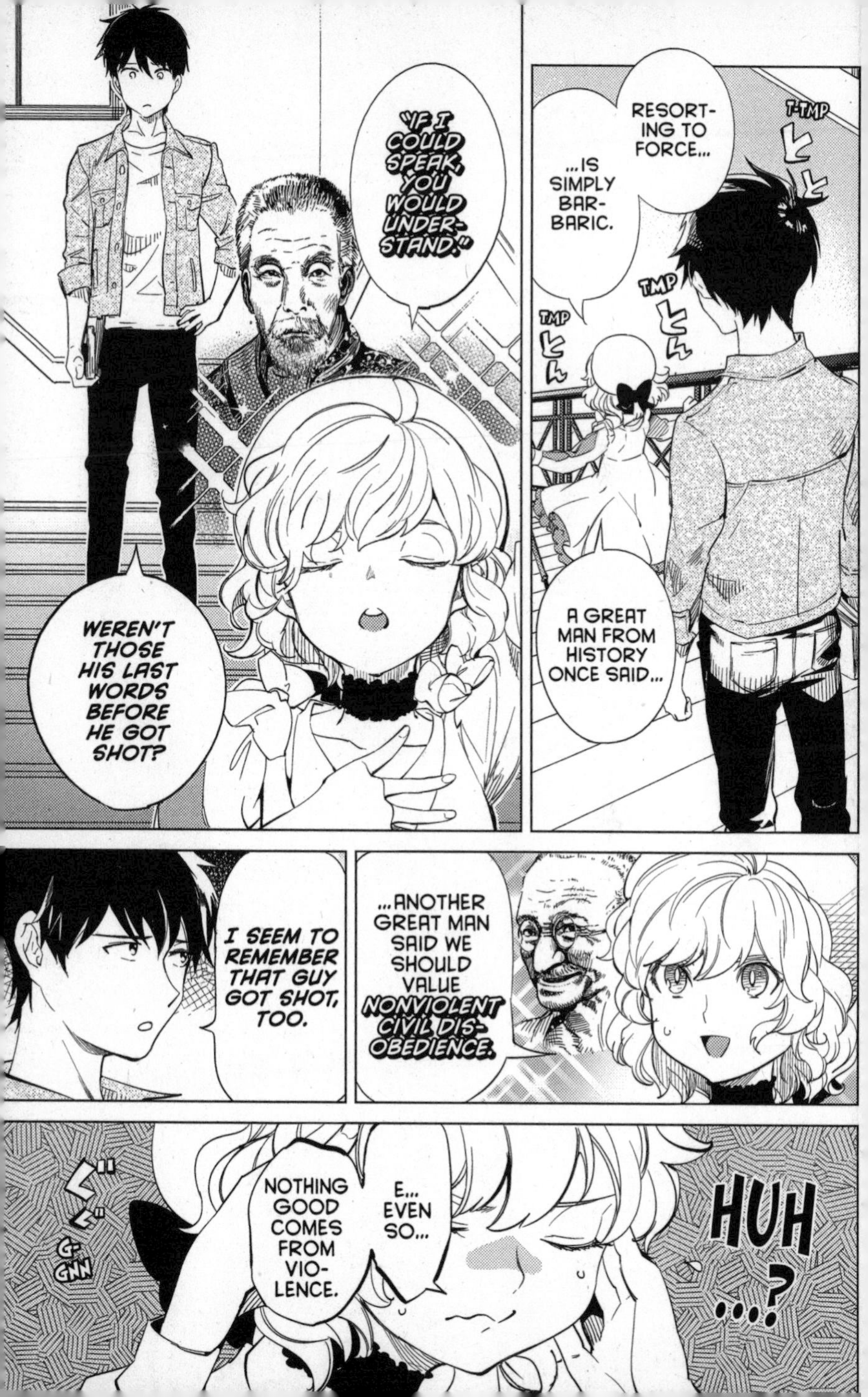
T-TMP
RESORTING TO FORCE...
...IS SIMPLY BARBARIC.
TMP
TMP
A GREAT MAN FROM HISTORY ONCE SAID...
"IF I COULD SPEAK, YOU WOULD UNDERSTAND."
WEREN'T THOSE HIS LAST WORDS BEFORE HE GOT SHOT?
...ANOTHER GREAT MAN SAID WE SHOULD VALUE NONVIOLENT CIVIL DISOBEDIENCE.
I SEEM TO REMEMBER THAT GUY GOT SHOT, TOO.
HUH...?
E... EVEN SO...
NOTHING GOOD COMES FROM VIOLENCE.
G-GNN

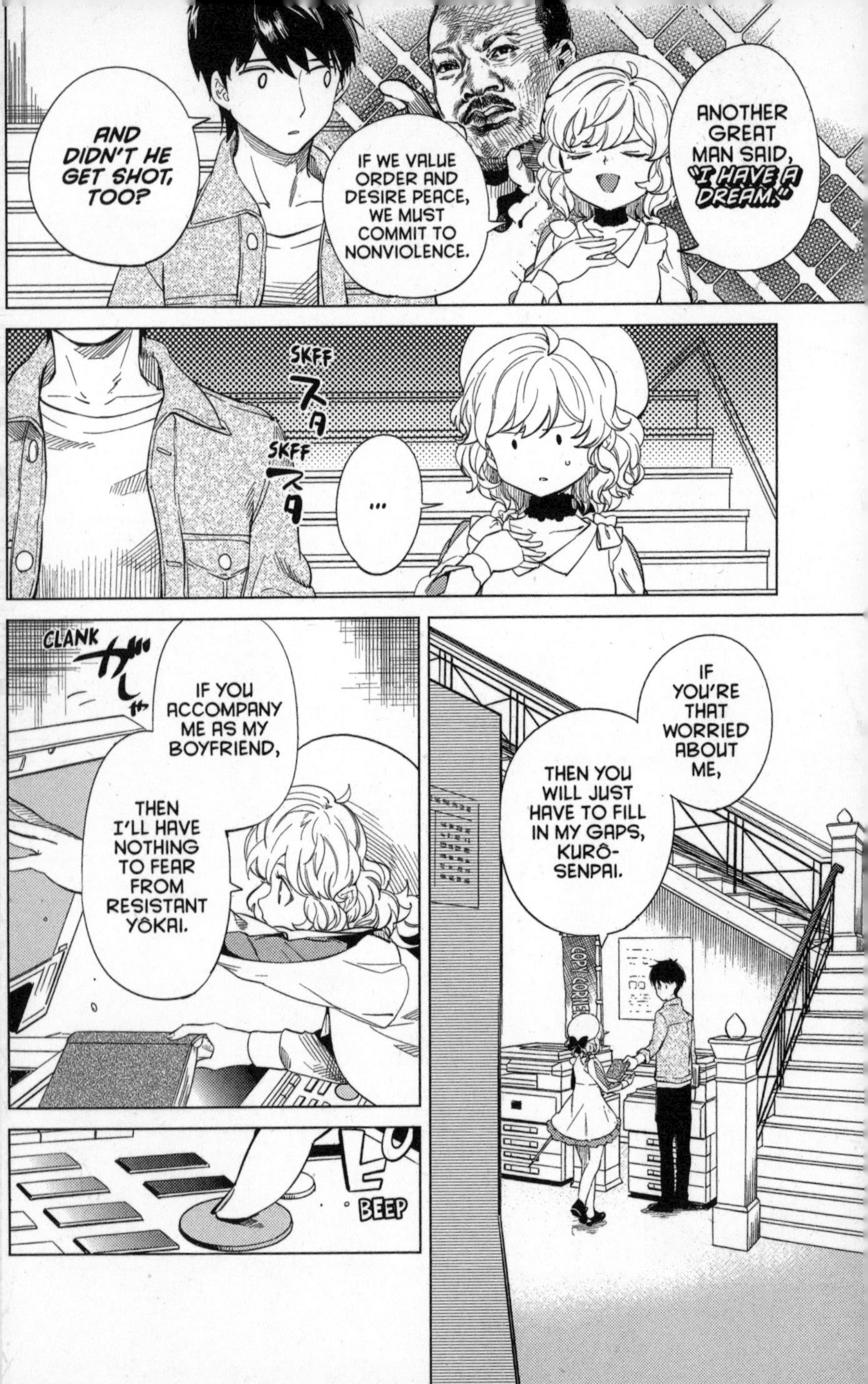
ANOTHER GREAT MAN SAID, "I HAVE A DREAM."
IF WE VALUE ORDER AND DESIRE PEACE, WE MUST COMMIT TO NONVIOLENCE.
AND DIDN'T HE GET SHOT, TOO?
...
SKFF
SKFF
IF YOU'RE THAT WORRIED ABOUT ME,
THEN YOU WILL JUST HAVE TO FILL IN MY GAPS, KURÔ-SENPAI.
CLANK
IF YOU ACCOMPANY ME AS MY BOYFRIEND,
THEN I'LL HAVE NOTHING TO FEAR FROM RESISTANT YÔKAI.
BEEP

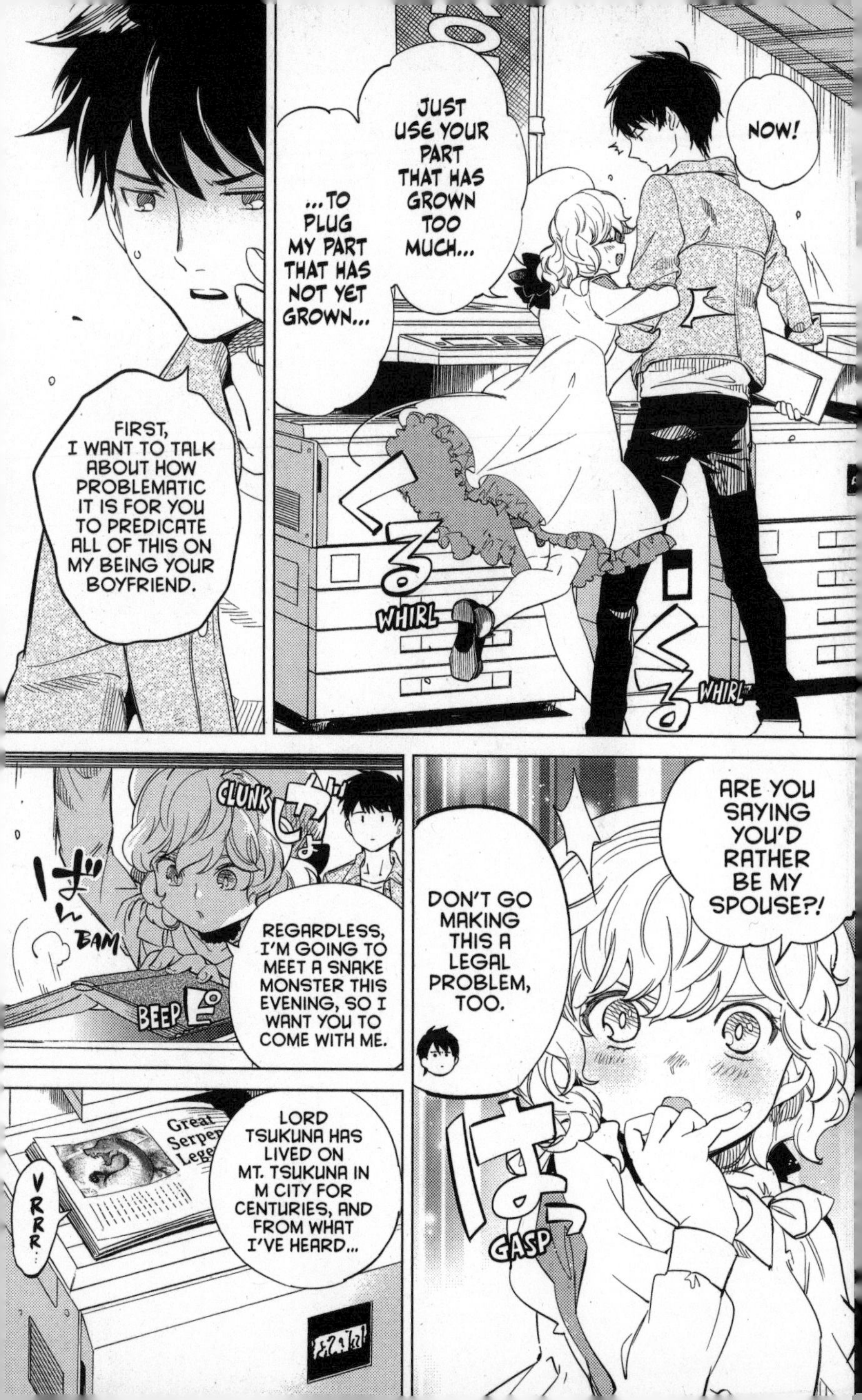
NOW!
JUST USE YOUR PART THAT HAS GROWN TOO MUCH...
...TO PLUG MY PART THAT HAS NOT YET GROWN...
WHIRL
WHIRL
FIRST, I WANT TO TALK ABOUT HOW PROBLEMATIC IT IS FOR YOU TO PREDICATE ALL OF THIS ON MY BEING YOUR BOYFRIEND.
ARE YOU SAYING YOU'D RATHER BE MY SPOUSE?!
DON'T GO MAKING THIS A LEGAL PROBLEM, TOO.
GASP
CLUNK
BAM
REGARDLESS, I'M GOING TO MEET A SNAKE MONSTER THIS EVENING, SO I WANT YOU TO COME WITH ME.
BEEP
Great
LORD TSUKUNA HAS LIVED ON MT. TSUKUNA IN M CITY FOR CENTURIES, AND FROM WHAT I'VE HEARD...
VRRR...

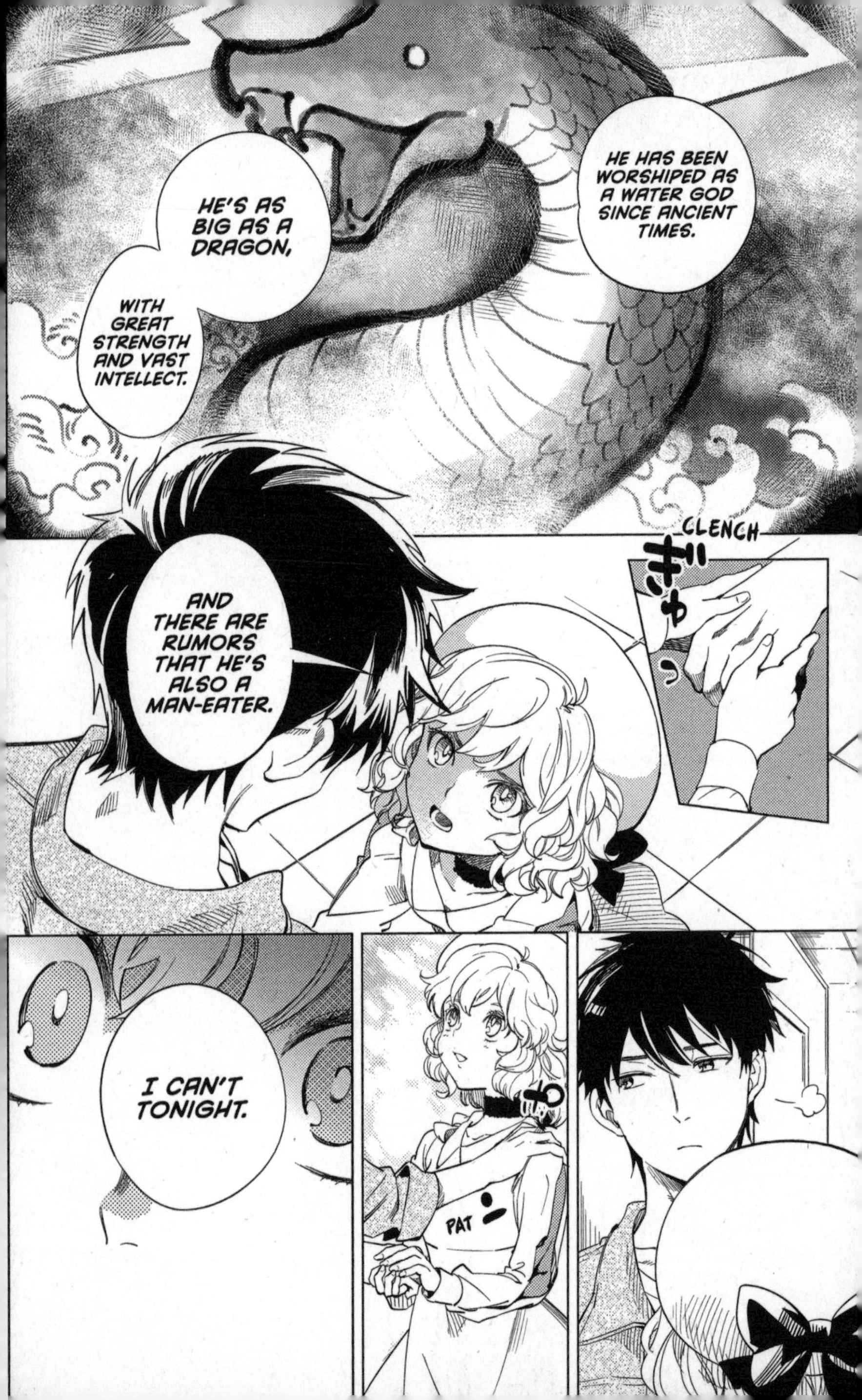
HE HAS BEEN WORSHIPED AS A WATER GOD SINCE ANCIENT TIMES.
HE'S AS BIG AS A DRAGON,
WITH GREAT STRENGTH AND VAST INTELLECT.
CLENCH
ぎゅっ
AND THERE ARE RUMORS THAT HE'S ALSO A MAN-EATER.
PAT
I CAN'T TONIGHT.

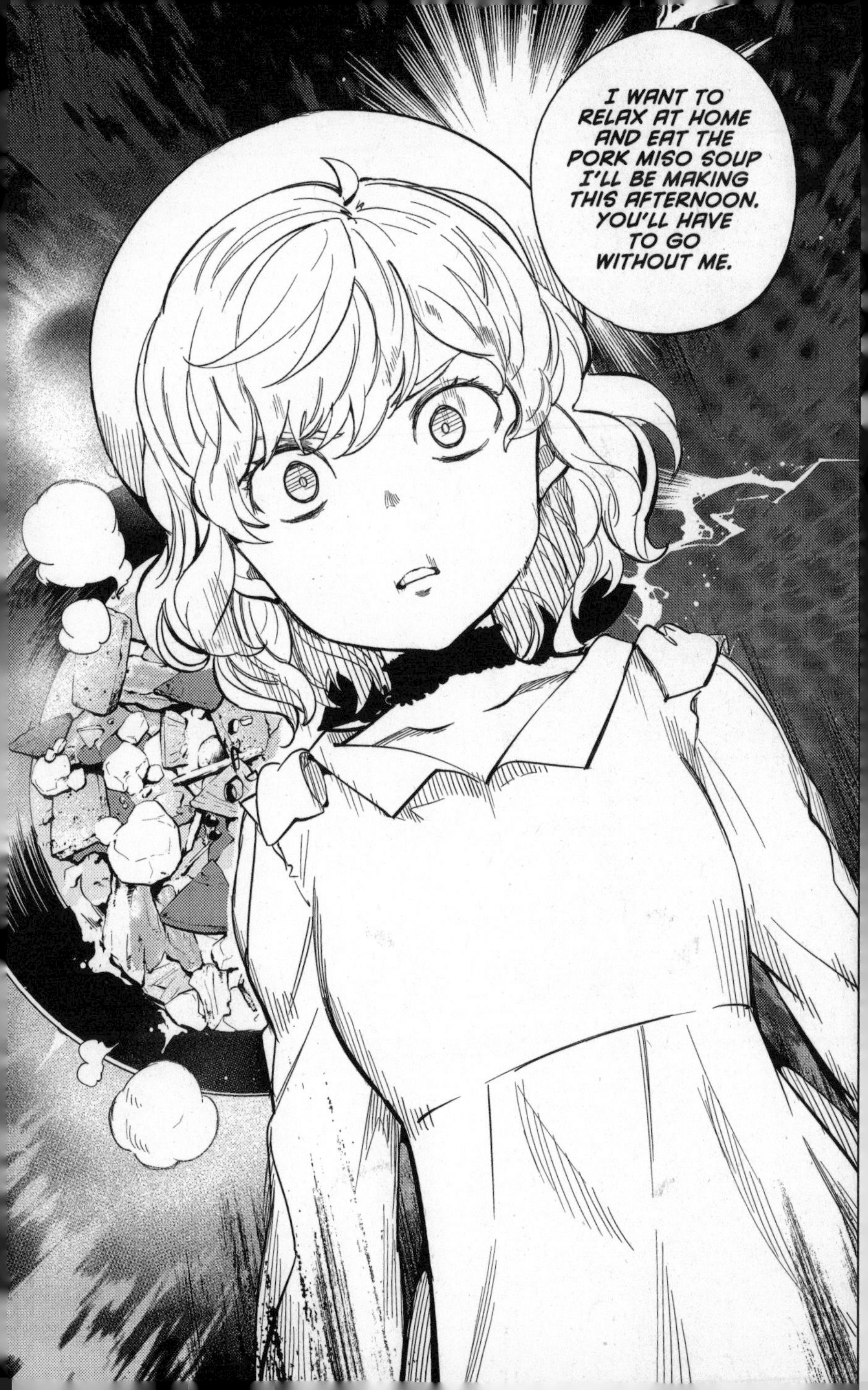
I WANT TO RELAX AT HOME AND EAT THE PORK MISO SOUP I'LL BE MAKING THIS AFTERNOON. YOU'LL HAVE TO GO WITHOUT ME.

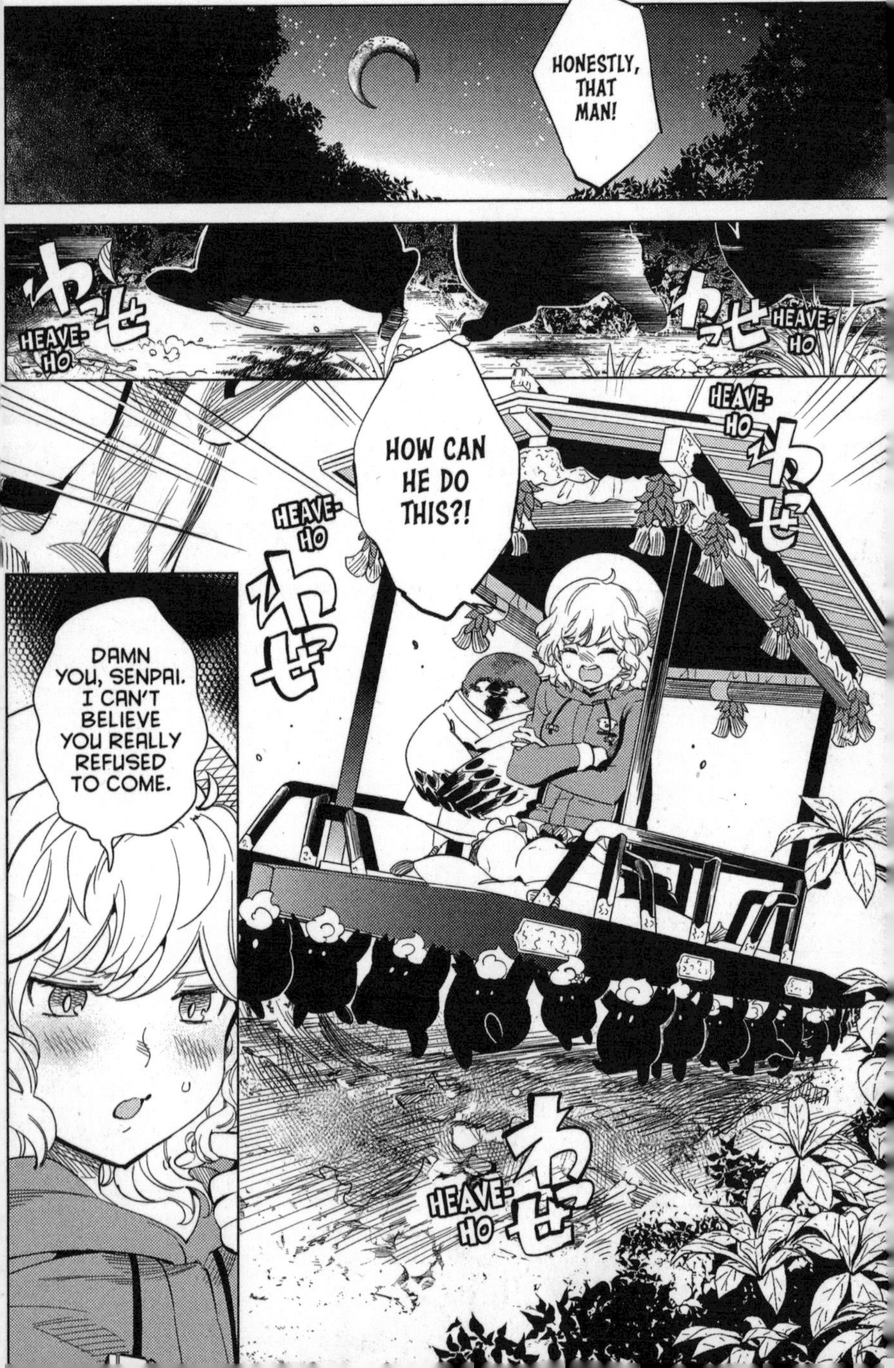
HONESTLY, THAT MAN!
わっせ
HEAVE-HO
わっせ
HEAVE-HO
HEAVE-HO
わっせ
HOW CAN HE DO THIS?!
HEAVE-HO
わっせ
わっせ
HEAVE-HO
DAMN YOU, SENPAI. I CAN'T BELIEVE YOU REALLY REFUSED TO COME.

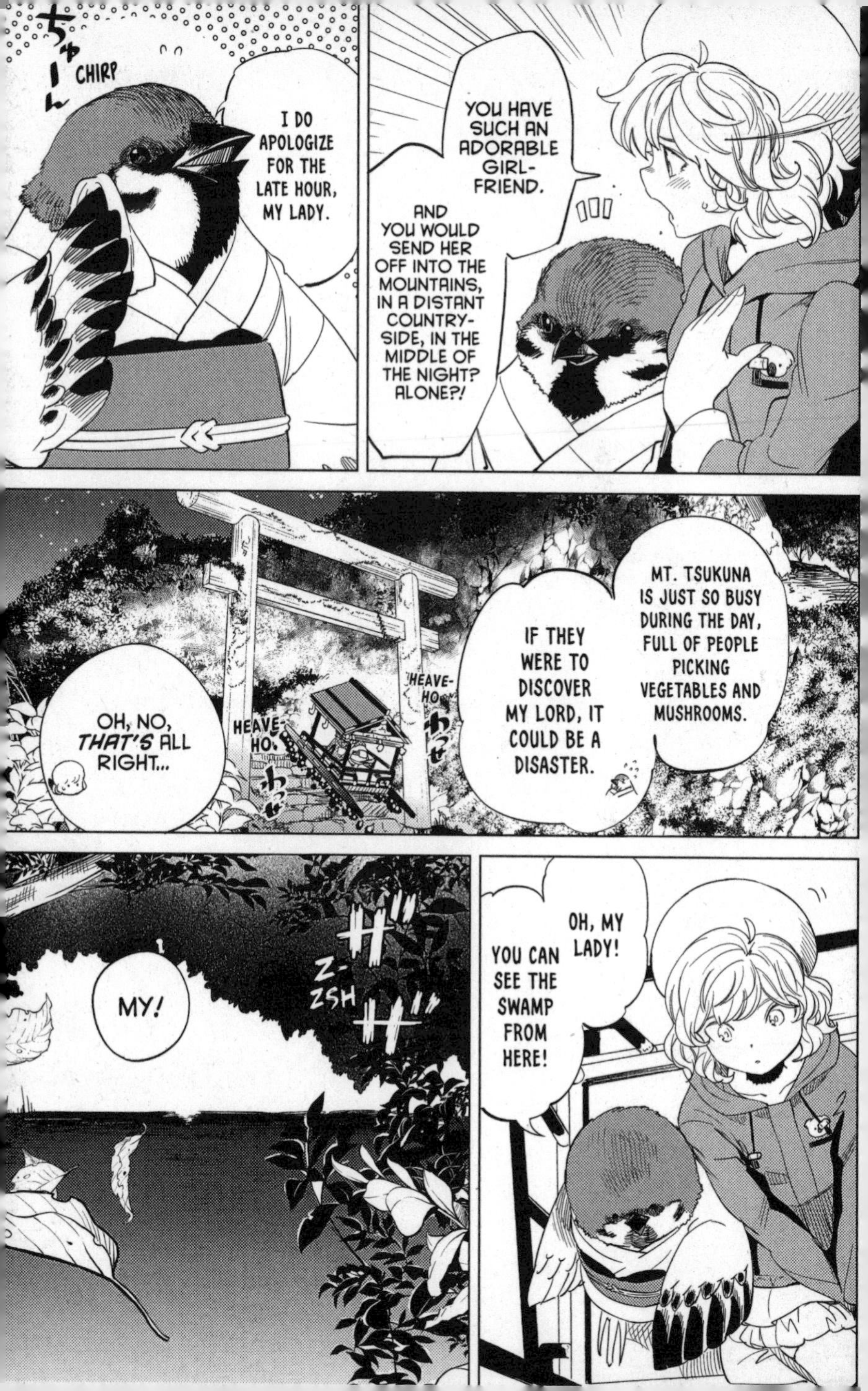
YOU HAVE SUCH AN ADORABLE GIRL-FRIEND.
AND YOU WOULD SEND HER OFF INTO THE MOUNTAINS, IN A DISTANT COUNTRY-SIDE, IN THE MIDDLE OF THE NIGHT? ALONE?!
CHIRP
I DO APOLOGIZE FOR THE LATE HOUR, MY LADY.
MT. TSUKUNA IS JUST SO BUSY DURING THE DAY, FULL OF PEOPLE PICKING VEGETABLES AND MUSHROOMS.
IF THEY WERE TO DISCOVER MY LORD, IT COULD BE A DISASTER.
HEAVE-HO
HEAVE-HO
OH, NO, *THAT'S* ALL RIGHT...
OH, MY LADY!
YOU CAN SEE THE SWAMP FROM HERE!
Z-ZSH
MY!

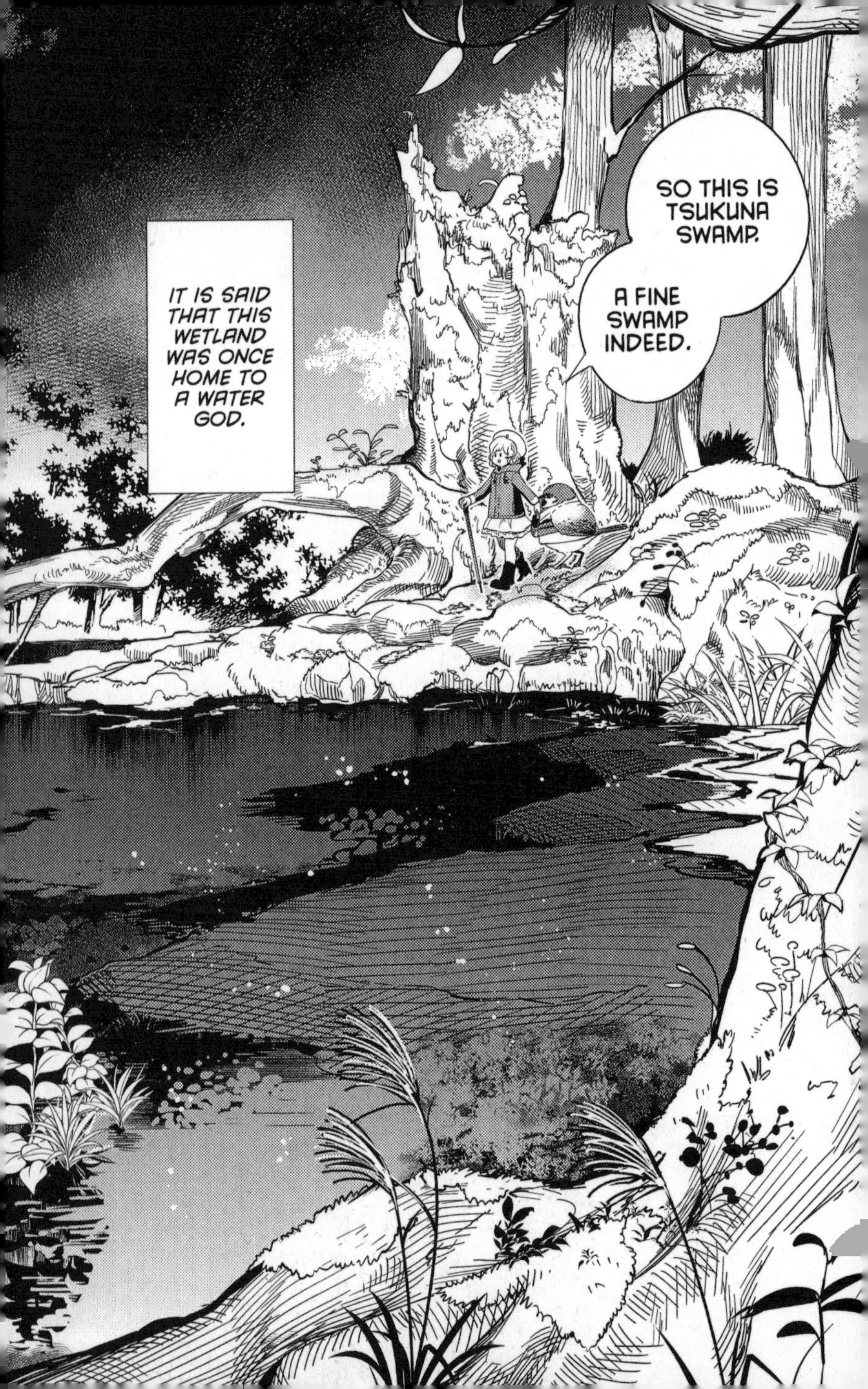

SO THIS IS TSUKUNA SWAMP.
A FINE SWAMP INDEED.
IT IS SAID THAT THIS WETLAND WAS ONCE HOME TO A WATER GOD.

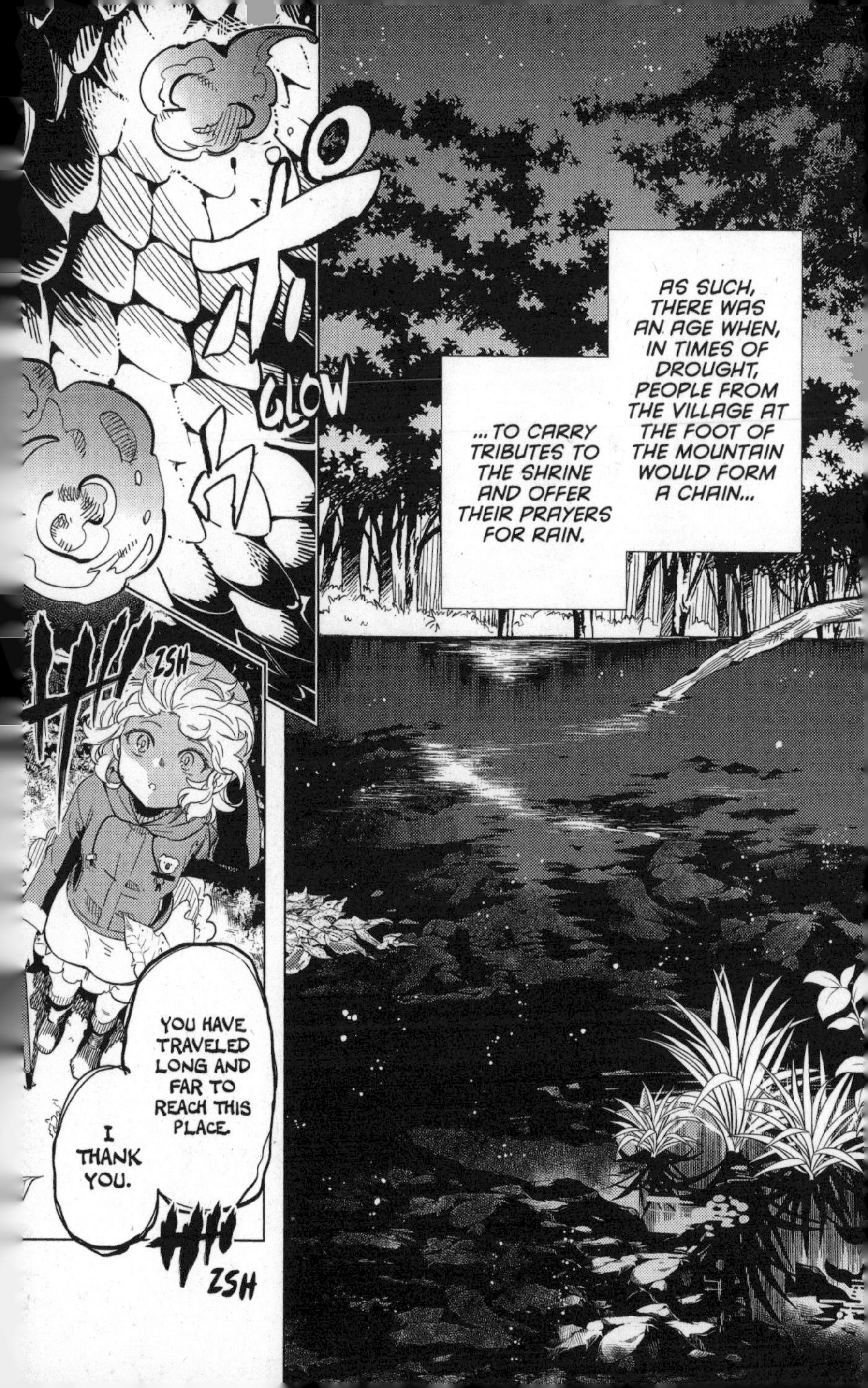
AS SUCH, THERE WAS AN AGE WHEN, IN TIMES OF DROUGHT, PEOPLE FROM THE VILLAGE AT THE FOOT OF THE MOUNTAIN WOULD FORM A CHAIN...
...TO CARRY TRIBUTES TO THE SHRINE AND OFFER THEIR PRAYERS FOR RAIN.
GLOW
ZSH
YOU HAVE TRAVELED LONG AND FAR TO REACH THIS PLACE.
I THANK YOU.
ZSH

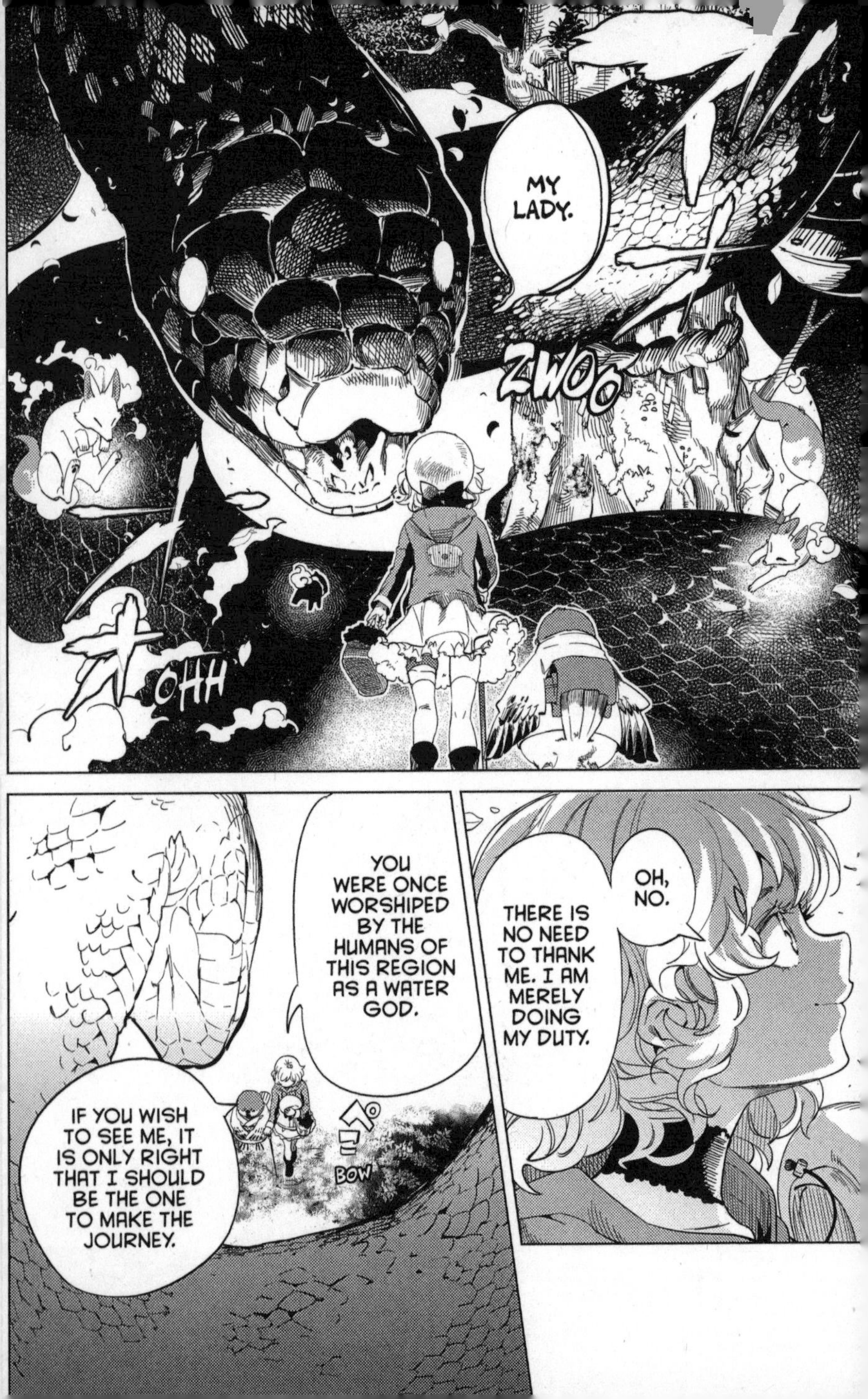
MY LADY.
ZWOO
OHH
OH, NO.
THERE IS NO NEED TO THANK ME. I AM MERELY DOING MY DUTY.
YOU WERE ONCE WORSHIPED BY THE HUMANS OF THIS REGION AS A WATER GOD.
IF YOU WISH TO SEE ME, IT IS ONLY RIGHT THAT I SHOULD BE THE ONE TO MAKE THE JOURNEY.
BOW

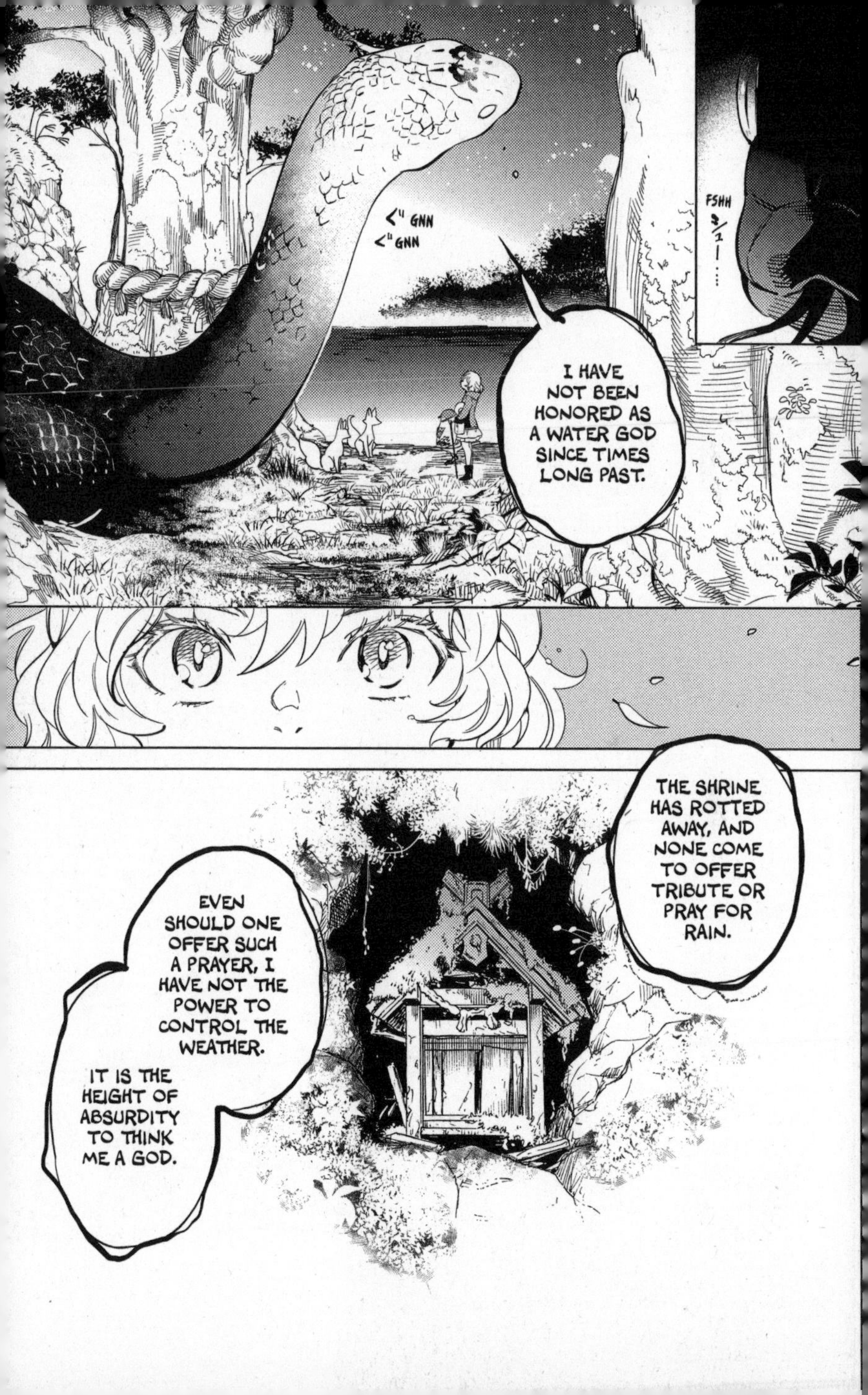
FSHH
...
<" GNN
<" GNN
I HAVE NOT BEEN HONORED AS A WATER GOD SINCE TIMES LONG PAST.
THE SHRINE HAS ROTTED AWAY, AND NONE COME TO OFFER TRIBUTE OR PRAY FOR RAIN.
EVEN SHOULD ONE OFFER SUCH A PRAYER, I HAVE NOT THE POWER TO CONTROL THE WEATHER.
IT IS THE HEIGHT OF ABSURDITY TO THINK ME A GOD.

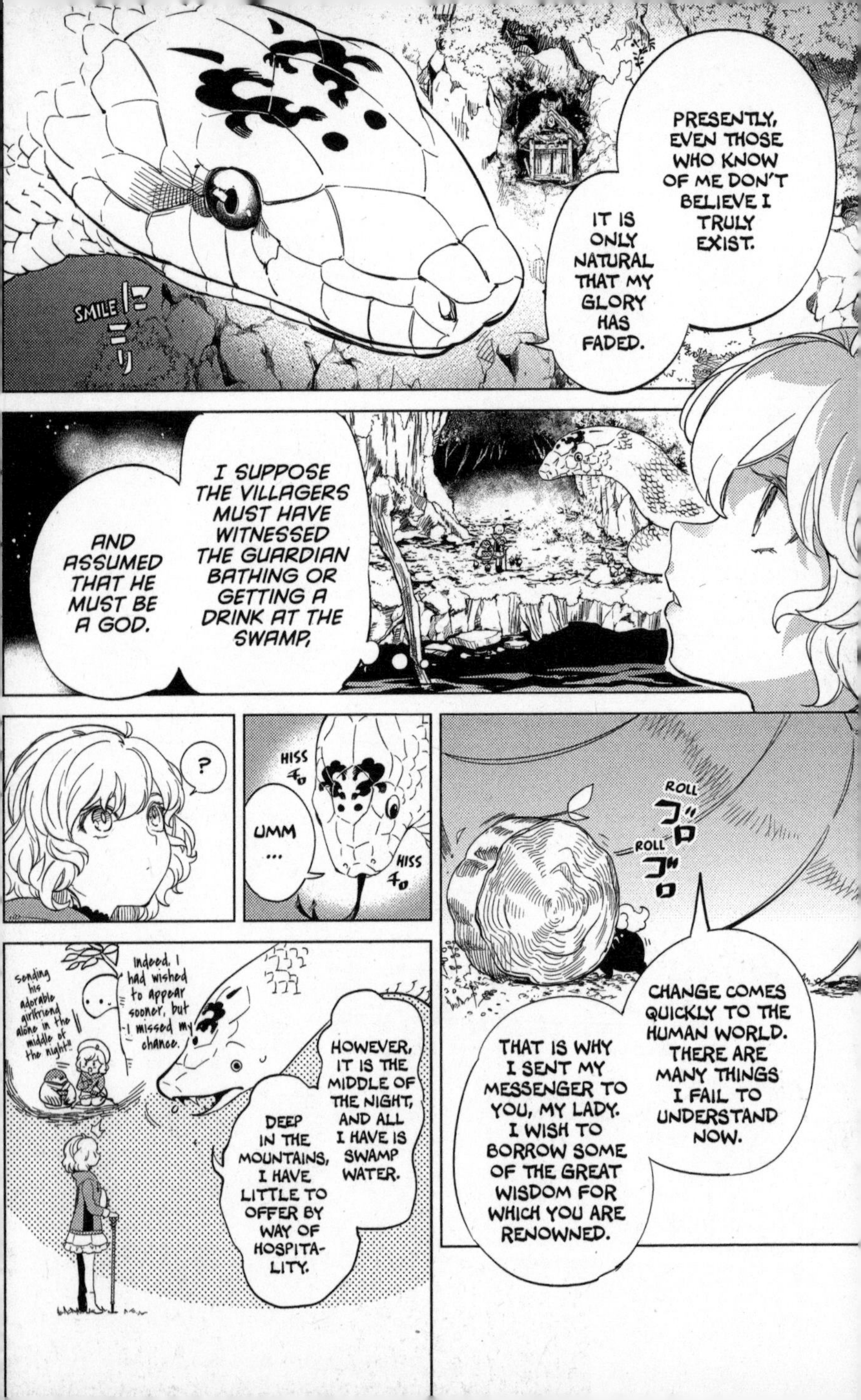
PRESENTLY, EVEN THOSE WHO KNOW OF ME DON'T BELIEVE I TRULY EXIST.
IT IS ONLY NATURAL THAT MY GLORY HAS FADED.
SMILE
I SUPPOSE THE VILLAGERS MUST HAVE WITNESSED THE GUARDIAN BATHING OR GETTING A DRINK AT THE SWAMP,
AND ASSUMED THAT HE MUST BE A GOD.
ROLL
ROLL
CHANGE COMES QUICKLY TO THE HUMAN WORLD. THERE ARE MANY THINGS I FAIL TO UNDERSTAND NOW.
THAT IS WHY I SENT MY MESSENGER TO YOU, MY LADY. I WISH TO BORROW SOME OF THE GREAT WISDOM FOR WHICH YOU ARE RENOWNED.
HISS
UMM...
HISS
?
HOWEVER, IT IS THE MIDDLE OF THE NIGHT, AND ALL I HAVE IS SWAMP WATER.
DEEP IN THE MOUNTAINS, I HAVE LITTLE TO OFFER BY WAY OF HOSPITALITY.
Indeed, I had wished to appear sooner, but I missed my chance.
Sending his adorable girlfriend alone in the middle of the night!!

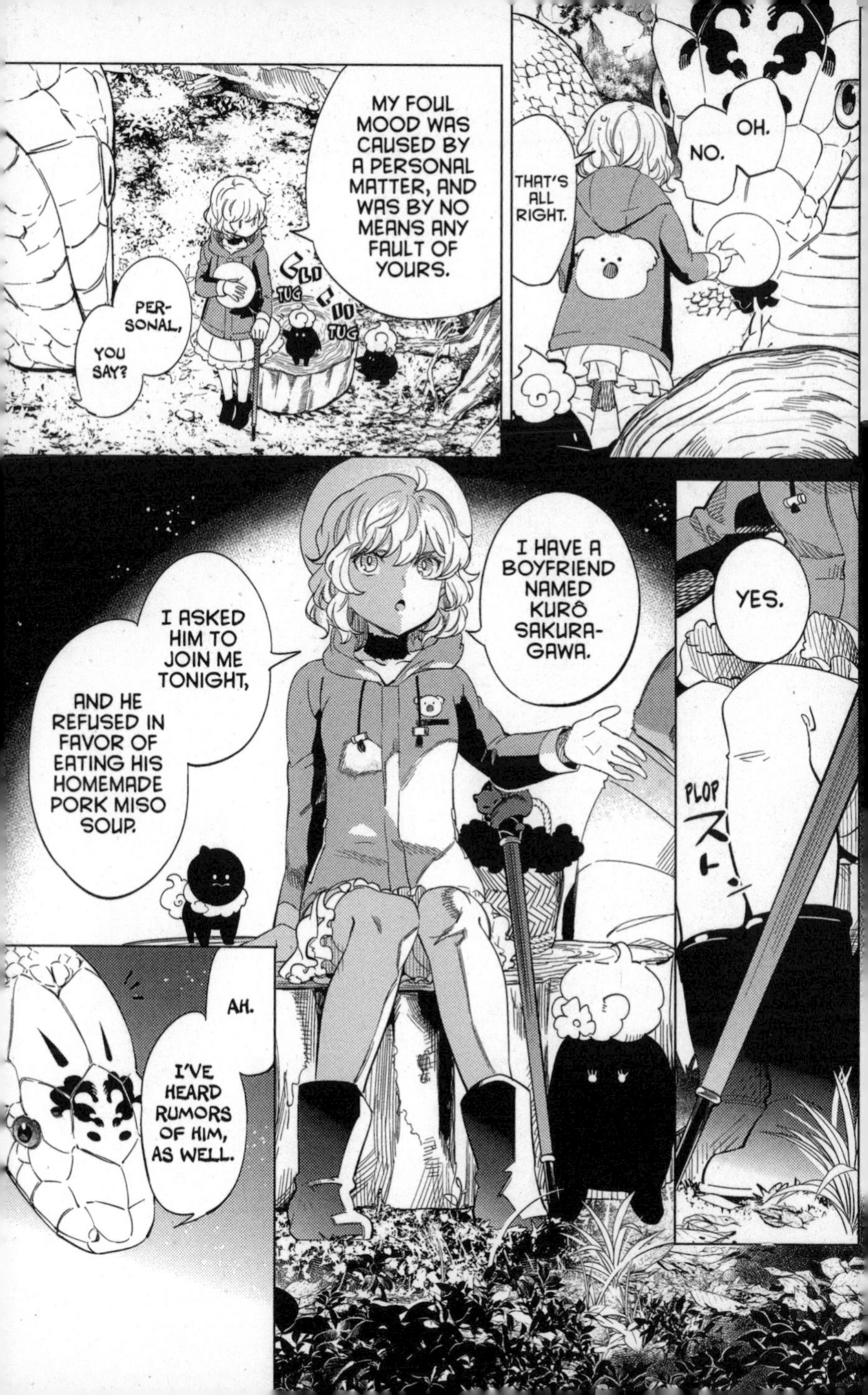
OH.
NO.
THAT'S ALL RIGHT.
MY FOUL MOOD WAS CAUSED BY A PERSONAL MATTER, AND WAS BY NO MEANS ANY FAULT OF YOURS.
TUG
TUG
PER-SONAL,
YOU SAY?
YES.
PLOP
I HAVE A BOYFRIEND NAMED KURÔ SAKURA-GAWA.
I ASKED HIM TO JOIN ME TONIGHT,
AND HE REFUSED IN FAVOR OF EATING HIS HOMEMADE PORK MISO SOUP.
AH.
I'VE HEARD RUMORS OF HIM, AS WELL.

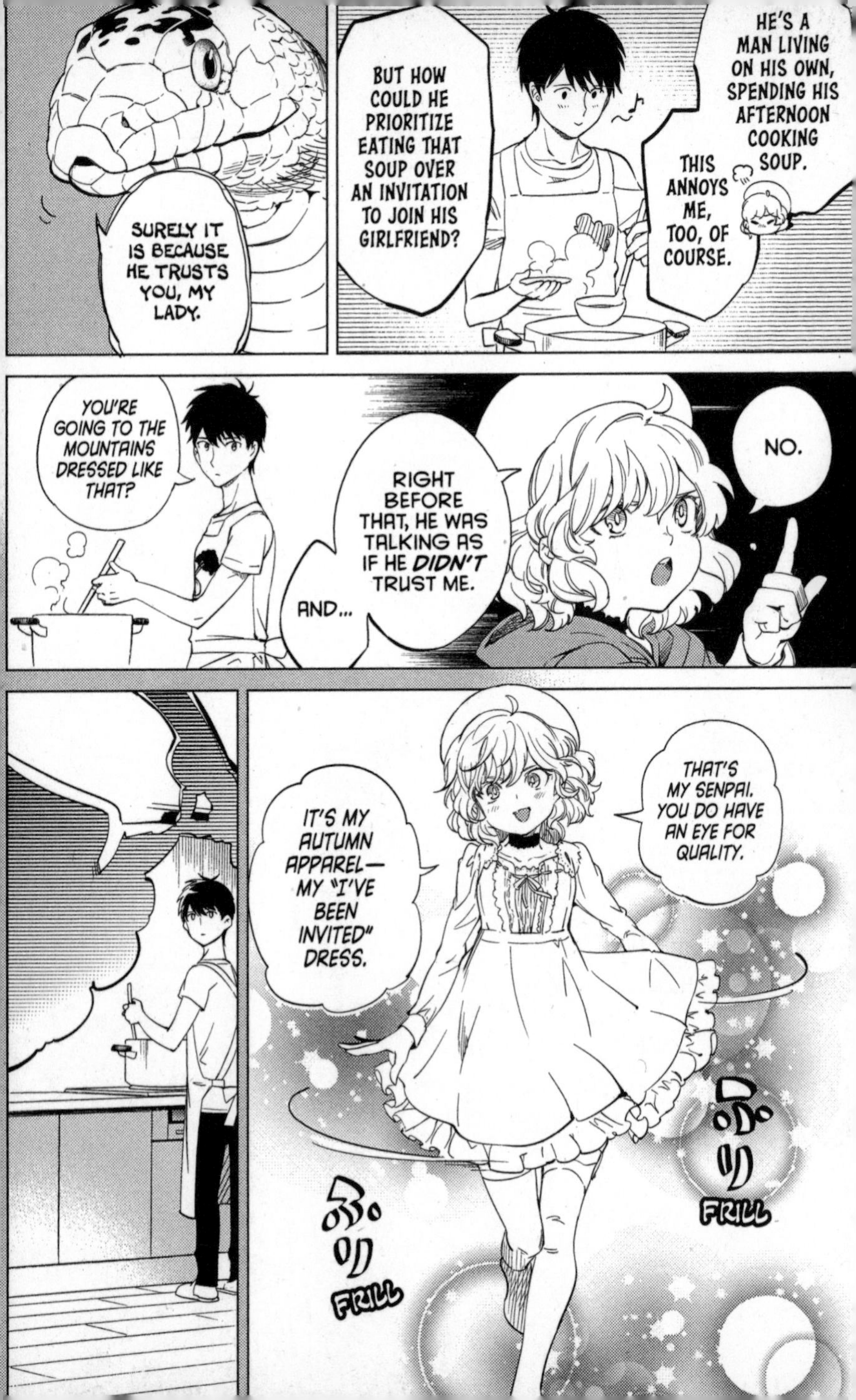
HE'S A MAN LIVING ON HIS OWN, SPENDING HIS AFTERNOON COOKING SOUP.
THIS ANNOYS ME, TOO, OF COURSE.
BUT HOW COULD HE PRIORITIZE EATING THAT SOUP OVER AN INVITATION TO JOIN HIS GIRLFRIEND?
SURELY IT IS BECAUSE HE TRUSTS YOU, MY LADY.
NO.
RIGHT BEFORE THAT, HE WAS TALKING AS IF HE *DIDN'T* TRUST ME.
AND...
YOU'RE GOING TO THE MOUNTAINS DRESSED LIKE THAT?
THAT'S MY SENPAI. YOU DO HAVE AN EYE FOR QUALITY.
IT'S MY AUTUMN APPAREL— MY "I'VE BEEN INVITED" DRESS.
FRILL
FRILL

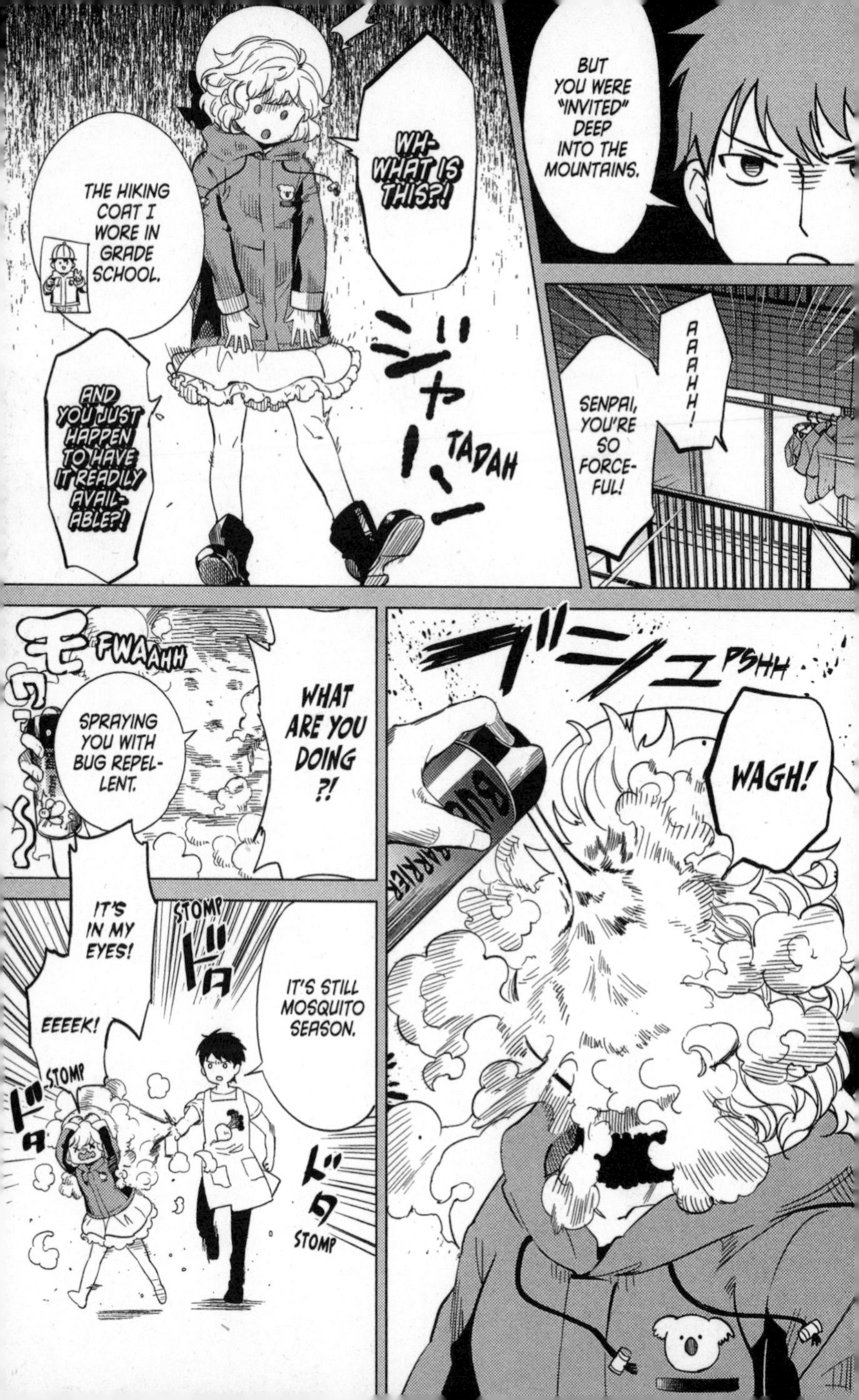

BUT YOU WERE "INVITED" DEEP INTO THE MOUNTAINS.
AAAHH!
SENPAI, YOU'RE SO FORCE-FUL!
WH-WHAT IS THIS?!
ジャーン
TADAH
THE HIKING COAT I WORE IN GRADE SCHOOL.
AND YOU JUST HAPPEN TO HAVE IT READILY AVAIL-ABLE?!
ブシュ
PSHH
WAGH!
BUG BARRIER
WHAT ARE YOU DOING?!
SPRAYING YOU WITH BUG REPEL-LENT.
FWAAHH
IT'S STILL MOSQUITO SEASON.
ドタ
STOMP
ドタ
STOMP
IT'S IN MY EYES!
EEEEK!
ドタ
STOMP

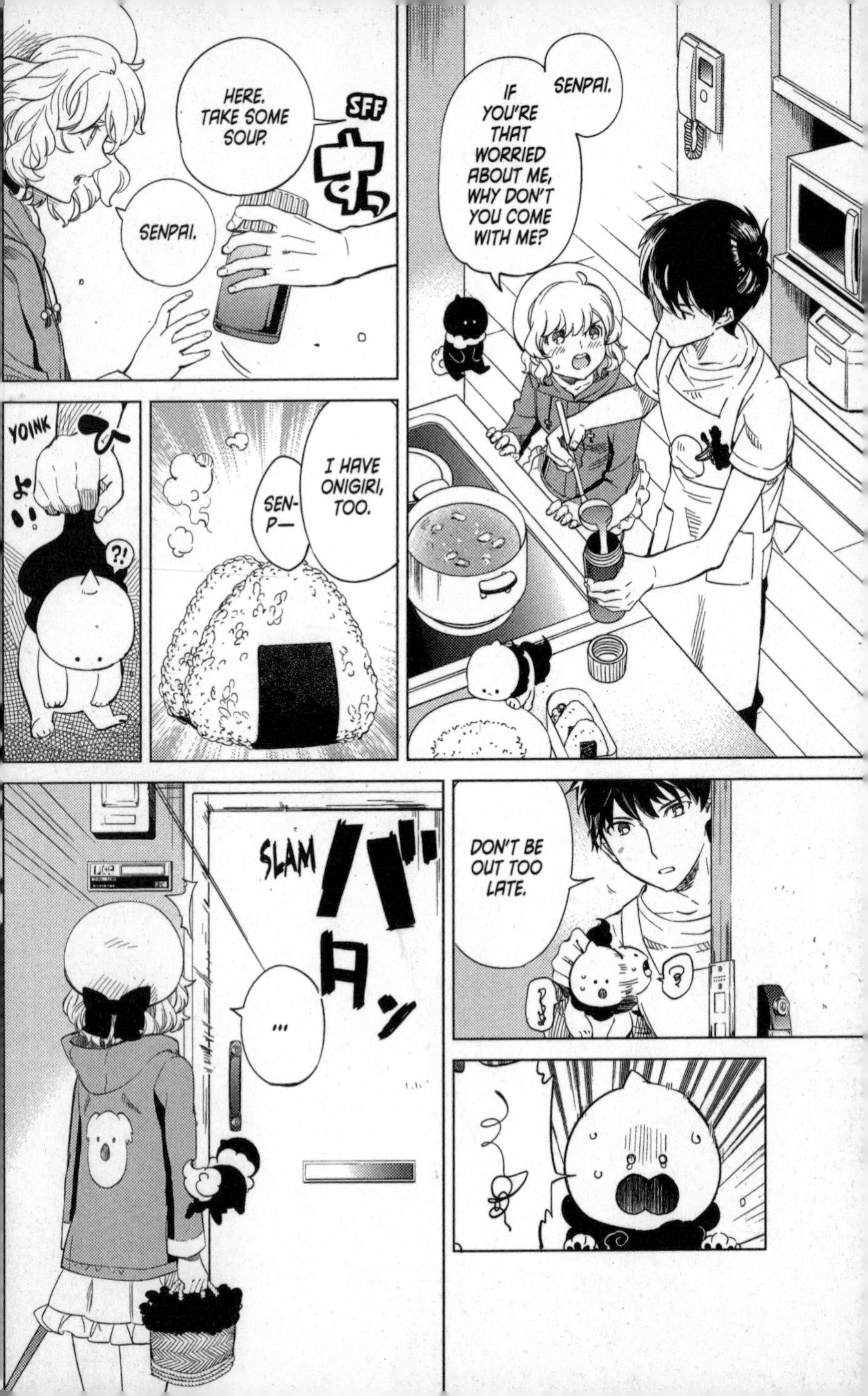
SENPAI.
IF YOU'RE THAT WORRIED ABOUT ME, WHY DON'T YOU COME WITH ME?
HERE. TAKE SOME SOUP.
SFF
SENPAI.
I HAVE ONIGIRI, TOO.
SEN-P—
YOINK
?!
DON'T BE OUT TOO LATE.
SLAM
...

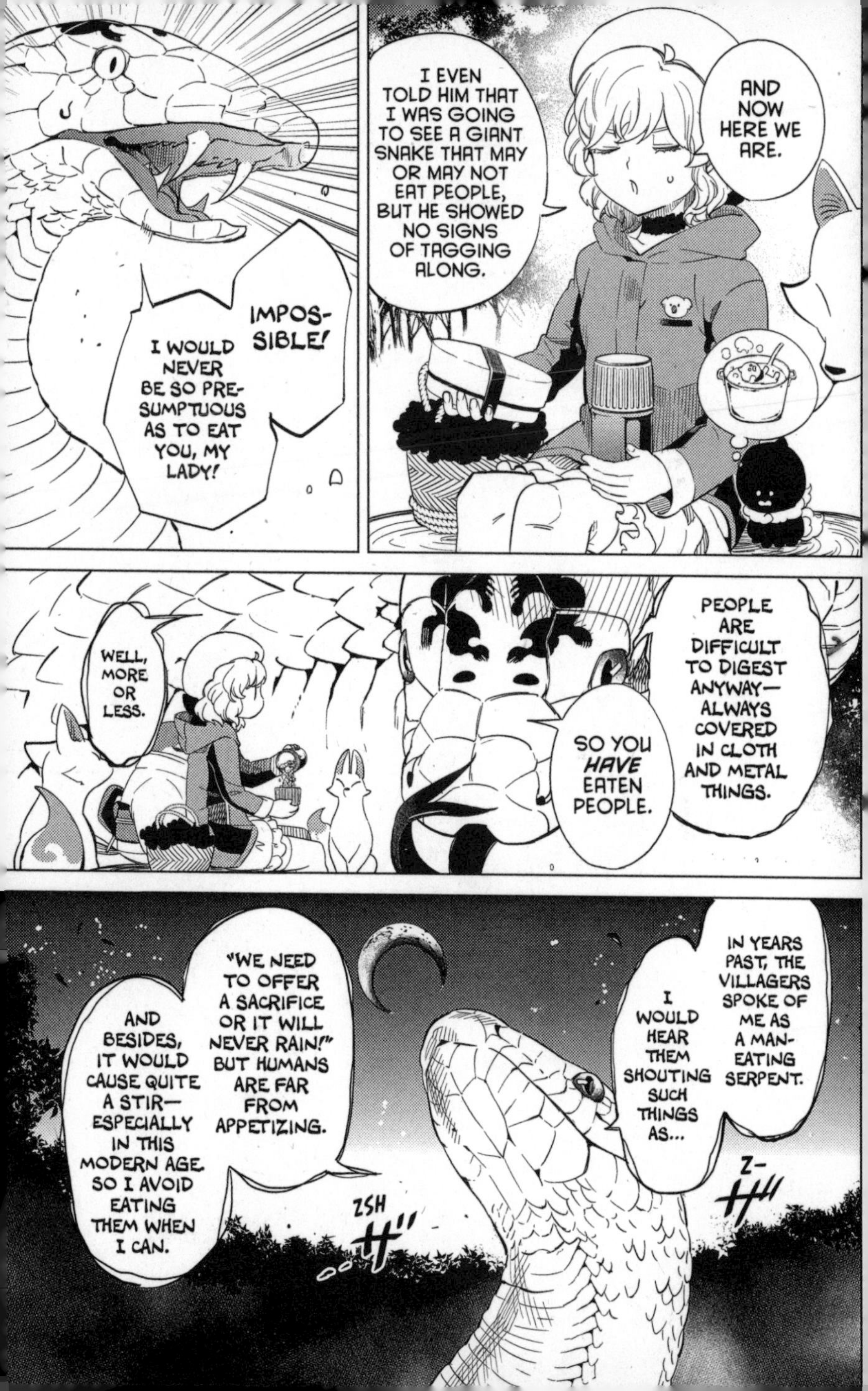
I EVEN TOLD HIM THAT I WAS GOING TO SEE A GIANT SNAKE THAT MAY OR MAY NOT EAT PEOPLE, BUT HE SHOWED NO SIGNS OF TAGGING ALONG.
AND NOW HERE WE ARE.
IMPOSSIBLE!
I WOULD NEVER BE SO PRESUMPTUOUS AS TO EAT YOU, MY LADY!
PEOPLE ARE DIFFICULT TO DIGEST ANYWAY—ALWAYS COVERED IN CLOTH AND METAL THINGS.
SO YOU *HAVE* EATEN PEOPLE.
WELL, MORE OR LESS.
IN YEARS PAST, THE VILLAGERS SPOKE OF ME AS A MAN-EATING SERPENT.
I WOULD HEAR THEM SHOUTING SUCH THINGS AS...
"WE NEED TO OFFER A SACRIFICE OR IT WILL NEVER RAIN!" BUT HUMANS ARE FAR FROM APPETIZING.
AND BESIDES, IT WOULD CAUSE QUITE A STIR—ESPECIALLY IN THIS MODERN AGE. SO I AVOID EATING THEM WHEN I CAN.
Z-
ZSH

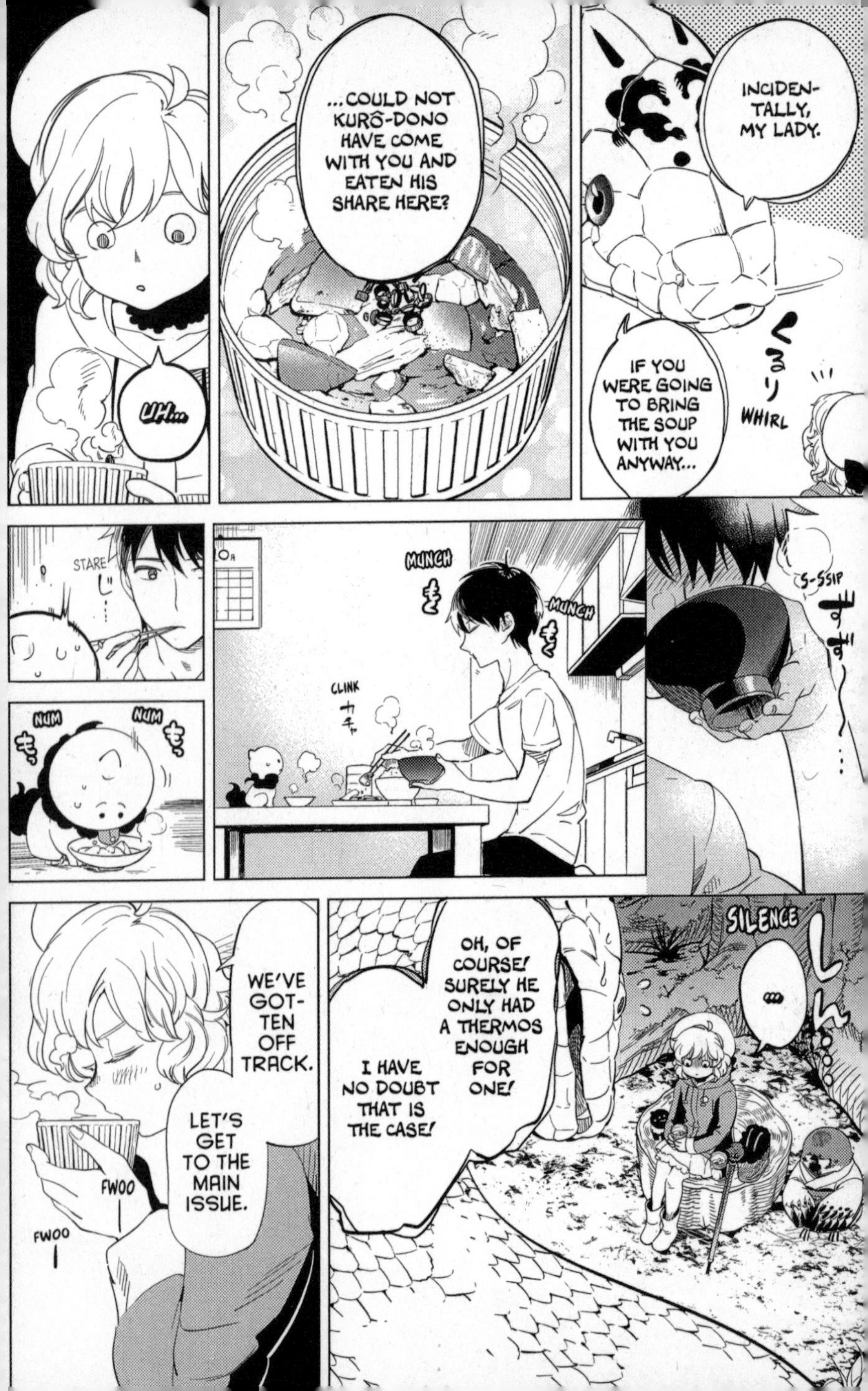
INCIDEN-TALLY, MY LADY.
くるり
WHIRL
IF YOU WERE GOING TO BRING THE SOUP WITH YOU ANYWAY...
...COULD NOT KURŌ-DONO HAVE COME WITH YOU AND EATEN HIS SHARE HERE?
UH...
S-SSIP
すず〜…
MUNCH
MUNCH
CLINK
カチャ
STARE
じー…
NUM
NUM
SILENCE
しん…
...
OH, OF COURSE! SURELY HE ONLY HAD A THERMOS ENOUGH FOR ONE!
I HAVE NO DOUBT THAT IS THE CASE!
WE'VE GOT-TEN OFF TRACK.
LET'S GET TO THE MAIN ISSUE.
FWOO
FWOO

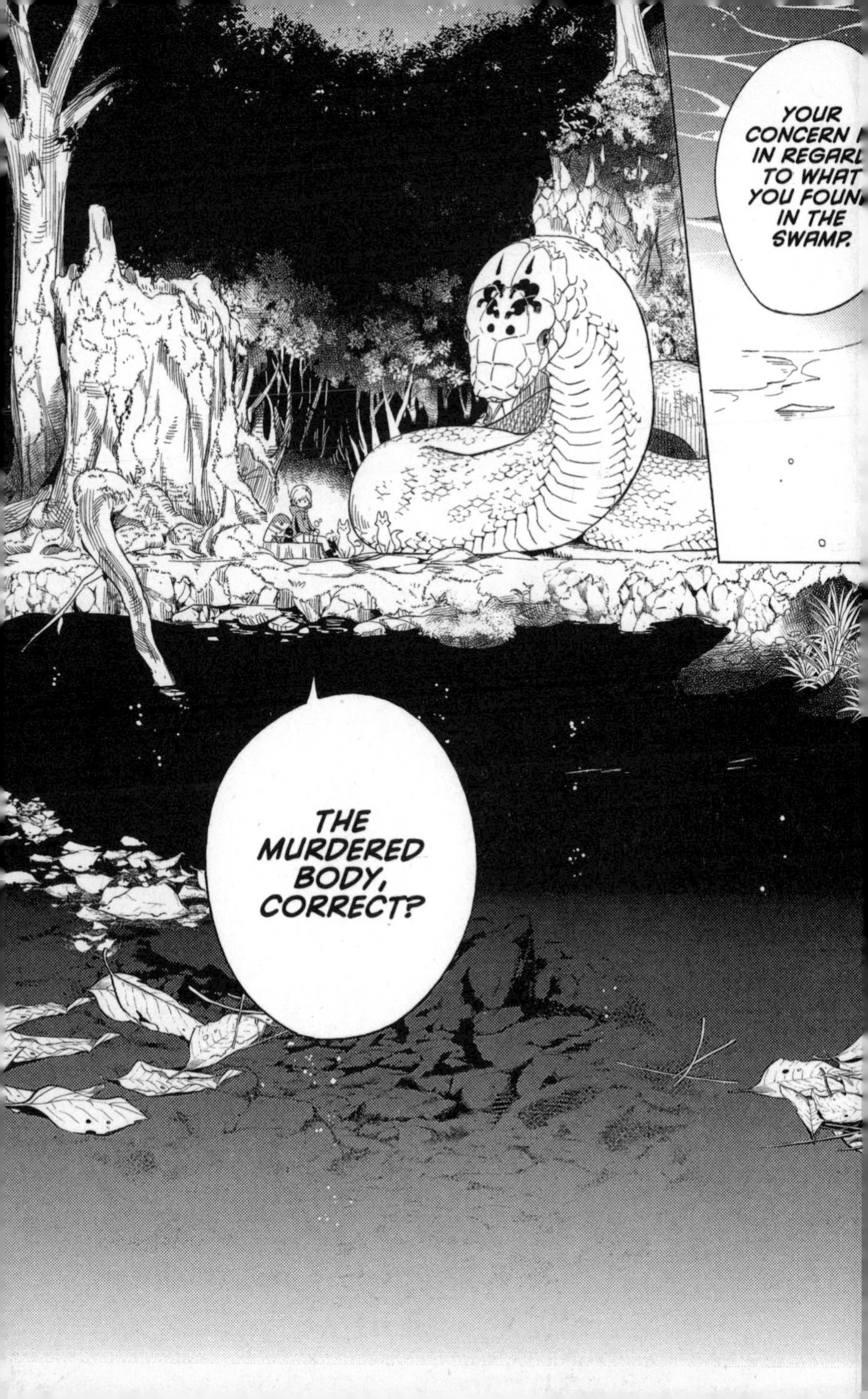
YOUR CONCERN I IN REGARL TO WHAT YOU FOUN IN THE SWAMP.
THE MURDERED BODY, CORRECT?

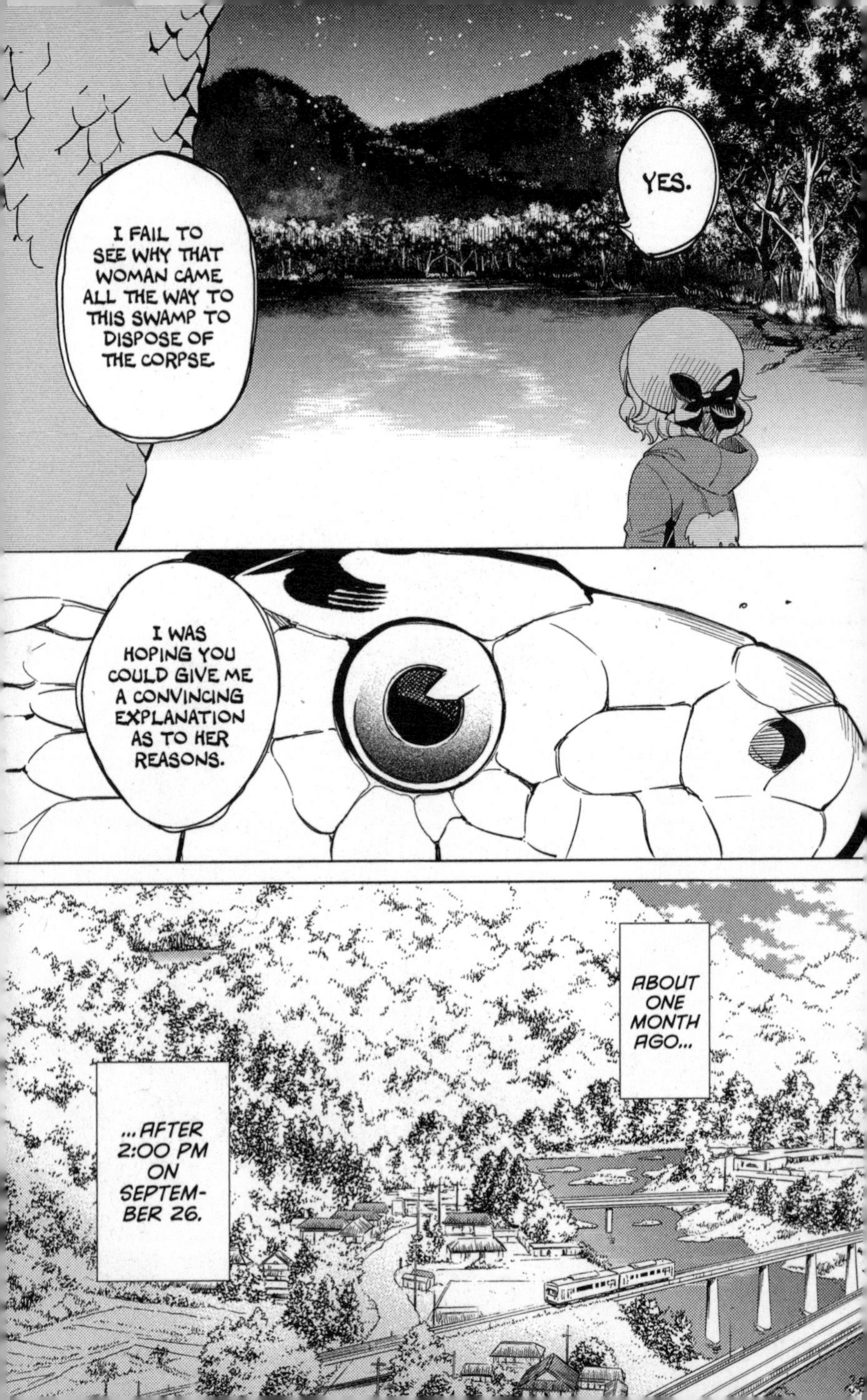
YES.
I FAIL TO SEE WHY THAT WOMAN CAME ALL THE WAY TO THIS SWAMP TO DISPOSE OF THE CORPSE.
I WAS HOPING YOU COULD GIVE ME A CONVINCING EXPLANATION AS TO HER REASONS.
ABOUT ONE MONTH AGO...
...AFTER 2:00 PM ON SEPTEMBER 26.

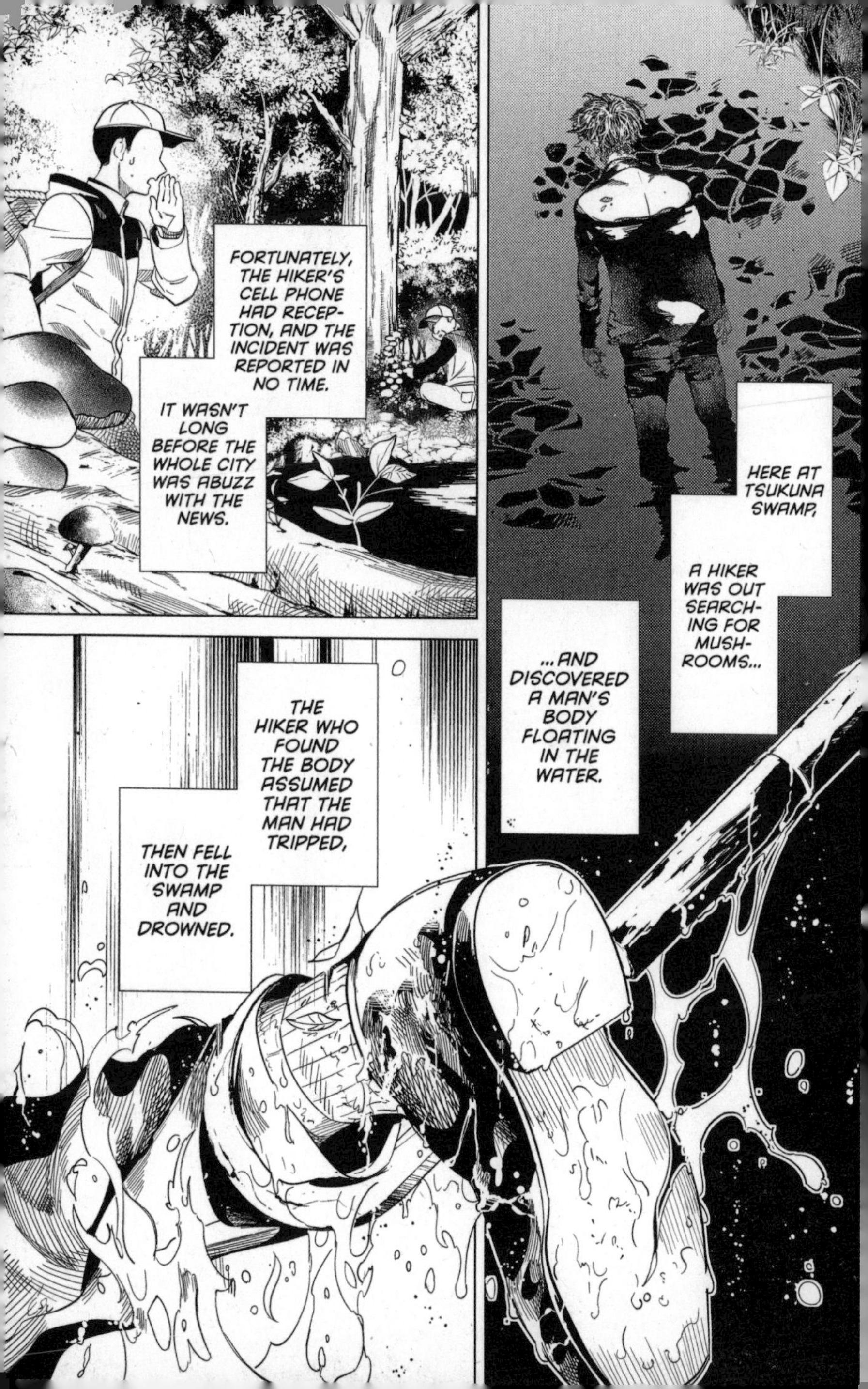
HERE AT TSUKUNA SWAMP,
A HIKER WAS OUT SEARCHING FOR MUSHROOMS...
...AND DISCOVERED A MAN'S BODY FLOATING IN THE WATER.
FORTUNATELY, THE HIKER'S CELL PHONE HAD RECEPTION, AND THE INCIDENT WAS REPORTED IN NO TIME.
IT WASN'T LONG BEFORE THE WHOLE CITY WAS ABUZZ WITH THE NEWS.
THE HIKER WHO FOUND THE BODY ASSUMED THAT THE MAN HAD TRIPPED,
THEN FELL INTO THE SWAMP AND DROWNED.

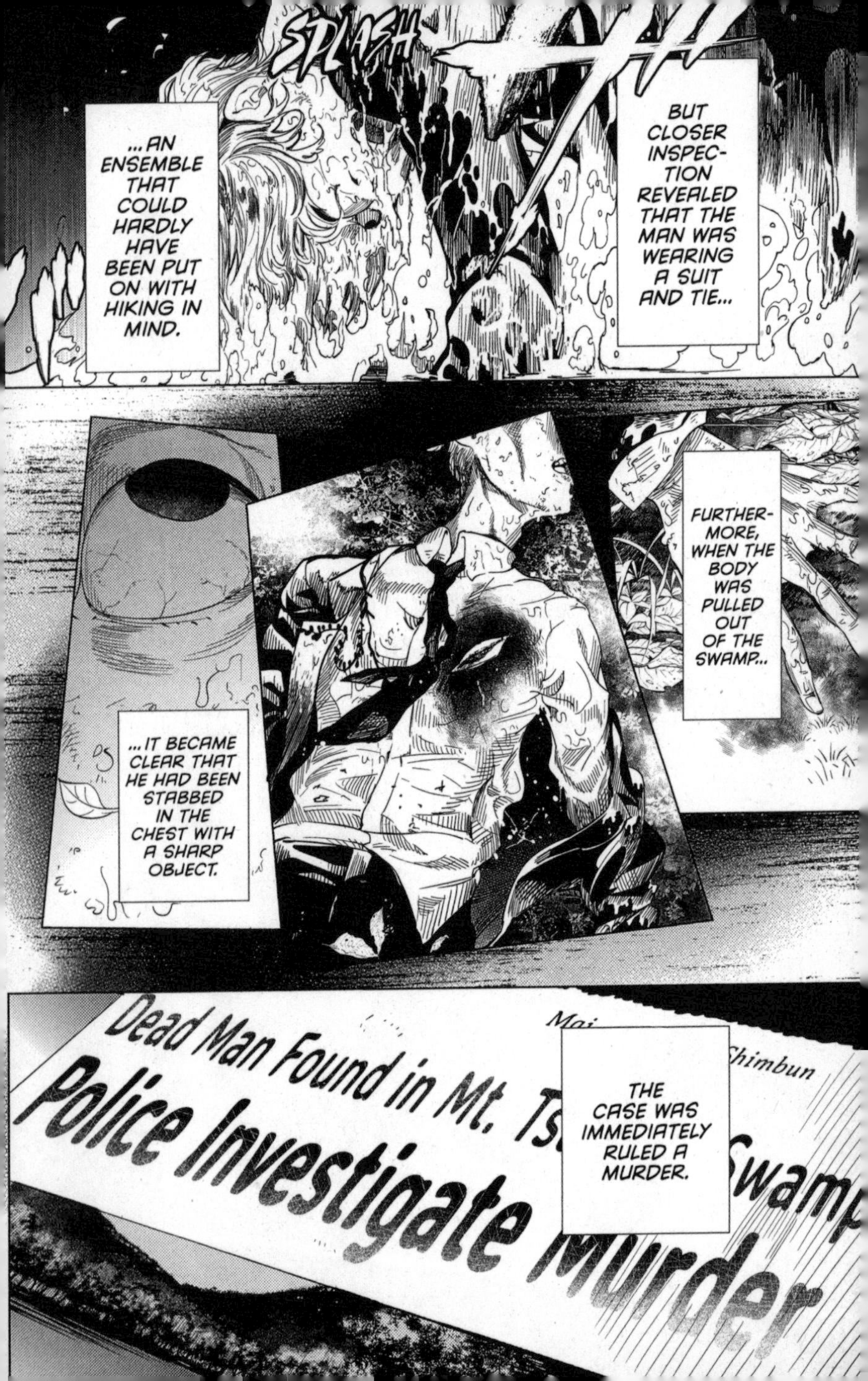
SPLASH
BUT CLOSER INSPECTION REVEALED THAT THE MAN WAS WEARING A SUIT AND TIE...
...AN ENSEMBLE THAT COULD HARDLY HAVE BEEN PUT ON WITH HIKING IN MIND.
FURTHERMORE, WHEN THE BODY WAS PULLED OUT OF THE SWAMP...
...IT BECAME CLEAR THAT HE HAD BEEN STABBED IN THE CHEST WITH A SHARP OBJECT.
Dead Man Found in Mt.
Police Investigate Murder
THE CASE WAS IMMEDIATELY RULED A MURDER.

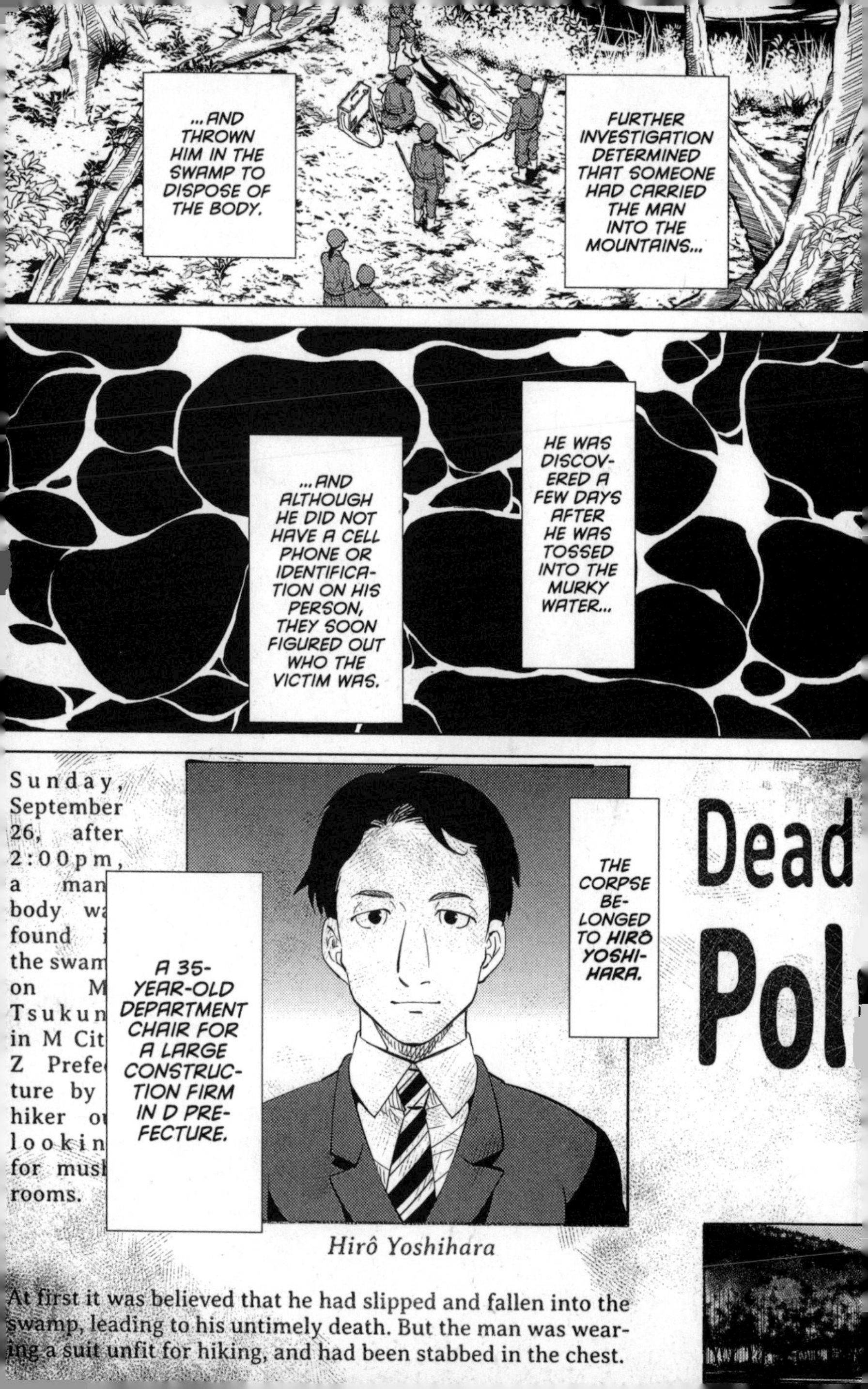
FURTHER INVESTIGATION DETERMINED THAT SOMEONE HAD CARRIED THE MAN INTO THE MOUNTAINS...
...AND THROWN HIM IN THE SWAMP TO DISPOSE OF THE BODY.
HE WAS DISCOVERED A FEW DAYS AFTER HE WAS TOSSED INTO THE MURKY WATER...
...AND ALTHOUGH HE DID NOT HAVE A CELL PHONE OR IDENTIFICATION ON HIS PERSON, THEY SOON FIGURED OUT WHO THE VICTIM WAS.
THE CORPSE BELONGED TO HIRÔ YOSHIHARA.
A 35-YEAR-OLD DEPARTMENT CHAIR FOR A LARGE CONSTRUCTION FIRM IN D PREFECTURE.
Hirô Yoshihara
At first it was believed that he had slipped and fallen into the swamp, leading to his untimely death. But the man was wearing a suit unfit for hiking, and had been stabbed in the chest.

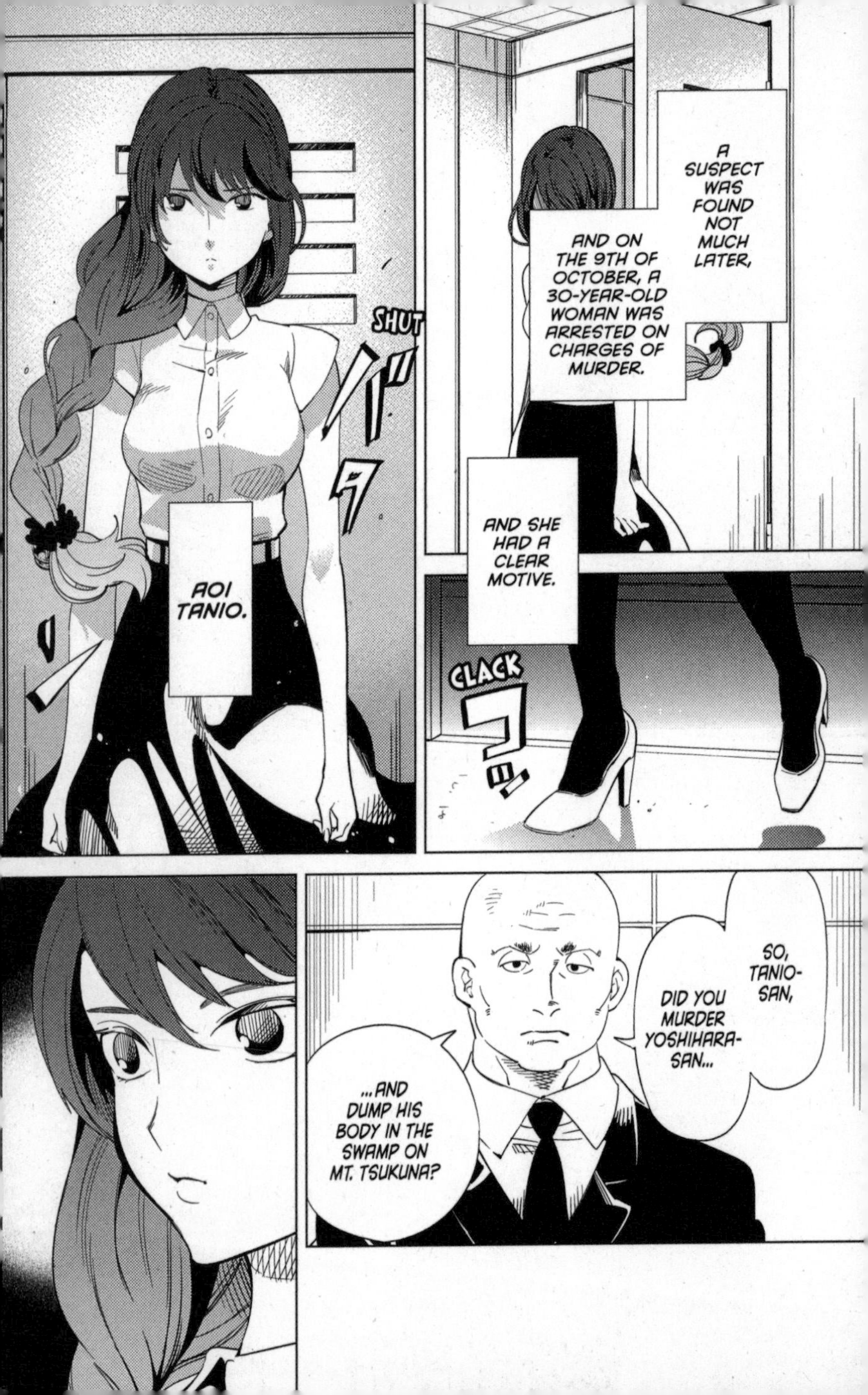
A SUSPECT WAS FOUND NOT MUCH LATER,
AND ON THE 9TH OF OCTOBER, A 30-YEAR-OLD WOMAN WAS ARRESTED ON CHARGES OF MURDER.
AND SHE HAD A CLEAR MOTIVE.
CLACK
SHUT
AOI TANIO.
SO, TANIO-SAN,
DID YOU MURDER YOSHIHARA-SAN...
...AND DUMP HIS BODY IN THE SWAMP ON MT. TSUKUNA?

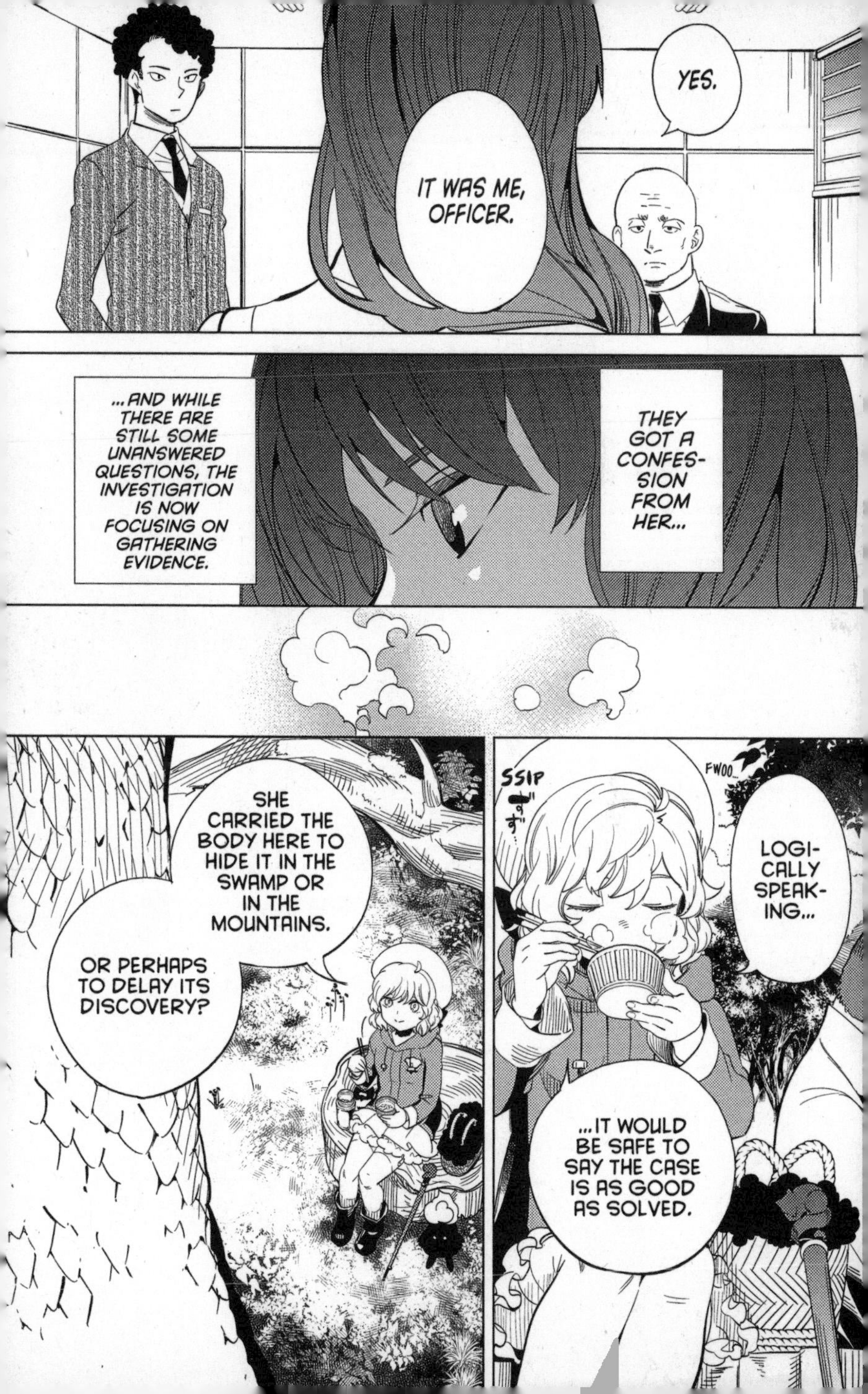
YES.
IT WAS ME, OFFICER.
THEY GOT A CONFESSION FROM HER...
...AND WHILE THERE ARE STILL SOME UNANSWERED QUESTIONS, THE INVESTIGATION IS NOW FOCUSING ON GATHERING EVIDENCE.
FWOO...
SSIP
LOGICALLY SPEAKING...
...IT WOULD BE SAFE TO SAY THE CASE IS AS GOOD AS SOLVED.
SHE CARRIED THE BODY HERE TO HIDE IT IN THE SWAMP OR IN THE MOUNTAINS.
OR PERHAPS TO DELAY ITS DISCOVERY?

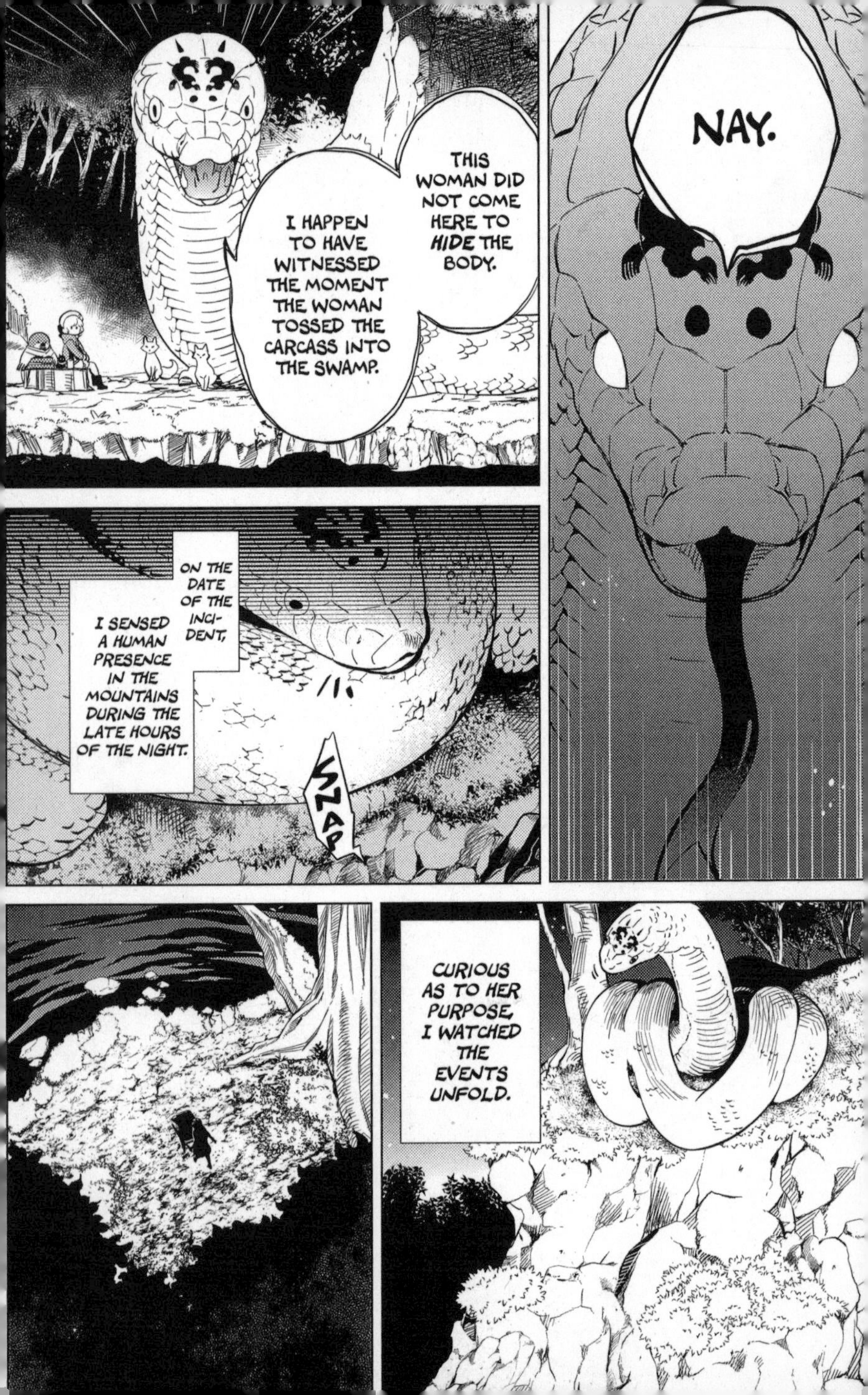
NAY.
THIS WOMAN DID NOT COME HERE TO *HIDE* THE BODY.
I HAPPEN TO HAVE WITNESSED THE MOMENT THE WOMAN TOSSED THE CARCASS INTO THE SWAMP.
ON THE DATE OF THE INCI-DENT,
I SENSED A HUMAN PRESENCE IN THE MOUNTAINS DURING THE LATE HOURS OF THE NIGHT.
SNAP
CURIOUS AS TO HER PURPOSE, I WATCHED THE EVENTS UNFOLD.

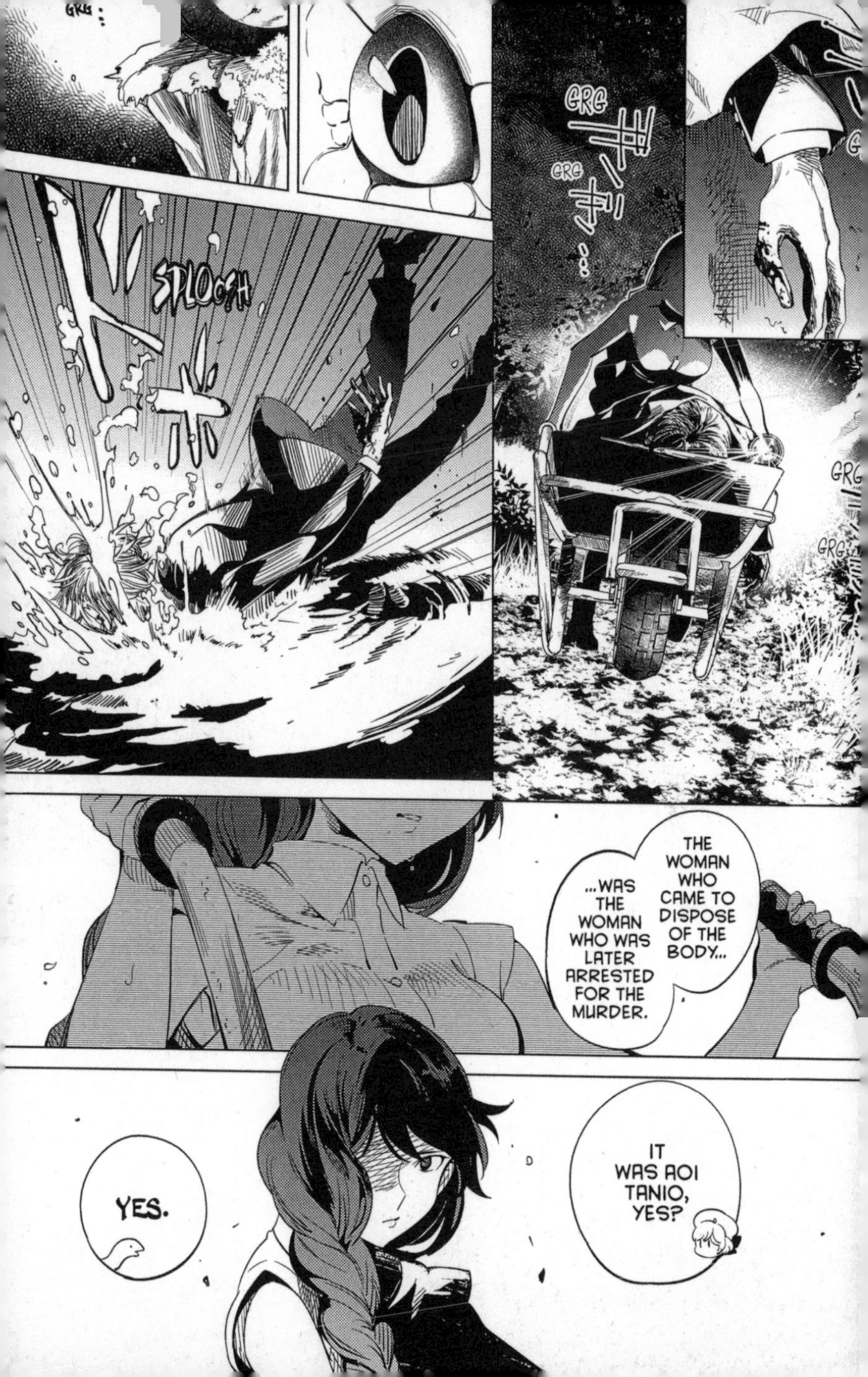
GRG
GRG
GRG
GRG
GRG...
SPLOOSH
THE WOMAN WHO CAME TO DISPOSE OF THE BODY...
...WAS THE WOMAN WHO WAS LATER ARRESTED FOR THE MURDER.
IT WAS AOI TANIO, YES?
YES.

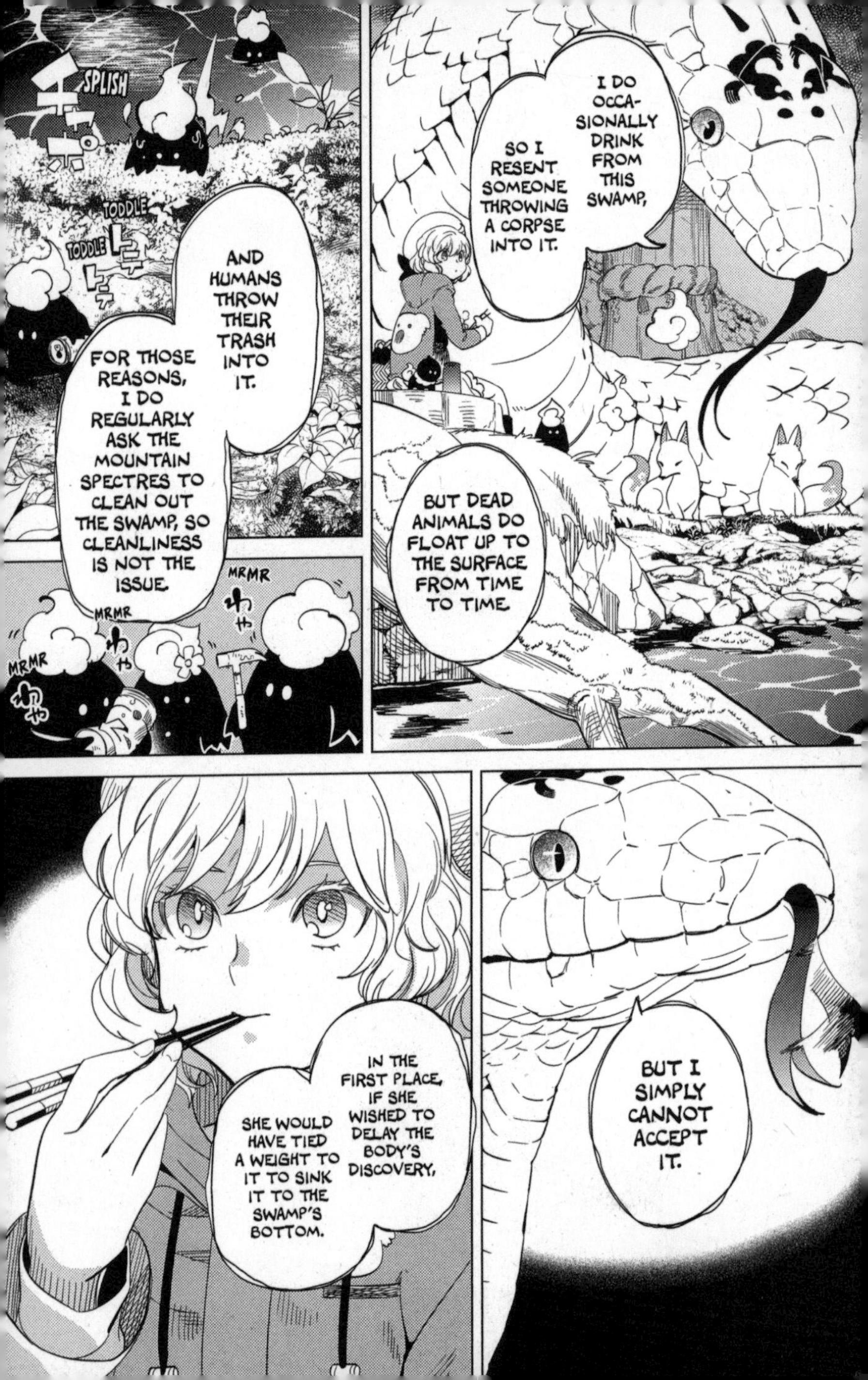
I DO OCCA-SIONALLY DRINK FROM THIS SWAMP,
SO I RESENT SOMEONE THROWING A CORPSE INTO IT.
SPLISH
AND HUMANS THROW THEIR TRASH INTO IT.
TODDLE TODDLE
FOR THOSE REASONS, I DO REGULARLY ASK THE MOUNTAIN SPECTRES TO CLEAN OUT THE SWAMP, SO CLEANLINESS IS NOT THE ISSUE.
MRMR
MRMR
MRMR
BUT DEAD ANIMALS DO FLOAT UP TO THE SURFACE FROM TIME TO TIME.
BUT I SIMPLY CANNOT ACCEPT IT.
IN THE FIRST PLACE, IF SHE WISHED TO DELAY THE BODY'S DISCOVERY,
SHE WOULD HAVE TIED A WEIGHT TO IT TO SINK IT TO THE SWAMP'S BOTTOM.

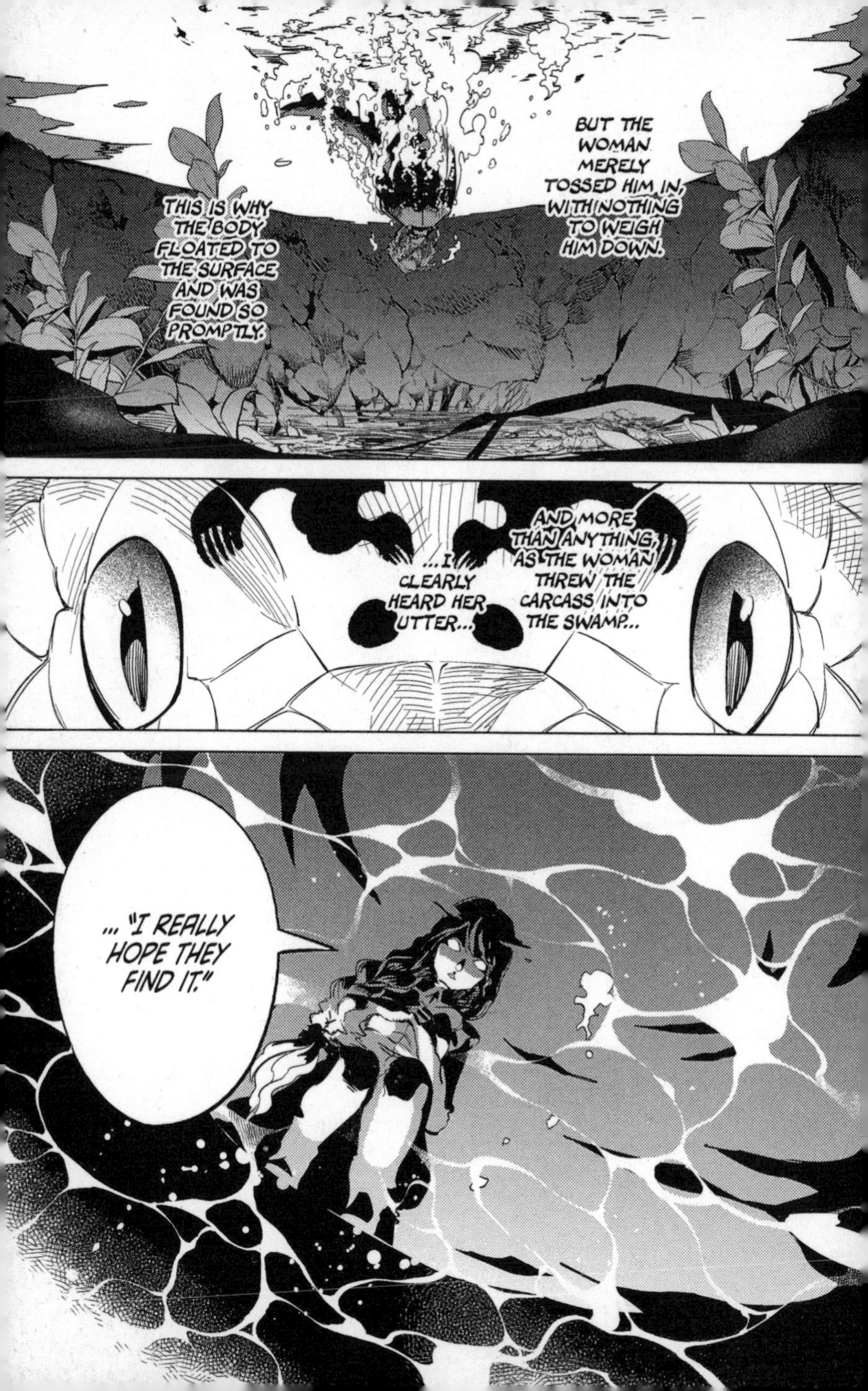
BUT THE WOMAN MERELY TOSSED HIM IN, WITH NOTHING TO WEIGH HIM DOWN.
THIS IS WHY THE BODY FLOATED TO THE SURFACE AND WAS FOUND SO PROMPTLY.
AND MORE THAN ANYTHING, AS THE WOMAN THREW THE CARCASS INTO THE SWAMP...
...I CLEARLY HEARD HER UTTER...
..."I REALLY HOPE THEY FIND IT."

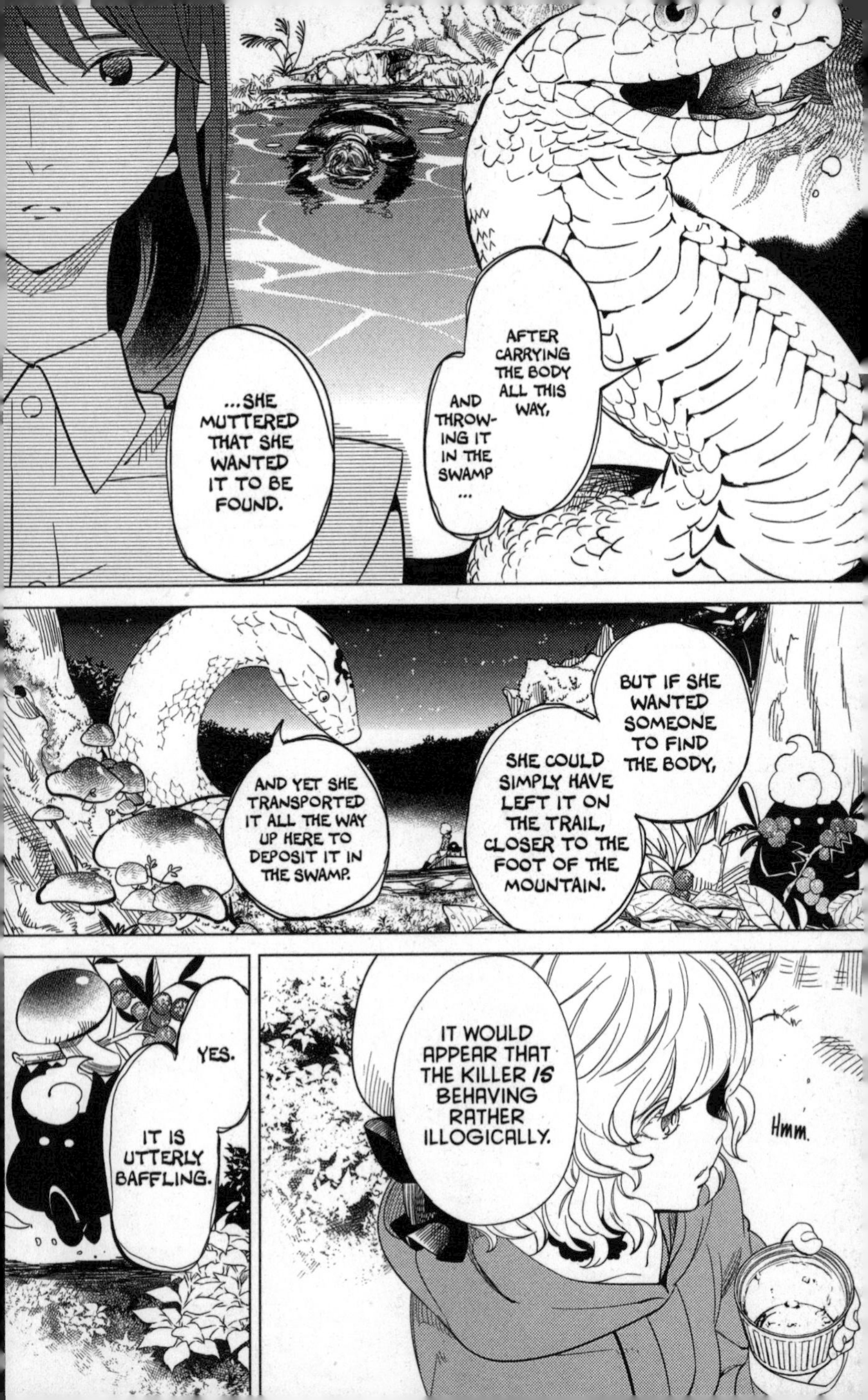
AFTER CARRYING THE BODY ALL THIS WAY,
AND THROWING IT IN THE SWAMP...
...SHE MUTTERED THAT SHE WANTED IT TO BE FOUND.
BUT IF SHE WANTED SOMEONE TO FIND THE BODY,
SHE COULD SIMPLY HAVE LEFT IT ON THE TRAIL, CLOSER TO THE FOOT OF THE MOUNTAIN.
AND YET SHE TRANSPORTED IT ALL THE WAY UP HERE TO DEPOSIT IT IN THE SWAMP.
Hmm.
IT WOULD APPEAR THAT THE KILLER *IS* BEHAVING RATHER ILLOGICALLY.
YES.
IT IS UTTERLY BAFFLING.

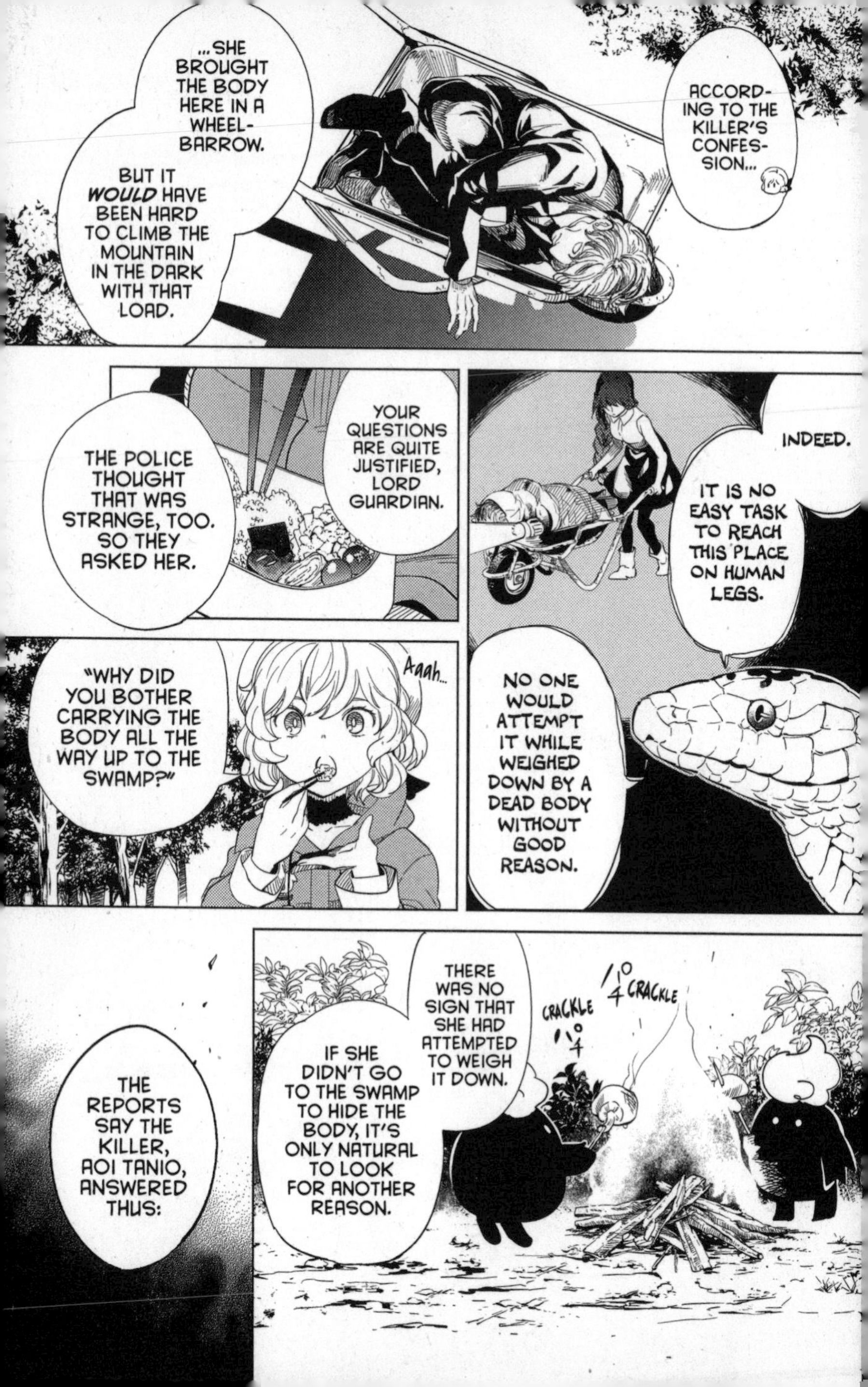
ACCORDING TO THE KILLER'S CONFESSION...
...SHE BROUGHT THE BODY HERE IN A WHEELBARROW.
BUT IT *WOULD* HAVE BEEN HARD TO CLIMB THE MOUNTAIN IN THE DARK WITH THAT LOAD.
INDEED.
IT IS NO EASY TASK TO REACH THIS PLACE ON HUMAN LEGS.
NO ONE WOULD ATTEMPT IT WHILE WEIGHED DOWN BY A DEAD BODY WITHOUT GOOD REASON.
YOUR QUESTIONS ARE QUITE JUSTIFIED, LORD GUARDIAN.
THE POLICE THOUGHT THAT WAS STRANGE, TOO. SO THEY ASKED HER.
Aaah...
"WHY DID YOU BOTHER CARRYING THE BODY ALL THE WAY UP TO THE SWAMP?"
CRACKLE
CRACKLE
THERE WAS NO SIGN THAT SHE HAD ATTEMPTED TO WEIGH IT DOWN.
IF SHE DIDN'T GO TO THE SWAMP TO HIDE THE BODY, IT'S ONLY NATURAL TO LOOK FOR ANOTHER REASON.
THE REPORTS SAY THE KILLER, AOI TANIO, ANSWERED THUS:

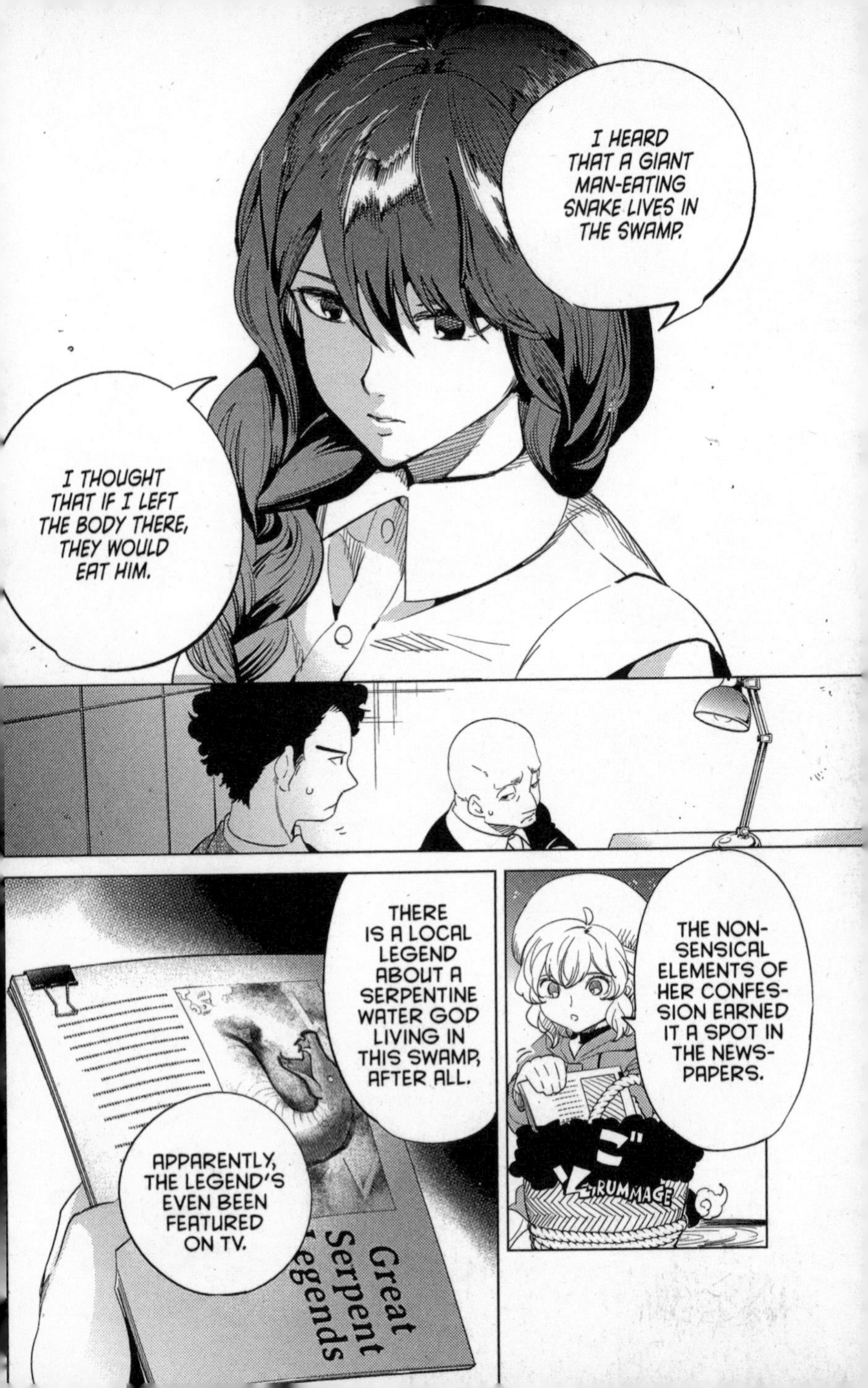
I HEARD THAT A GIANT MAN-EATING SNAKE LIVES IN THE SWAMP.
I THOUGHT THAT IF I LEFT THE BODY THERE, THEY WOULD EAT HIM.
THE NONSENSICAL ELEMENTS OF HER CONFESSION EARNED IT A SPOT IN THE NEWSPAPERS.
RUMMAGE
THERE IS A LOCAL LEGEND ABOUT A SERPENTINE WATER GOD LIVING IN THIS SWAMP, AFTER ALL.
APPARENTLY, THE LEGEND'S EVEN BEEN FEATURED ON TV.
Great Serpent Legends

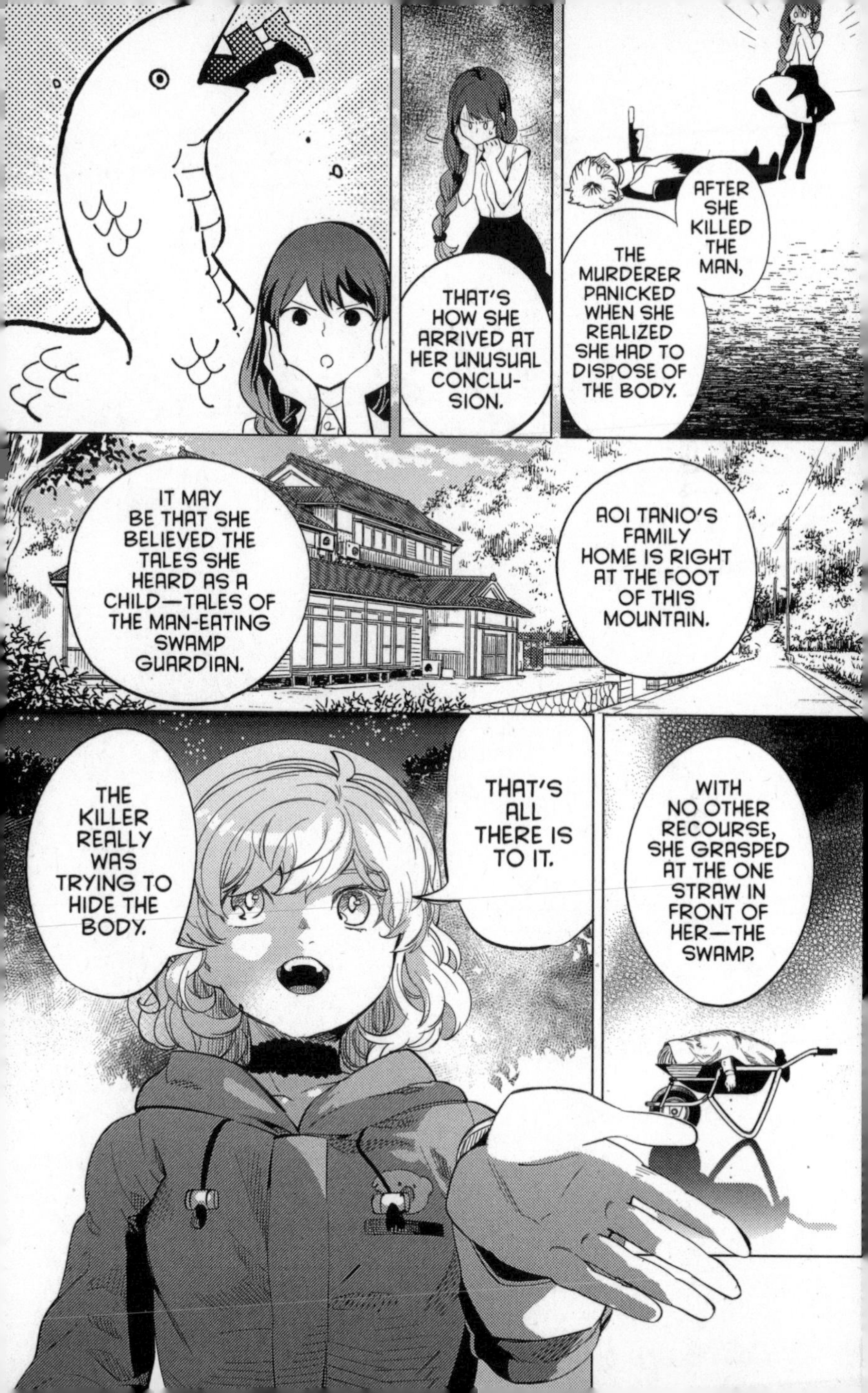
AFTER SHE KILLED THE MAN,
THE MURDERER PANICKED WHEN SHE REALIZED SHE HAD TO DISPOSE OF THE BODY.
THAT'S HOW SHE ARRIVED AT HER UNUSUAL CONCLUSION.
AOI TANIO'S FAMILY HOME IS RIGHT AT THE FOOT OF THIS MOUNTAIN.
IT MAY BE THAT SHE BELIEVED THE TALES SHE HEARD AS A CHILD—TALES OF THE MAN-EATING SWAMP GUARDIAN.
WITH NO OTHER RECOURSE, SHE GRASPED AT THE ONE STRAW IN FRONT OF HER—THE SWAMP.
THAT'S ALL THERE IS TO IT.
THE KILLER REALLY WAS TRYING TO HIDE THE BODY.

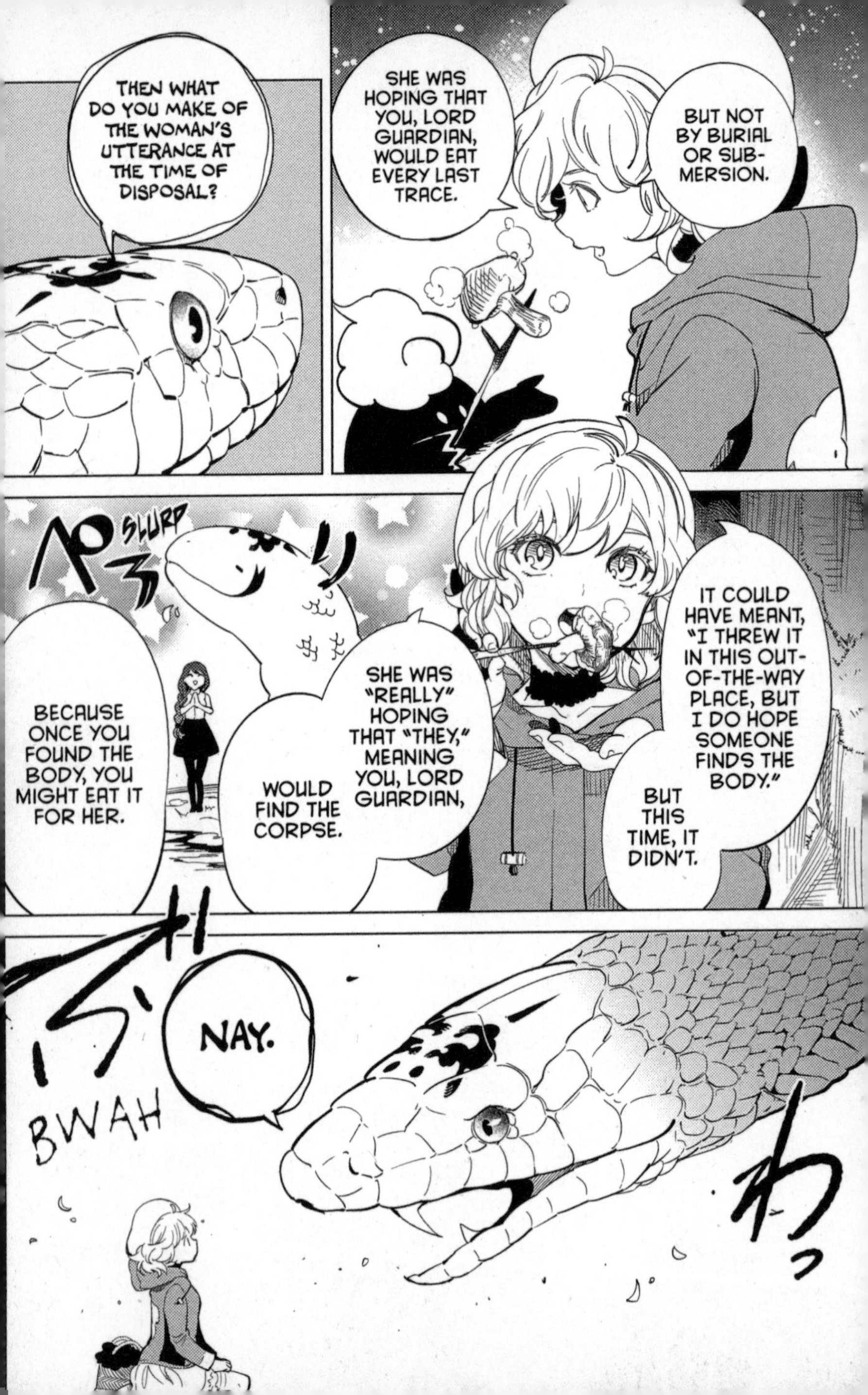
BUT NOT BY BURIAL OR SUB-MERSION.
SHE WAS HOPING THAT YOU, LORD GUARDIAN, WOULD EAT EVERY LAST TRACE.
THEN WHAT DO YOU MAKE OF THE WOMAN'S UTTERANCE AT THE TIME OF DISPOSAL?
IT COULD HAVE MEANT, "I THREW IT IN THIS OUT-OF-THE-WAY PLACE, BUT I DO HOPE SOMEONE FINDS THE BODY."
BUT THIS TIME, IT DIDN'T.
SHE WAS "REALLY" HOPING THAT "THEY," MEANING YOU, LORD GUARDIAN,
WOULD FIND THE CORPSE.
SLURP
BECAUSE ONCE YOU FOUND THE BODY, YOU MIGHT EAT IT FOR HER.
NAY.
BWAH

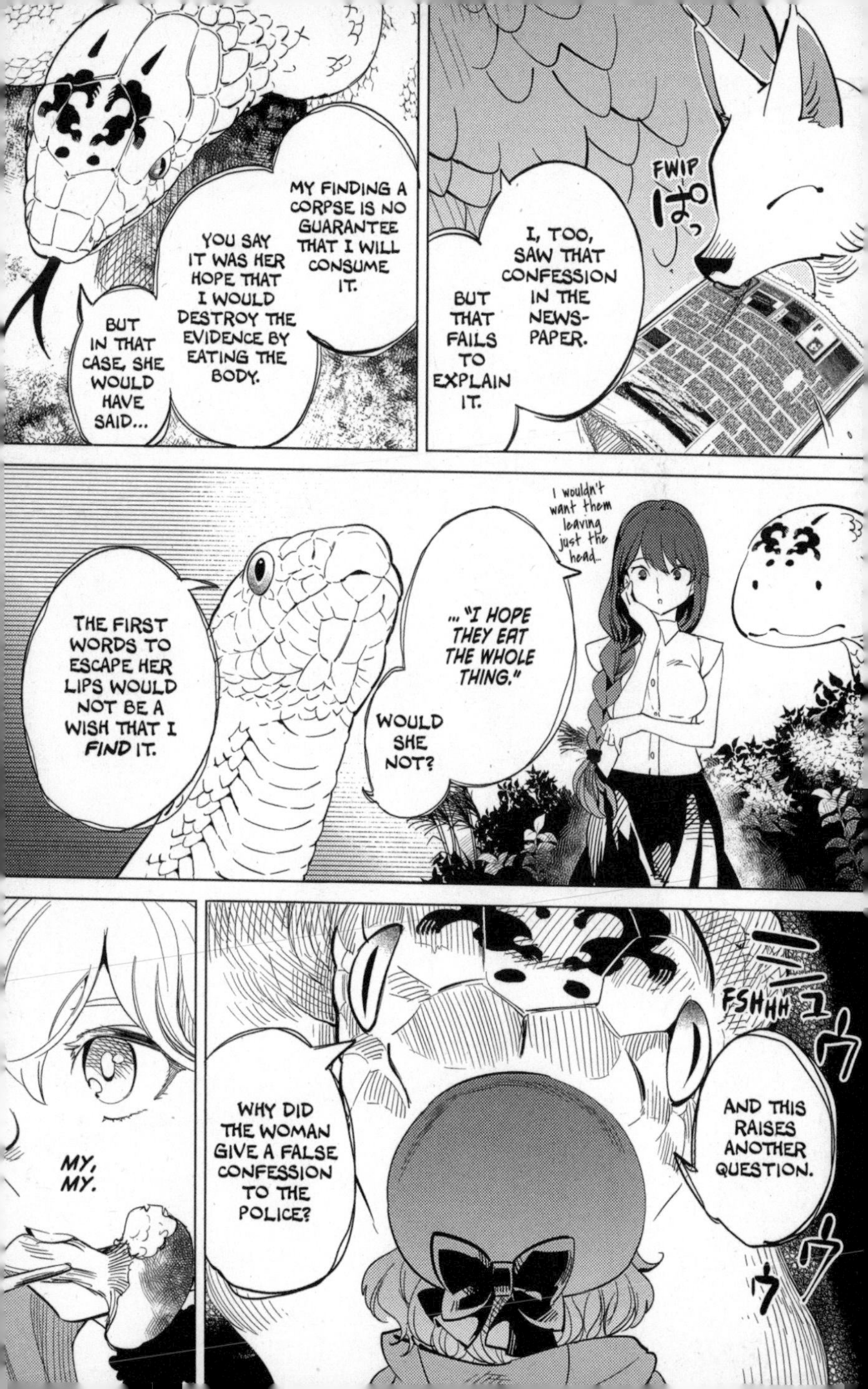
FWIP
ぱっ
I, TOO, SAW THAT CONFESSION IN THE NEWSPAPER.
BUT THAT FAILS TO EXPLAIN IT.
MY FINDING A CORPSE IS NO GUARANTEE THAT I WILL CONSUME IT.
YOU SAY IT WAS HER HOPE THAT I WOULD DESTROY THE EVIDENCE BY EATING THE BODY.
BUT IN THAT CASE, SHE WOULD HAVE SAID...
I wouldn't want them leaving just the head...
..."I HOPE THEY EAT THE WHOLE THING."
WOULD SHE NOT?
THE FIRST WORDS TO ESCAPE HER LIPS WOULD NOT BE A WISH THAT I *FIND* IT.
FSHHH
AND THIS RAISES ANOTHER QUESTION.
WHY DID THE WOMAN GIVE A FALSE CONFESSION TO THE POLICE?
MY, MY.

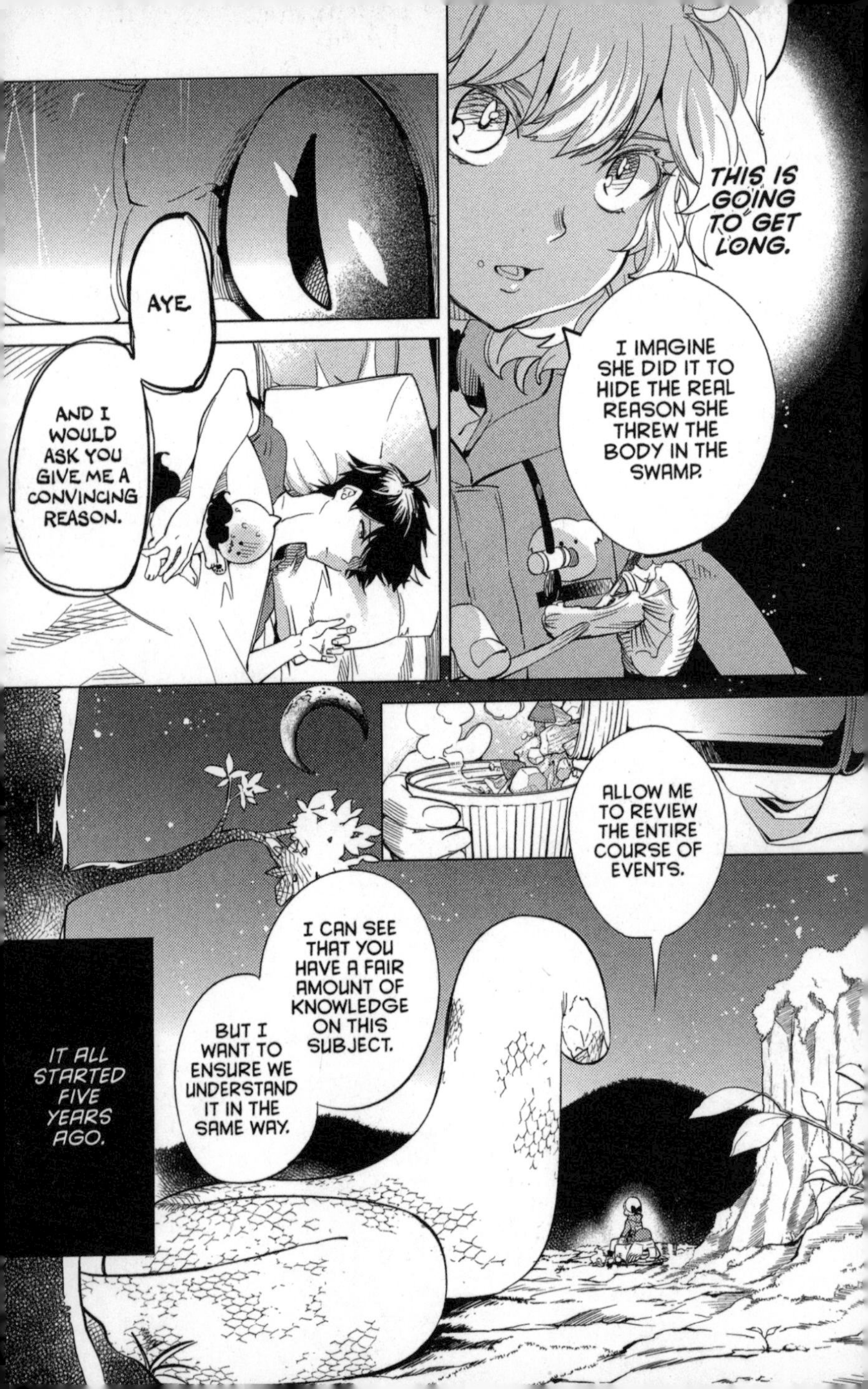
THIS IS GOING TO GET LONG.
I IMAGINE SHE DID IT TO HIDE THE REAL REASON SHE THREW THE BODY IN THE SWAMP.
AYE.
AND I WOULD ASK YOU GIVE ME A CONVINCING REASON.
ALLOW ME TO REVIEW THE ENTIRE COURSE OF EVENTS.
I CAN SEE THAT YOU HAVE A FAIR AMOUNT OF KNOWLEDGE ON THIS SUBJECT.
BUT I WANT TO ENSURE WE UNDERSTAND IT IN THE SAME WAY.
IT ALL STARTED FIVE YEARS AGO.

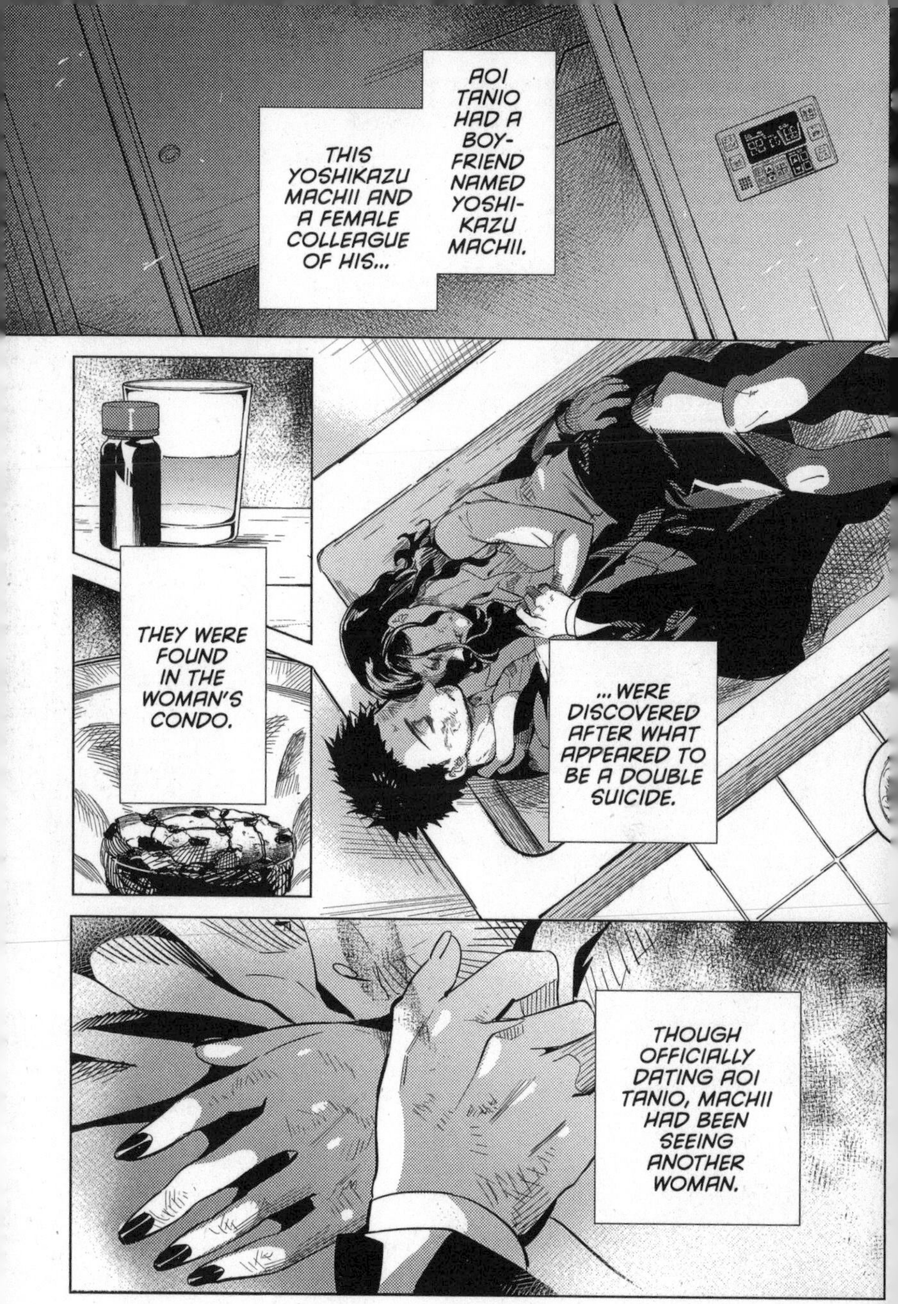
AOI TANIO HAD A BOY-FRIEND NAMED YOSHI-KAZU MACHII.
THIS YOSHIKAZU MACHII AND A FEMALE COLLEAGUE OF HIS...
...WERE DISCOVERED AFTER WHAT APPEARED TO BE A DOUBLE SUICIDE.
THEY WERE FOUND IN THE WOMAN'S CONDO.
THOUGH OFFICIALLY DATING AOI TANIO, MACHII HAD BEEN SEEING ANOTHER WOMAN.

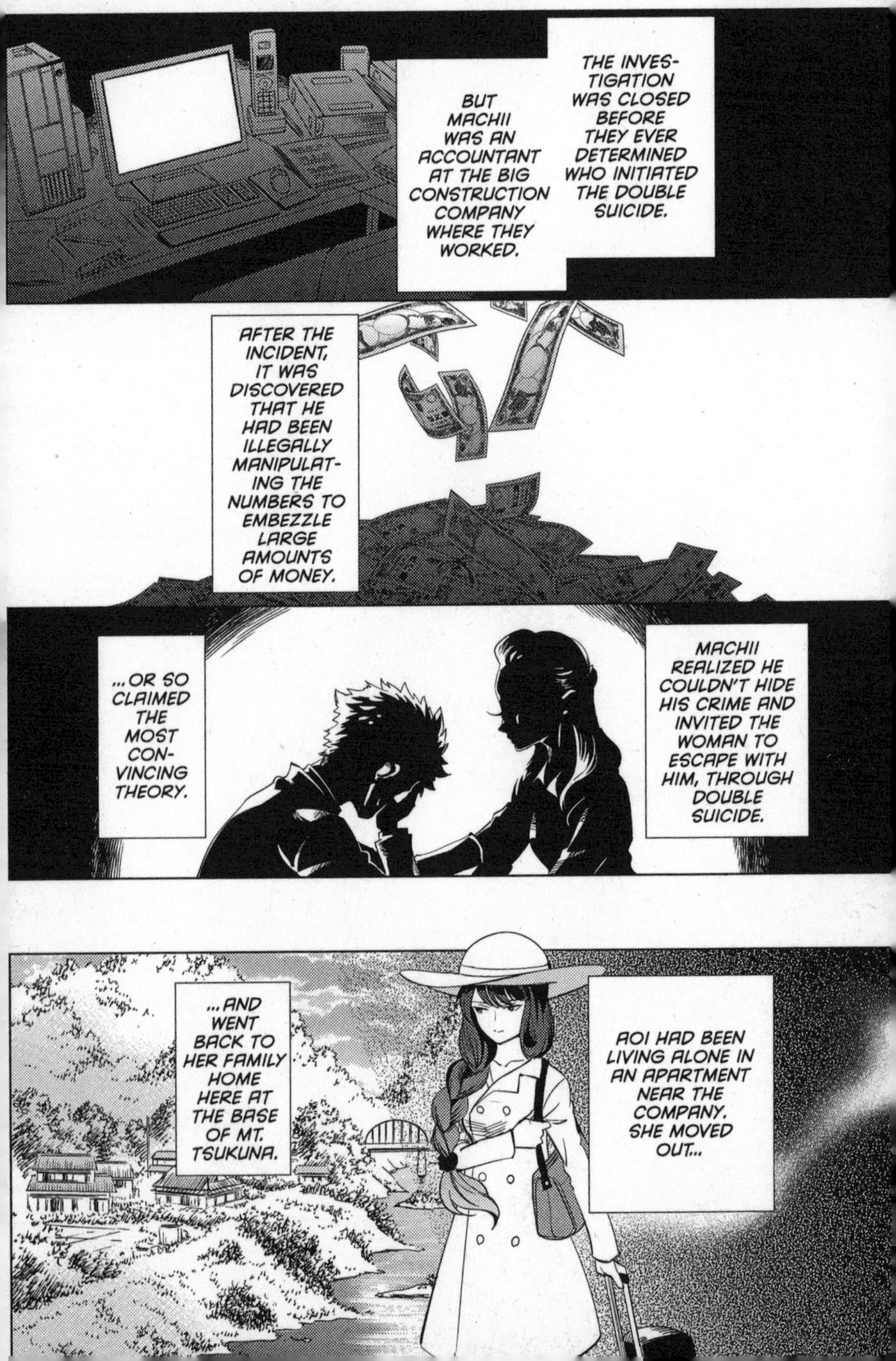
THE INVES-TIGATION WAS CLOSED BEFORE THEY EVER DETERMINED WHO INITIATED THE DOUBLE SUICIDE.
BUT MACHII WAS AN ACCOUNTANT AT THE BIG CONSTRUCTION COMPANY WHERE THEY WORKED.
AFTER THE INCIDENT, IT WAS DISCOVERED THAT HE HAD BEEN ILLEGALLY MANIPULAT-ING THE NUMBERS TO EMBEZZLE LARGE AMOUNTS OF MONEY.
MACHII REALIZED HE COULDN'T HIDE HIS CRIME AND INVITED THE WOMAN TO ESCAPE WITH HIM, THROUGH DOUBLE SUICIDE.
...OR SO CLAIMED THE MOST CON-VINCING THEORY.
AOI HAD BEEN LIVING ALONE IN AN APARTMENT NEAR THE COMPANY. SHE MOVED OUT...
...AND WENT BACK TO HER FAMILY HOME HERE AT THE BASE OF MT. TSUKUNA.

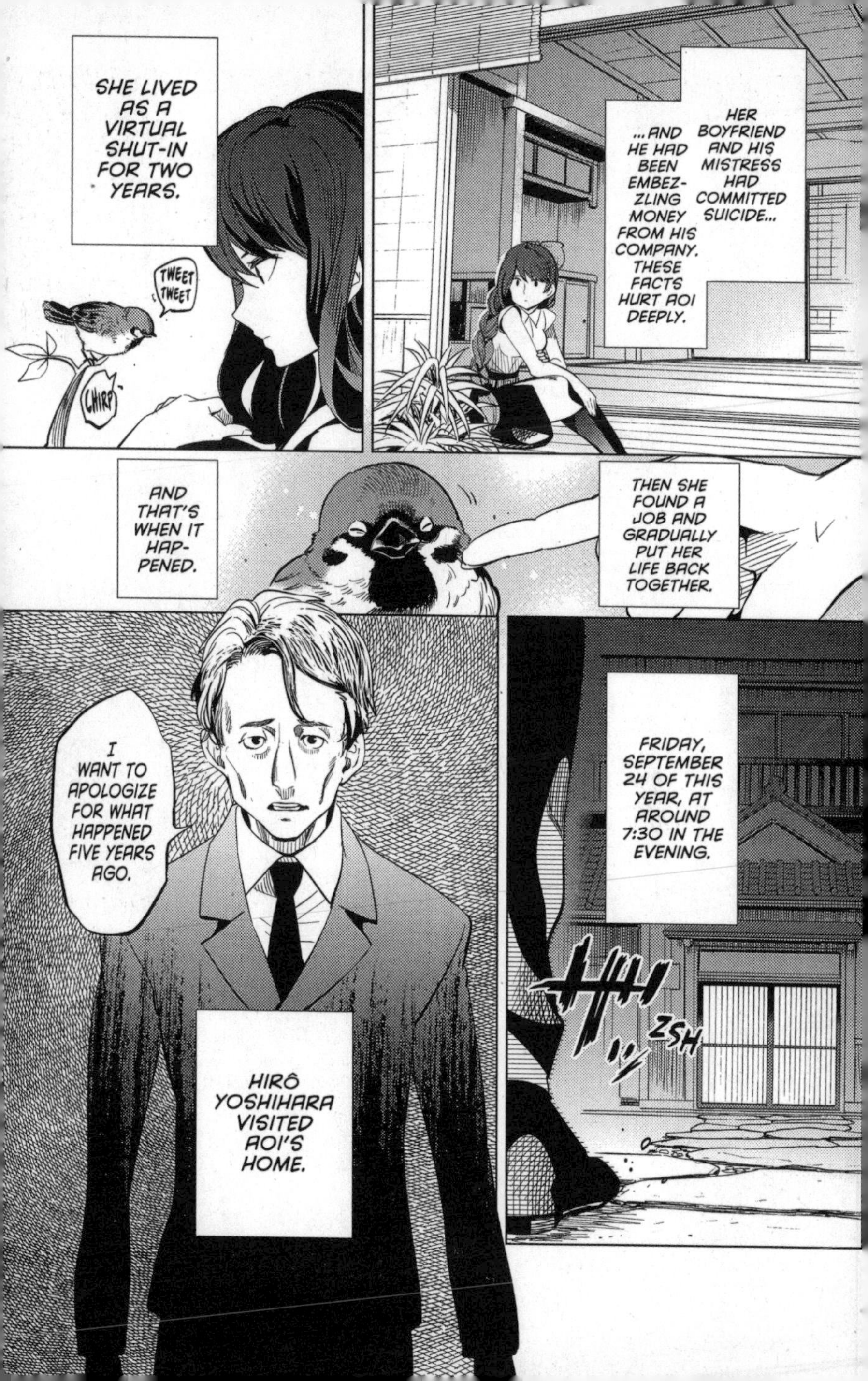
HER BOYFRIEND AND HIS MISTRESS HAD COMMITTED SUICIDE...
...AND HE HAD BEEN EMBEZ-ZLING MONEY FROM HIS COMPANY. THESE FACTS HURT AOI DEEPLY.
SHE LIVED AS A VIRTUAL SHUT-IN FOR TWO YEARS.
TWEET TWEET
CHIRP
THEN SHE FOUND A JOB AND GRADUALLY PUT HER LIFE BACK TOGETHER.
AND THAT'S WHEN IT HAP-PENED.
FRIDAY, SEPTEMBER 24 OF THIS YEAR, AT AROUND 7:30 IN THE EVENING.
ZSH
I WANT TO APOLOGIZE FOR WHAT HAPPENED FIVE YEARS AGO.
HIRÔ YOSHIHARA VISITED AOI'S HOME.

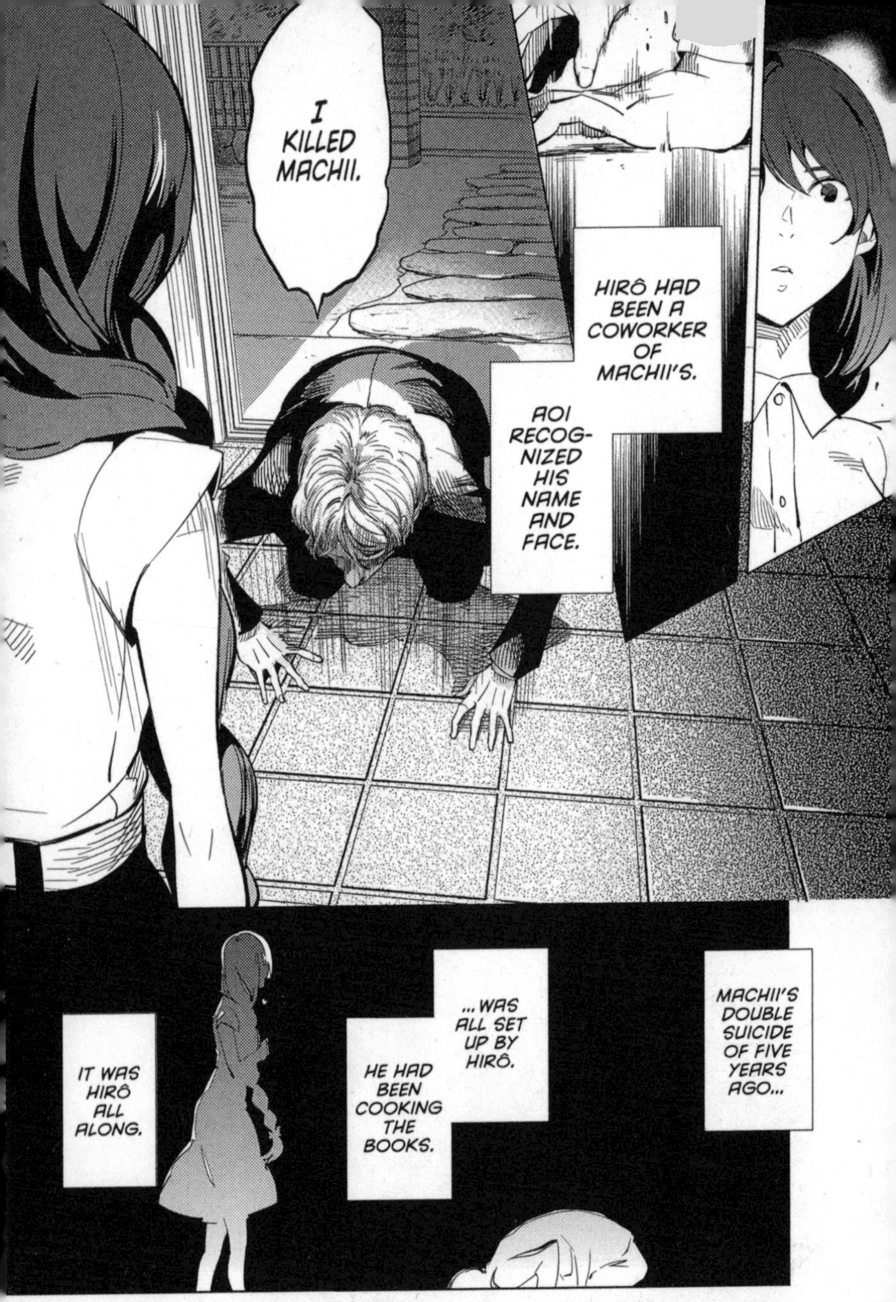
I KILLED MACHII.
HIRÔ HAD BEEN A COWORKER OF MACHII'S.
AOI RECOGNIZED HIS NAME AND FACE.
MACHII'S DOUBLE SUICIDE OF FIVE YEARS AGO...
...WAS ALL SET UP BY HIRÔ.
HE HAD BEEN COOKING THE BOOKS.
IT WAS HIRÔ ALL ALONG.

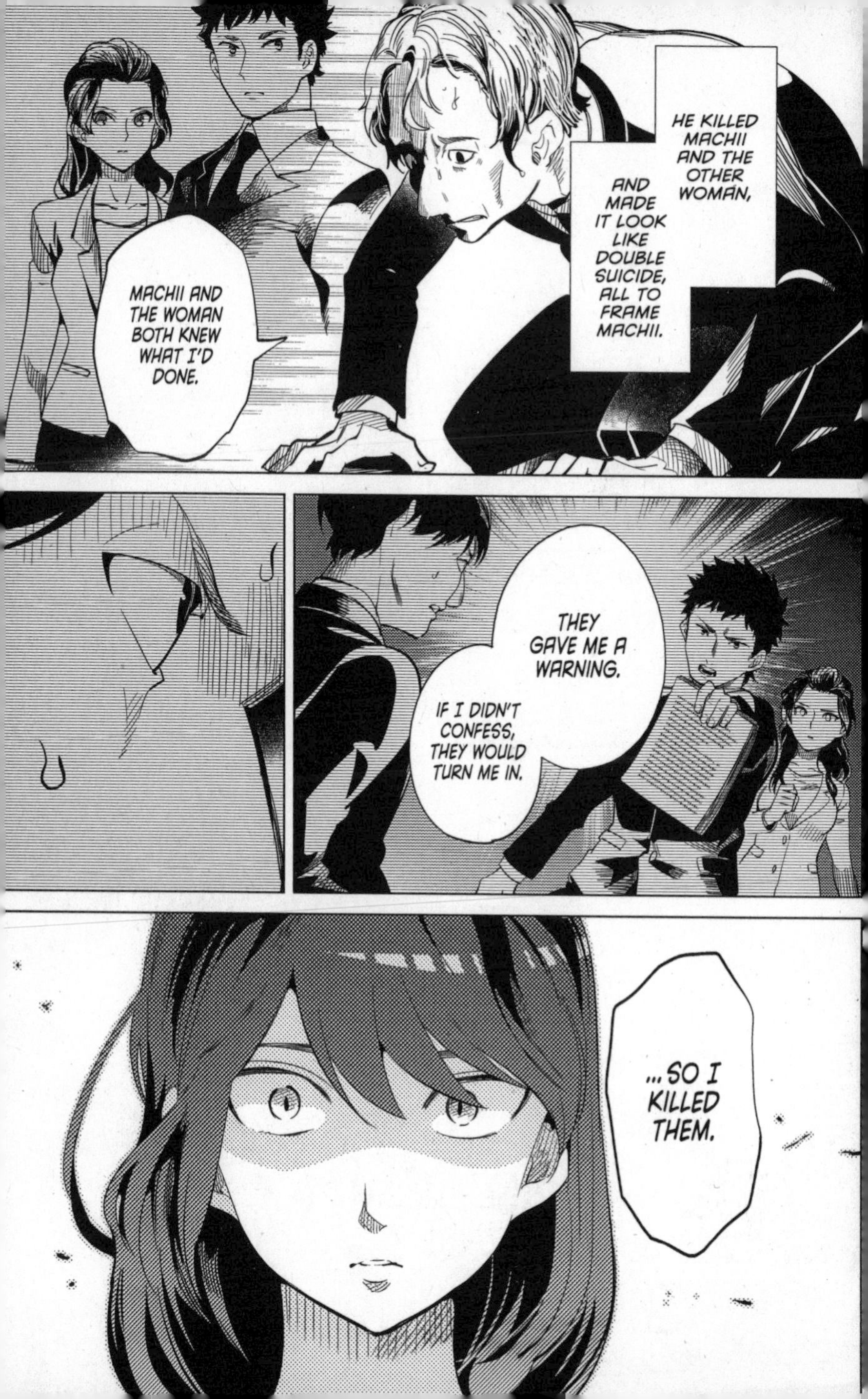
HE KILLED MACHII AND THE OTHER WOMAN,
AND MADE IT LOOK LIKE DOUBLE SUICIDE, ALL TO FRAME MACHII.
MACHII AND THE WOMAN BOTH KNEW WHAT I'D DONE.
THEY GAVE ME A WARNING.
IF I DIDN'T CONFESS, THEY WOULD TURN ME IN.
...SO I KILLED THEM.

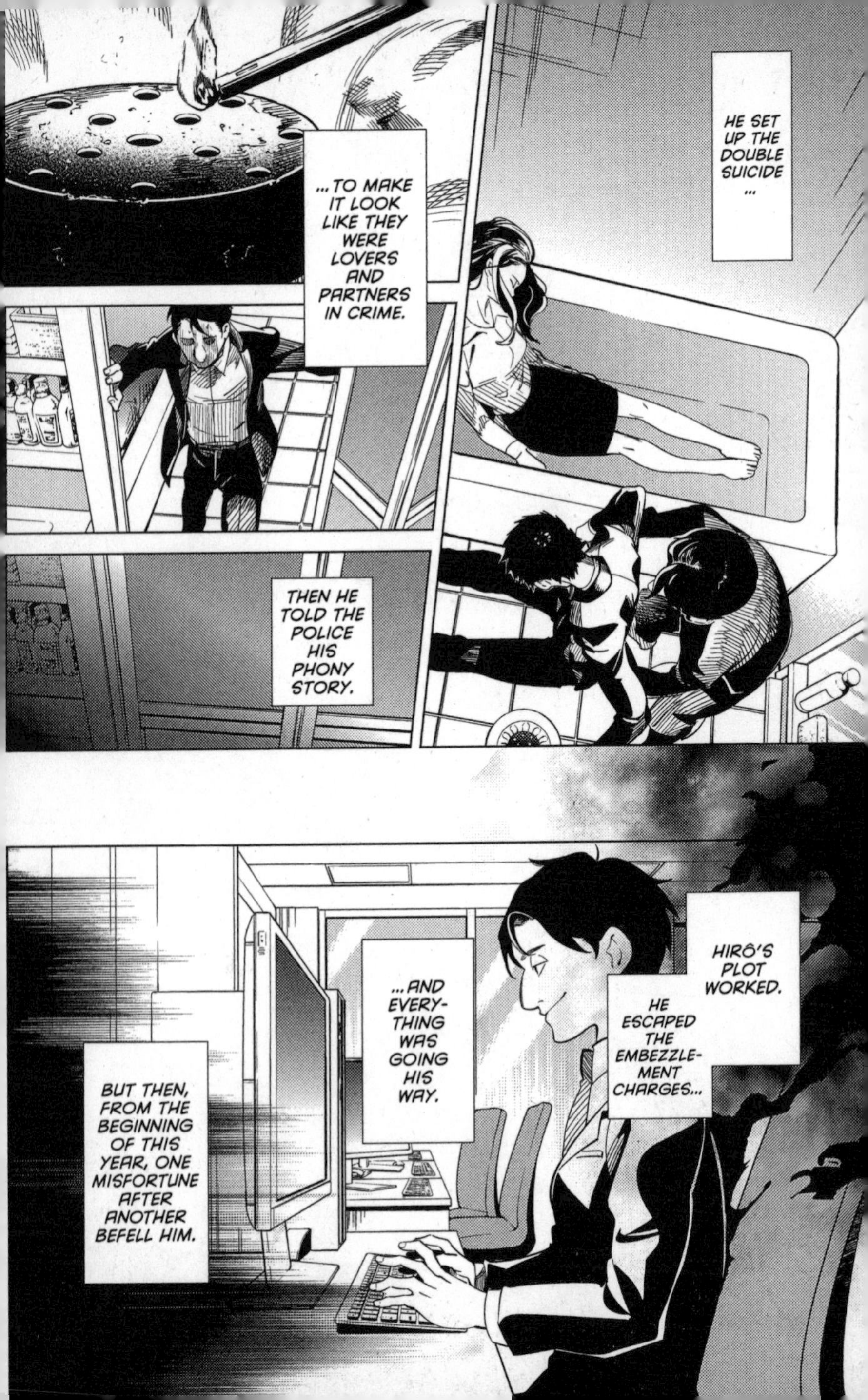
HE SET UP THE DOUBLE SUICIDE ...
...TO MAKE IT LOOK LIKE THEY WERE LOVERS AND PARTNERS IN CRIME.
THEN HE TOLD THE POLICE HIS PHONY STORY.
HIRÔ'S PLOT WORKED.
HE ESCAPED THE EMBEZZLEMENT CHARGES...
...AND EVERYTHING WAS GOING HIS WAY.
BUT THEN, FROM THE BEGINNING OF THIS YEAR, ONE MISFORTUNE AFTER ANOTHER BEFELL HIM.

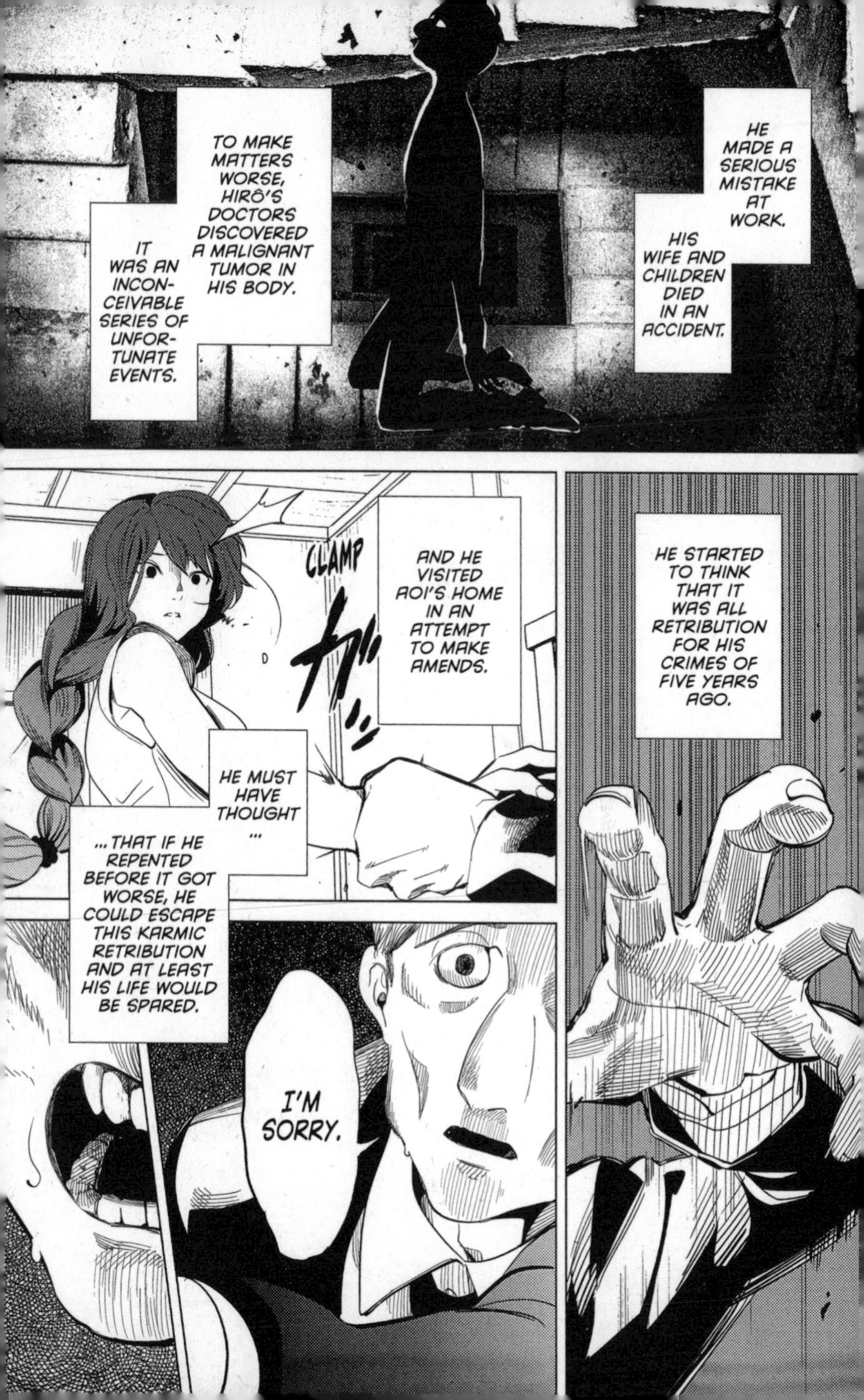
HE MADE A SERIOUS MISTAKE AT WORK.
HIS WIFE AND CHILDREN DIED IN AN ACCIDENT.
TO MAKE MATTERS WORSE, HIRÔ'S DOCTORS DISCOVERED A MALIGNANT TUMOR IN HIS BODY.
IT WAS AN INCON-CEIVABLE SERIES OF UNFOR-TUNATE EVENTS.
HE STARTED TO THINK THAT IT WAS ALL RETRIBUTION FOR HIS CRIMES OF FIVE YEARS AGO.
AND HE VISITED AOI'S HOME IN AN ATTEMPT TO MAKE AMENDS.
CLAMP
HE MUST HAVE THOUGHT...
...THAT IF HE REPENTED BEFORE IT GOT WORSE, HE COULD ESCAPE THIS KARMIC RETRIBUTION AND AT LEAST HIS LIFE WOULD BE SPARED.
I'M SORRY.

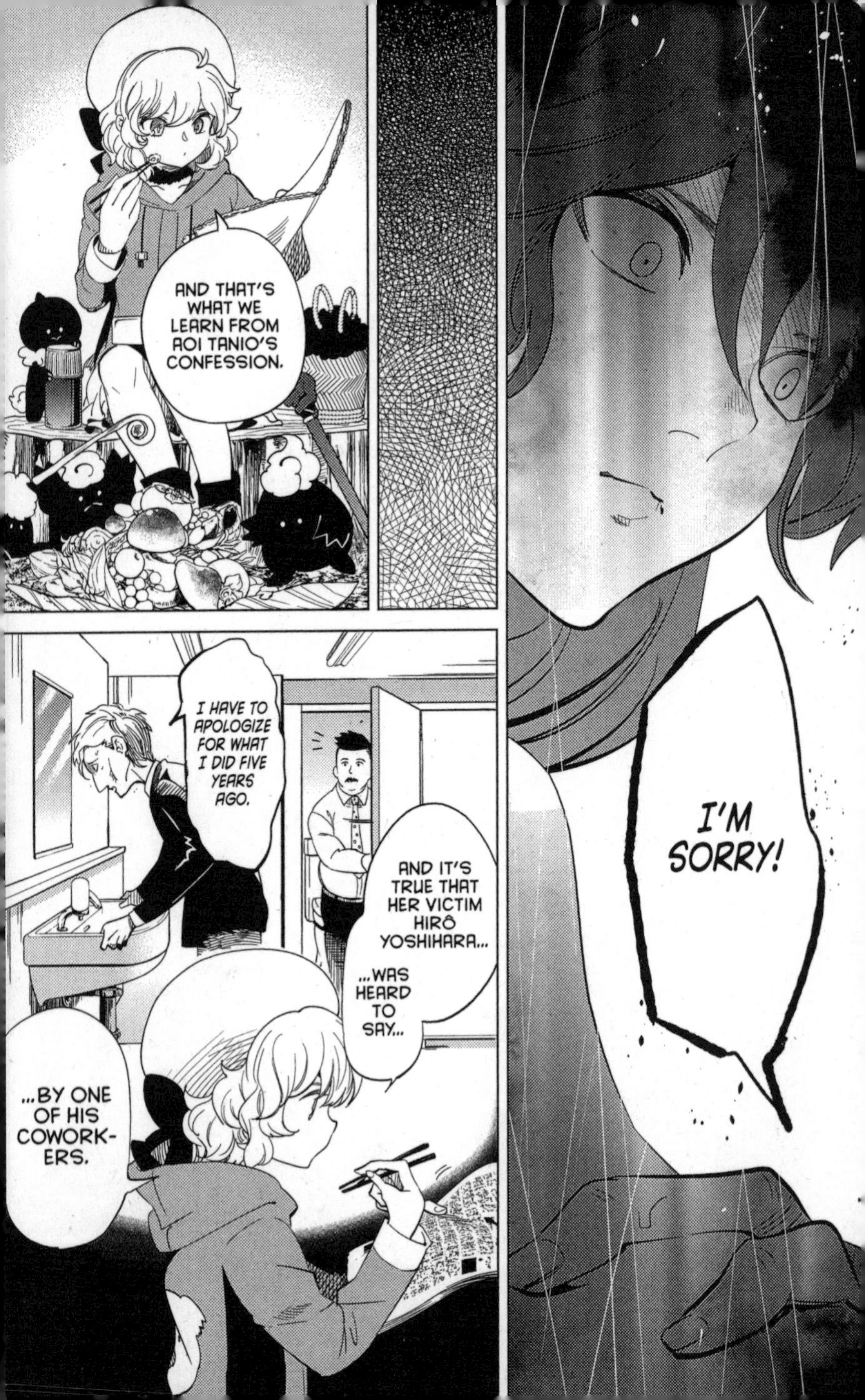
I'M SORRY!
AND THAT'S WHAT WE LEARN FROM AOI TANIO'S CONFESSION.
I HAVE TO APOLOGIZE FOR WHAT I DID FIVE YEARS AGO.
AND IT'S TRUE THAT HER VICTIM HIRÔ YOSHIHARA...
...WAS HEARD TO SAY...
...BY ONE OF HIS COWORKERS.

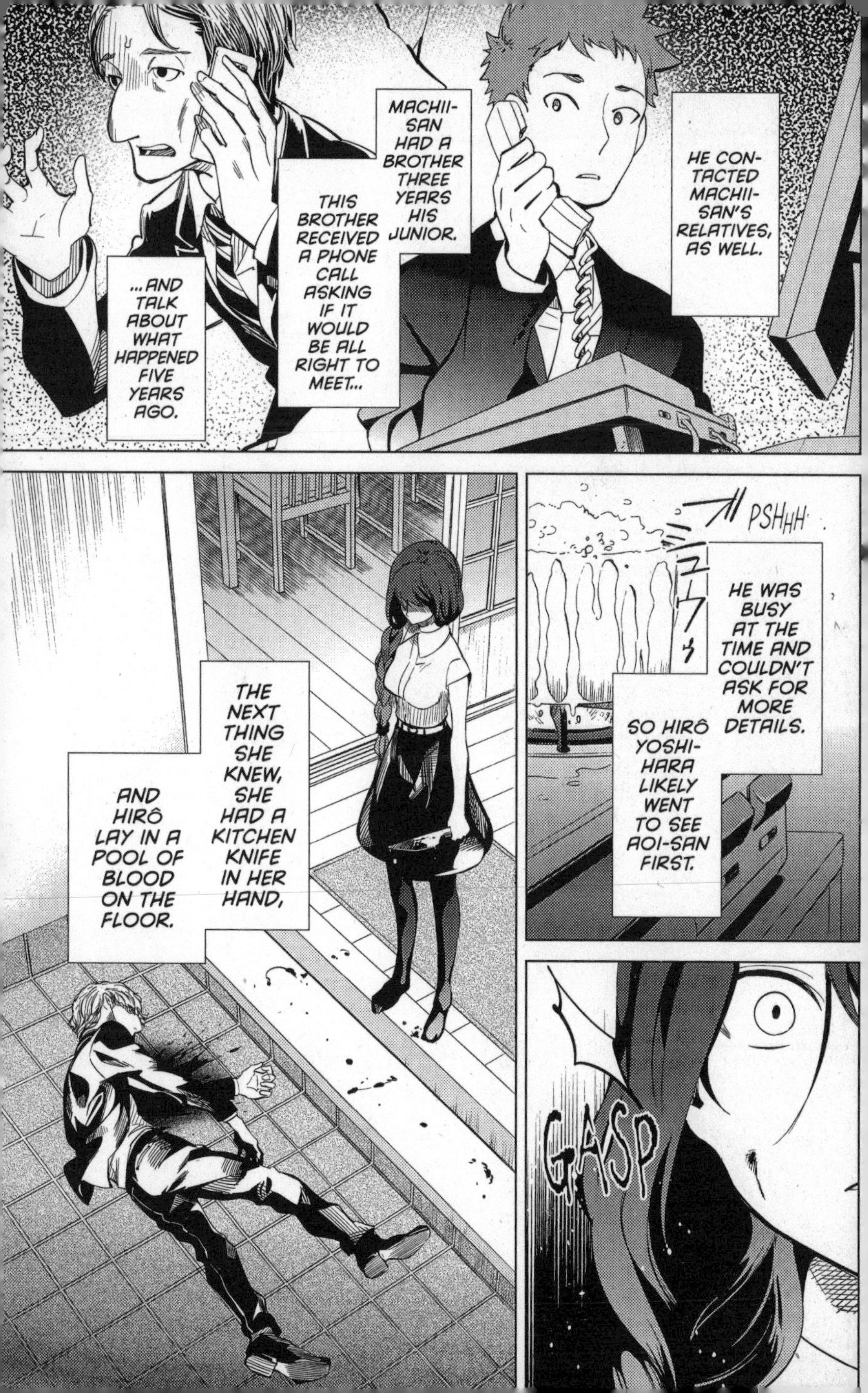
HE CONTACTED MACHII-SAN'S RELATIVES, AS WELL.
MACHII-SAN HAD A BROTHER THREE YEARS HIS JUNIOR.
THIS BROTHER RECEIVED A PHONE CALL ASKING IF IT WOULD BE ALL RIGHT TO MEET...
...AND TALK ABOUT WHAT HAPPENED FIVE YEARS AGO.
PSHHH
HE WAS BUSY AT THE TIME AND COULDN'T ASK FOR MORE DETAILS.
SO HIRÔ YOSHIHARA LIKELY WENT TO SEE AOI-SAN FIRST.
GASP
THE NEXT THING SHE KNEW, SHE HAD A KITCHEN KNIFE IN HER HAND,
AND HIRÔ LAY IN A POOL OF BLOOD ON THE FLOOR.

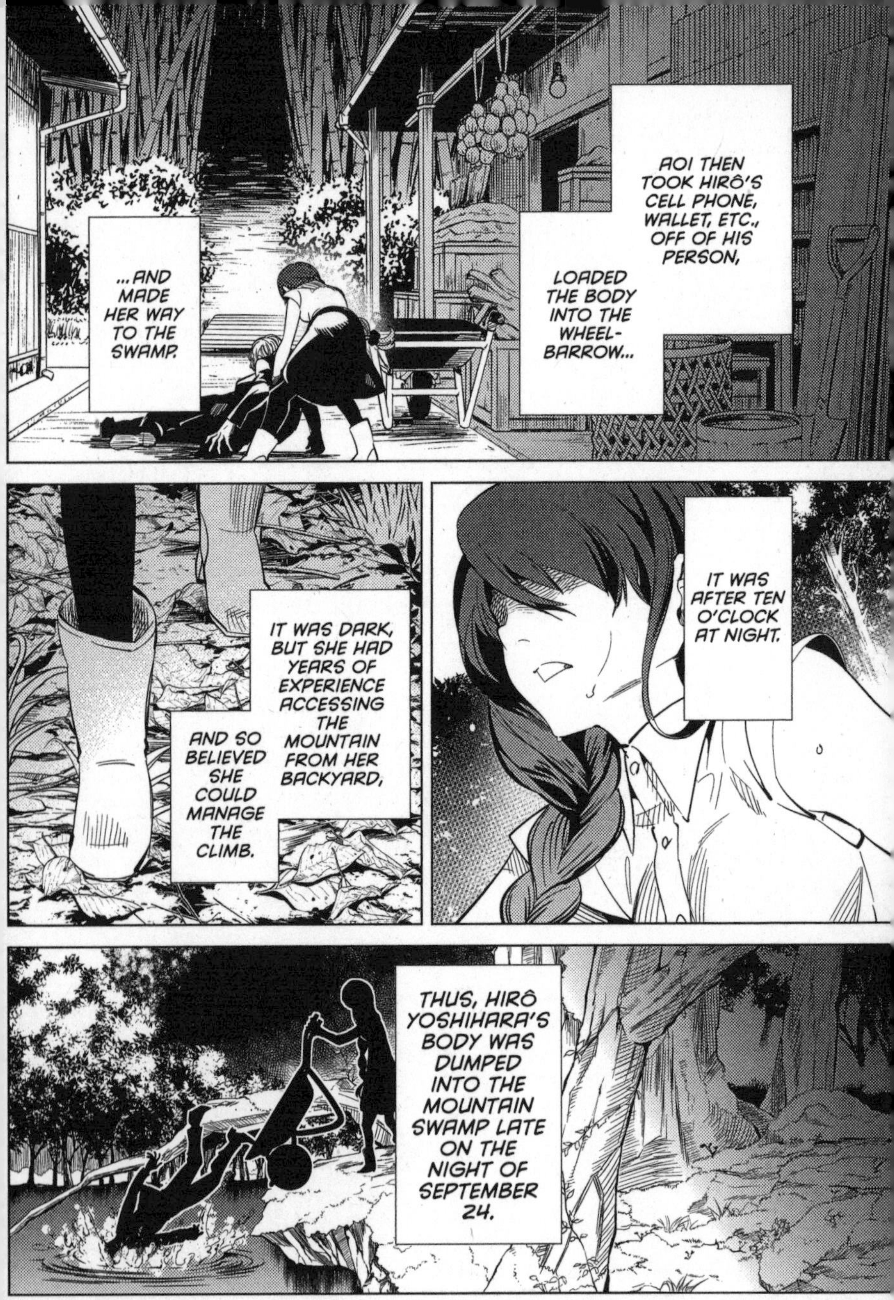
AOI THEN TOOK HIRÔ'S CELL PHONE, WALLET, ETC., OFF OF HIS PERSON,
LOADED THE BODY INTO THE WHEEL-BARROW...
...AND MADE HER WAY TO THE SWAMP.
IT WAS AFTER TEN O'CLOCK AT NIGHT.
IT WAS DARK, BUT SHE HAD YEARS OF EXPERIENCE ACCESSING THE MOUNTAIN FROM HER BACKYARD,
AND SO BELIEVED SHE COULD MANAGE THE CLIMB.
THUS, HIRÔ YOSHIHARA'S BODY WAS DUMPED INTO THE MOUNTAIN SWAMP LATE ON THE NIGHT OF SEPTEMBER 24.

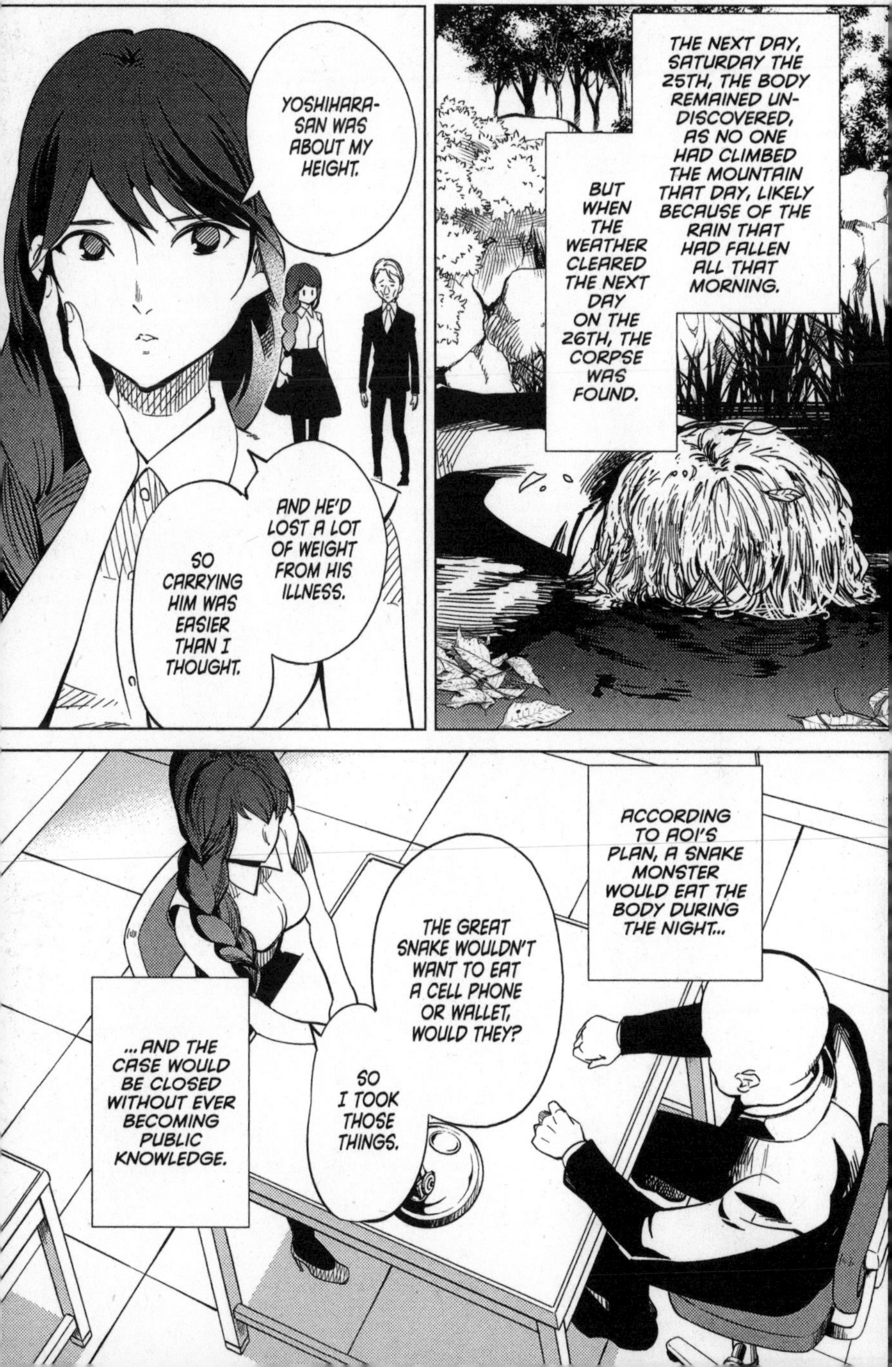
THE NEXT DAY, SATURDAY THE 25TH, THE BODY REMAINED UN-DISCOVERED, AS NO ONE HAD CLIMBED THE MOUNTAIN THAT DAY, LIKELY BECAUSE OF THE RAIN THAT HAD FALLEN ALL THAT MORNING.
BUT WHEN THE WEATHER CLEARED THE NEXT DAY ON THE 26TH, THE CORPSE WAS FOUND.
YOSHIHARA-SAN WAS ABOUT MY HEIGHT.
AND HE'D LOST A LOT OF WEIGHT FROM HIS ILLNESS.
SO CARRYING HIM WAS EASIER THAN I THOUGHT.
ACCORDING TO AOI'S PLAN, A SNAKE MONSTER WOULD EAT THE BODY DURING THE NIGHT...
THE GREAT SNAKE WOULDN'T WANT TO EAT A CELL PHONE OR WALLET, WOULD THEY?
SO I TOOK THOSE THINGS.
...AND THE CASE WOULD BE CLOSED WITHOUT EVER BECOMING PUBLIC KNOWLEDGE.

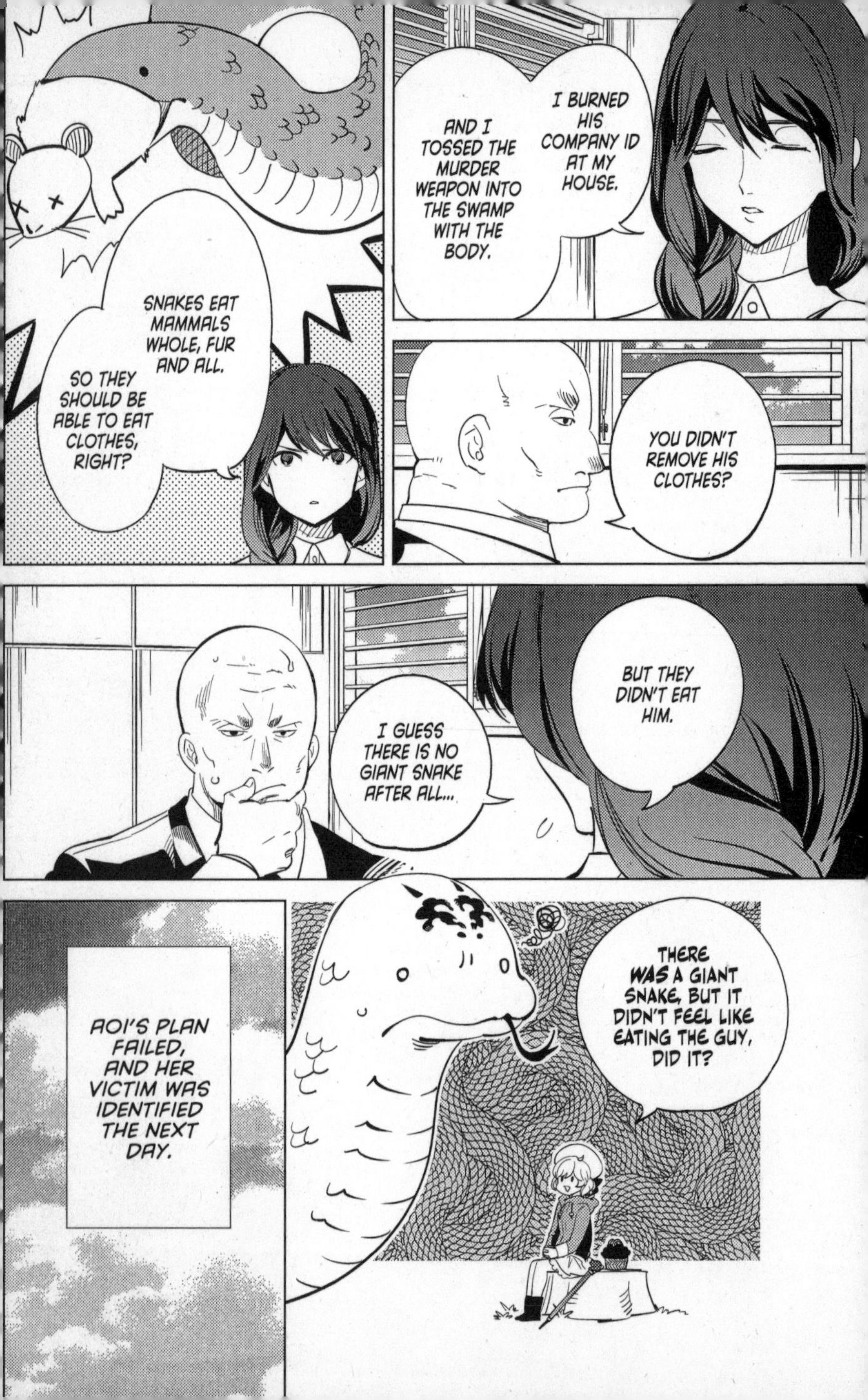
I BURNED HIS COMPANY ID AT MY HOUSE.
AND I TOSSED THE MURDER WEAPON INTO THE SWAMP WITH THE BODY.
YOU DIDN'T REMOVE HIS CLOTHES?
SNAKES EAT MAMMALS WHOLE, FUR AND ALL.
SO THEY SHOULD BE ABLE TO EAT CLOTHES, RIGHT?
BUT THEY DIDN'T EAT HIM.
I GUESS THERE IS NO GIANT SNAKE AFTER ALL...
THERE **WAS** A GIANT SNAKE, BUT IT DIDN'T FEEL LIKE EATING THE GUY, DID IT?
AOI'S PLAN FAILED, AND HER VICTIM WAS IDENTIFIED THE NEXT DAY.

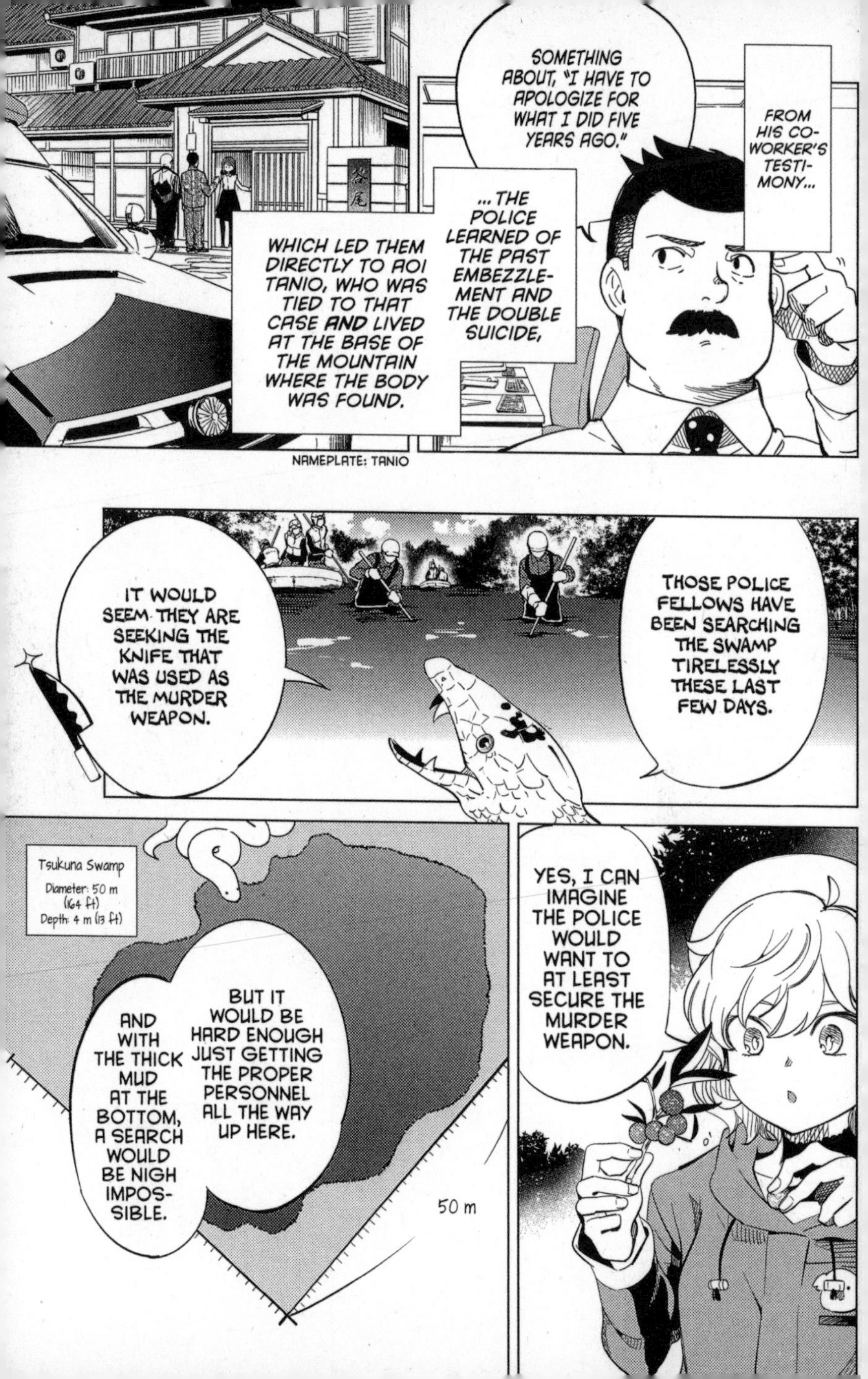
FROM HIS CO-WORKER'S TESTIMONY...
SOMETHING ABOUT, "I HAVE TO APOLOGIZE FOR WHAT I DID FIVE YEARS AGO."
...THE POLICE LEARNED OF THE PAST EMBEZZLEMENT AND THE DOUBLE SUICIDE,
WHICH LED THEM DIRECTLY TO AOI TANIO, WHO WAS TIED TO THAT CASE AND LIVED AT THE BASE OF THE MOUNTAIN WHERE THE BODY WAS FOUND.
NAMEPLATE: TANIO
THOSE POLICE FELLOWS HAVE BEEN SEARCHING THE SWAMP TIRELESSLY THESE LAST FEW DAYS.
IT WOULD SEEM THEY ARE SEEKING THE KNIFE THAT WAS USED AS THE MURDER WEAPON.
YES, I CAN IMAGINE THE POLICE WOULD WANT TO AT LEAST SECURE THE MURDER WEAPON.
Tsukuna Swamp
Diameter: 50 m (164 ft)
Depth: 4 m (13 ft)
BUT IT WOULD BE HARD ENOUGH JUST GETTING THE PROPER PERSONNEL ALL THE WAY UP HERE.
AND WITH THE THICK MUD AT THE BOTTOM, A SEARCH WOULD BE NIGH IMPOSSIBLE.
50 m

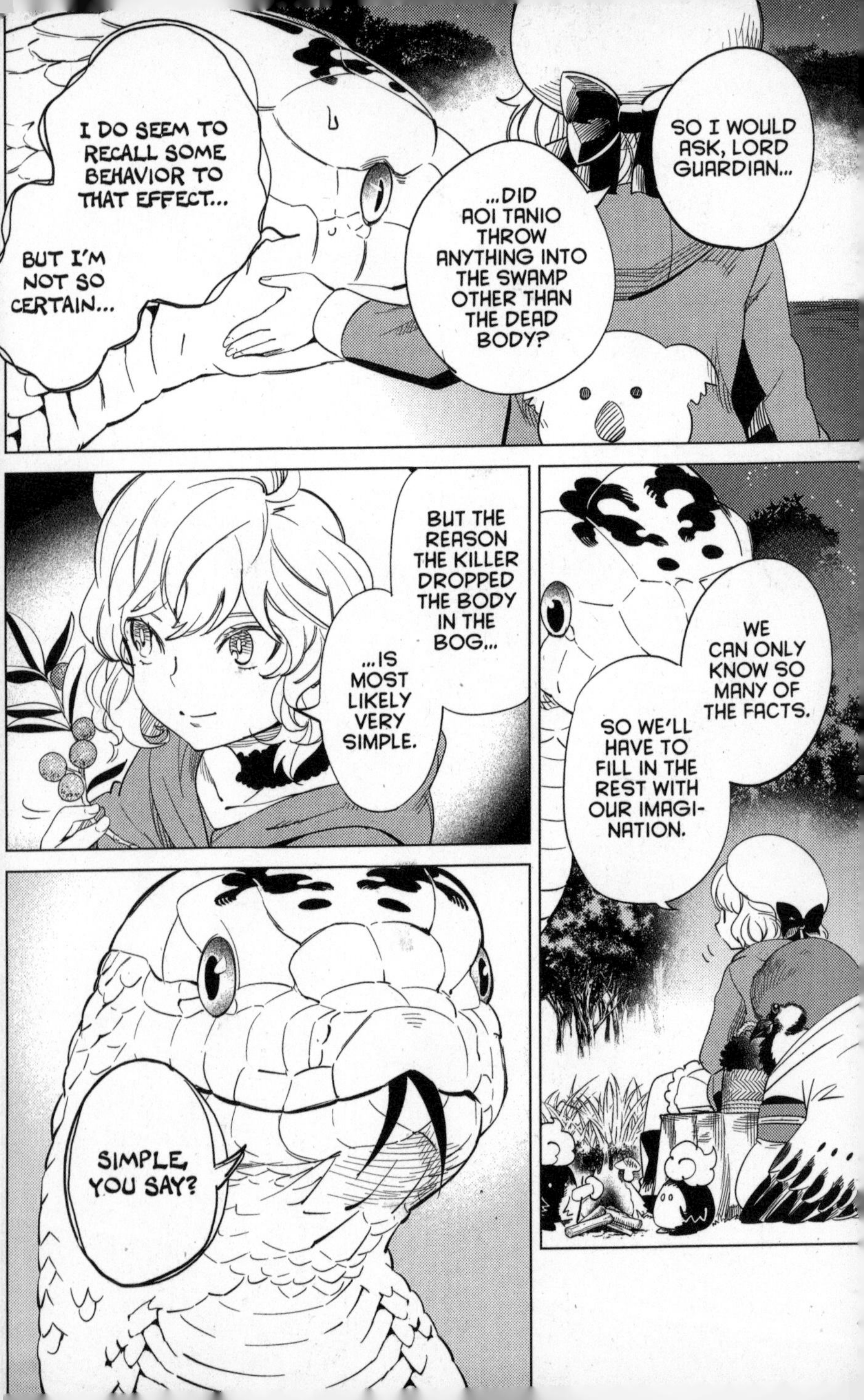
SO I WOULD ASK, LORD GUARDIAN...
...DID AOI TANIO THROW ANYTHING INTO THE SWAMP OTHER THAN THE DEAD BODY?
I DO SEEM TO RECALL SOME BEHAVIOR TO THAT EFFECT...
BUT I'M NOT SO CERTAIN...
WE CAN ONLY KNOW SO MANY OF THE FACTS.
SO WE'LL HAVE TO FILL IN THE REST WITH OUR IMAGINATION.
BUT THE REASON THE KILLER DROPPED THE BODY IN THE BOG...
...IS MOST LIKELY VERY SIMPLE.
SIMPLE, YOU SAY?

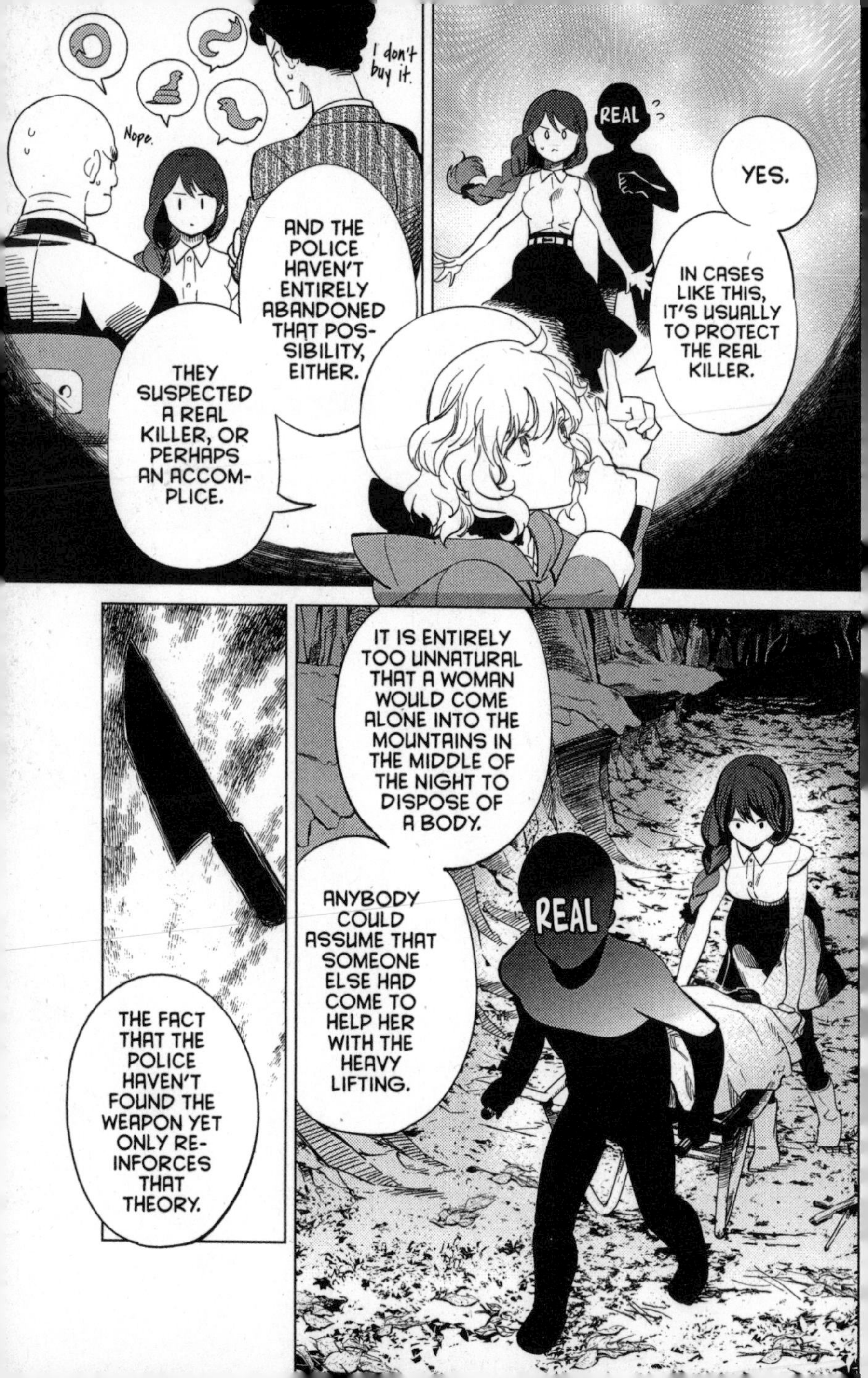
REAL
YES.
IN CASES LIKE THIS, IT'S USUALLY TO PROTECT THE REAL KILLER.
I don't buy it.
Nope.
AND THE POLICE HAVEN'T ENTIRELY ABANDONED THAT POSSIBILITY, EITHER.
THEY SUSPECTED A REAL KILLER, OR PERHAPS AN ACCOMPLICE.
IT IS ENTIRELY TOO UNNATURAL THAT A WOMAN WOULD COME ALONE INTO THE MOUNTAINS IN THE MIDDLE OF THE NIGHT TO DISPOSE OF A BODY.
ANYBODY COULD ASSUME THAT SOMEONE ELSE HAD COME TO HELP HER WITH THE HEAVY LIFTING.
REAL
THE FACT THAT THE POLICE HAVEN'T FOUND THE WEAPON YET ONLY REINFORCES THAT THEORY.

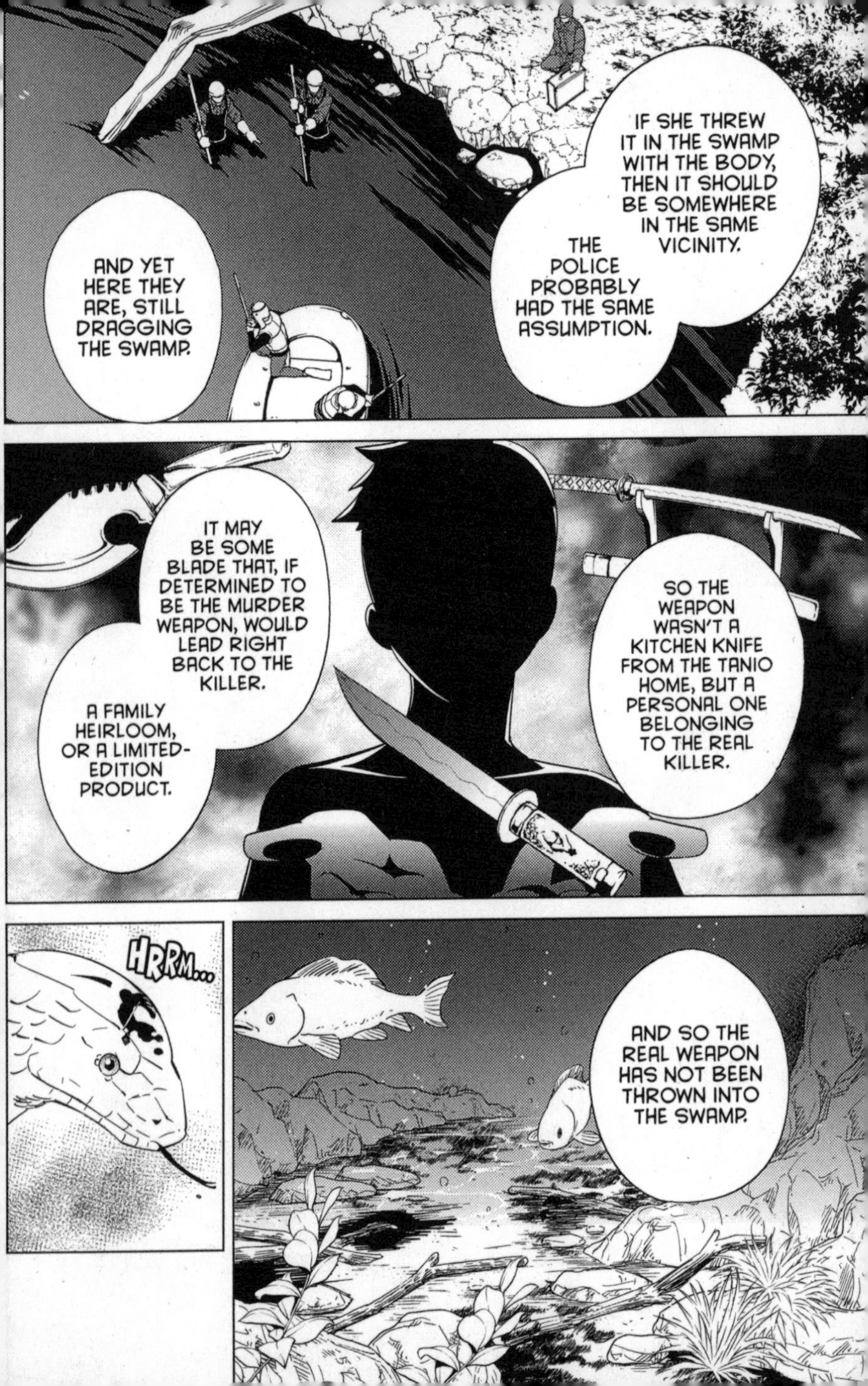
IF SHE THREW IT IN THE SWAMP WITH THE BODY, THEN IT SHOULD BE SOMEWHERE IN THE SAME VICINITY.
THE POLICE PROBABLY HAD THE SAME ASSUMPTION.
AND YET HERE THEY ARE, STILL DRAGGING THE SWAMP.
SO THE WEAPON WASN'T A KITCHEN KNIFE FROM THE TANIO HOME, BUT A PERSONAL ONE BELONGING TO THE REAL KILLER.
IT MAY BE SOME BLADE THAT, IF DETERMINED TO BE THE MURDER WEAPON, WOULD LEAD RIGHT BACK TO THE KILLER.
A FAMILY HEIRLOOM, OR A LIMITED-EDITION PRODUCT.
AND SO THE REAL WEAPON HAS NOT BEEN THROWN INTO THE SWAMP.
HRRM...

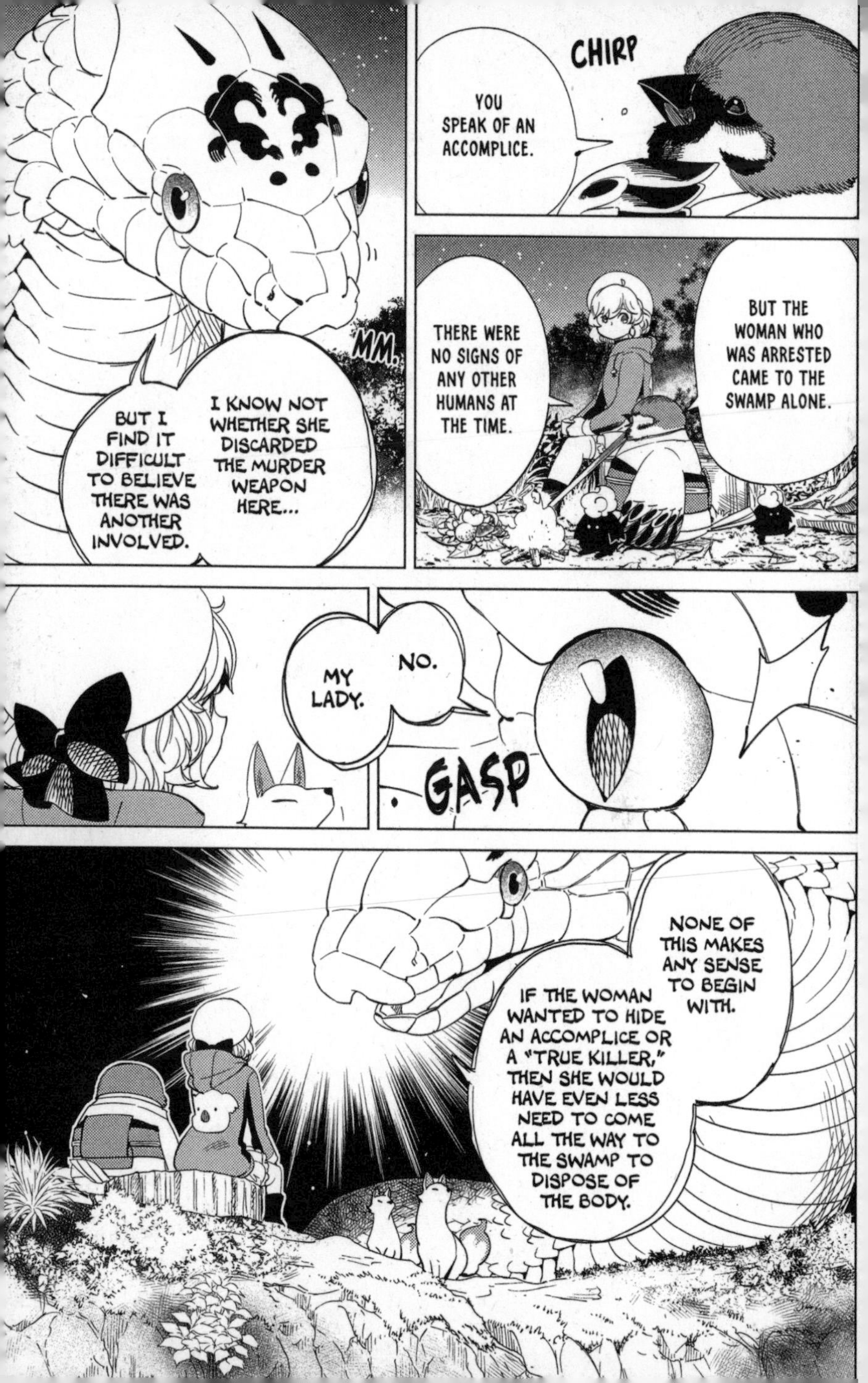
CHIRP
YOU SPEAK OF AN ACCOMPLICE.
BUT THE WOMAN WHO WAS ARRESTED CAME TO THE SWAMP ALONE.
THERE WERE NO SIGNS OF ANY OTHER HUMANS AT THE TIME.
MM.
I KNOW NOT WHETHER SHE DISCARDED THE MURDER WEAPON HERE...
BUT I FIND IT DIFFICULT TO BELIEVE THERE WAS ANOTHER INVOLVED.
NO. MY LADY.
GASP
NONE OF THIS MAKES ANY SENSE TO BEGIN WITH.
IF THE WOMAN WANTED TO HIDE AN ACCOMPLICE OR A "TRUE KILLER," THEN SHE WOULD HAVE EVEN LESS NEED TO COME ALL THE WAY TO THE SWAMP TO DISPOSE OF THE BODY.

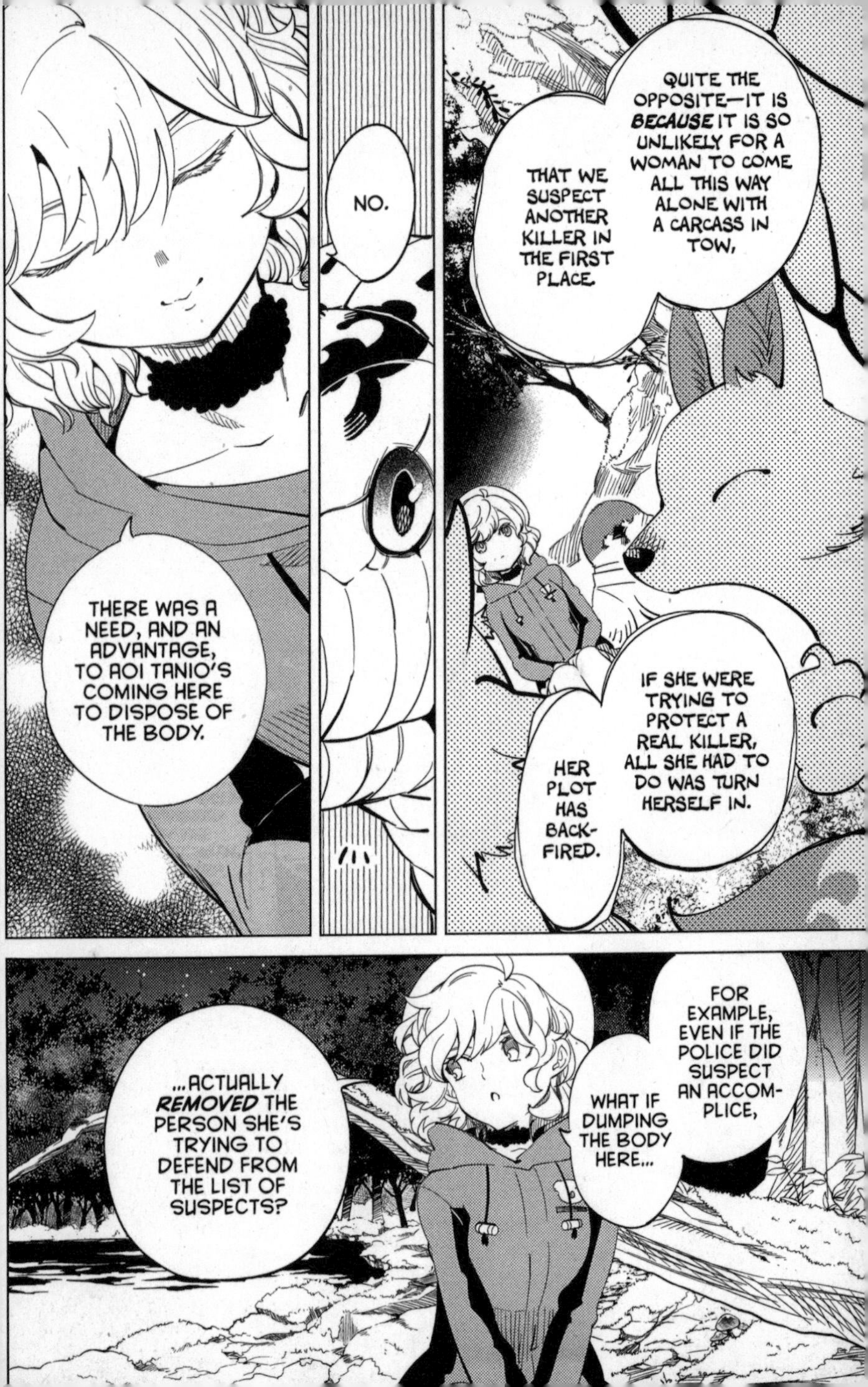
QUITE THE OPPOSITE—IT IS *BECAUSE* IT IS SO UNLIKELY FOR A WOMAN TO COME ALL THIS WAY ALONE WITH A CARCASS IN TOW,
THAT WE SUSPECT ANOTHER KILLER IN THE FIRST PLACE.
IF SHE WERE TRYING TO PROTECT A REAL KILLER, ALL SHE HAD TO DO WAS TURN HERSELF IN.
HER PLOT HAS BACK-FIRED.
NO.
THERE WAS A NEED, AND AN ADVANTAGE, TO AOI TANIO'S COMING HERE TO DISPOSE OF THE BODY.
FOR EXAMPLE, EVEN IF THE POLICE DID SUSPECT AN ACCOM-PLICE,
WHAT IF DUMPING THE BODY HERE...
...ACTUALLY ***REMOVED*** THE PERSON SHE'S TRYING TO DEFEND FROM THE LIST OF SUSPECTS?

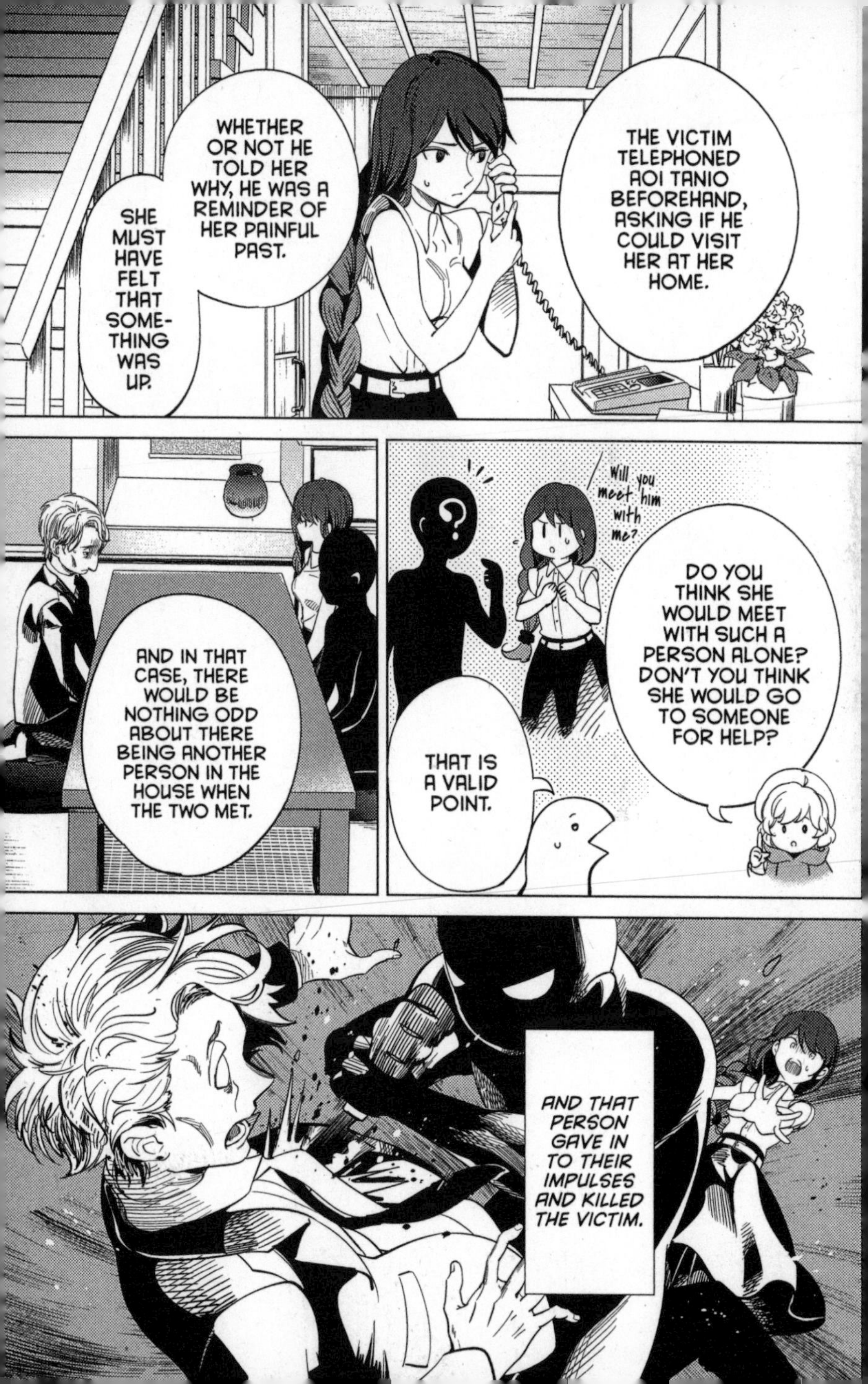
THE VICTIM TELEPHONED AOI TANIO BEFOREHAND, ASKING IF HE COULD VISIT HER AT HER HOME.
WHETHER OR NOT HE TOLD HER WHY, HE WAS A REMINDER OF HER PAINFUL PAST.
SHE MUST HAVE FELT THAT SOME-THING WAS UP.
Will you meet him with me?
DO YOU THINK SHE WOULD MEET WITH SUCH A PERSON ALONE? DON'T YOU THINK SHE WOULD GO TO SOMEONE FOR HELP?
THAT IS A VALID POINT.
AND IN THAT CASE, THERE WOULD BE NOTHING ODD ABOUT THERE BEING ANOTHER PERSON IN THE HOUSE WHEN THE TWO MET.
AND THAT PERSON GAVE IN TO THEIR IMPULSES AND KILLED THE VICTIM.

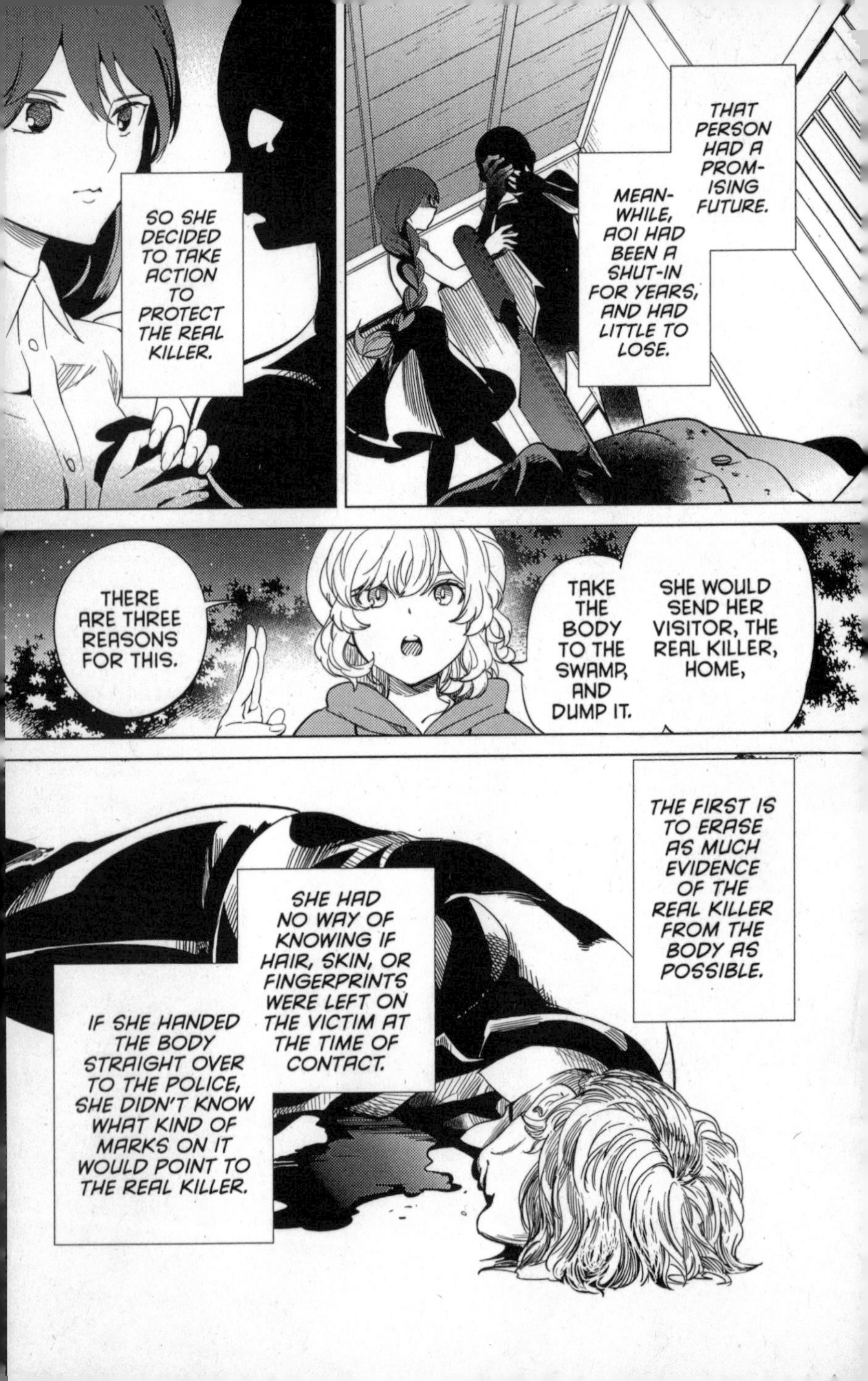
THAT PERSON HAD A PROMISING FUTURE.
MEANWHILE, AOI HAD BEEN A SHUT-IN FOR YEARS, AND HAD LITTLE TO LOSE.
SO SHE DECIDED TO TAKE ACTION TO PROTECT THE REAL KILLER.
SHE WOULD SEND HER VISITOR, THE REAL KILLER, HOME,
TAKE THE BODY TO THE SWAMP, AND DUMP IT.
THERE ARE THREE REASONS FOR THIS.
THE FIRST IS TO ERASE AS MUCH EVIDENCE OF THE REAL KILLER FROM THE BODY AS POSSIBLE.
SHE HAD NO WAY OF KNOWING IF HAIR, SKIN, OR FINGERPRINTS WERE LEFT ON THE VICTIM AT THE TIME OF CONTACT.
IF SHE HANDED THE BODY STRAIGHT OVER TO THE POLICE, SHE DIDN'T KNOW WHAT KIND OF MARKS ON IT WOULD POINT TO THE REAL KILLER.

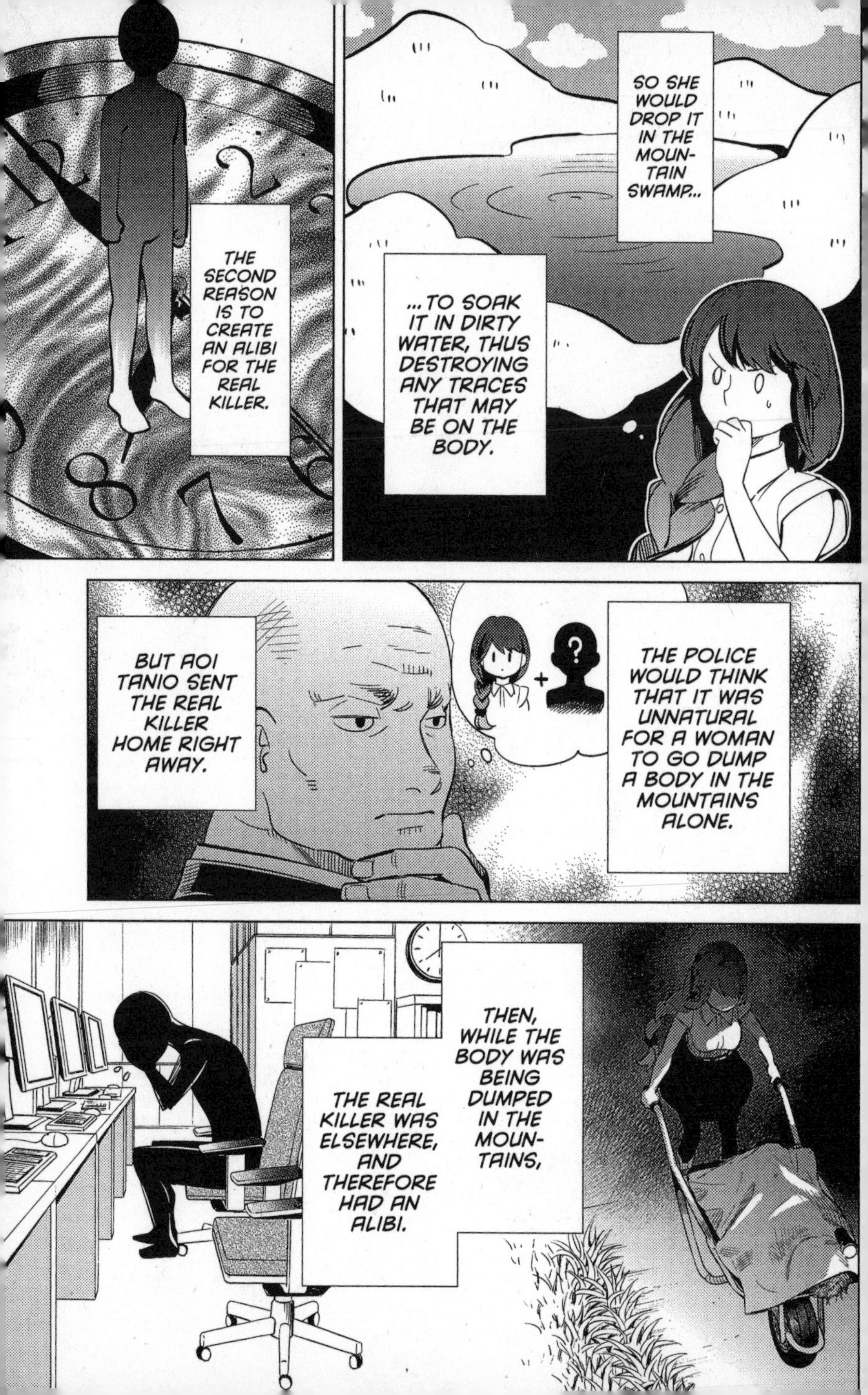
SO SHE WOULD DROP IT IN THE MOUNTAIN SWAMP...
...TO SOAK IT IN DIRTY WATER, THUS DESTROYING ANY TRACES THAT MAY BE ON THE BODY.
THE SECOND REASON IS TO CREATE AN ALIBI FOR THE REAL KILLER.
THE POLICE WOULD THINK THAT IT WAS UNNATURAL FOR A WOMAN TO GO DUMP A BODY IN THE MOUNTAINS ALONE.
BUT AOI TANIO SENT THE REAL KILLER HOME RIGHT AWAY.
THEN, WHILE THE BODY WAS BEING DUMPED IN THE MOUNTAINS,
THE REAL KILLER WAS ELSEWHERE, AND THEREFORE HAD AN ALIBI.

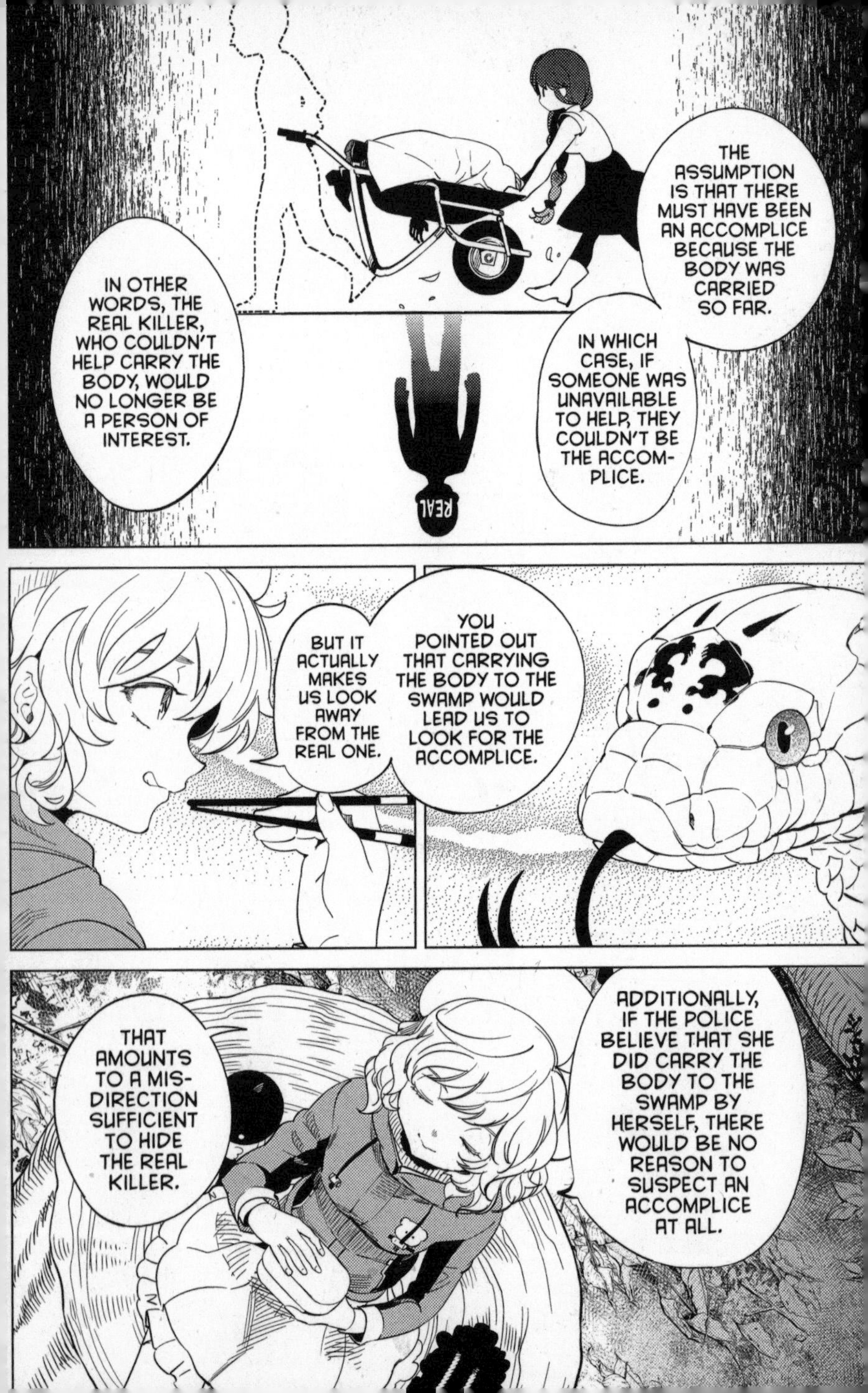
THE ASSUMPTION IS THAT THERE MUST HAVE BEEN AN ACCOMPLICE BECAUSE THE BODY WAS CARRIED SO FAR.
IN WHICH CASE, IF SOMEONE WAS UNAVAILABLE TO HELP, THEY COULDN'T BE THE ACCOMPLICE.
REAL
IN OTHER WORDS, THE REAL KILLER, WHO COULDN'T HELP CARRY THE BODY, WOULD NO LONGER BE A PERSON OF INTEREST.
YOU POINTED OUT THAT CARRYING THE BODY TO THE SWAMP WOULD LEAD US TO LOOK FOR THE ACCOMPLICE.
BUT IT ACTUALLY MAKES US LOOK AWAY FROM THE REAL ONE.
ADDITIONALLY, IF THE POLICE BELIEVE THAT SHE DID CARRY THE BODY TO THE SWAMP BY HERSELF, THERE WOULD BE NO REASON TO SUSPECT AN ACCOMPLICE AT ALL.
THAT AMOUNTS TO A MIS-DIRECTION SUFFICIENT TO HIDE THE REAL KILLER.

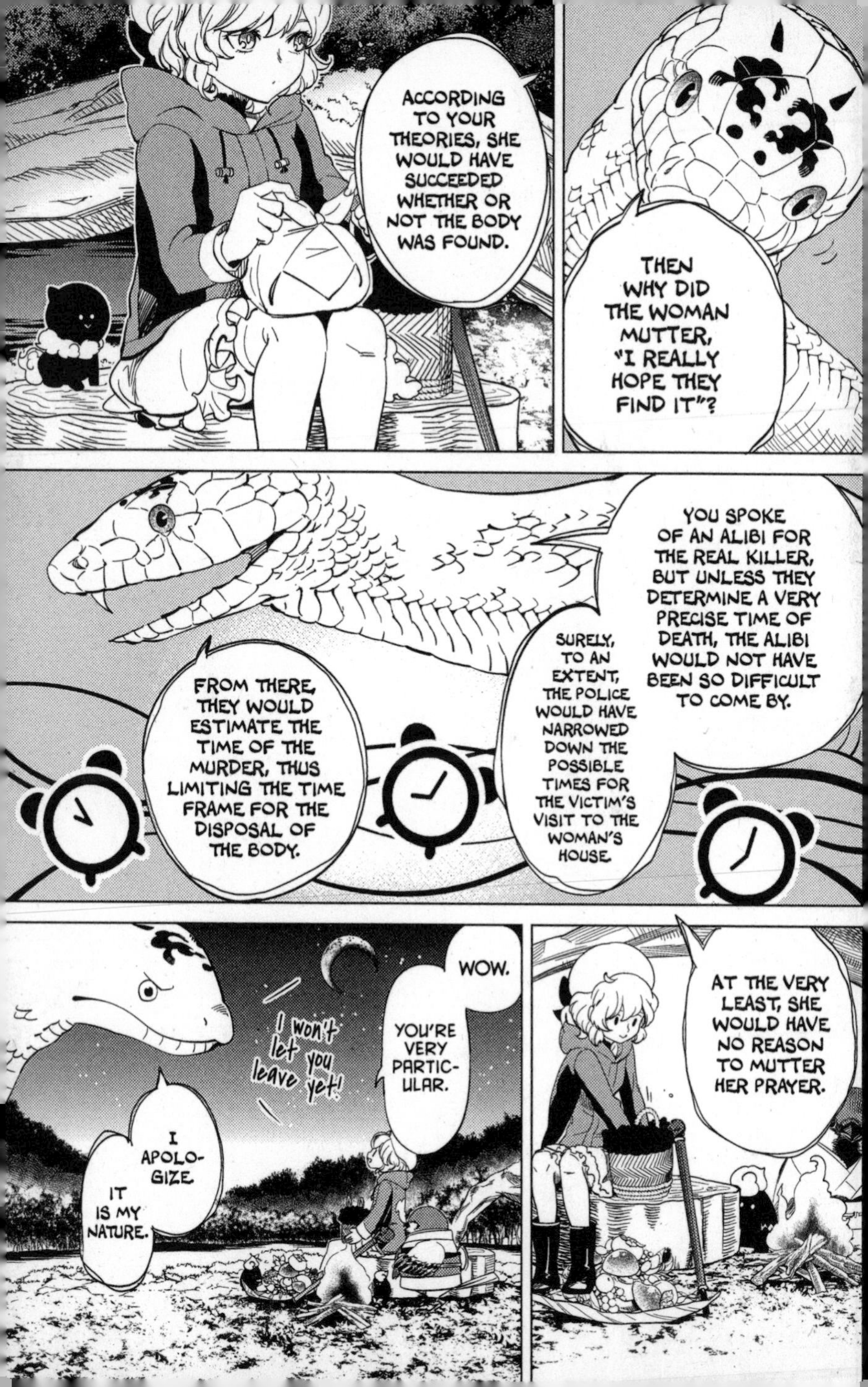
THEN WHY DID THE WOMAN MUTTER, "I REALLY HOPE THEY FIND IT"?
ACCORDING TO YOUR THEORIES, SHE WOULD HAVE SUCCEEDED WHETHER OR NOT THE BODY WAS FOUND.
YOU SPOKE OF AN ALIBI FOR THE REAL KILLER, BUT UNLESS THEY DETERMINE A VERY PRECISE TIME OF DEATH, THE ALIBI WOULD NOT HAVE BEEN SO DIFFICULT TO COME BY.
SURELY, TO AN EXTENT, THE POLICE WOULD HAVE NARROWED DOWN THE POSSIBLE TIMES FOR THE VICTIM'S VISIT TO THE WOMAN'S HOUSE.
FROM THERE, THEY WOULD ESTIMATE THE TIME OF THE MURDER, THUS LIMITING THE TIME FRAME FOR THE DISPOSAL OF THE BODY.
AT THE VERY LEAST, SHE WOULD HAVE NO REASON TO MUTTER HER PRAYER.
WOW.
YOU'RE VERY PARTICULAR.
I won't let you leave yet!
I APOLOGIZE.
IT IS MY NATURE.

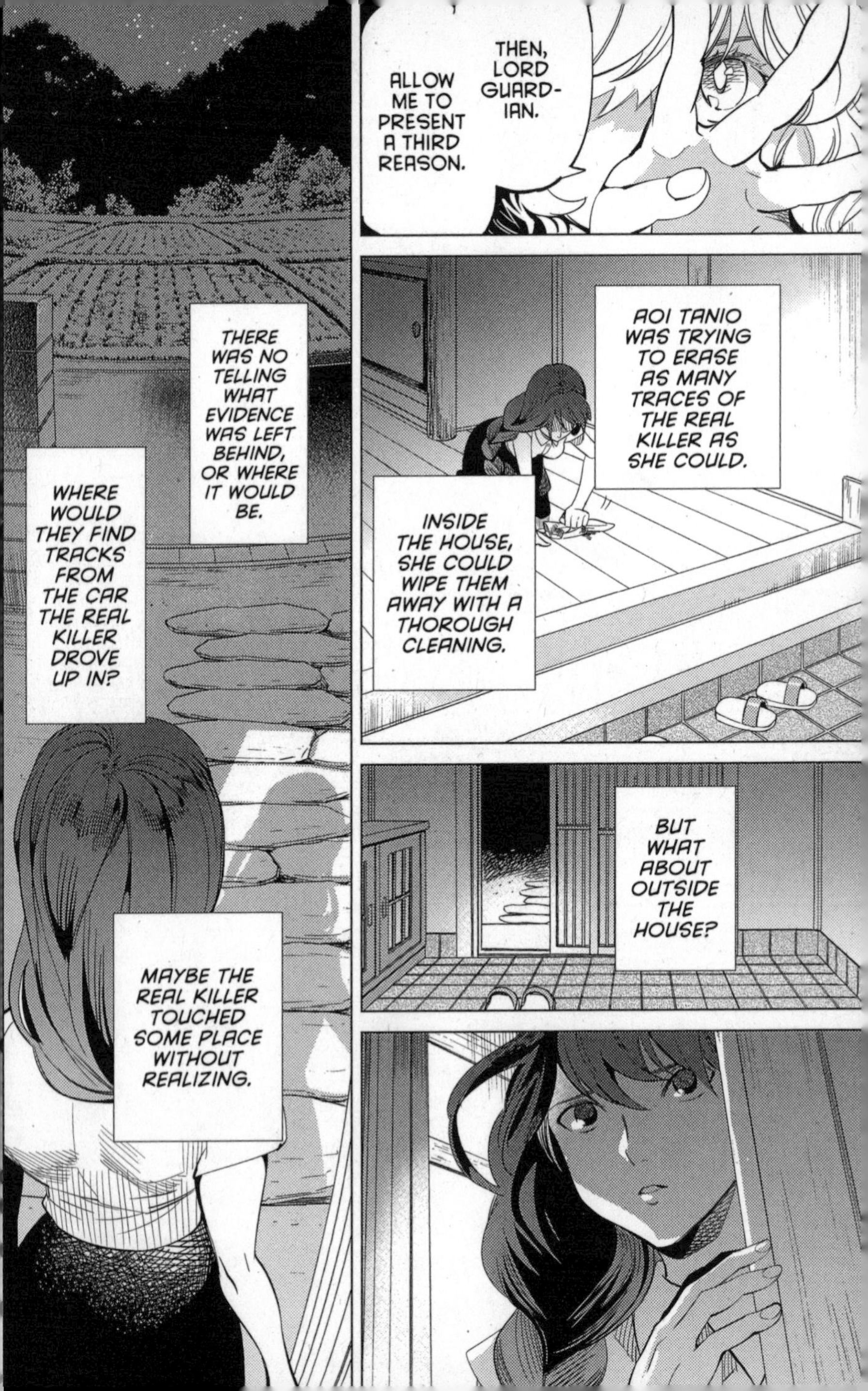
THEN, LORD GUARD-IAN.
ALLOW ME TO PRESENT A THIRD REASON.
AOI TANIO WAS TRYING TO ERASE AS MANY TRACES OF THE REAL KILLER AS SHE COULD.
INSIDE THE HOUSE, SHE COULD WIPE THEM AWAY WITH A THOROUGH CLEANING.
BUT WHAT ABOUT OUTSIDE THE HOUSE?
THERE WAS NO TELLING WHAT EVIDENCE WAS LEFT BEHIND, OR WHERE IT WOULD BE.
WHERE WOULD THEY FIND TRACKS FROM THE CAR THE REAL KILLER DROVE UP IN?
MAYBE THE REAL KILLER TOUCHED SOME PLACE WITHOUT REALIZING.

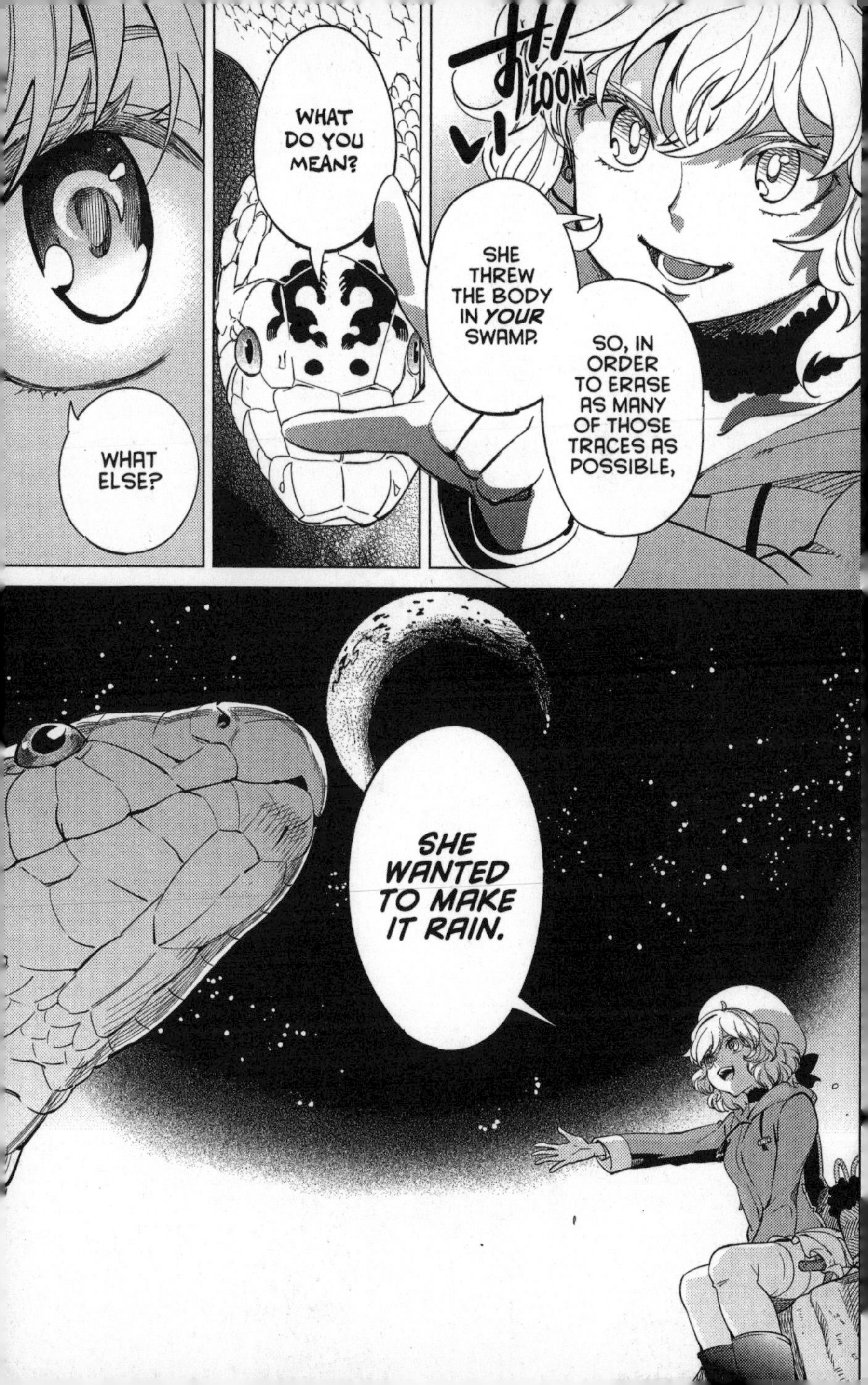
ZOOM
SHE THREW THE BODY IN *YOUR* SWAMP.
SO, IN ORDER TO ERASE AS MANY OF THOSE TRACES AS POSSIBLE,
WHAT DO YOU MEAN?
WHAT ELSE?
SHE WANTED TO MAKE IT RAIN.

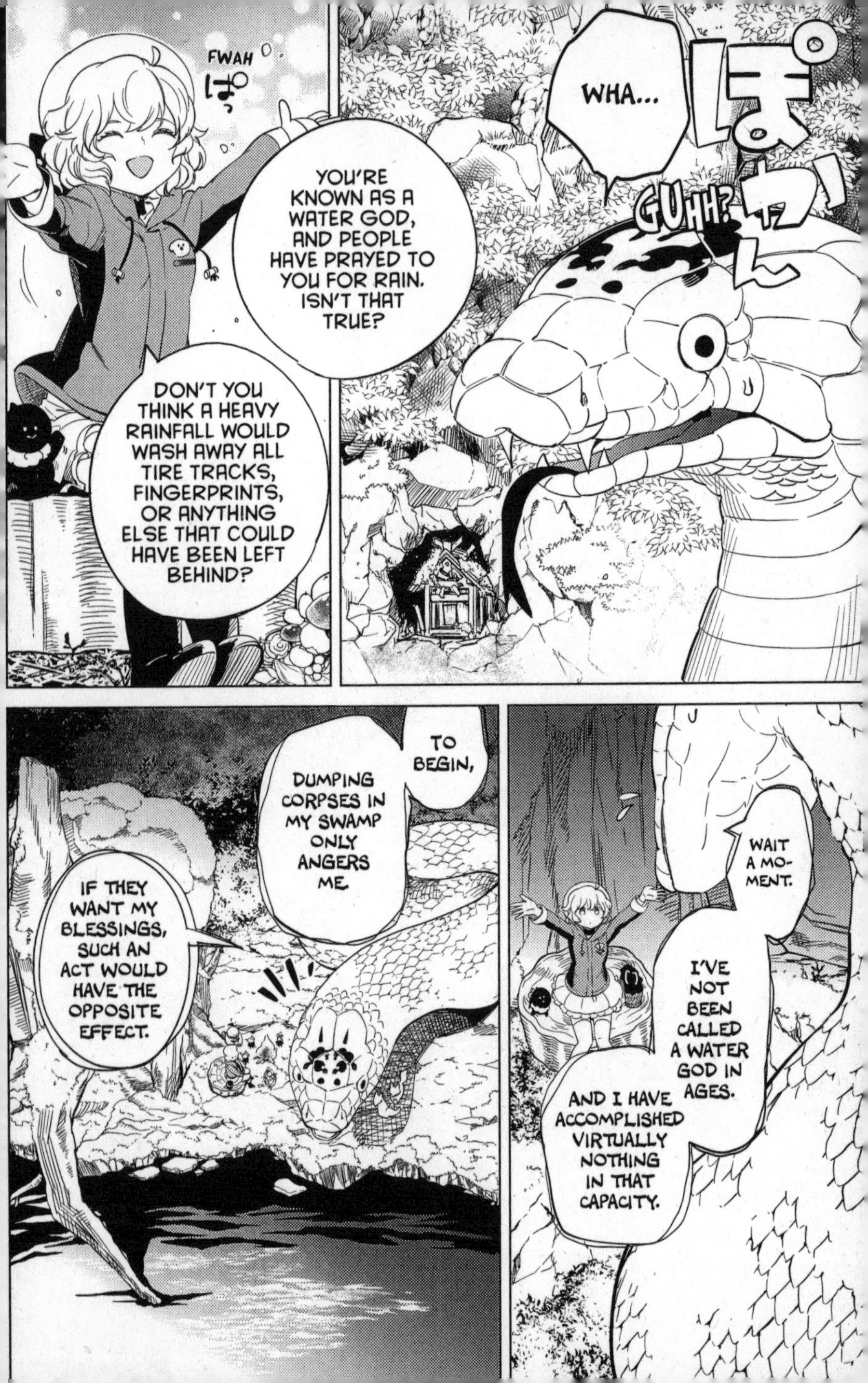
WHA...
GUHH?
ぽかん
FWAH
ぱっ
YOU'RE KNOWN AS A WATER GOD, AND PEOPLE HAVE PRAYED TO YOU FOR RAIN. ISN'T THAT TRUE?
DON'T YOU THINK A HEAVY RAINFALL WOULD WASH AWAY ALL TIRE TRACKS, FINGERPRINTS, OR ANYTHING ELSE THAT COULD HAVE BEEN LEFT BEHIND?
WAIT A MO-MENT.
I'VE NOT BEEN CALLED A WATER GOD IN AGES.
AND I HAVE ACCOMPLISHED VIRTUALLY NOTHING IN THAT CAPACITY.
TO BEGIN,
DUMPING CORPSES IN MY SWAMP ONLY ANGERS ME.
IF THEY WANT MY BLESSINGS, SUCH AN ACT WOULD HAVE THE OPPOSITE EFFECT.

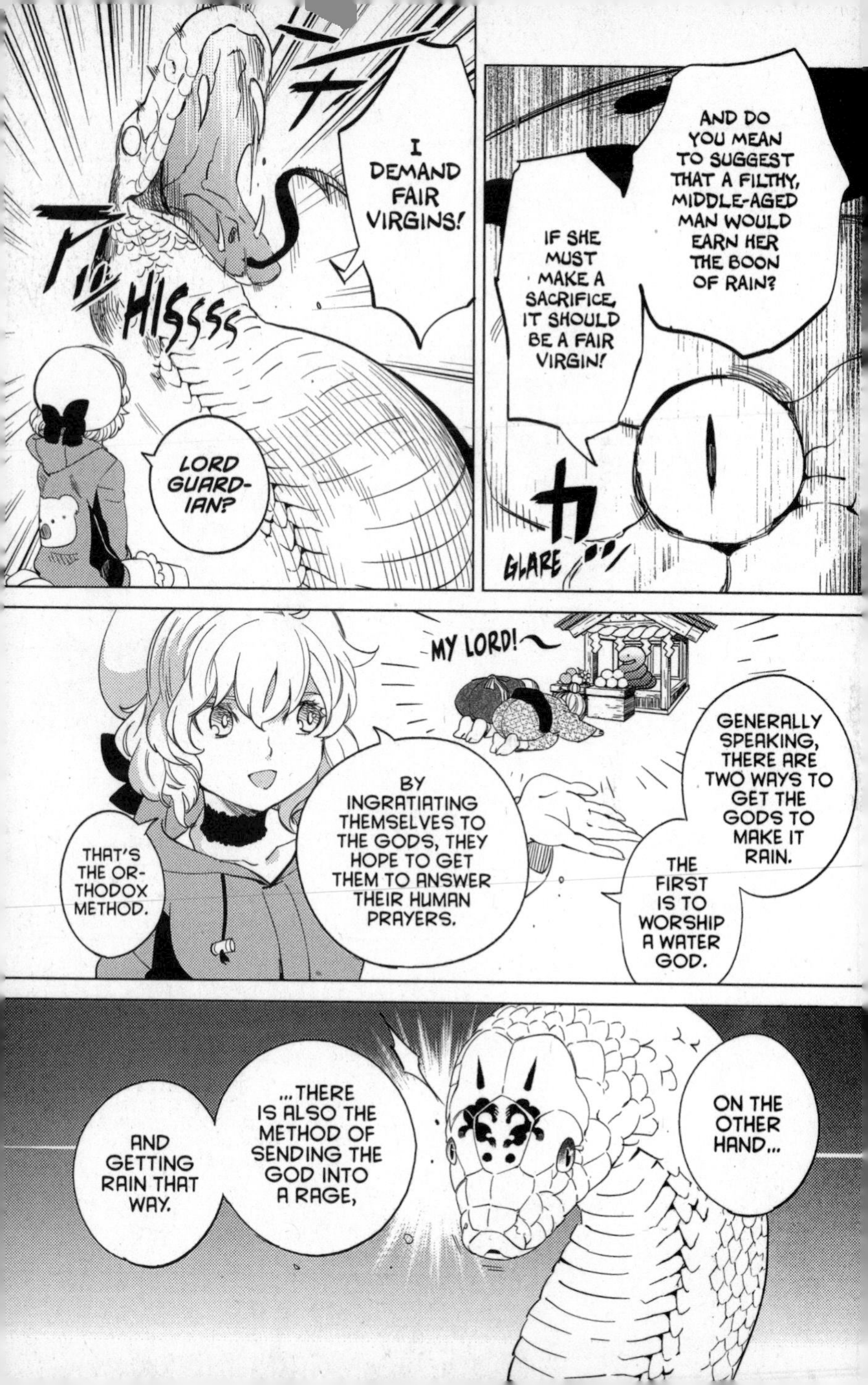
AND DO YOU MEAN TO SUGGEST THAT A FILTHY, MIDDLE-AGED MAN WOULD EARN HER THE BOON OF RAIN?
IF SHE MUST MAKE A SACRIFICE, IT SHOULD BE A FAIR VIRGIN!
GLARE
I DEMAND FAIR VIRGINS!
HISSSSS
LORD GUARDIAN?
MY LORD!~
GENERALLY SPEAKING, THERE ARE TWO WAYS TO GET THE GODS TO MAKE IT RAIN.
THE FIRST IS TO WORSHIP A WATER GOD.
BY INGRATIATING THEMSELVES TO THE GODS, THEY HOPE TO GET THEM TO ANSWER THEIR HUMAN PRAYERS.
THAT'S THE ORTHODOX METHOD.
ON THE OTHER HAND...
...THERE IS ALSO THE METHOD OF SENDING THE GOD INTO A RAGE,
AND GETTING RAIN THAT WAY.

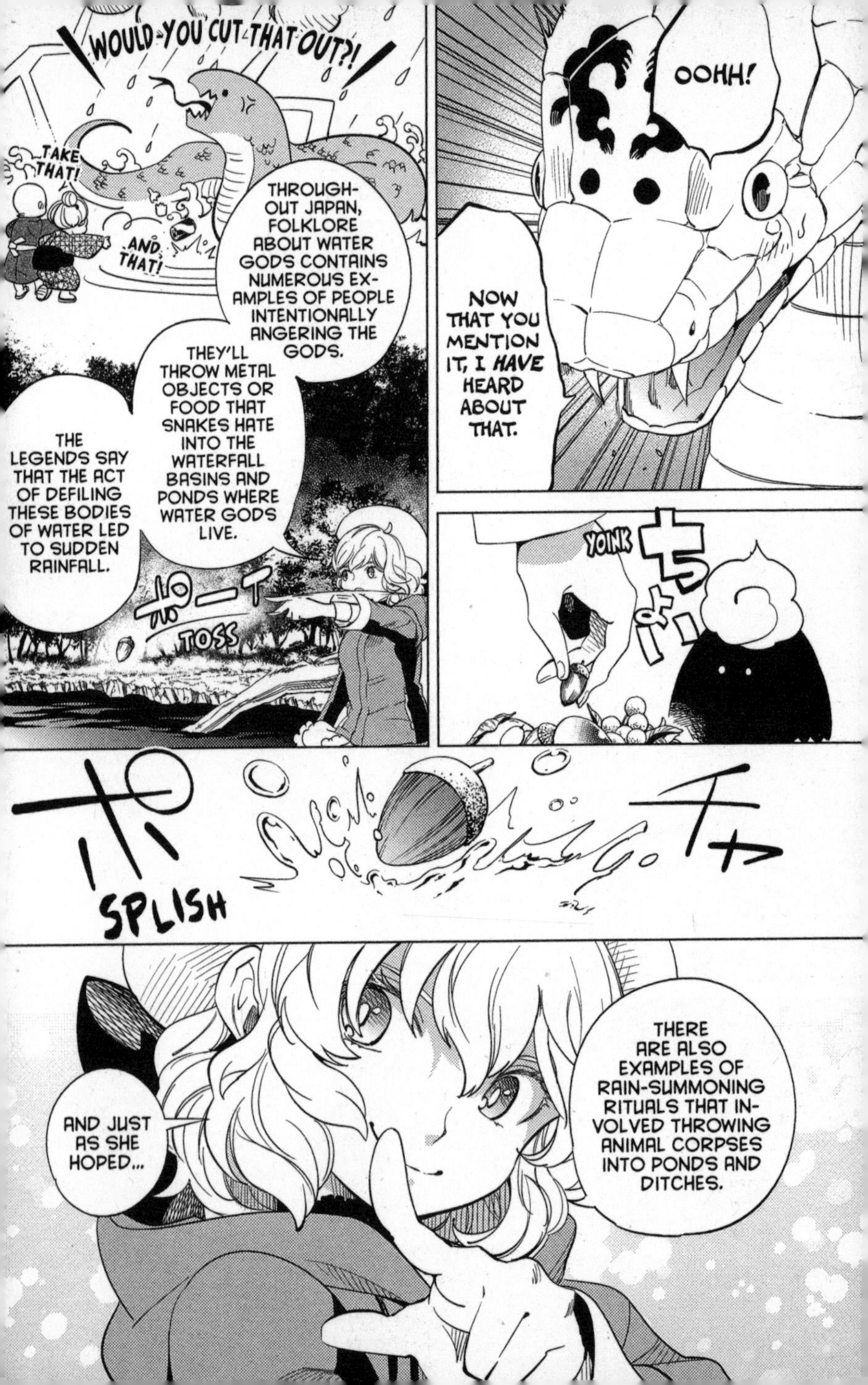
OOHH!
NOW THAT YOU MENTION IT, I *HAVE* HEARD ABOUT THAT.
YOINK
ちょい
WOULD YOU CUT THAT OUT?!
TAKE THAT!
AND THAT!
THROUGH-OUT JAPAN, FOLKLORE ABOUT WATER GODS CONTAINS NUMEROUS EX-AMPLES OF PEOPLE INTENTIONALLY ANGERING THE GODS.
THEY'LL THROW METAL OBJECTS OR FOOD THAT SNAKES HATE INTO THE WATERFALL BASINS AND PONDS WHERE WATER GODS LIVE.
THE LEGENDS SAY THAT THE ACT OF DEFILING THESE BODIES OF WATER LED TO SUDDEN RAINFALL.
ポーイ
TOSS
ポチャ
SPLISH
THERE ARE ALSO EXAMPLES OF RAIN-SUMMONING RITUALS THAT IN-VOLVED THROWING ANIMAL CORPSES INTO PONDS AND DITCHES.
AND JUST AS SHE HOPED...

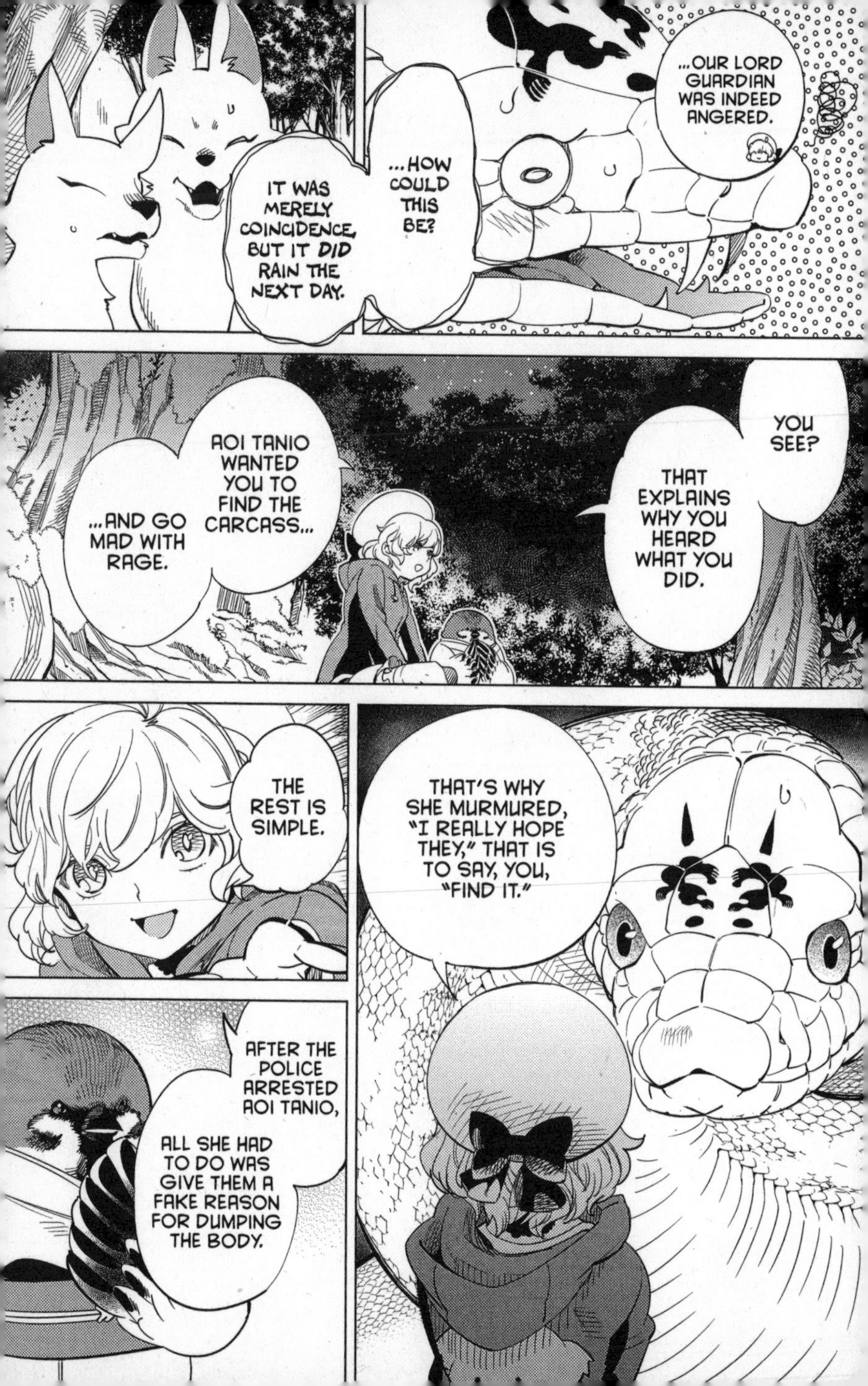
...OUR LORD GUARDIAN WAS INDEED ANGERED.
...HOW COULD THIS BE?
IT WAS MERELY COINCIDENCE, BUT IT DID RAIN THE NEXT DAY.
YOU SEE?
THAT EXPLAINS WHY YOU HEARD WHAT YOU DID.
AOI TANIO WANTED YOU TO FIND THE CARCASS...
...AND GO MAD WITH RAGE.
THAT'S WHY SHE MURMURED, "I REALLY HOPE THEY," THAT IS TO SAY, YOU, "FIND IT."
THE REST IS SIMPLE.
AFTER THE POLICE ARRESTED AOI TANIO,
ALL SHE HAD TO DO WAS GIVE THEM A FAKE REASON FOR DUMPING THE BODY.

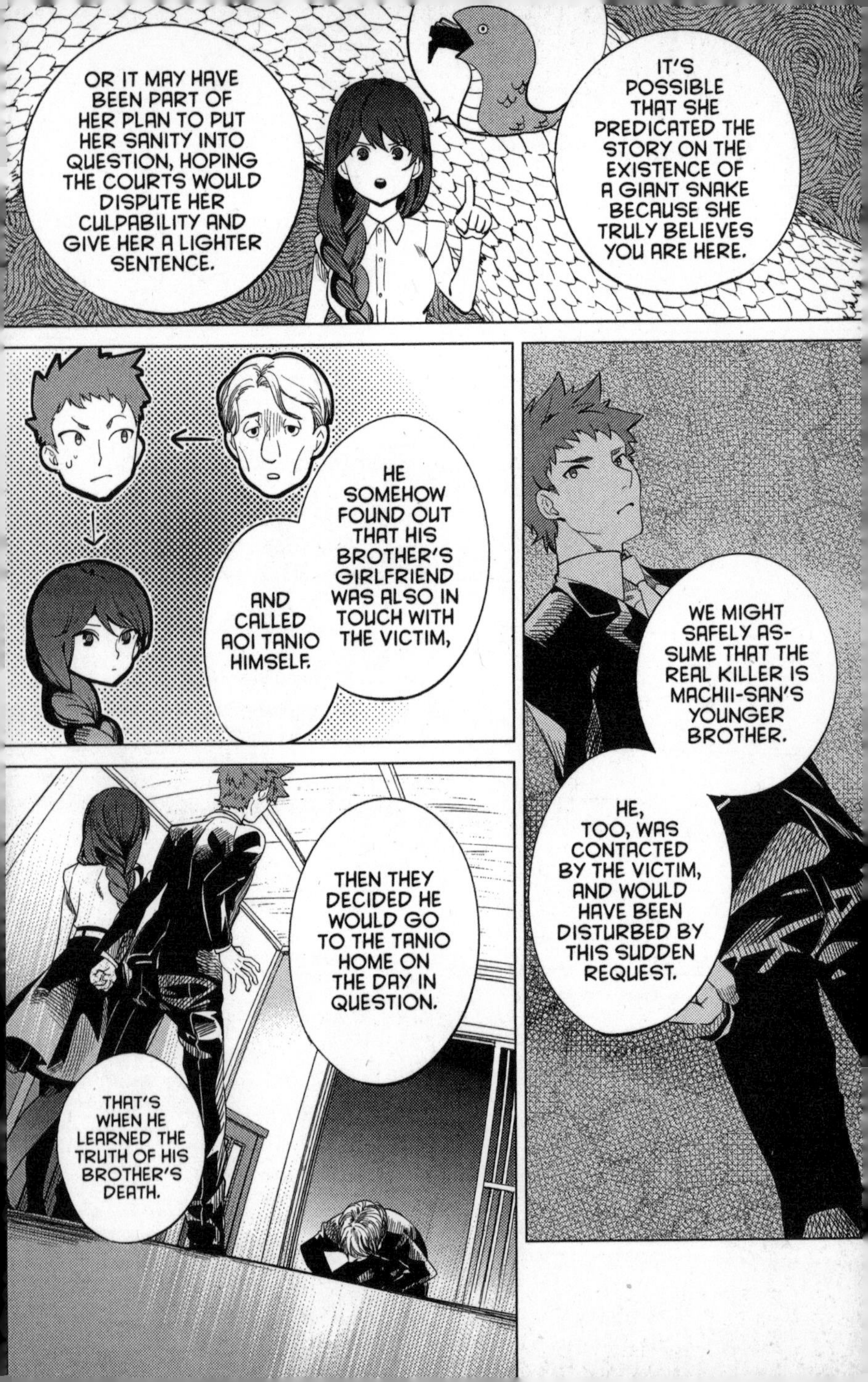
IT'S POSSIBLE THAT SHE PREDICATED THE STORY ON THE EXISTENCE OF A GIANT SNAKE BECAUSE SHE TRULY BELIEVES YOU ARE HERE.
OR IT MAY HAVE BEEN PART OF HER PLAN TO PUT HER SANITY INTO QUESTION, HOPING THE COURTS WOULD DISPUTE HER CULPABILITY AND GIVE HER A LIGHTER SENTENCE.
WE MIGHT SAFELY AS-SUME THAT THE REAL KILLER IS MACHII-SAN'S YOUNGER BROTHER.
HE, TOO, WAS CONTACTED BY THE VICTIM, AND WOULD HAVE BEEN DISTURBED BY THIS SUDDEN REQUEST.
HE SOMEHOW FOUND OUT THAT HIS BROTHER'S GIRLFRIEND WAS ALSO IN TOUCH WITH THE VICTIM,
AND CALLED AOI TANIO HIMSELF.
THEN THEY DECIDED HE WOULD GO TO THE TANIO HOME ON THE DAY IN QUESTION.
THAT'S WHEN HE LEARNED THE TRUTH OF HIS BROTHER'S DEATH.

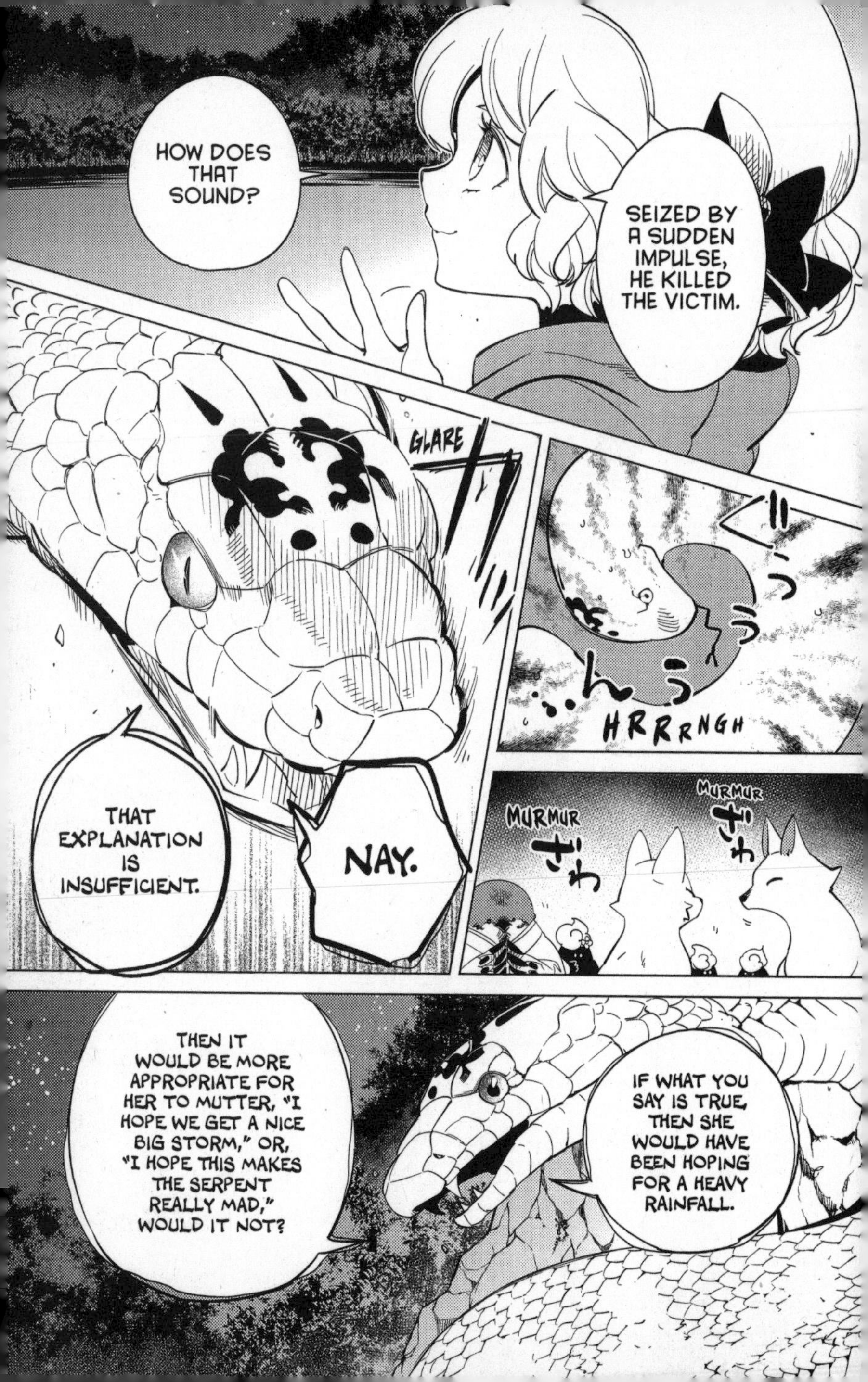
SEIZED BY A SUDDEN IMPULSE, HE KILLED THE VICTIM.
HOW DOES THAT SOUND?
HRRRNGH
MURMUR
ざわ
MURMUR
ざわ
GLARE
NAY.
THAT EXPLANATION IS INSUFFICIENT.
IF WHAT YOU SAY IS TRUE, THEN SHE WOULD HAVE BEEN HOPING FOR A HEAVY RAINFALL.
THEN IT WOULD BE MORE APPROPRIATE FOR HER TO MUTTER, "I HOPE WE GET A NICE BIG STORM," OR, "I HOPE THIS MAKES THE SERPENT REALLY MAD," WOULD IT NOT?

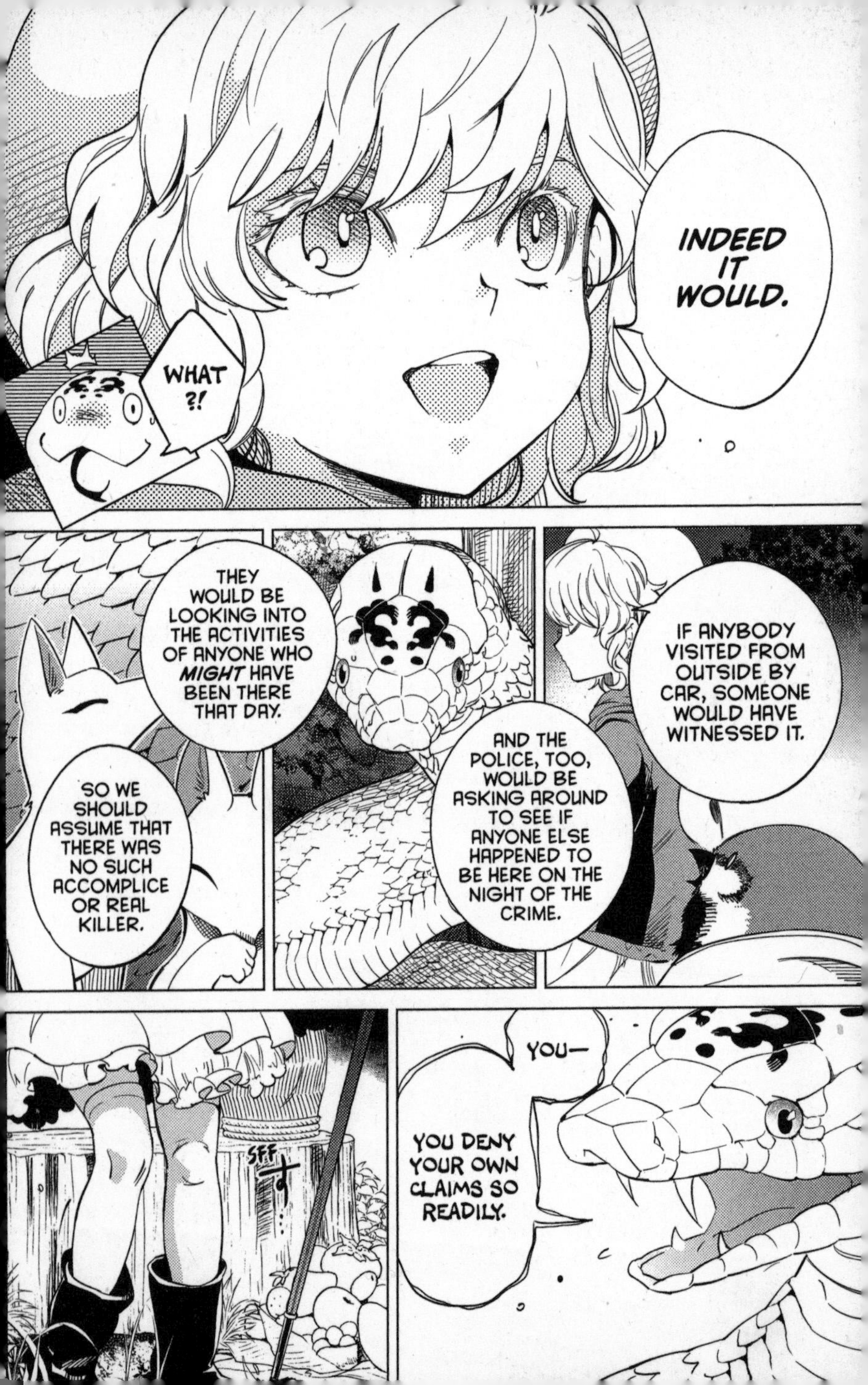
INDEED IT WOULD.
WHAT ?!
IF ANYBODY VISITED FROM OUTSIDE BY CAR, SOMEONE WOULD HAVE WITNESSED IT.
AND THE POLICE, TOO, WOULD BE ASKING AROUND TO SEE IF ANYONE ELSE HAPPENED TO BE HERE ON THE NIGHT OF THE CRIME.
THEY WOULD BE LOOKING INTO THE ACTIVITIES OF ANYONE WHO *MIGHT* HAVE BEEN THERE THAT DAY.
SO WE SHOULD ASSUME THAT THERE WAS NO SUCH ACCOMPLICE OR REAL KILLER.
YOU—
YOU DENY YOUR OWN CLAIMS SO READILY.
SFF

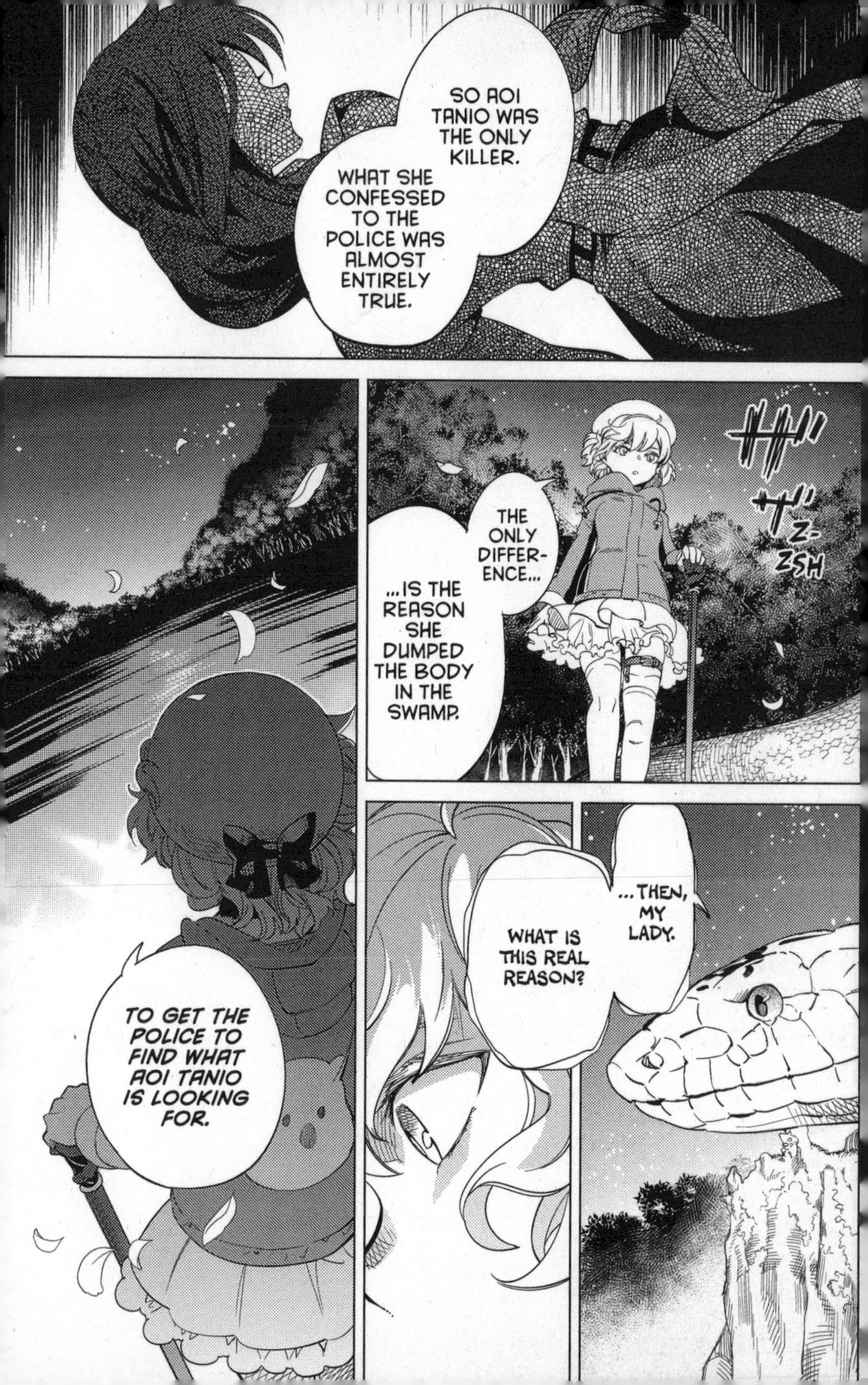
SO AOI TANIO WAS THE ONLY KILLER.
WHAT SHE CONFESSED TO THE POLICE WAS ALMOST ENTIRELY TRUE.
Z-ZSH
THE ONLY DIFFERENCE...
...IS THE REASON SHE DUMPED THE BODY IN THE SWAMP.
...THEN, MY LADY.
WHAT IS THIS REAL REASON?
TO GET THE POLICE TO FIND WHAT AOI TANIO IS LOOKING FOR.

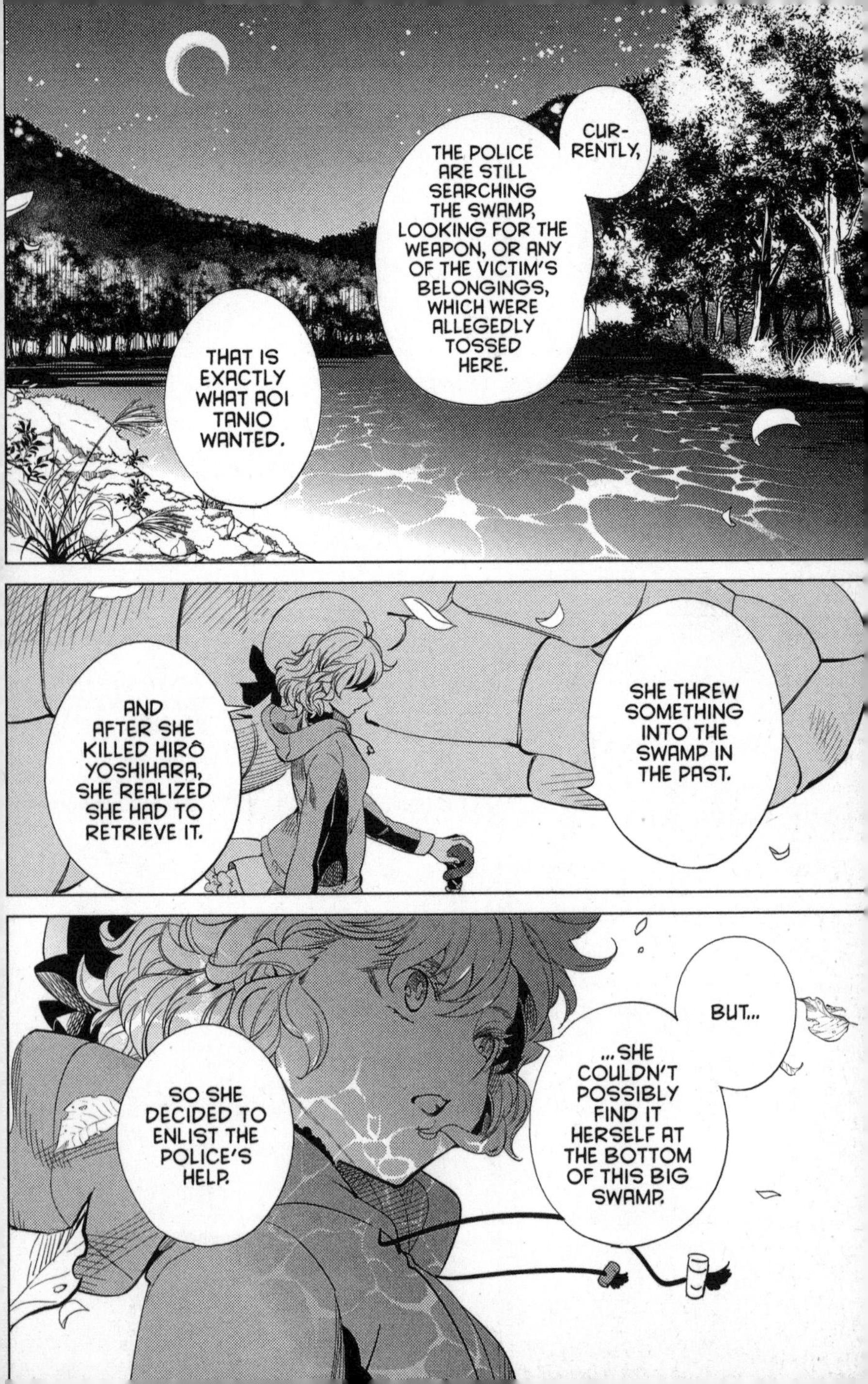
CUR-RENTLY,
THE POLICE ARE STILL SEARCHING THE SWAMP, LOOKING FOR THE WEAPON, OR ANY OF THE VICTIM'S BELONGINGS, WHICH WERE ALLEGEDLY TOSSED HERE.
THAT IS EXACTLY WHAT AOI TANIO WANTED.
SHE THREW SOMETHING INTO THE SWAMP IN THE PAST.
AND AFTER SHE KILLED HIRÔ YOSHIHARA, SHE REALIZED SHE HAD TO RETRIEVE IT.
BUT...
...SHE COULDN'T POSSIBLY FIND IT HERSELF AT THE BOTTOM OF THIS BIG SWAMP.
SO SHE DECIDED TO ENLIST THE POLICE'S HELP.

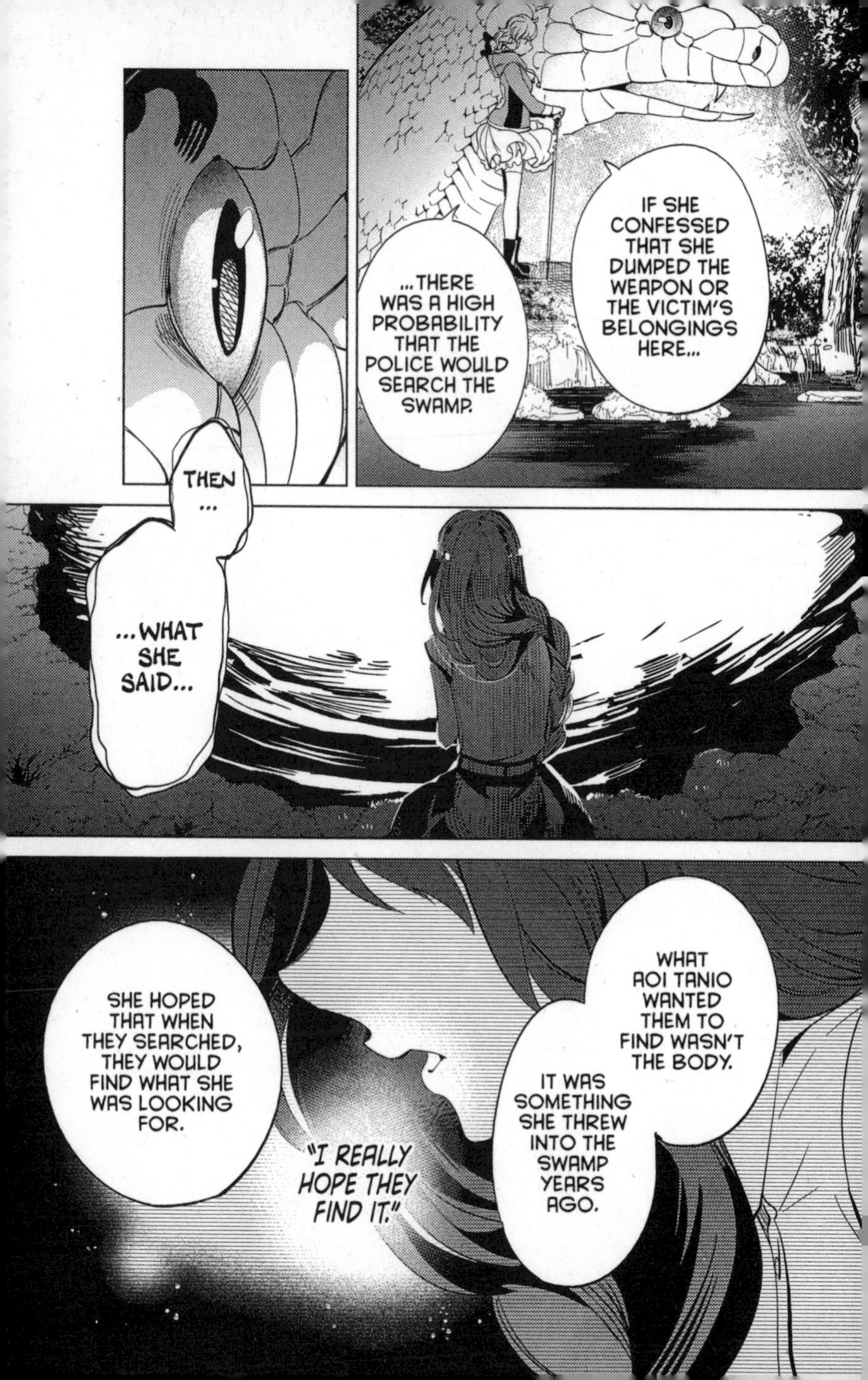
IF SHE CONFESSED THAT SHE DUMPED THE WEAPON OR THE VICTIM'S BELONGINGS HERE...
...THERE WAS A HIGH PROBABILITY THAT THE POLICE WOULD SEARCH THE SWAMP.
THEN ...
...WHAT SHE SAID...
WHAT AOI TANIO WANTED THEM TO FIND WASN'T THE BODY.
IT WAS SOMETHING SHE THREW INTO THE SWAMP YEARS AGO.
"I REALLY HOPE THEY FIND IT."
SHE HOPED THAT WHEN THEY SEARCHED, THEY WOULD FIND WHAT SHE WAS LOOKING FOR.

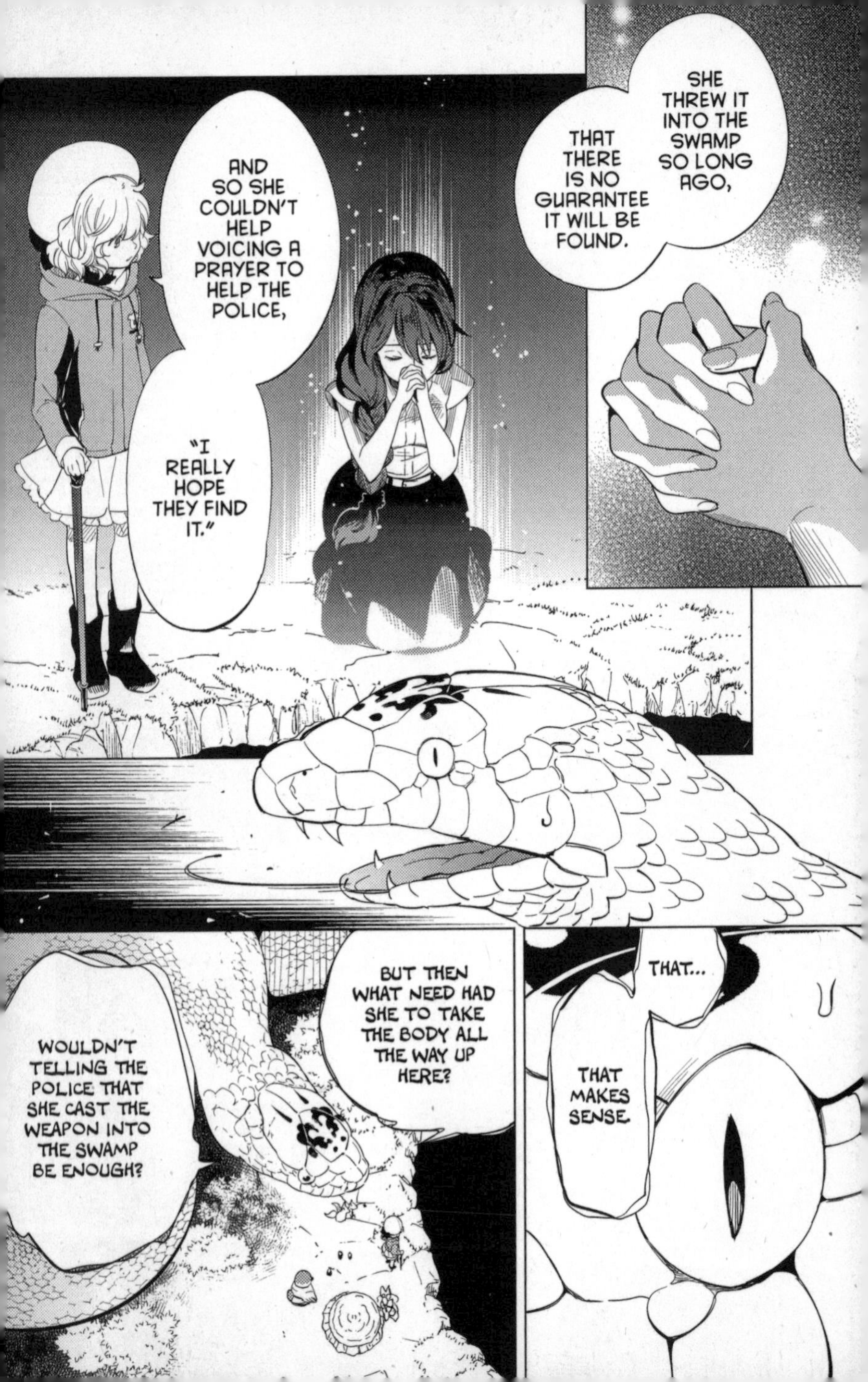
SHE THREW IT INTO THE SWAMP SO LONG AGO,
THAT THERE IS NO GUARANTEE IT WILL BE FOUND.
AND SO SHE COULDN'T HELP VOICING A PRAYER TO HELP THE POLICE,
"I REALLY HOPE THEY FIND IT."
THAT...
THAT MAKES SENSE.
BUT THEN WHAT NEED HAD SHE TO TAKE THE BODY ALL THE WAY UP HERE?
WOULDN'T TELLING THE POLICE THAT SHE CAST THE WEAPON INTO THE SWAMP BE ENOUGH?

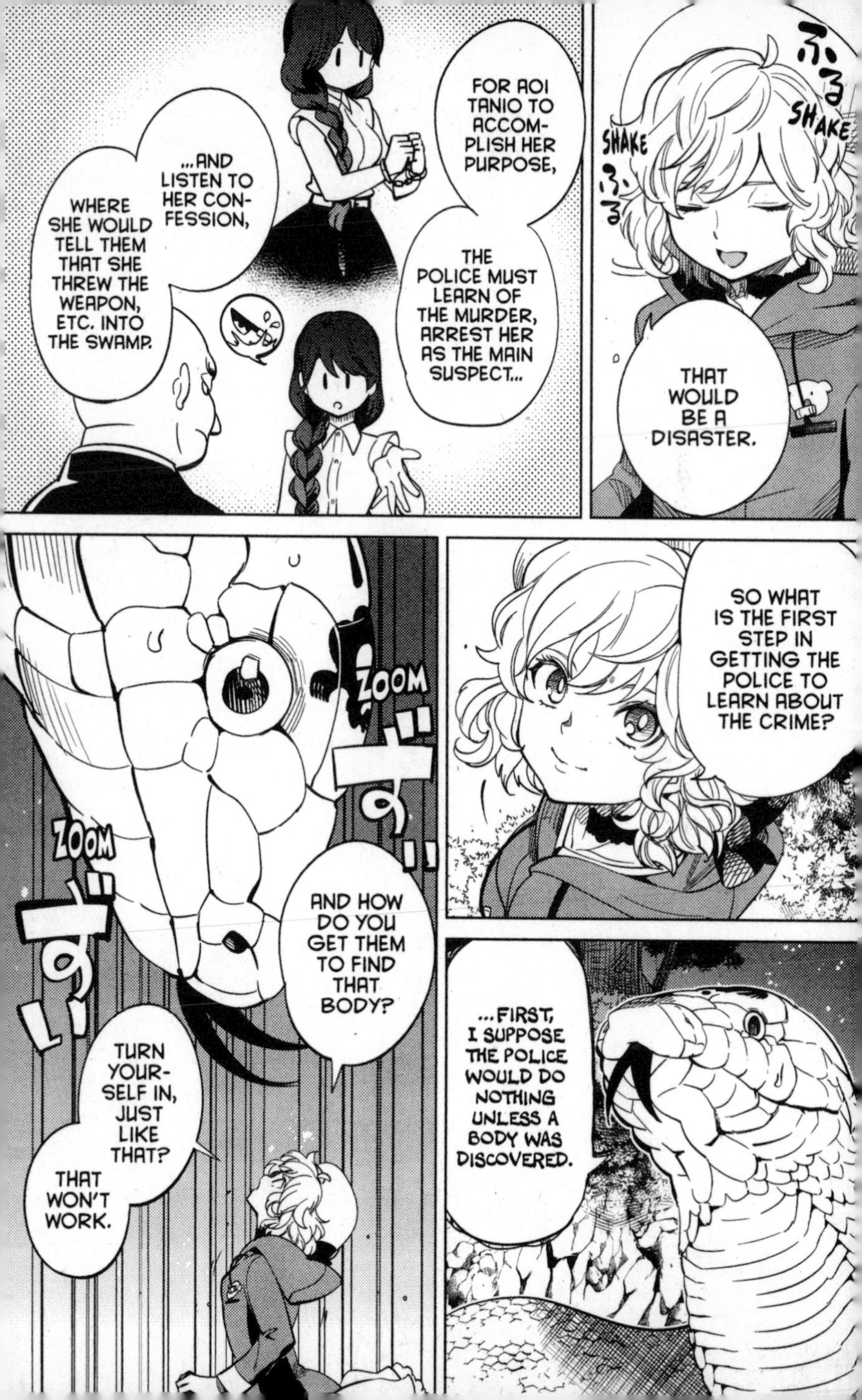
ふる
SHAKE
SHAKE
ふる
THAT WOULD BE A DISASTER.
FOR AOI TANIO TO ACCOMPLISH HER PURPOSE,
THE POLICE MUST LEARN OF THE MURDER, ARREST HER AS THE MAIN SUSPECT...
...AND LISTEN TO HER CONFESSION,
WHERE SHE WOULD TELL THEM THAT SHE THREW THE WEAPON, ETC. INTO THE SWAMP.
SO WHAT IS THE FIRST STEP IN GETTING THE POLICE TO LEARN ABOUT THE CRIME?
...FIRST, I SUPPOSE THE POLICE WOULD DO NOTHING UNLESS A BODY WAS DISCOVERED.
ZOOM
ずい
AND HOW DO YOU GET THEM TO FIND THAT BODY?
ZOOM
ずい
TURN YOURSELF IN, JUST LIKE THAT?
THAT WON'T WORK.

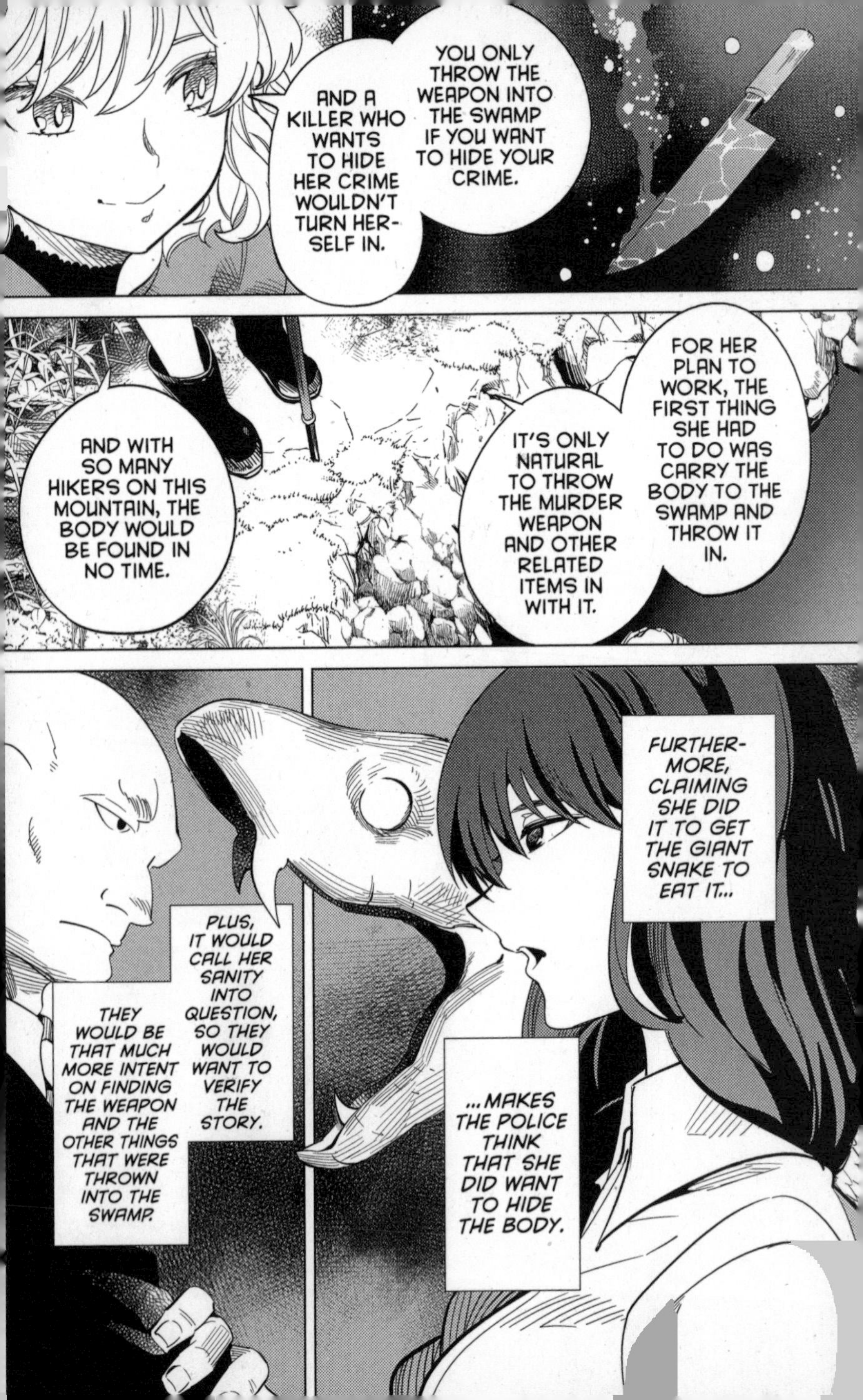
YOU ONLY THROW THE WEAPON INTO THE SWAMP IF YOU WANT TO HIDE YOUR CRIME.
AND A KILLER WHO WANTS TO HIDE HER CRIME WOULDN'T TURN HER-SELF IN.
FOR HER PLAN TO WORK, THE FIRST THING SHE HAD TO DO WAS CARRY THE BODY TO THE SWAMP AND THROW IT IN.
IT'S ONLY NATURAL TO THROW THE MURDER WEAPON AND OTHER RELATED ITEMS IN WITH IT.
AND WITH SO MANY HIKERS ON THIS MOUNTAIN, THE BODY WOULD BE FOUND IN NO TIME.
FURTHER-MORE, CLAIMING SHE DID IT TO GET THE GIANT SNAKE TO EAT IT...
...MAKES THE POLICE THINK THAT SHE DID WANT TO HIDE THE BODY.
PLUS, IT WOULD CALL HER SANITY INTO QUESTION, SO THEY WOULD WANT TO VERIFY THE STORY.
THEY WOULD BE THAT MUCH MORE INTENT ON FINDING THE WEAPON AND THE OTHER THINGS THAT WERE THROWN INTO THE SWAMP.

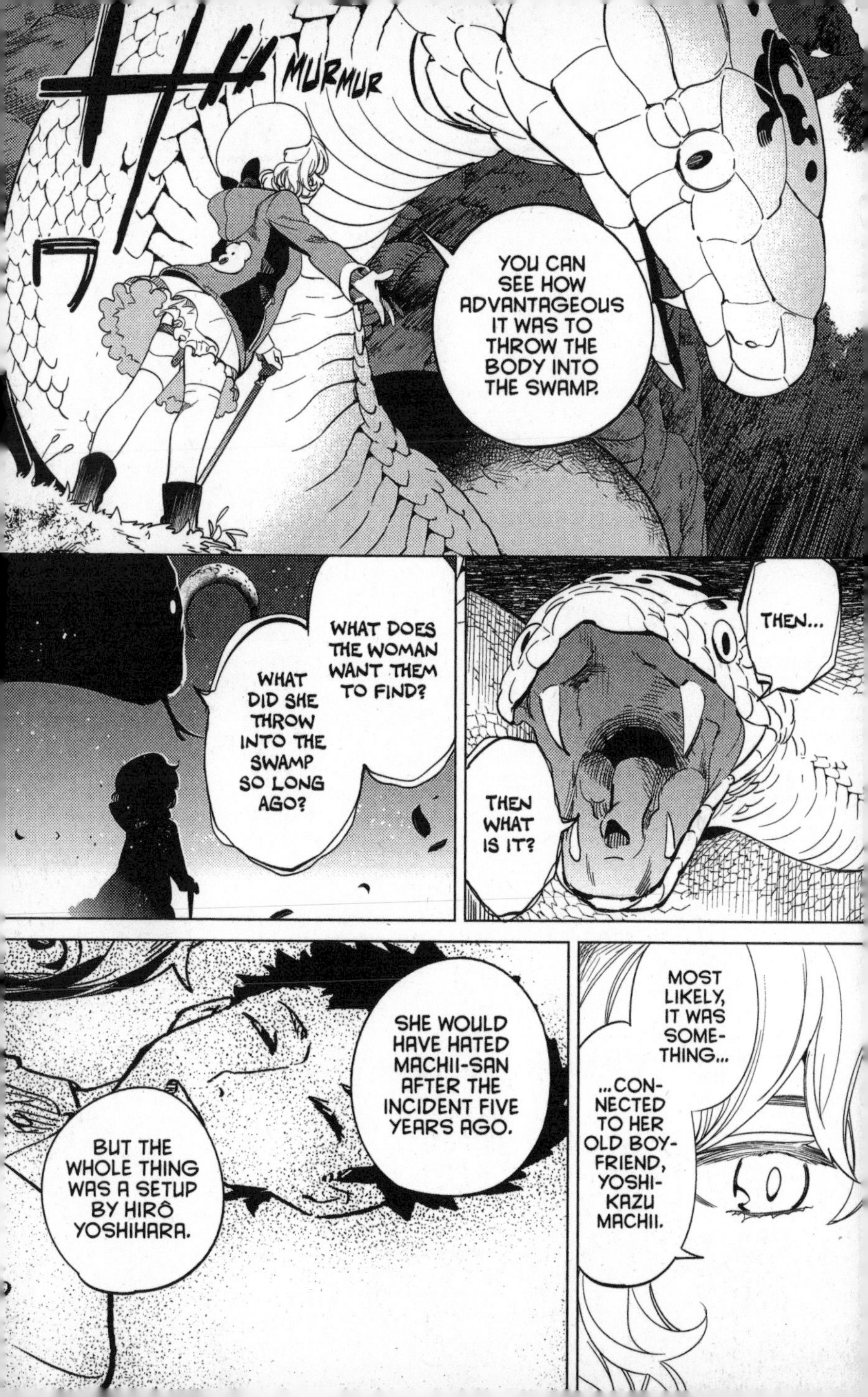
MURMUR
YOU CAN SEE HOW ADVANTAGEOUS IT WAS TO THROW THE BODY INTO THE SWAMP.
THEN...
THEN WHAT IS IT?
WHAT DOES THE WOMAN WANT THEM TO FIND?
WHAT DID SHE THROW INTO THE SWAMP SO LONG AGO?
MOST LIKELY, IT WAS SOME-THING...
...CON-NECTED TO HER OLD BOY-FRIEND, YOSHI-KAZU MACHII.
SHE WOULD HAVE HATED MACHII-SAN AFTER THE INCIDENT FIVE YEARS AGO.
BUT THE WHOLE THING WAS A SETUP BY HIRÔ YOSHIHARA.

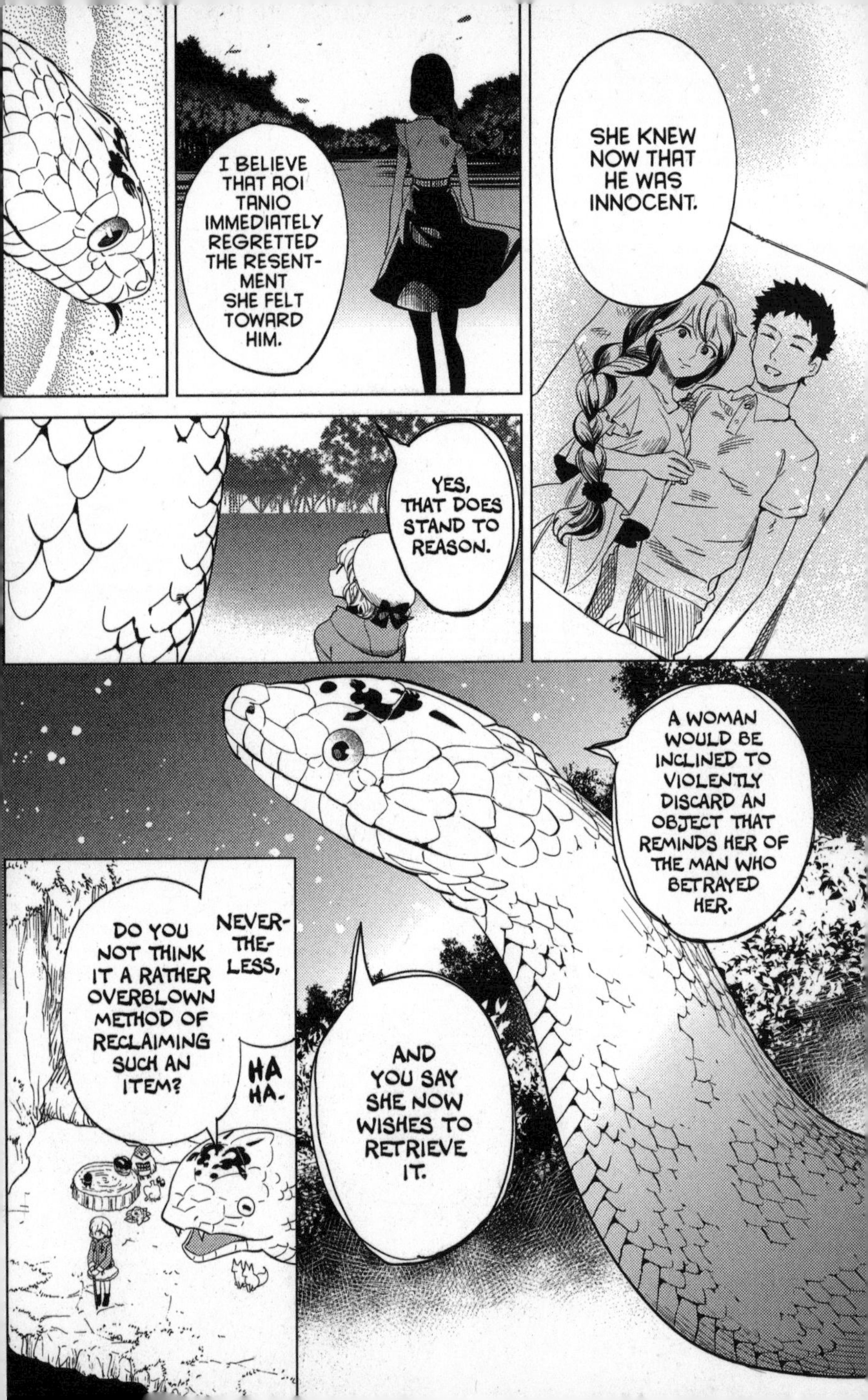
SHE KNEW NOW THAT HE WAS INNOCENT.
I BELIEVE THAT AOI TANIO IMMEDIATELY REGRETTED THE RESENTMENT SHE FELT TOWARD HIM.
YES, THAT DOES STAND TO REASON.
A WOMAN WOULD BE INCLINED TO VIOLENTLY DISCARD AN OBJECT THAT REMINDS HER OF THE MAN WHO BETRAYED HER.
AND YOU SAY SHE NOW WISHES TO RETRIEVE IT.
NEVER-THE-LESS,
DO YOU NOT THINK IT A RATHER OVERBLOWN METHOD OF RECLAIMING SUCH AN ITEM?
HA HA.

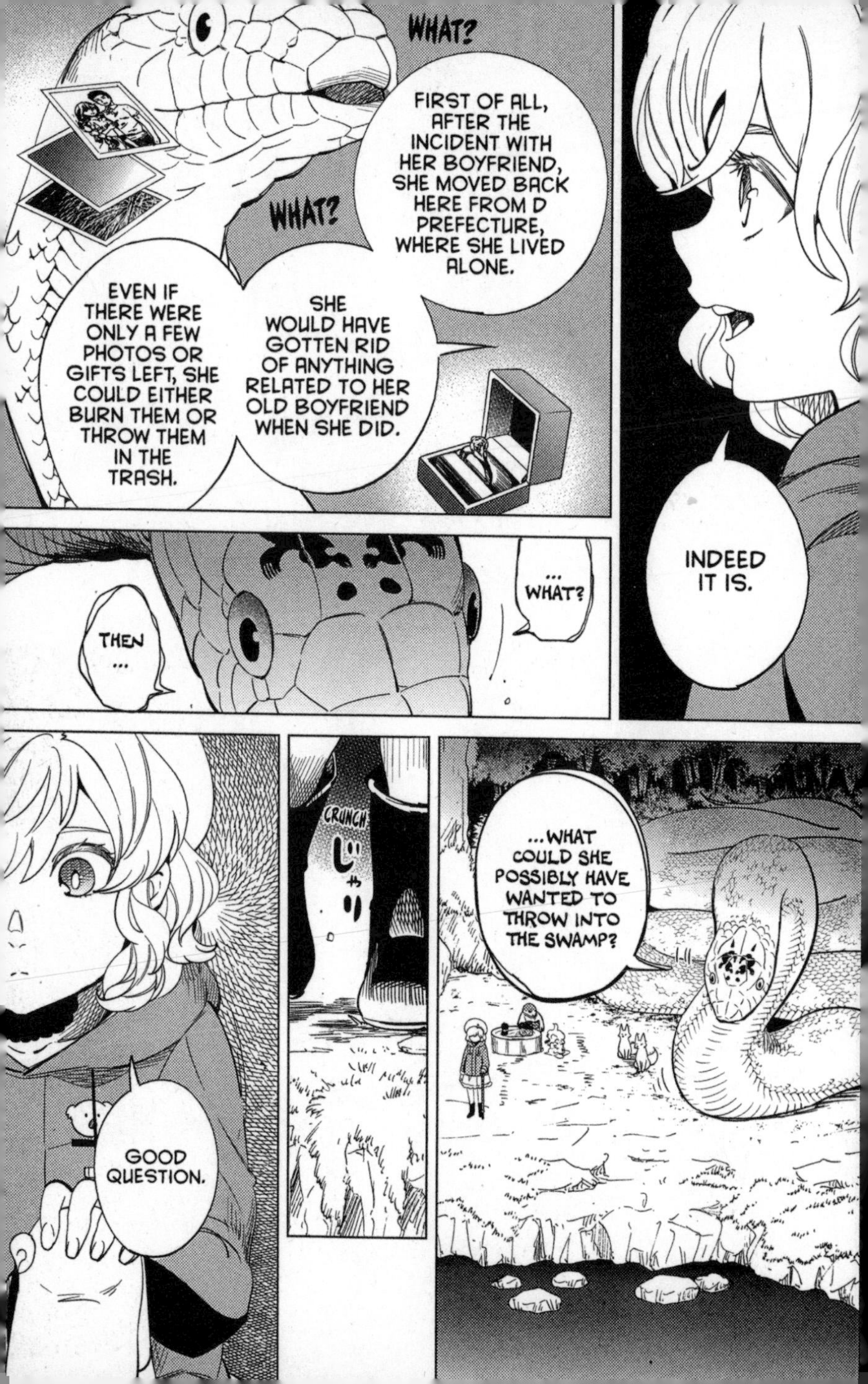
INDEED IT IS.
WHAT?
FIRST OF ALL, AFTER THE INCIDENT WITH HER BOYFRIEND, SHE MOVED BACK HERE FROM D PREFECTURE, WHERE SHE LIVED ALONE.
WHAT?
SHE WOULD HAVE GOTTEN RID OF ANYTHING RELATED TO HER OLD BOYFRIEND WHEN SHE DID.
EVEN IF THERE WERE ONLY A FEW PHOTOS OR GIFTS LEFT, SHE COULD EITHER BURN THEM OR THROW THEM IN THE TRASH.
...WHAT?
THEN ...
...WHAT COULD SHE POSSIBLY HAVE WANTED TO THROW INTO THE SWAMP?
CRUNCH
GOOD QUESTION.

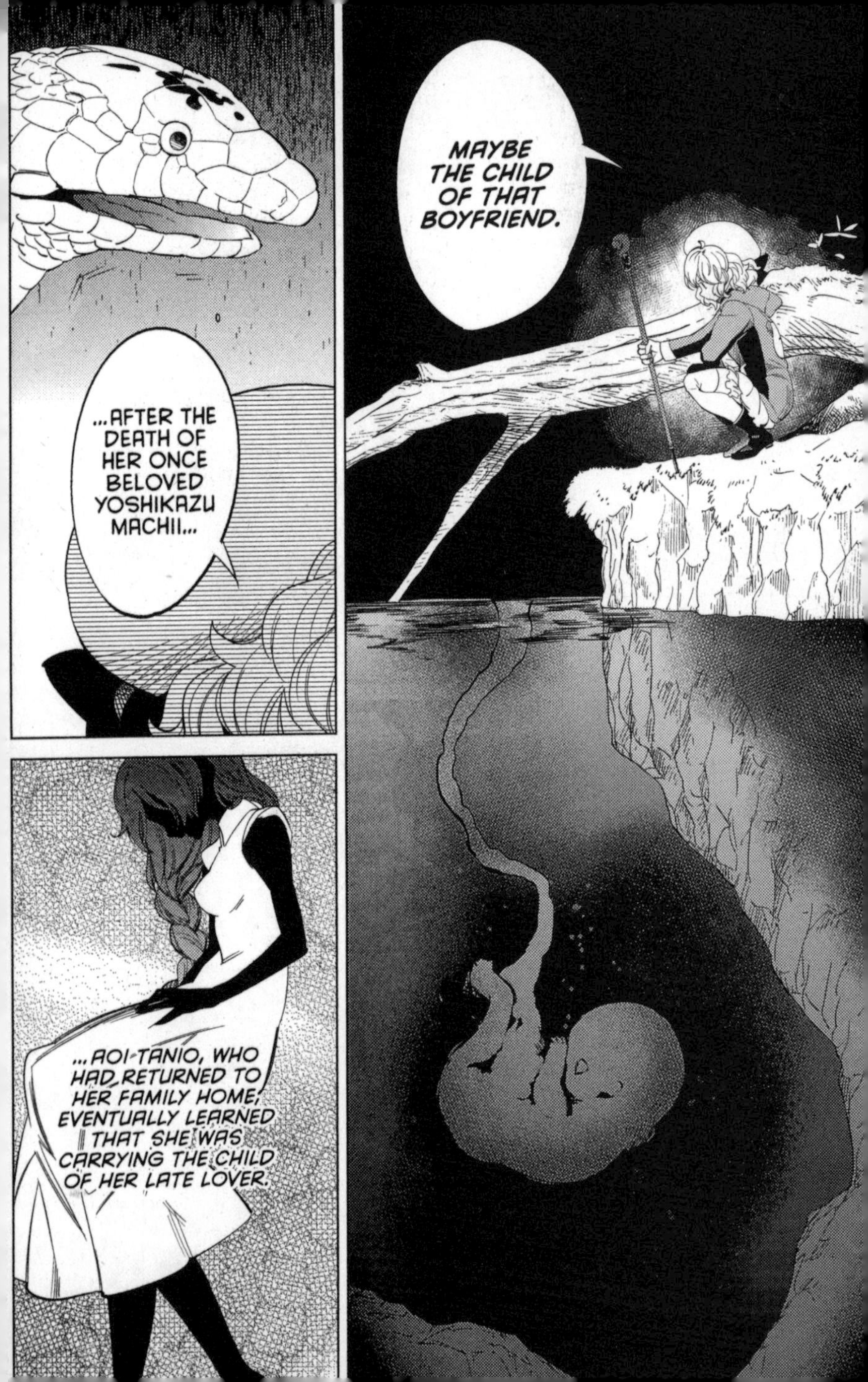
MAYBE THE CHILD OF THAT BOYFRIEND.
...AFTER THE DEATH OF HER ONCE BELOVED YOSHIKAZU MACHII...
...AOI TANIO, WHO HAD RETURNED TO HER FAMILY HOME, EVENTUALLY LEARNED THAT SHE WAS CARRYING THE CHILD OF HER LATE LOVER.

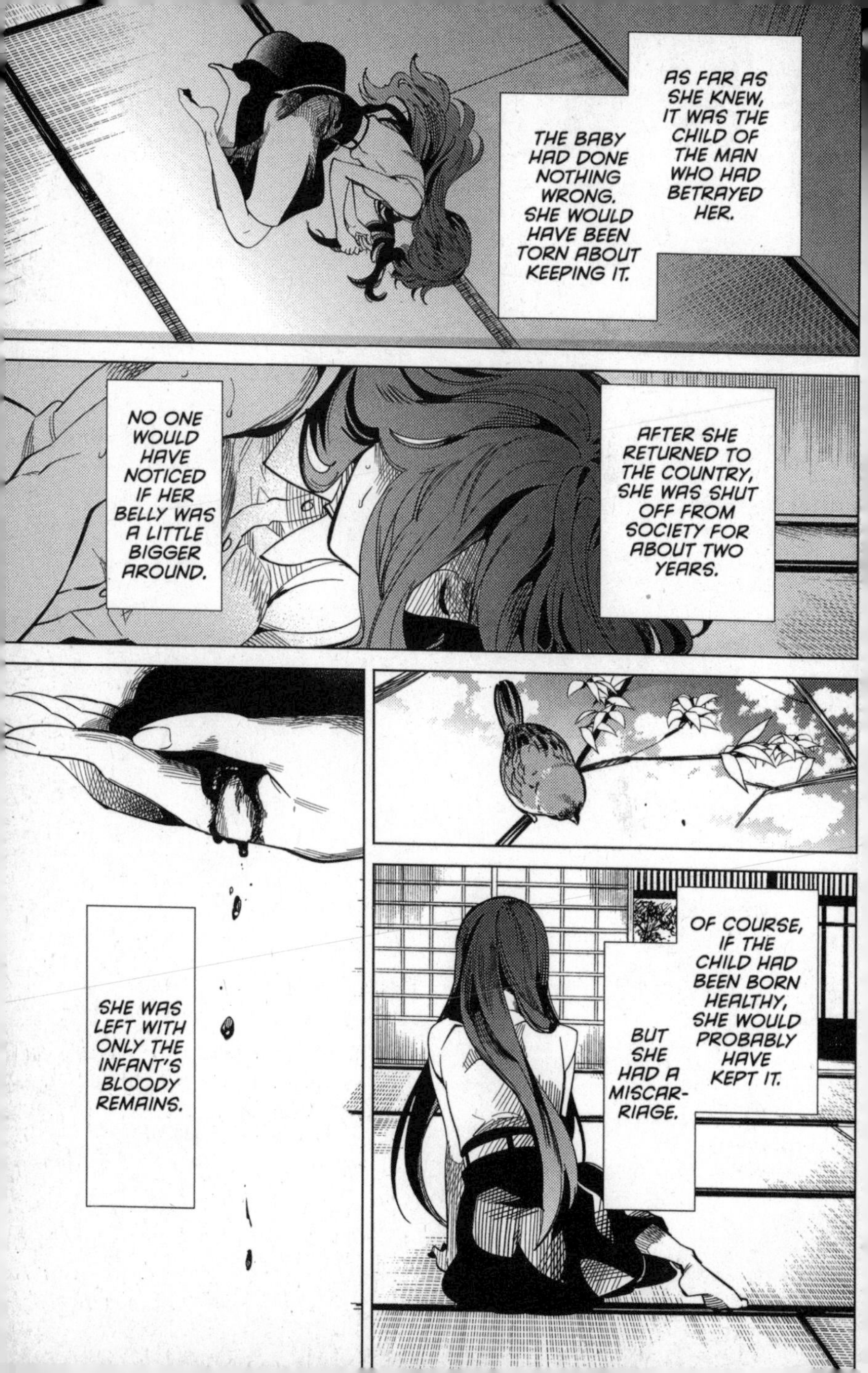
AS FAR AS SHE KNEW, IT WAS THE CHILD OF THE MAN WHO HAD BETRAYED HER.
THE BABY HAD DONE NOTHING WRONG. SHE WOULD HAVE BEEN TORN ABOUT KEEPING IT.
AFTER SHE RETURNED TO THE COUNTRY, SHE WAS SHUT OFF FROM SOCIETY FOR ABOUT TWO YEARS.
NO ONE WOULD HAVE NOTICED IF HER BELLY WAS A LITTLE BIGGER AROUND.
OF COURSE, IF THE CHILD HAD BEEN BORN HEALTHY, SHE WOULD PROBABLY HAVE KEPT IT.
BUT SHE HAD A MISCAR-RIAGE.
SHE WAS LEFT WITH ONLY THE INFANT'S BLOODY REMAINS.

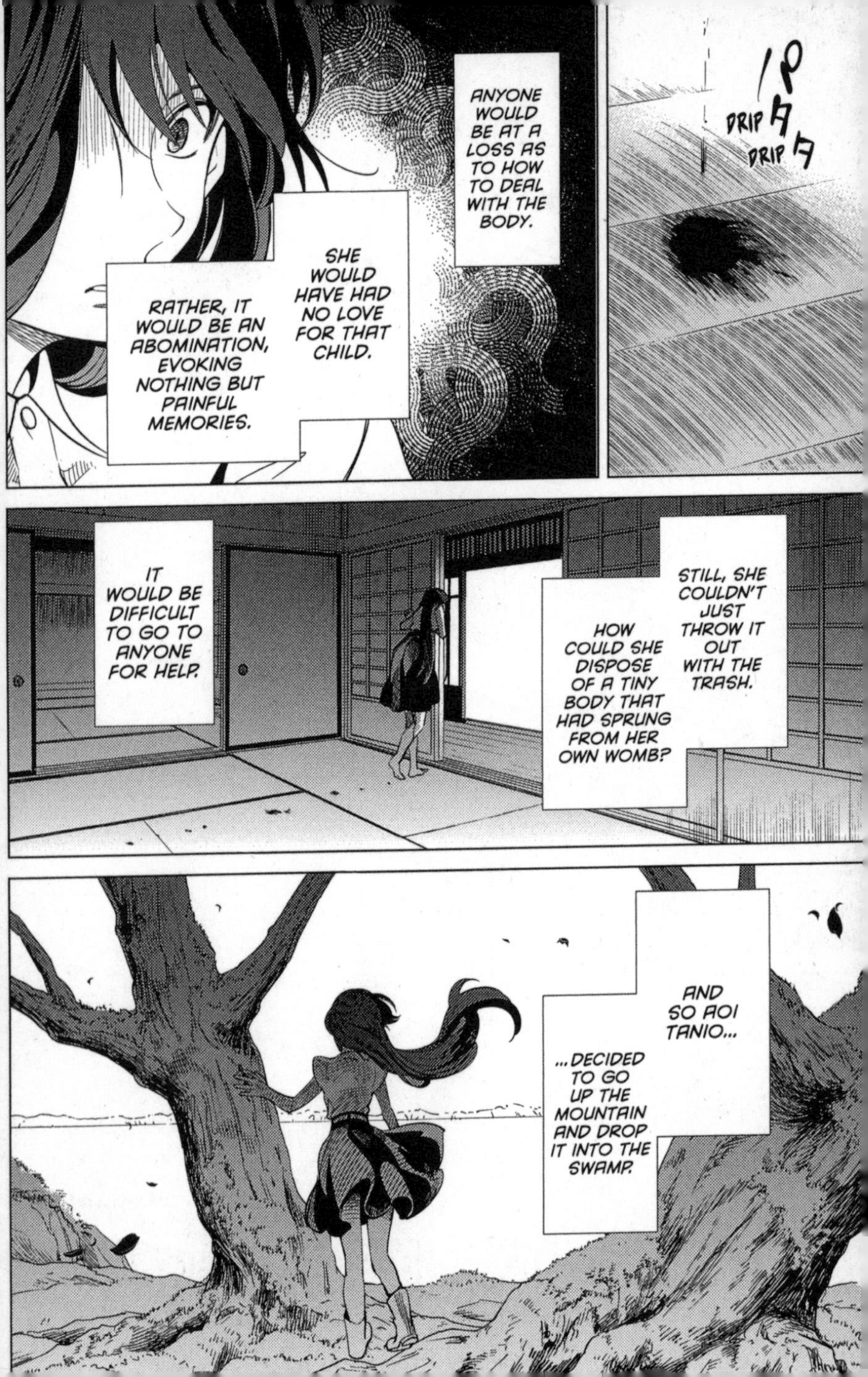
パタタ
DRIP
DRIP
ANYONE WOULD BE AT A LOSS AS TO HOW TO DEAL WITH THE BODY.
SHE WOULD HAVE HAD NO LOVE FOR THAT CHILD.
RATHER, IT WOULD BE AN ABOMINATION, EVOKING NOTHING BUT PAINFUL MEMORIES.
STILL, SHE COULDN'T JUST THROW IT OUT WITH THE TRASH.
HOW COULD SHE DISPOSE OF A TINY BODY THAT HAD SPRUNG FROM HER OWN WOMB?
IT WOULD BE DIFFICULT TO GO TO ANYONE FOR HELP.
AND SO AOI TANIO...
...DECIDED TO GO UP THE MOUNTAIN AND DROP IT INTO THE SWAMP.

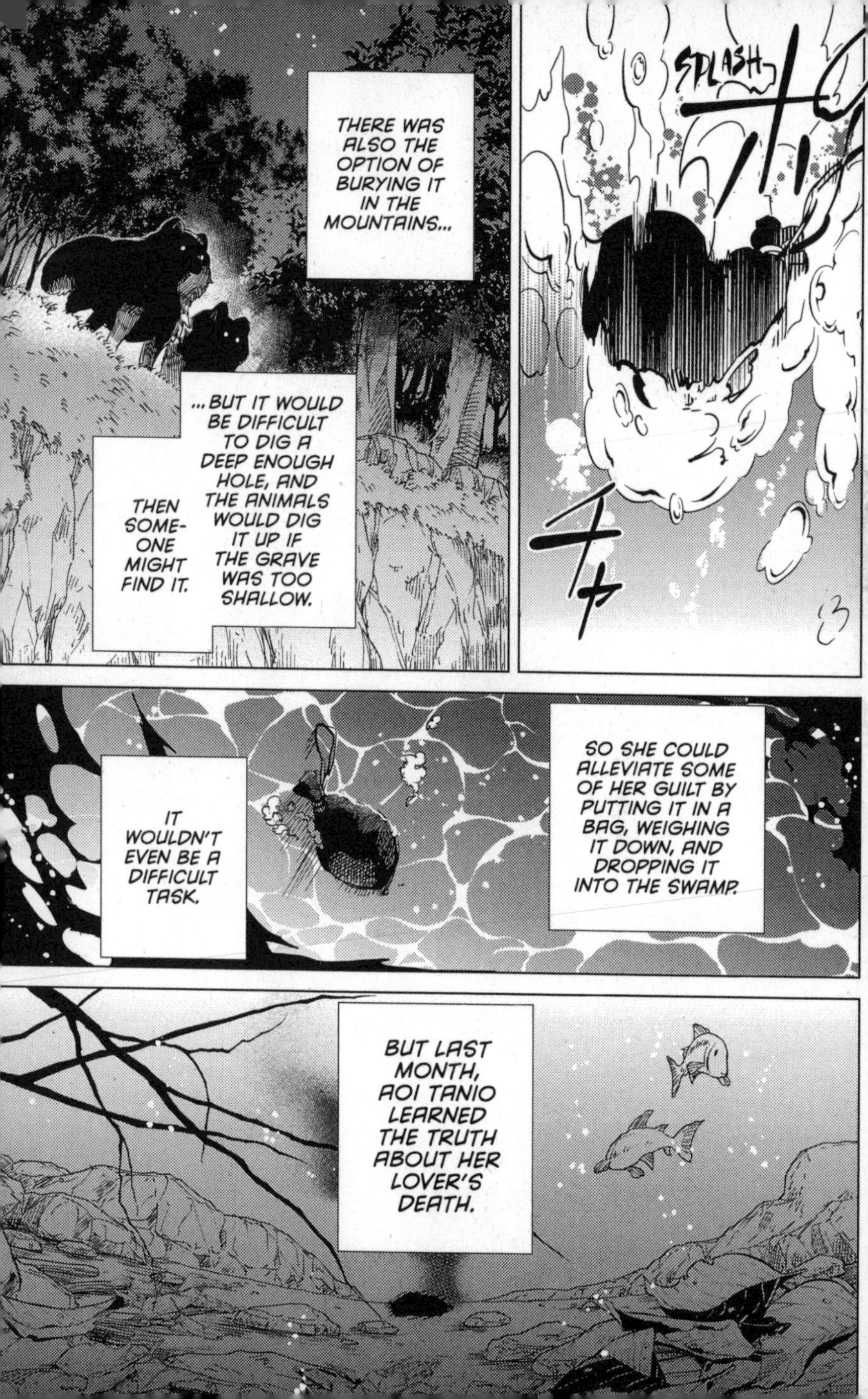
SPLASH
THERE WAS ALSO THE OPTION OF BURYING IT IN THE MOUNTAINS...
...BUT IT WOULD BE DIFFICULT TO DIG A DEEP ENOUGH HOLE, AND THE ANIMALS WOULD DIG IT UP IF THE GRAVE WAS TOO SHALLOW.
THEN SOME-ONE MIGHT FIND IT.
SO SHE COULD ALLEVIATE SOME OF HER GUILT BY PUTTING IT IN A BAG, WEIGHING IT DOWN, AND DROPPING IT INTO THE SWAMP.
IT WOULDN'T EVEN BE A DIFFICULT TASK.
BUT LAST MONTH, AOI TANIO LEARNED THE TRUTH ABOUT HER LOVER'S DEATH.

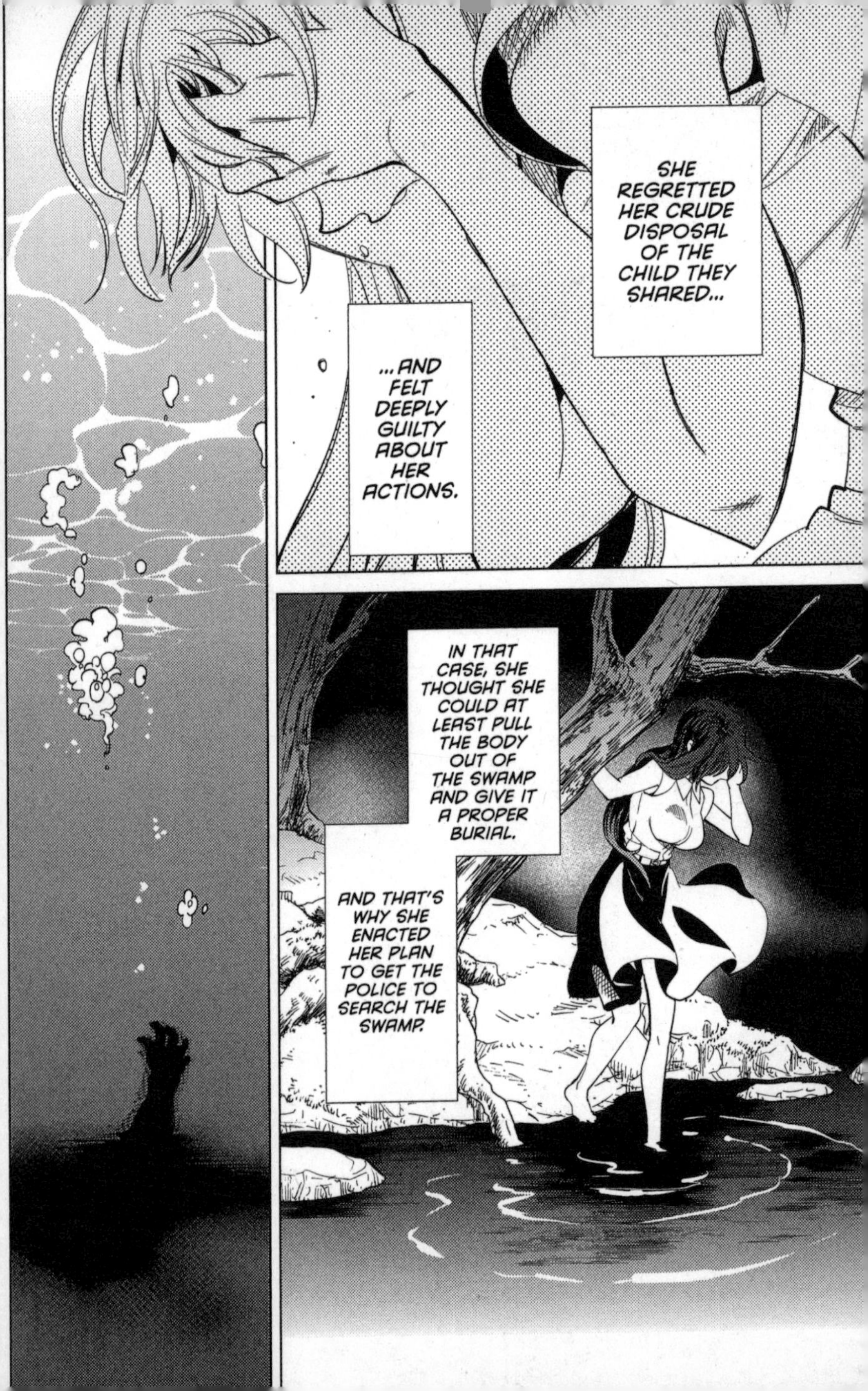
SHE REGRETTED HER CRUDE DISPOSAL OF THE CHILD THEY SHARED...
...AND FELT DEEPLY GUILTY ABOUT HER ACTIONS.
IN THAT CASE, SHE THOUGHT SHE COULD AT LEAST PULL THE BODY OUT OF THE SWAMP AND GIVE IT A PROPER BURIAL.
AND THAT'S WHY SHE ENACTED HER PLAN TO GET THE POLICE TO SEARCH THE SWAMP.

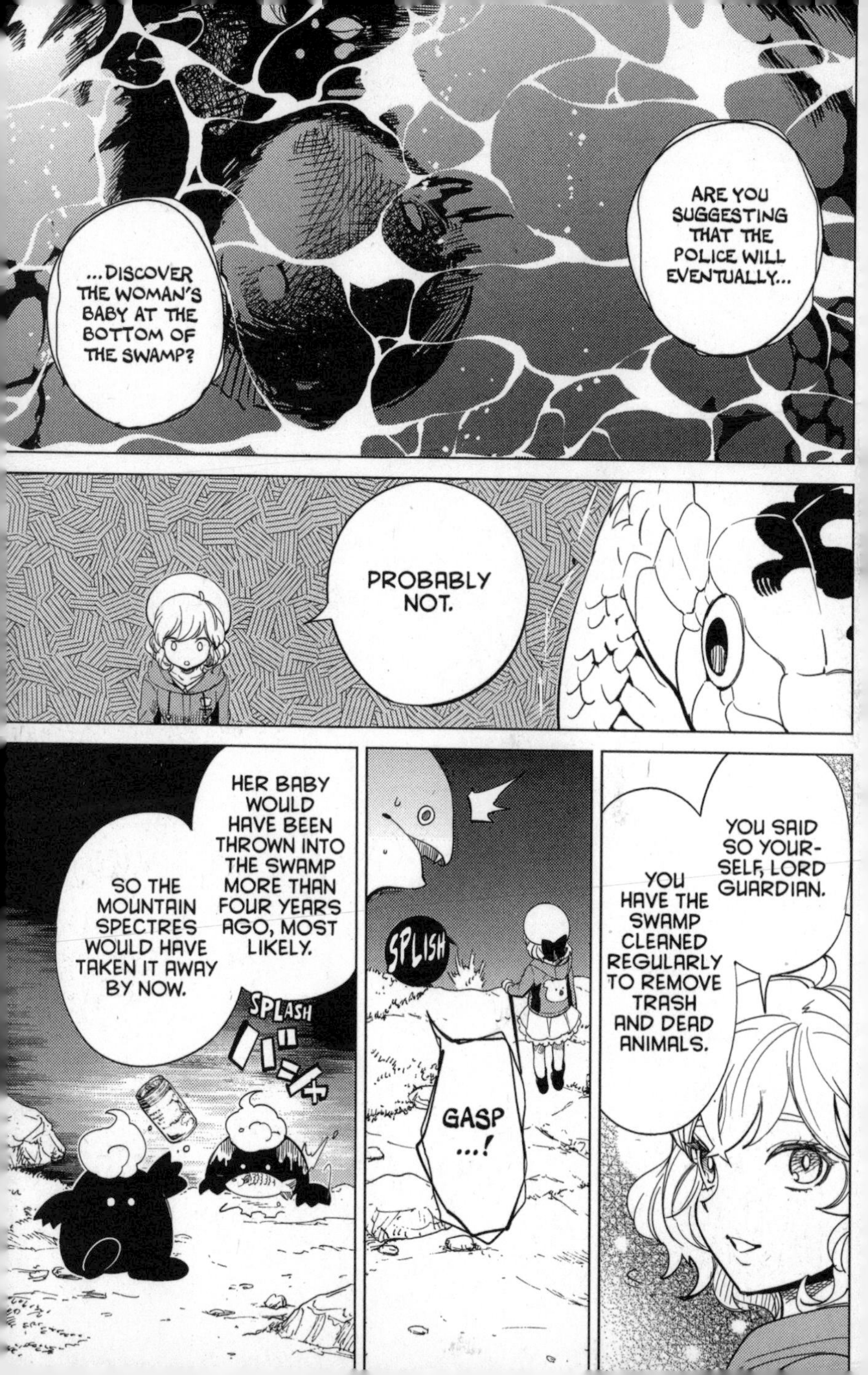
ARE YOU SUGGESTING THAT THE POLICE WILL EVENTUALLY...
...DISCOVER THE WOMAN'S BABY AT THE BOTTOM OF THE SWAMP?
PROBABLY NOT.
YOU SAID SO YOURSELF, LORD GUARDIAN.
YOU HAVE THE SWAMP CLEANED REGULARLY TO REMOVE TRASH AND DEAD ANIMALS.
SPLISH
GASP ...!
HER BABY WOULD HAVE BEEN THROWN INTO THE SWAMP MORE THAN FOUR YEARS AGO, MOST LIKELY.
SO THE MOUNTAIN SPECTRES WOULD HAVE TAKEN IT AWAY BY NOW.
SPLASH

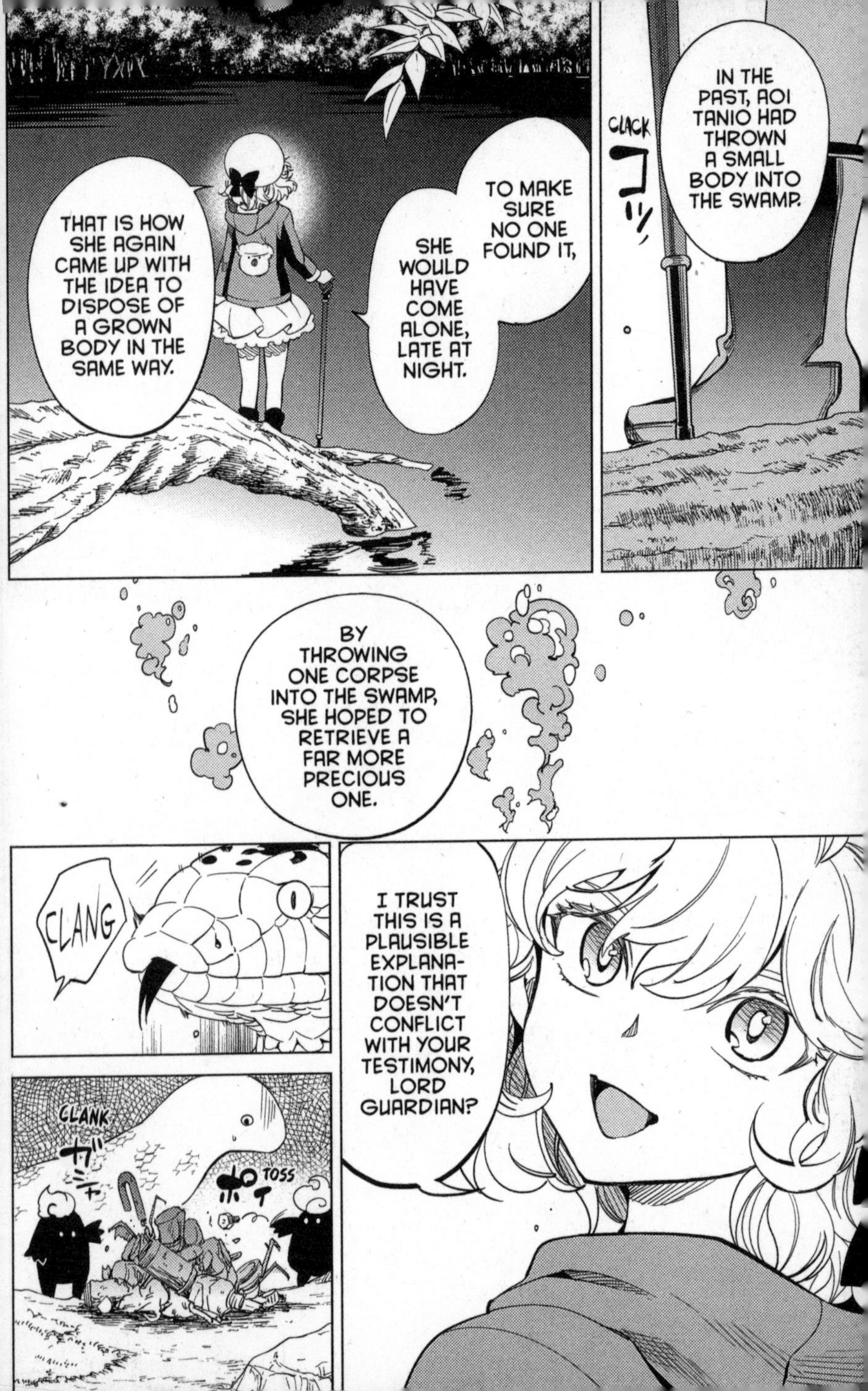
CLACK
IN THE PAST, AOI TANIO HAD THROWN A SMALL BODY INTO THE SWAMP.
TO MAKE SURE NO ONE FOUND IT,
SHE WOULD HAVE COME ALONE, LATE AT NIGHT.
THAT IS HOW SHE AGAIN CAME UP WITH THE IDEA TO DISPOSE OF A GROWN BODY IN THE SAME WAY.
BY THROWING ONE CORPSE INTO THE SWAMP, SHE HOPED TO RETRIEVE A FAR MORE PRECIOUS ONE.
I TRUST THIS IS A PLAUSIBLE EXPLANATION THAT DOESN'T CONFLICT WITH YOUR TESTIMONY, LORD GUARDIAN?
CLANG
CLANK
TOSS

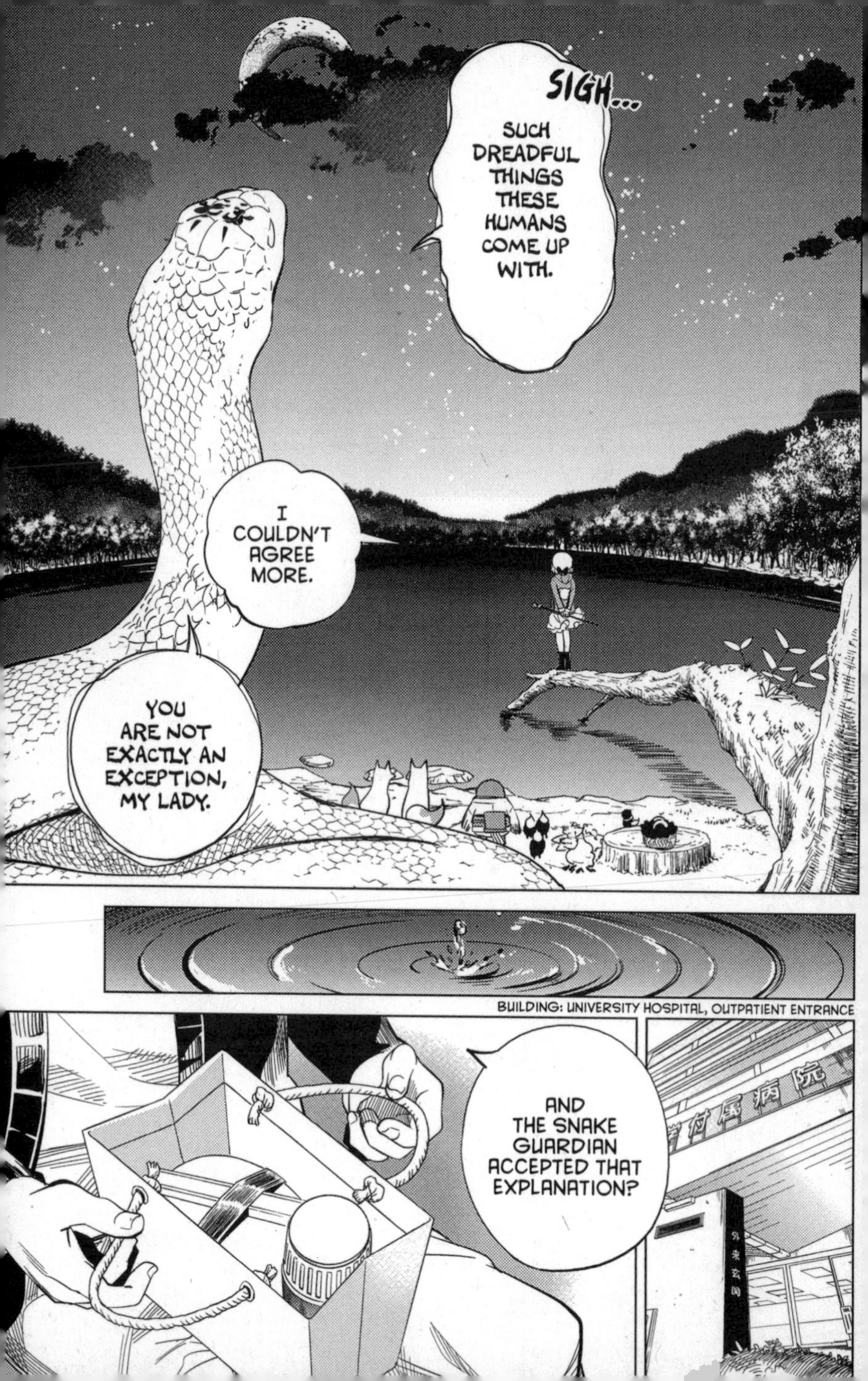
SIGH...
SUCH DREADFUL THINGS THESE HUMANS COME UP WITH.
I COULDN'T AGREE MORE.
YOU ARE NOT EXACTLY AN EXCEPTION, MY LADY.
BUILDING: UNIVERSITY HOSPITAL, OUTPATIENT ENTRANCE
AND THE SNAKE GUARDIAN ACCEPTED THAT EXPLANATION?

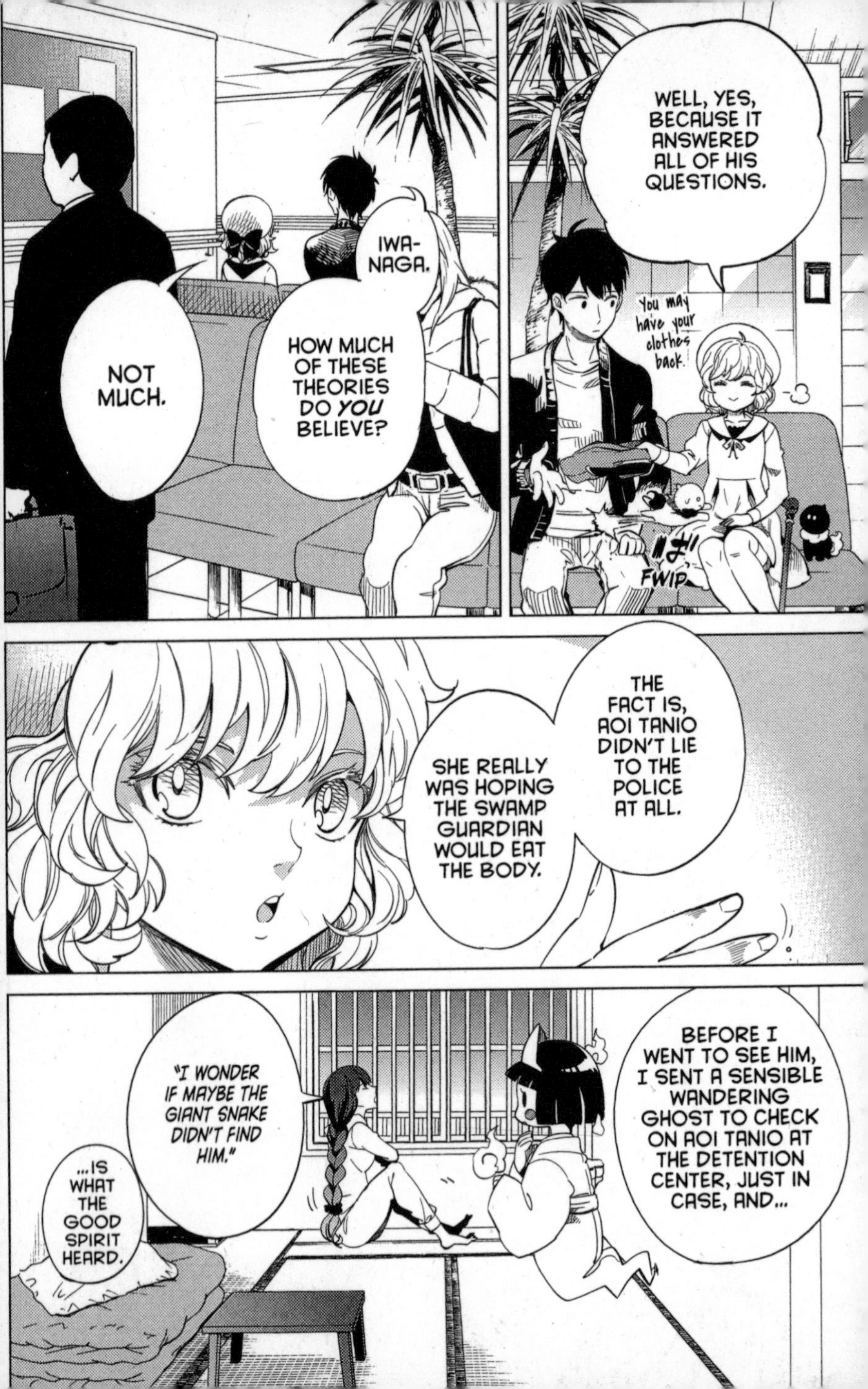
WELL, YES, BECAUSE IT ANSWERED ALL OF HIS QUESTIONS.
You may have your clothes back.
FWIP
IWA-NAGA.
HOW MUCH OF THESE THEORIES DO *YOU* BELIEVE?
NOT MUCH.
THE FACT IS, AOI TANIO DIDN'T LIE TO THE POLICE AT ALL.
SHE REALLY WAS HOPING THE SWAMP GUARDIAN WOULD EAT THE BODY.
BEFORE I WENT TO SEE HIM, I SENT A SENSIBLE WANDERING GHOST TO CHECK ON AOI TANIO AT THE DETENTION CENTER, JUST IN CASE, AND...
"I WONDER IF MAYBE THE GIANT SNAKE DIDN'T FIND HIM."
...IS WHAT THE GOOD SPIRIT HEARD.

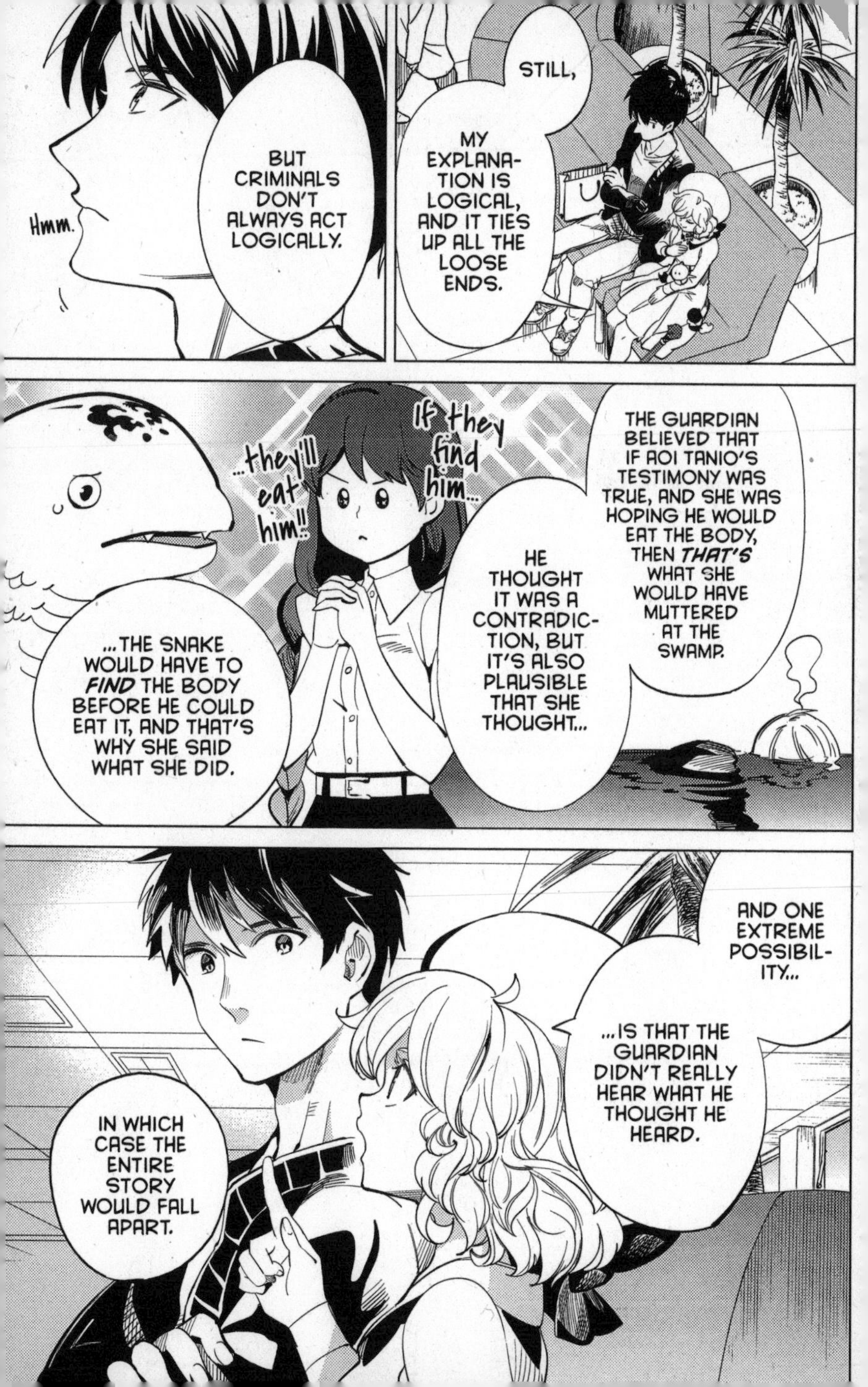
STILL,
MY EXPLANATION IS LOGICAL, AND IT TIES UP ALL THE LOOSE ENDS.
BUT CRIMINALS DON'T ALWAYS ACT LOGICALLY.
Hmm.
THE GUARDIAN BELIEVED THAT IF AOI TANIO'S TESTIMONY WAS TRUE, AND SHE WAS HOPING HE WOULD EAT THE BODY, THEN *THAT'S* WHAT SHE WOULD HAVE MUTTERED AT THE SWAMP.
HE THOUGHT IT WAS A CONTRADICTION, BUT IT'S ALSO PLAUSIBLE THAT SHE THOUGHT...
If they find him...
...they'll eat him!!
...THE SNAKE WOULD HAVE TO *FIND* THE BODY BEFORE HE COULD EAT IT, AND THAT'S WHY SHE SAID WHAT SHE DID.
AND ONE EXTREME POSSIBILITY...
...IS THAT THE GUARDIAN DIDN'T REALLY HEAR WHAT HE THOUGHT HE HEARD.
IN WHICH CASE THE ENTIRE STORY WOULD FALL APART.

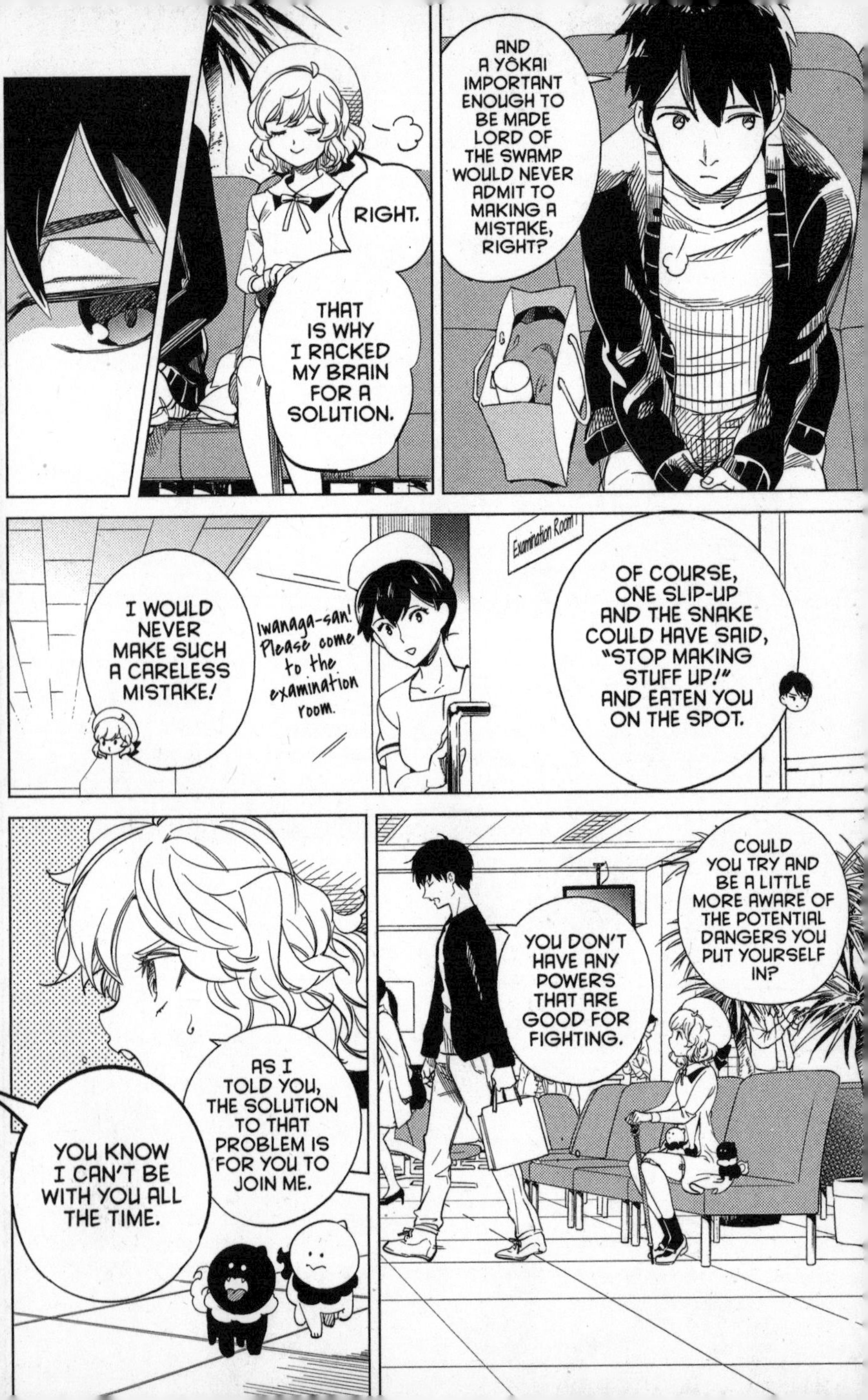
AND A YÔKAI IMPORTANT ENOUGH TO BE MADE LORD OF THE SWAMP WOULD NEVER ADMIT TO MAKING A MISTAKE, RIGHT?
RIGHT.
THAT IS WHY I RACKED MY BRAIN FOR A SOLUTION.
Examination Room 1
OF COURSE, ONE SLIP-UP AND THE SNAKE COULD HAVE SAID, "STOP MAKING STUFF UP!" AND EATEN YOU ON THE SPOT.
Iwanaga-san! Please come to the examination room.
I WOULD NEVER MAKE SUCH A CARELESS MISTAKE!
COULD YOU TRY AND BE A LITTLE MORE AWARE OF THE POTENTIAL DANGERS YOU PUT YOURSELF IN?
YOU DON'T HAVE ANY POWERS THAT ARE GOOD FOR FIGHTING.
AS I TOLD YOU, THE SOLUTION TO THAT PROBLEM IS FOR YOU TO JOIN ME.
YOU KNOW I CAN'T BE WITH YOU ALL THE TIME.

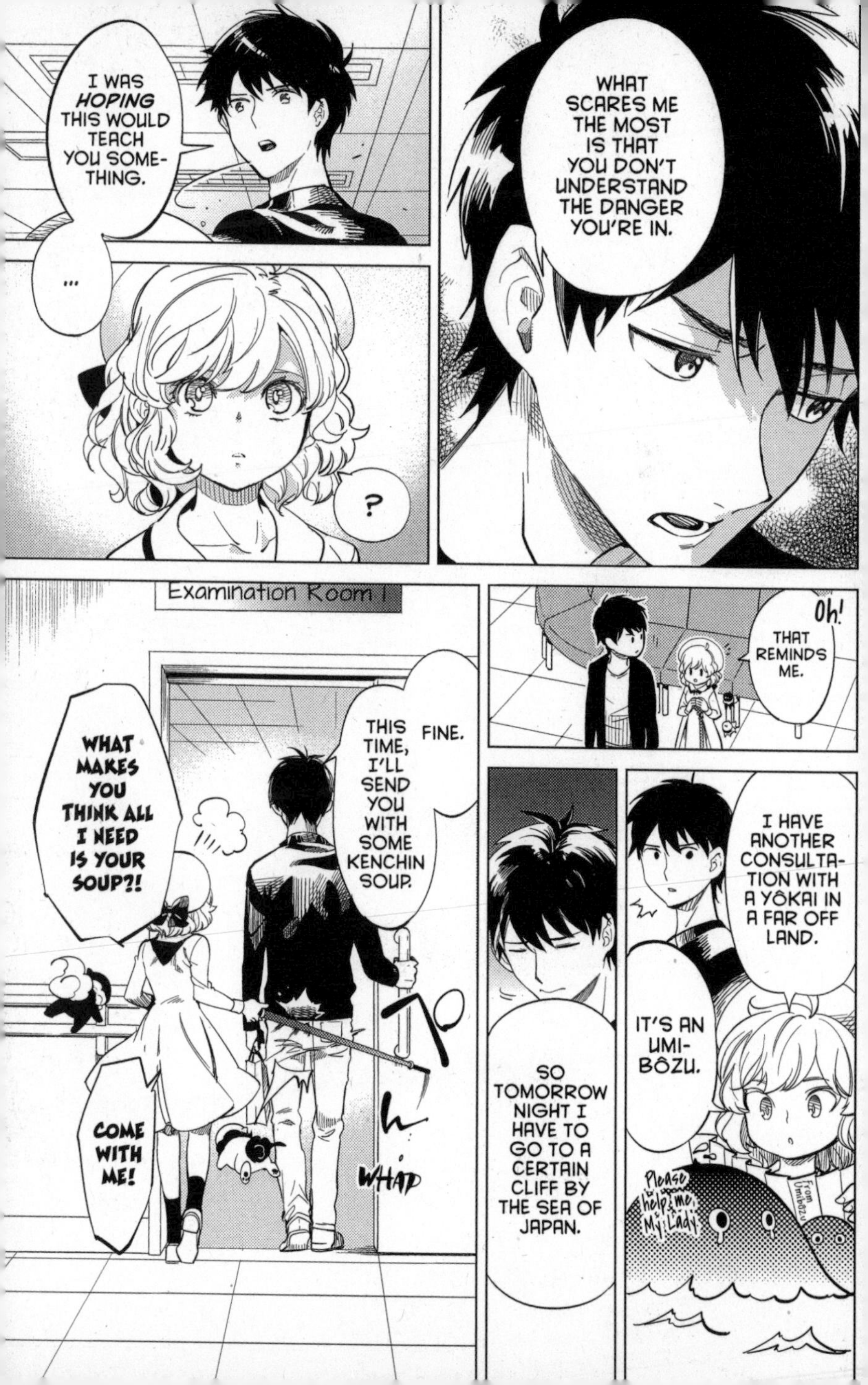
WHAT SCARES ME THE MOST IS THAT YOU DON'T UNDERSTAND THE DANGER YOU'RE IN.
I WAS *HOPING* THIS WOULD TEACH YOU SOME-THING.
...
?
Oh!
THAT REMINDS ME.
I HAVE ANOTHER CONSULTA-TION WITH A YÔKAI IN A FAR OFF LAND.
IT'S AN UMI-BÔZU.
SO TOMORROW NIGHT I HAVE TO GO TO A CERTAIN CLIFF BY THE SEA OF JAPAN.
From Umibozu
Please help me, My Lady
Examination Room 1
FINE.
THIS TIME, I'LL SEND YOU WITH SOME KENCHIN SOUP.
WHAT MAKES YOU THINK ALL I NEED IS YOUR SOUP?!
COME WITH ME!
WHAP

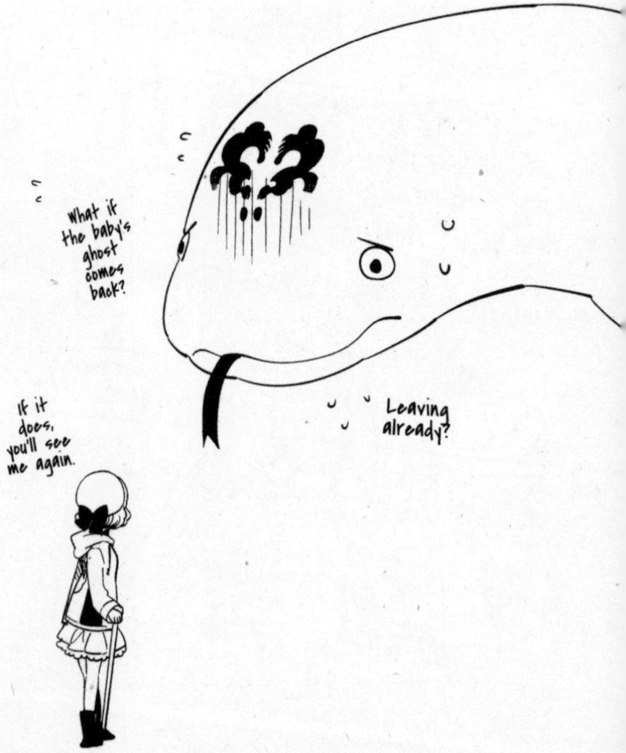
Leaving already?
What if the baby's ghost comes back?
If it does, you'll see me again.

CHAPTER 16: "LUCKY DAY AT THE UNAGI RESTAURANT"

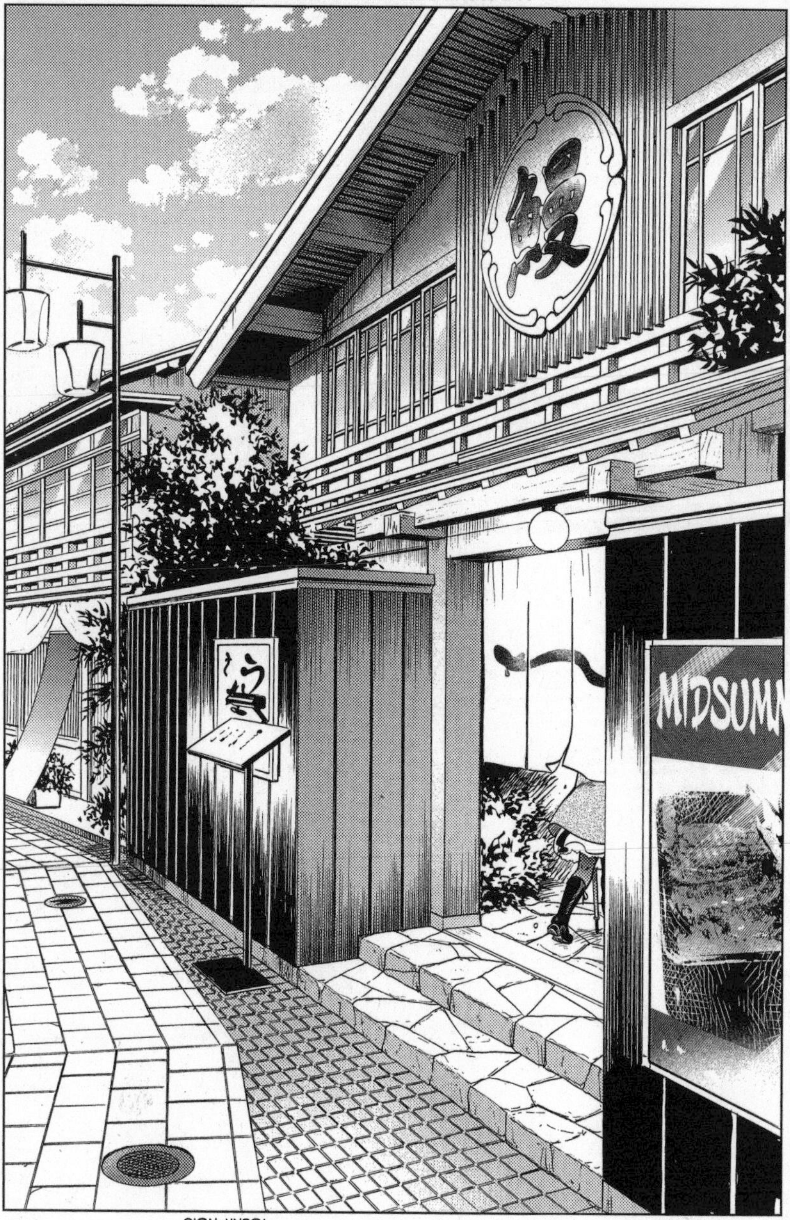
MIDSUMM

SIGN: UNAGI

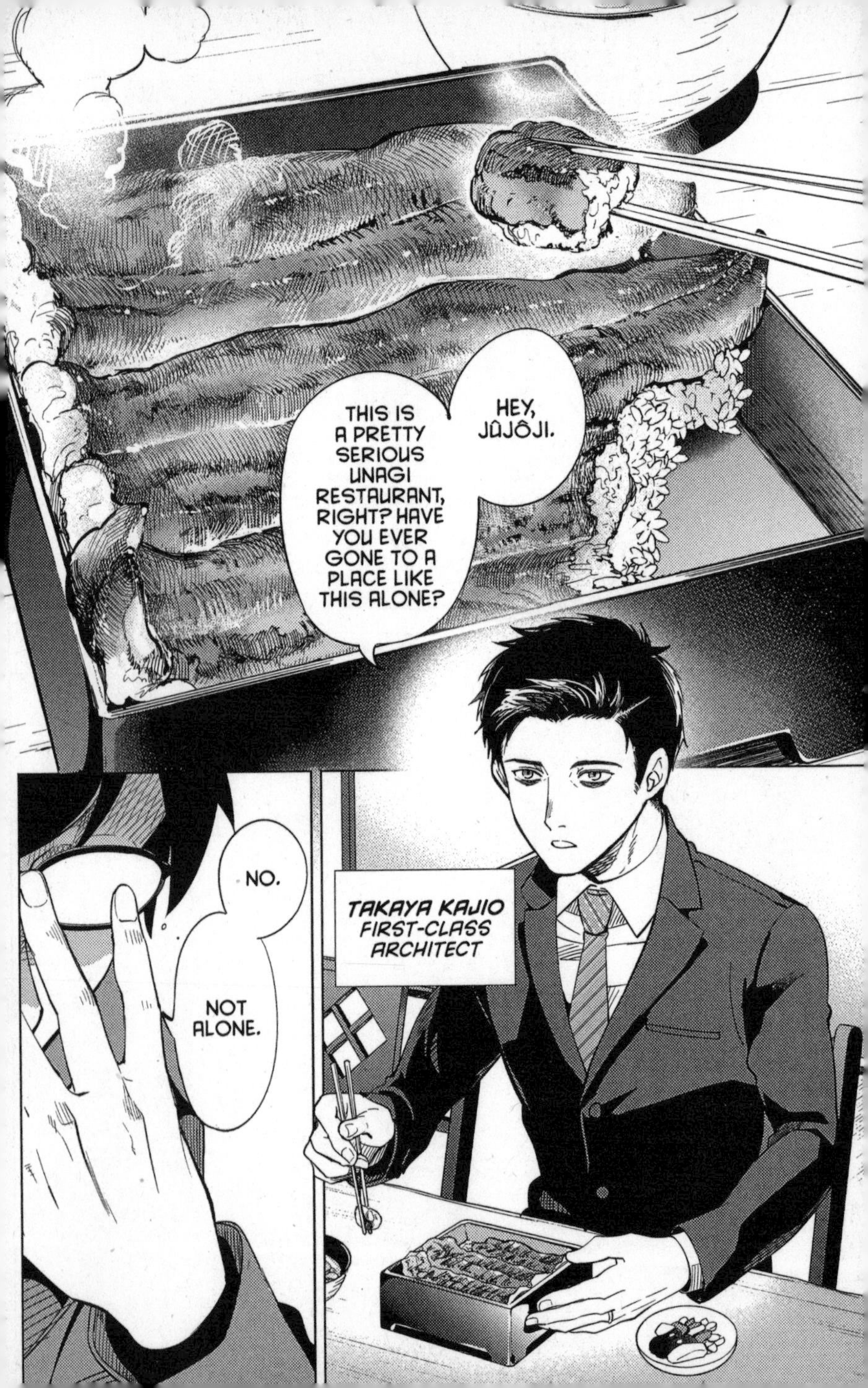
HEY, JÛJÔJI.
THIS IS A PRETTY SERIOUS UNAGI RESTAURANT, RIGHT? HAVE YOU EVER GONE TO A PLACE LIKE THIS ALONE?
TAKAYA KAJIO FIRST-CLASS ARCHITECT
NO.
NOT ALONE.

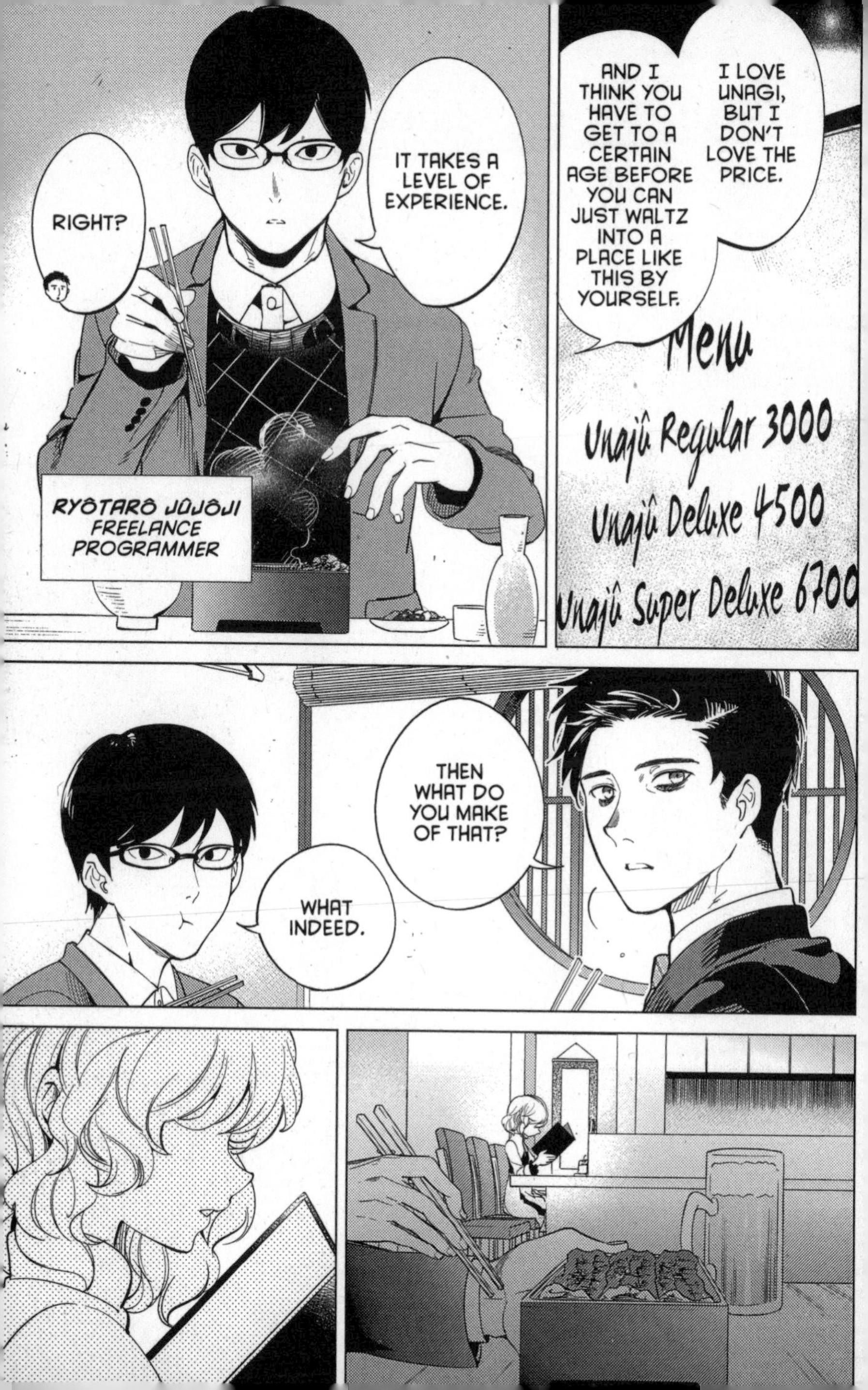
I LOVE UNAGI, BUT I DON'T LOVE THE PRICE.
AND I THINK YOU HAVE TO GET TO A CERTAIN AGE BEFORE YOU CAN JUST WALTZ INTO A PLACE LIKE THIS BY YOURSELF.
Menu
Unajû Regular 3000
Unajû Deluxe 4500
Unajû Super Deluxe 6700
IT TAKES A LEVEL OF EXPERIENCE.
RIGHT?
RYÔTARÔ JÛJÔJI
FREELANCE PROGRAMMER
THEN WHAT DO YOU MAKE OF THAT?
WHAT INDEED.

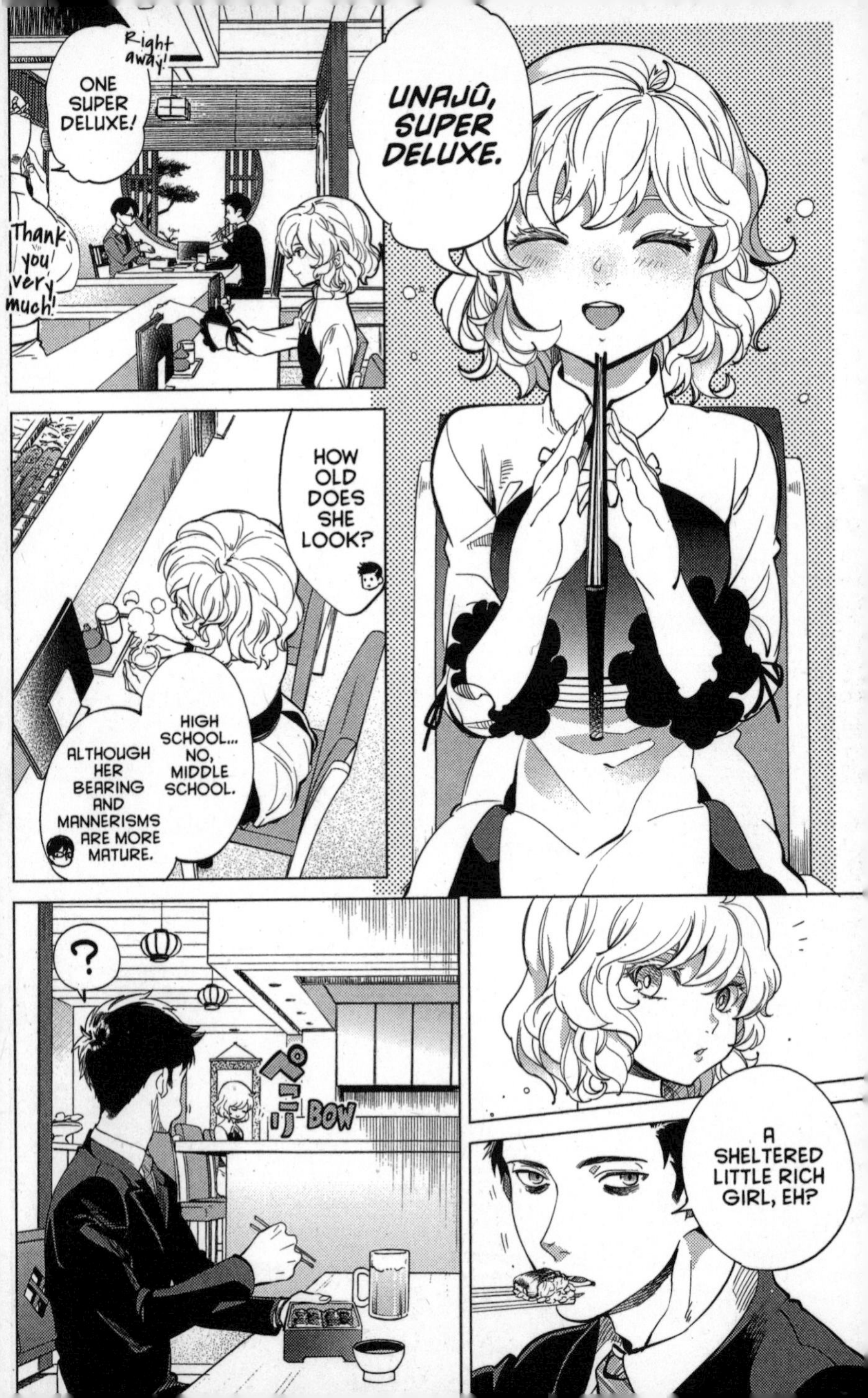
UNAJÛ, SUPER DELUXE.
ONE SUPER DELUXE!
Right away!
Thank you very much!
HOW OLD DOES SHE LOOK?
HIGH SCHOOL... NO, MIDDLE SCHOOL.
ALTHOUGH HER BEARING AND MANNERISMS ARE MORE MATURE.
A SHELTERED LITTLE RICH GIRL, EH?
?
BOW

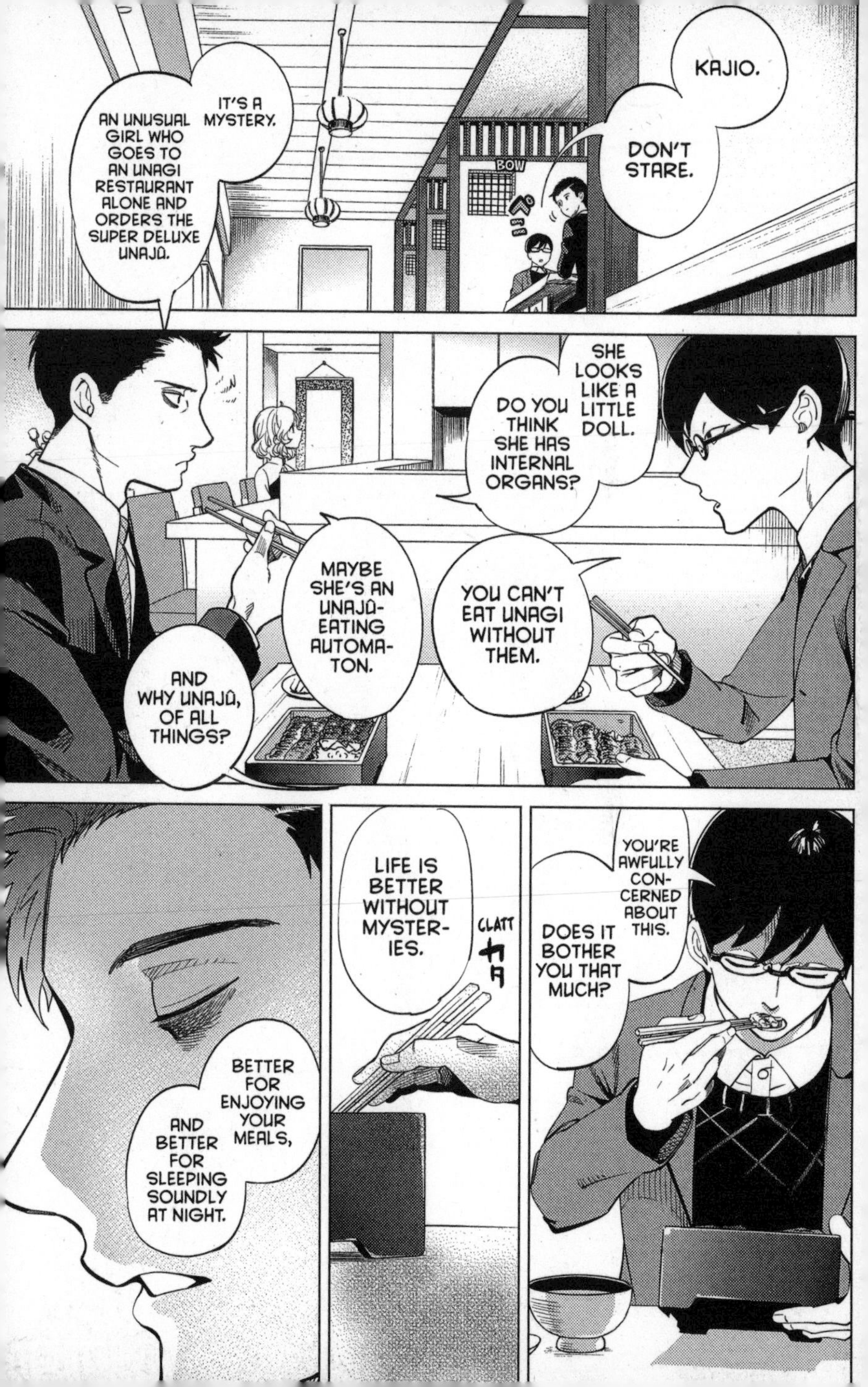
KAJIO.
DON'T STARE.
BOW
IT'S A MYSTERY.
AN UNUSUAL GIRL WHO GOES TO AN UNAGI RESTAURANT ALONE AND ORDERS THE SUPER DELUXE UNAJÛ.
SHE LOOKS LIKE A LITTLE DOLL.
DO YOU THINK SHE HAS INTERNAL ORGANS?
YOU CAN'T EAT UNAGI WITHOUT THEM.
MAYBE SHE'S AN UNAJÛ-EATING AUTOMA-TON.
AND WHY UNAJÛ, OF ALL THINGS?
YOU'RE AWFULLY CON-CERNED ABOUT THIS.
DOES IT BOTHER YOU THAT MUCH?
LIFE IS BETTER WITHOUT MYSTER-IES.
CLATT
BETTER FOR ENJOYING YOUR MEALS,
AND BETTER FOR SLEEPING SOUNDLY AT NIGHT.

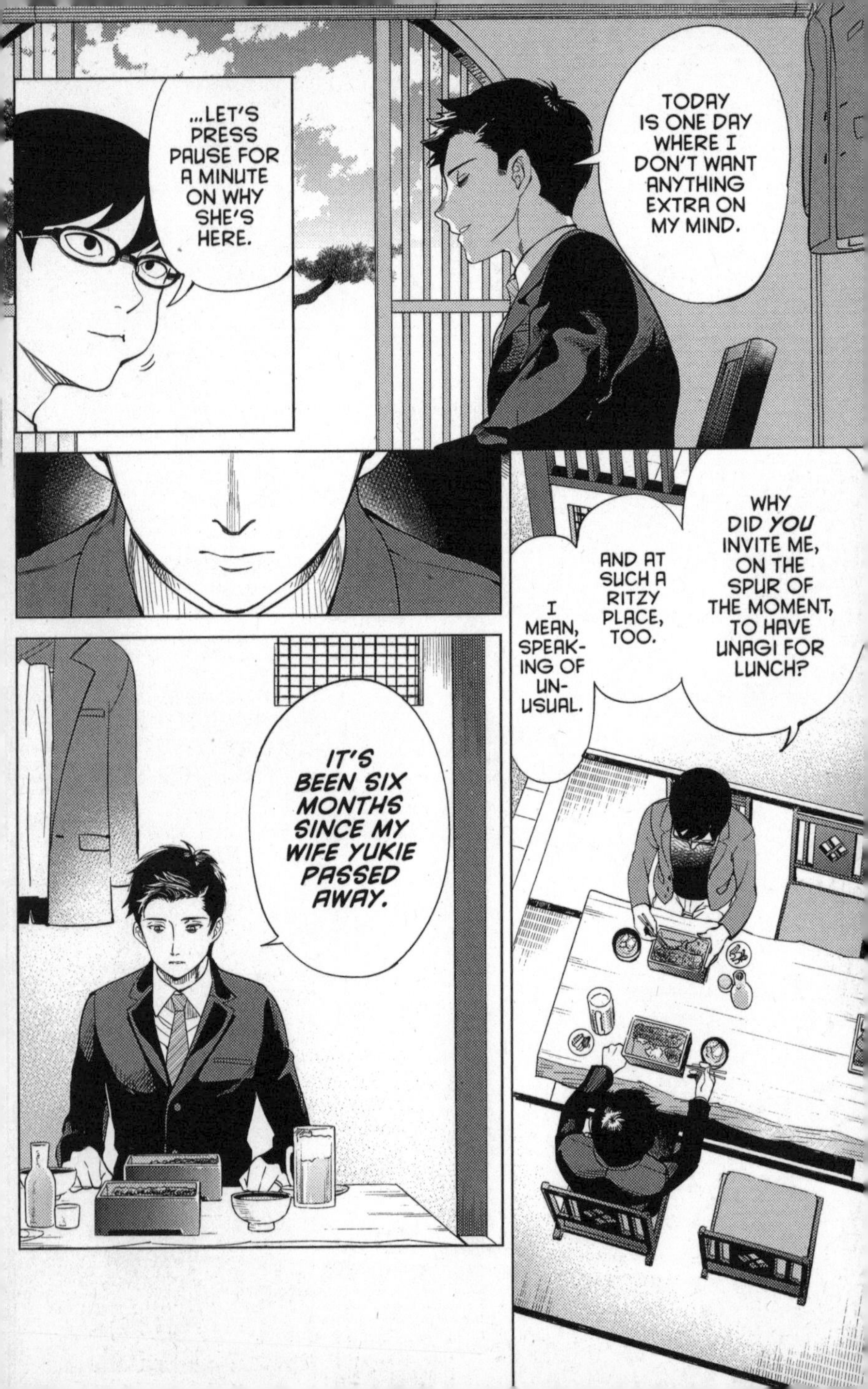
TODAY IS ONE DAY WHERE I DON'T WANT ANYTHING EXTRA ON MY MIND.
...LET'S PRESS PAUSE FOR A MINUTE ON WHY SHE'S HERE.
WHY DID *YOU* INVITE ME, ON THE SPUR OF THE MOMENT, TO HAVE UNAGI FOR LUNCH?
AND AT SUCH A RITZY PLACE, TOO.
I MEAN, SPEAK-ING OF UN-USUAL.
IT'S BEEN SIX MONTHS SINCE MY WIFE YUKIE PASSED AWAY.

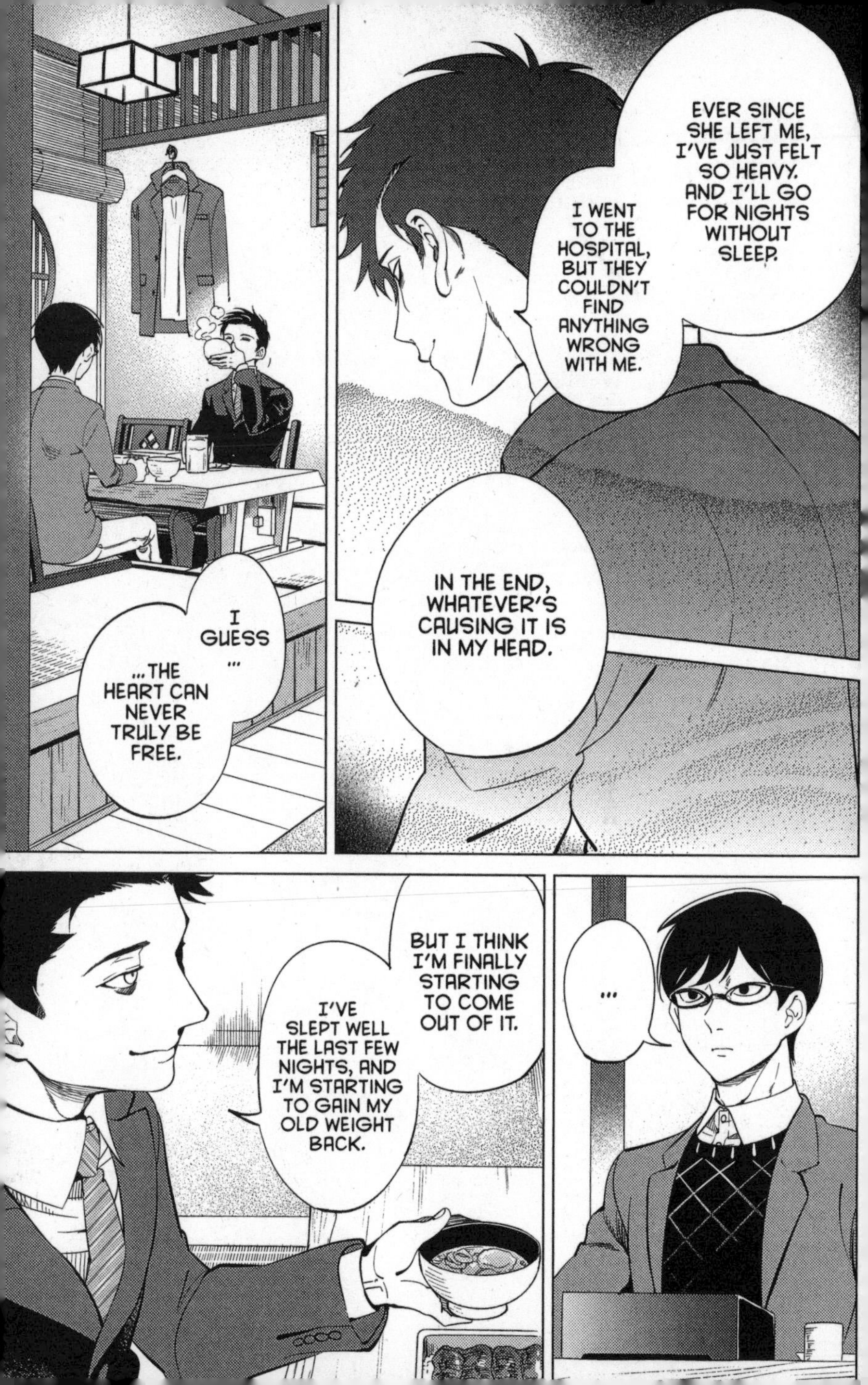
EVER SINCE SHE LEFT ME, I'VE JUST FELT SO HEAVY. AND I'LL GO FOR NIGHTS WITHOUT SLEEP.
I WENT TO THE HOSPITAL, BUT THEY COULDN'T FIND ANYTHING WRONG WITH ME.
IN THE END, WHATEVER'S CAUSING IT IS IN MY HEAD.
I GUESS ...
...THE HEART CAN NEVER TRULY BE FREE.
...
BUT I THINK I'M FINALLY STARTING TO COME OUT OF IT.
I'VE SLEPT WELL THE LAST FEW NIGHTS, AND I'M STARTING TO GAIN MY OLD WEIGHT BACK.

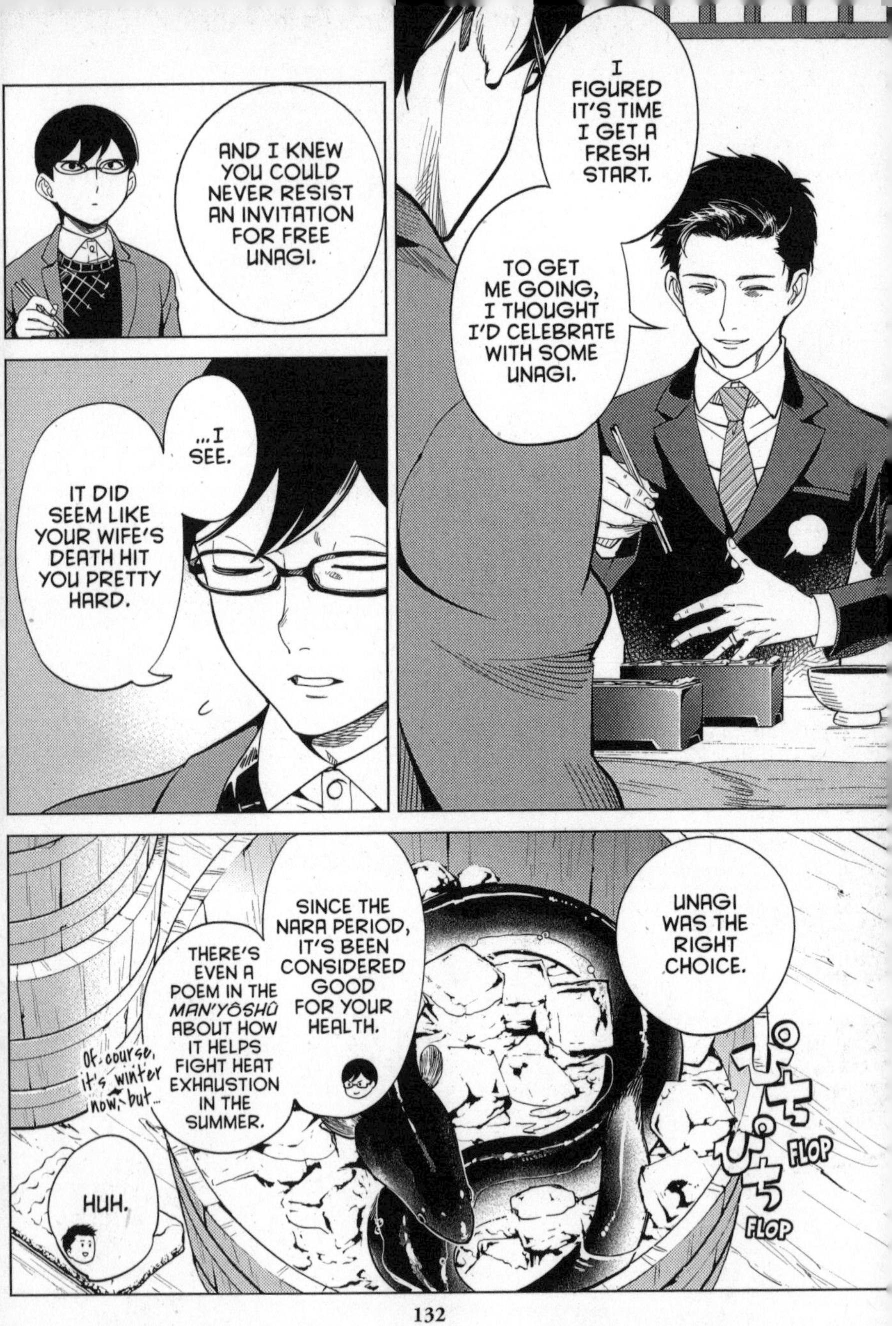
I FIGURED IT'S TIME I GET A FRESH START.
TO GET ME GOING, I THOUGHT I'D CELEBRATE WITH SOME UNAGI.
AND I KNEW YOU COULD NEVER RESIST AN INVITATION FOR FREE UNAGI.
...I SEE.
IT DID SEEM LIKE YOUR WIFE'S DEATH HIT YOU PRETTY HARD.
UNAGI WAS THE RIGHT CHOICE.
ぴち FLOP
ぴち FLOP
SINCE THE NARA PERIOD, IT'S BEEN CONSIDERED GOOD FOR YOUR HEALTH.
THERE'S EVEN A POEM IN THE *MAN'YÔSHÛ* ABOUT HOW IT HELPS FIGHT HEAT EXHAUSTION IN THE SUMMER.
Of course, it's winter now, but...
HUH.

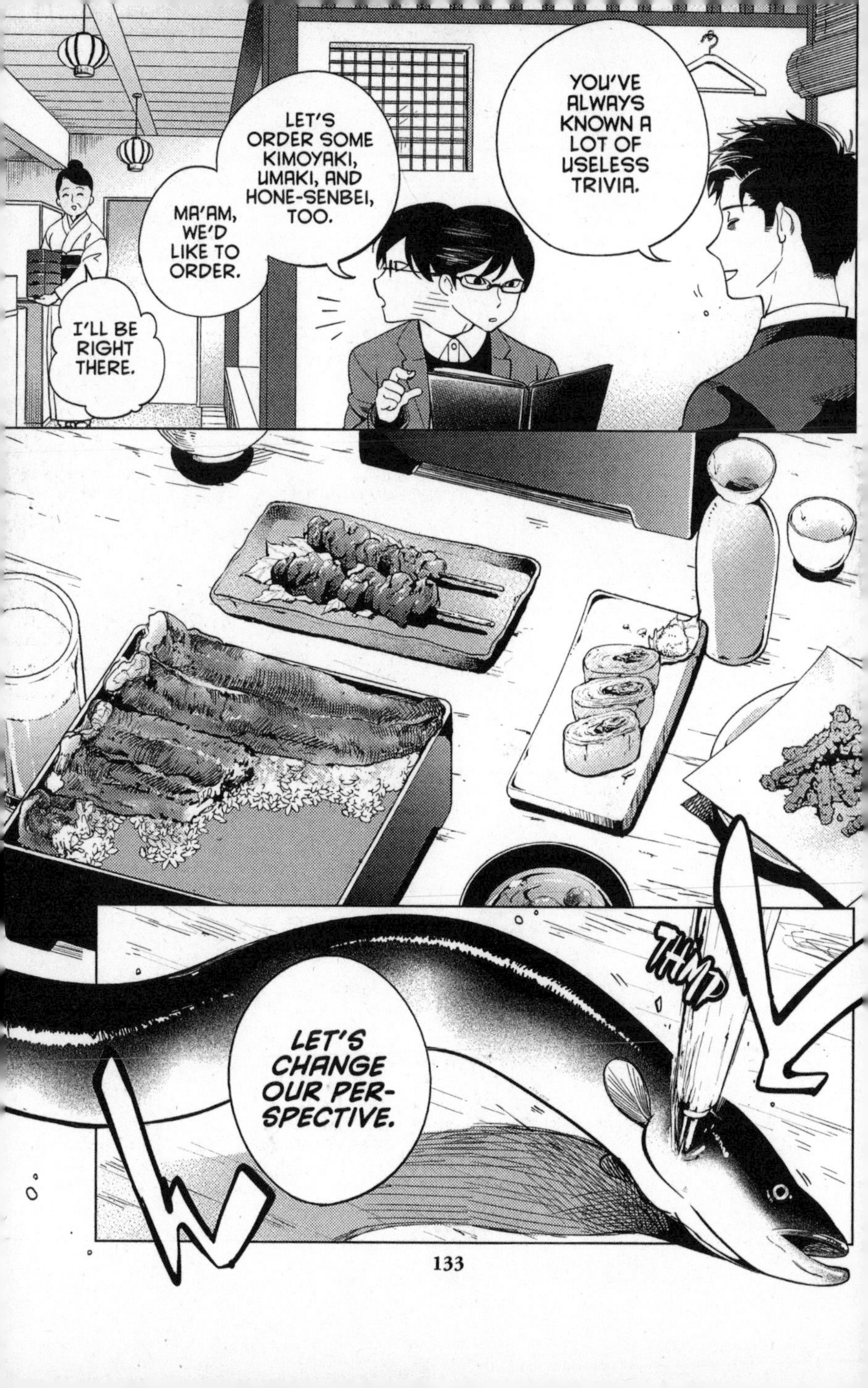
YOU'VE ALWAYS KNOWN A LOT OF USELESS TRIVIA.
LET'S ORDER SOME KIMOYAKI, UMAKI, AND HONE-SENBEI, TOO.
MA'AM, WE'D LIKE TO ORDER.
I'LL BE RIGHT THERE.
THMP
LET'S CHANGE OUR PER-SPECTIVE.

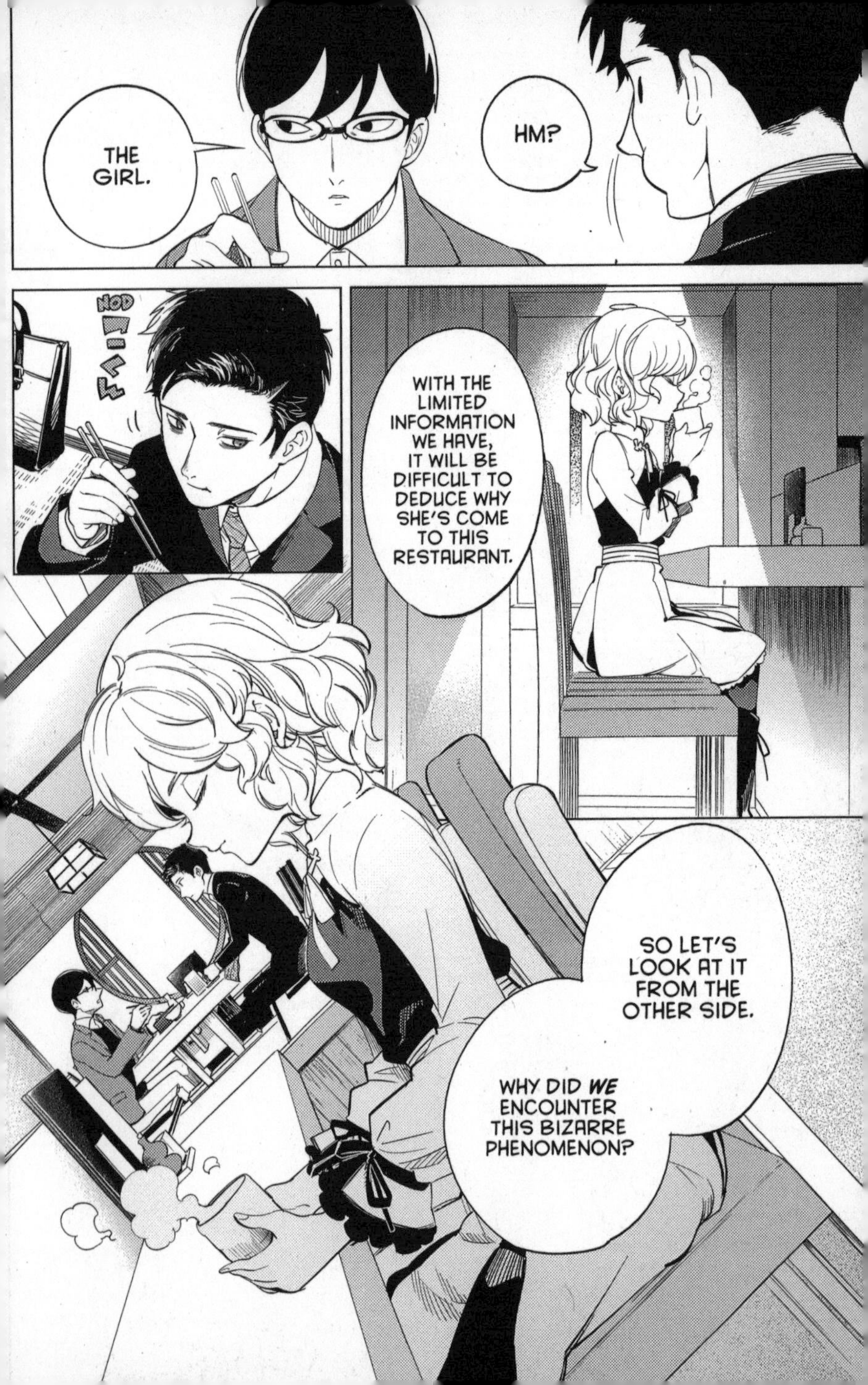
HM?
THE GIRL.
WITH THE LIMITED INFORMATION WE HAVE, IT WILL BE DIFFICULT TO DEDUCE WHY SHE'S COME TO THIS RESTAURANT.
NOD
SO LET'S LOOK AT IT FROM THE OTHER SIDE.
WHY DID *WE* ENCOUNTER THIS BIZARRE PHENOMENON?

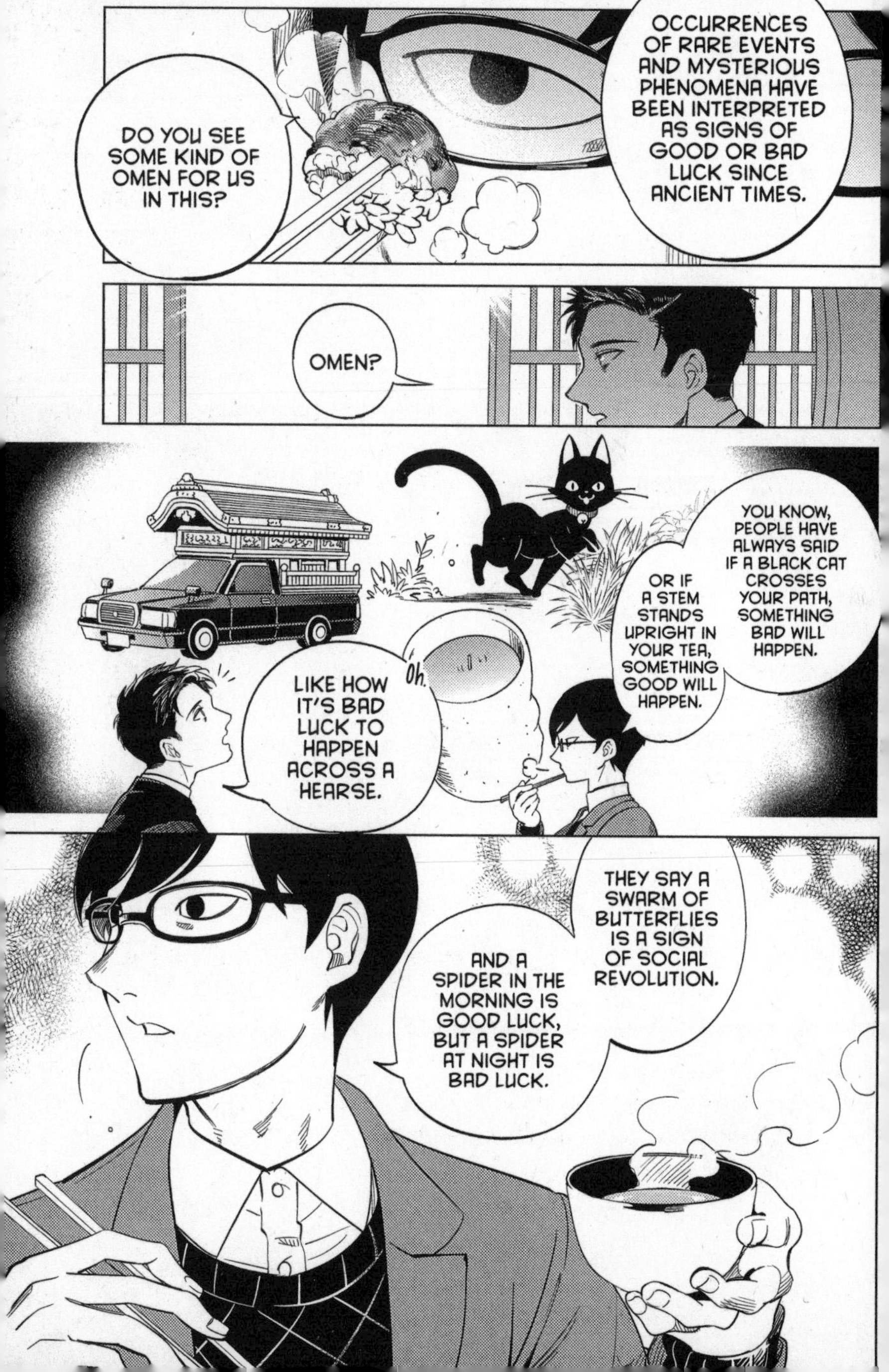
OCCURRENCES OF RARE EVENTS AND MYSTERIOUS PHENOMENA HAVE BEEN INTERPRETED AS SIGNS OF GOOD OR BAD LUCK SINCE ANCIENT TIMES.
DO YOU SEE SOME KIND OF OMEN FOR US IN THIS?
OMEN?
YOU KNOW, PEOPLE HAVE ALWAYS SAID IF A BLACK CAT CROSSES YOUR PATH, SOMETHING BAD WILL HAPPEN.
OR IF A STEM STANDS UPRIGHT IN YOUR TEA, SOMETHING GOOD WILL HAPPEN.
Oh.
LIKE HOW IT'S BAD LUCK TO HAPPEN ACROSS A HEARSE.
THEY SAY A SWARM OF BUTTERFLIES IS A SIGN OF SOCIAL REVOLUTION.
AND A SPIDER IN THE MORNING IS GOOD LUCK, BUT A SPIDER AT NIGHT IS BAD LUCK.

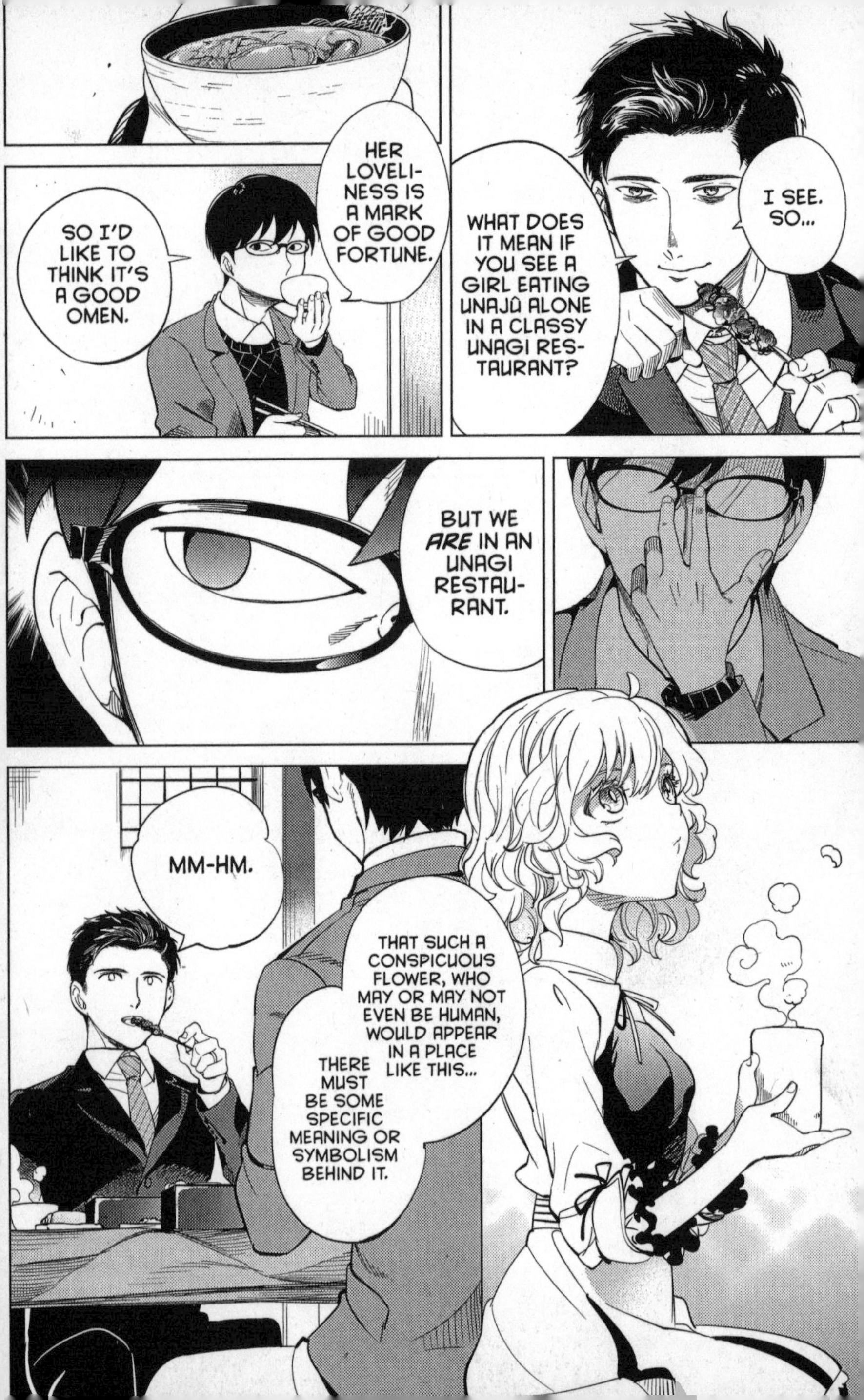
I SEE. SO...
WHAT DOES IT MEAN IF YOU SEE A GIRL EATING UNAJÛ ALONE IN A CLASSY UNAGI RESTAURANT?
HER LOVELINESS IS A MARK OF GOOD FORTUNE.
SO I'D LIKE TO THINK IT'S A GOOD OMEN.
BUT WE *ARE* IN AN UNAGI RESTAURANT.
THAT SUCH A CONSPICUOUS FLOWER, WHO MAY OR MAY NOT EVEN BE HUMAN, WOULD APPEAR IN A PLACE LIKE THIS...
THERE MUST BE SOME SPECIFIC MEANING OR SYMBOLISM BEHIND IT.
MM-HM.

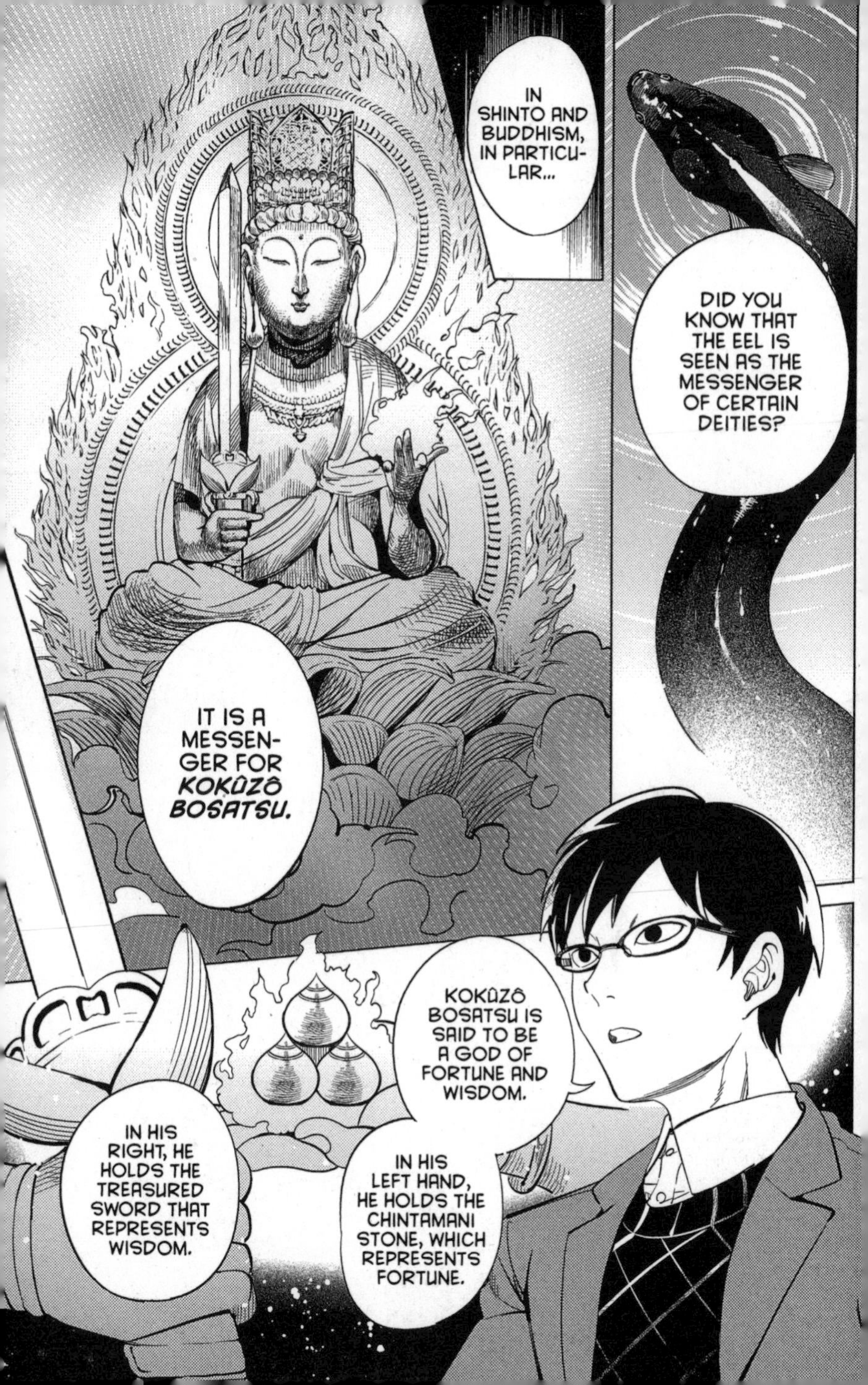
DID YOU KNOW THAT THE EEL IS SEEN AS THE MESSENGER OF CERTAIN DEITIES?
IN SHINTO AND BUDDHISM, IN PARTICULAR...
IT IS A MESSENGER FOR *KOKÛZÔ BOSATSU.*
KOKÛZÔ BOSATSU IS SAID TO BE A GOD OF FORTUNE AND WISDOM.
IN HIS LEFT HAND, HE HOLDS THE CHINTAMANI STONE, WHICH REPRESENTS FORTUNE.
IN HIS RIGHT, HE HOLDS THE TREASURED SWORD THAT REPRESENTS WISDOM.

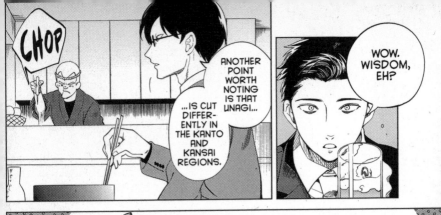

WOW. WISDOM, EH?
CHOP
ANOTHER POINT WORTH NOTING IS THAT UNAGI...
...IS CUT DIFFERENTLY IN THE KANTO AND KANSAI REGIONS.
East
RIGHT, IN KANTO THEY SLICE IT FROM THE BACK, AND IN KANSAI, THEY SLICE IT FROM THE BELLY.
West
I HEARD THAT'S BECAUSE THERE ARE A LOT OF WARRIORS IN KANTO, AND THEY WANTED TO AVOID ANYTHING THAT WAS TOO MUCH LIKE RITUAL SUICIDE.
THAT'S THE POPULAR THEORY, BUT THEY ALSO SAY IT'S BECAUSE THE DIFFERENT REGIONS USE DIFFERENT COOKING METHODS.
THIS RESTAURANT'S UNAGI...
PSHH
...APPEARS TO USE THE KANSAI STYLE OF COOKING.

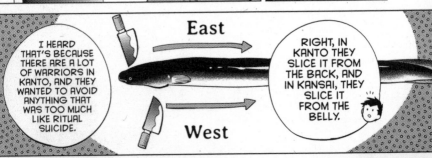

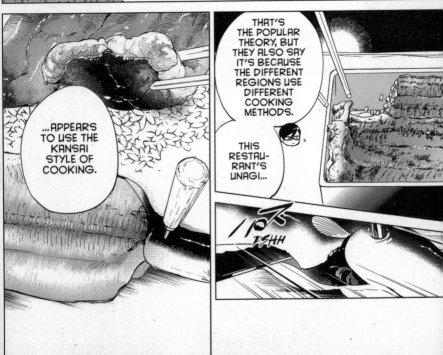

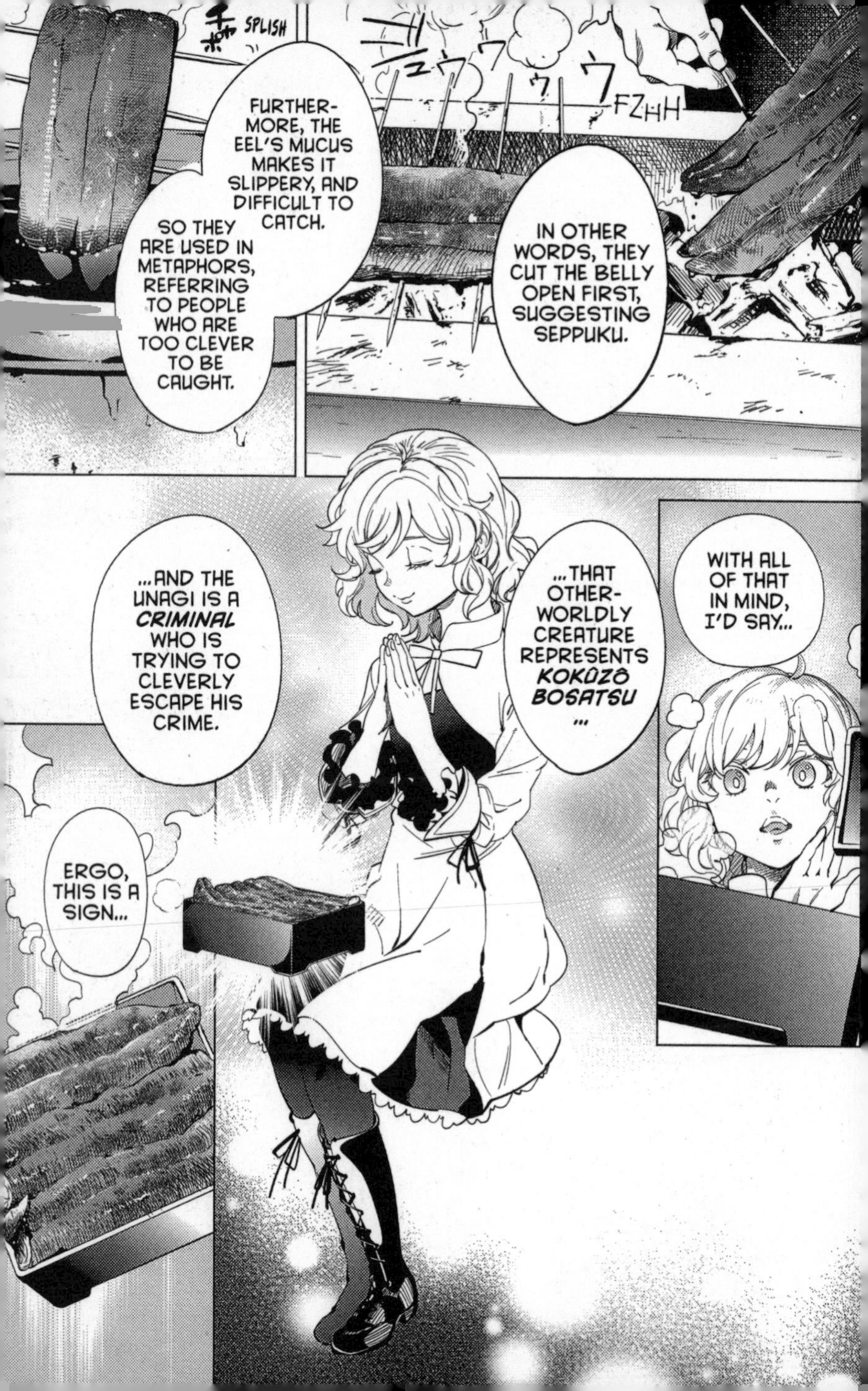
FZHH
IN OTHER WORDS, THEY CUT THE BELLY OPEN FIRST, SUGGESTING SEPPUKU.
SPLISH
FURTHER-MORE, THE EEL'S MUCUS MAKES IT SLIPPERY, AND DIFFICULT TO CATCH.
SO THEY ARE USED IN METAPHORS, REFERRING TO PEOPLE WHO ARE TOO CLEVER TO BE CAUGHT.
WITH ALL OF THAT IN MIND, I'D SAY...
...THAT OTHER-WORLDLY CREATURE REPRESENTS *KOKŪZŌ BOSATSU*...
...AND THE UNAGI IS A *CRIMINAL* WHO IS TRYING TO CLEVERLY ESCAPE HIS CRIME.
ERGO, THIS IS A SIGN...

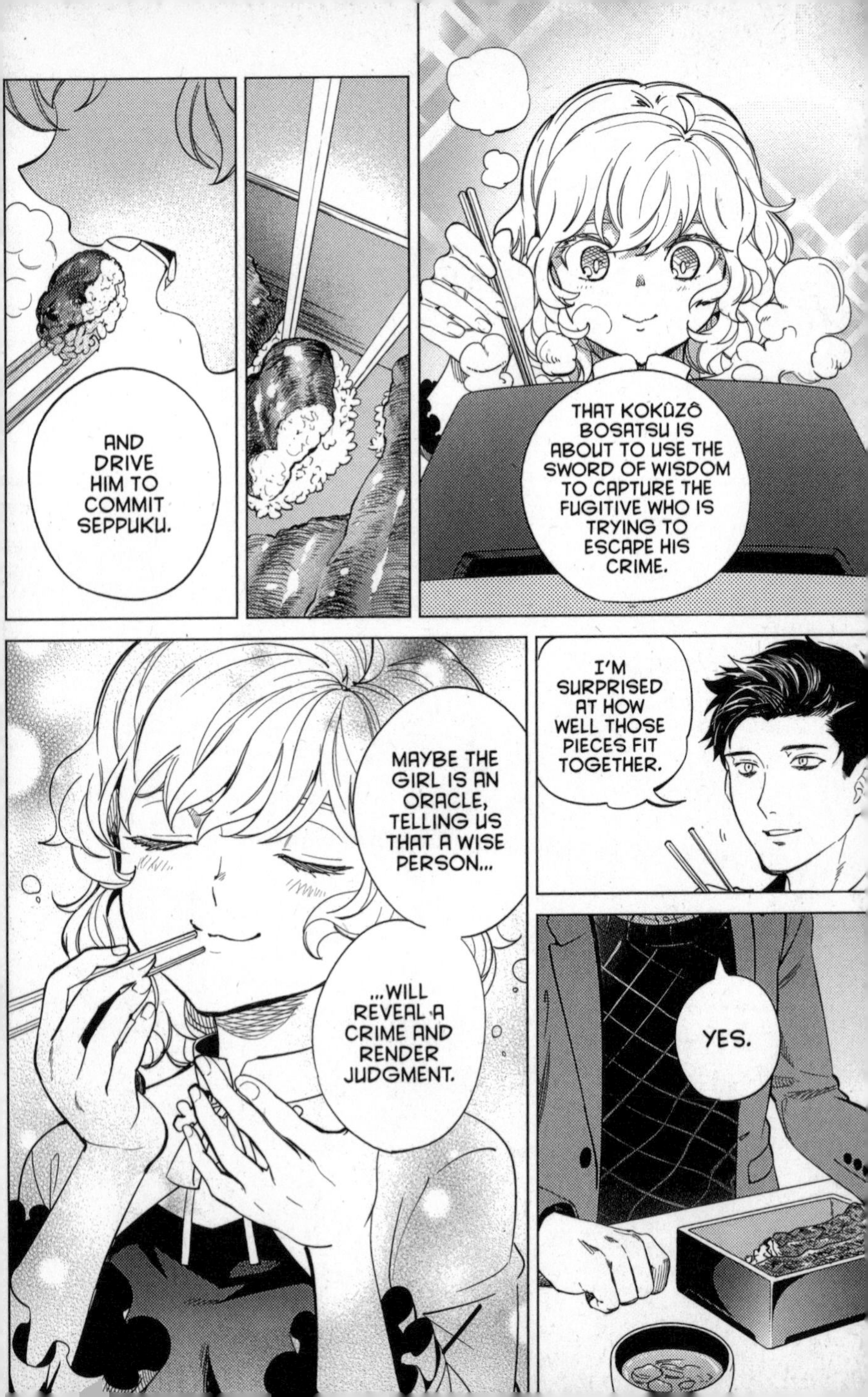
THAT KOKÛZÔ BOSATSU IS ABOUT TO USE THE SWORD OF WISDOM TO CAPTURE THE FUGITIVE WHO IS TRYING TO ESCAPE HIS CRIME.
AND DRIVE HIM TO COMMIT SEPPUKU.
I'M SURPRISED AT HOW WELL THOSE PIECES FIT TOGETHER.
YES.
MAYBE THE GIRL IS AN ORACLE, TELLING US THAT A WISE PERSON...
...WILL REVEAL A CRIME AND RENDER JUDGMENT.

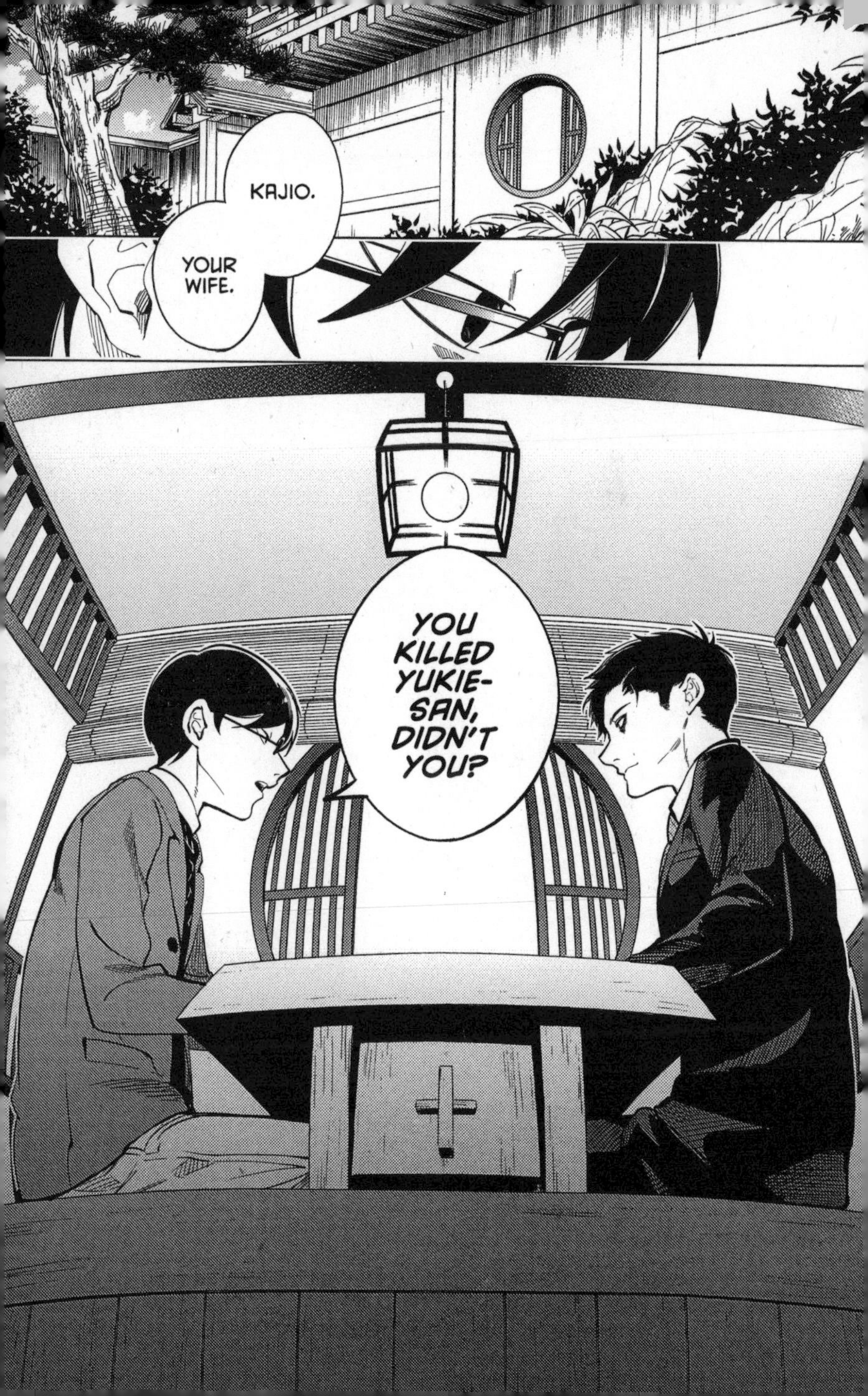
KAJIO.
YOUR WIFE.
YOU KILLED YUKIE-SAN, DIDN'T YOU?

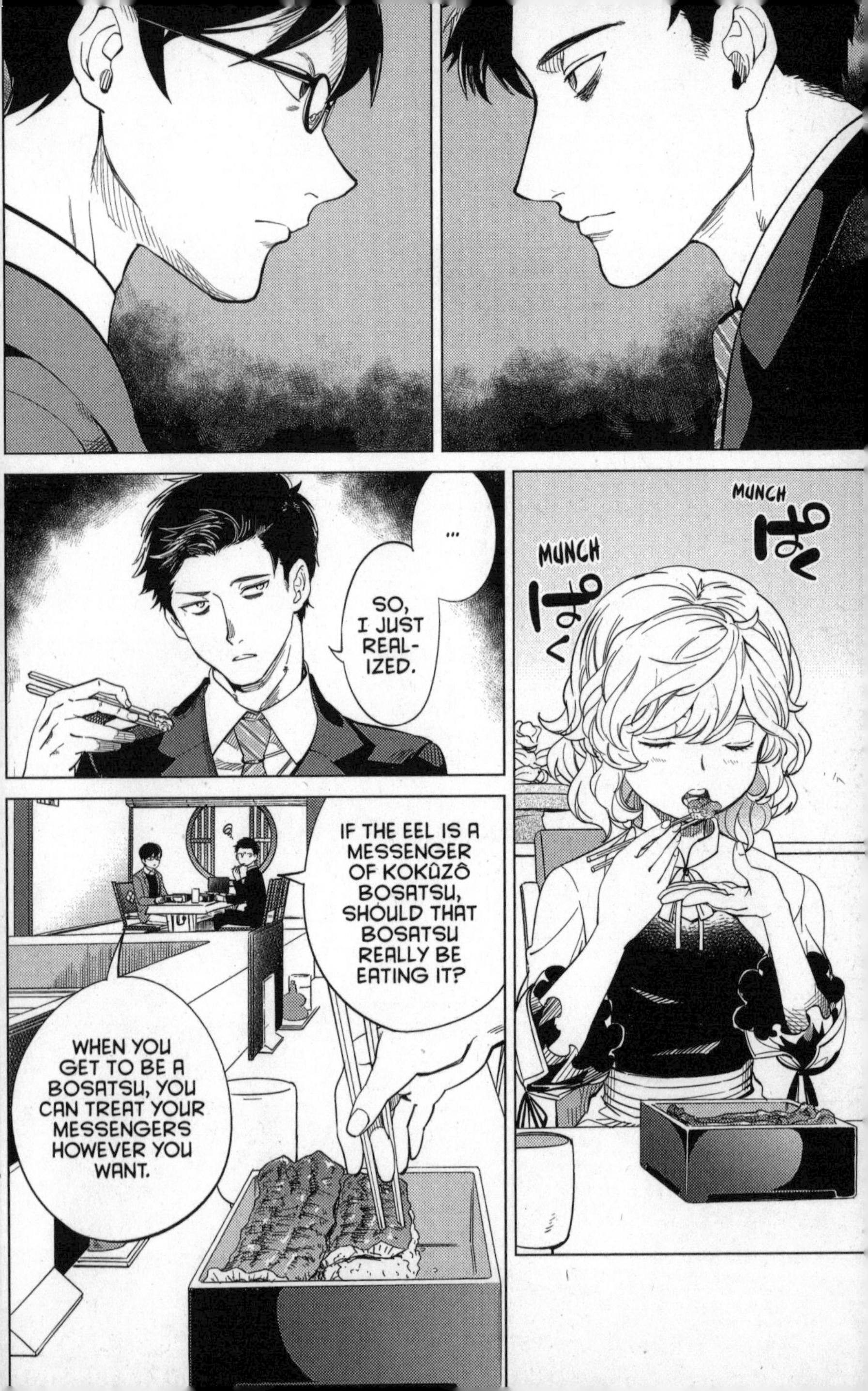

MUNCH
ぱく
MUNCH
ぱく
...
SO, I JUST REALIZED.
IF THE EEL IS A MESSENGER OF KOKÛZÔ BOSATSU, SHOULD THAT BOSATSU REALLY BE EATING IT?
WHEN YOU GET TO BE A BOSATSU, YOU CAN TREAT YOUR MESSENGERS HOWEVER YOU WANT.

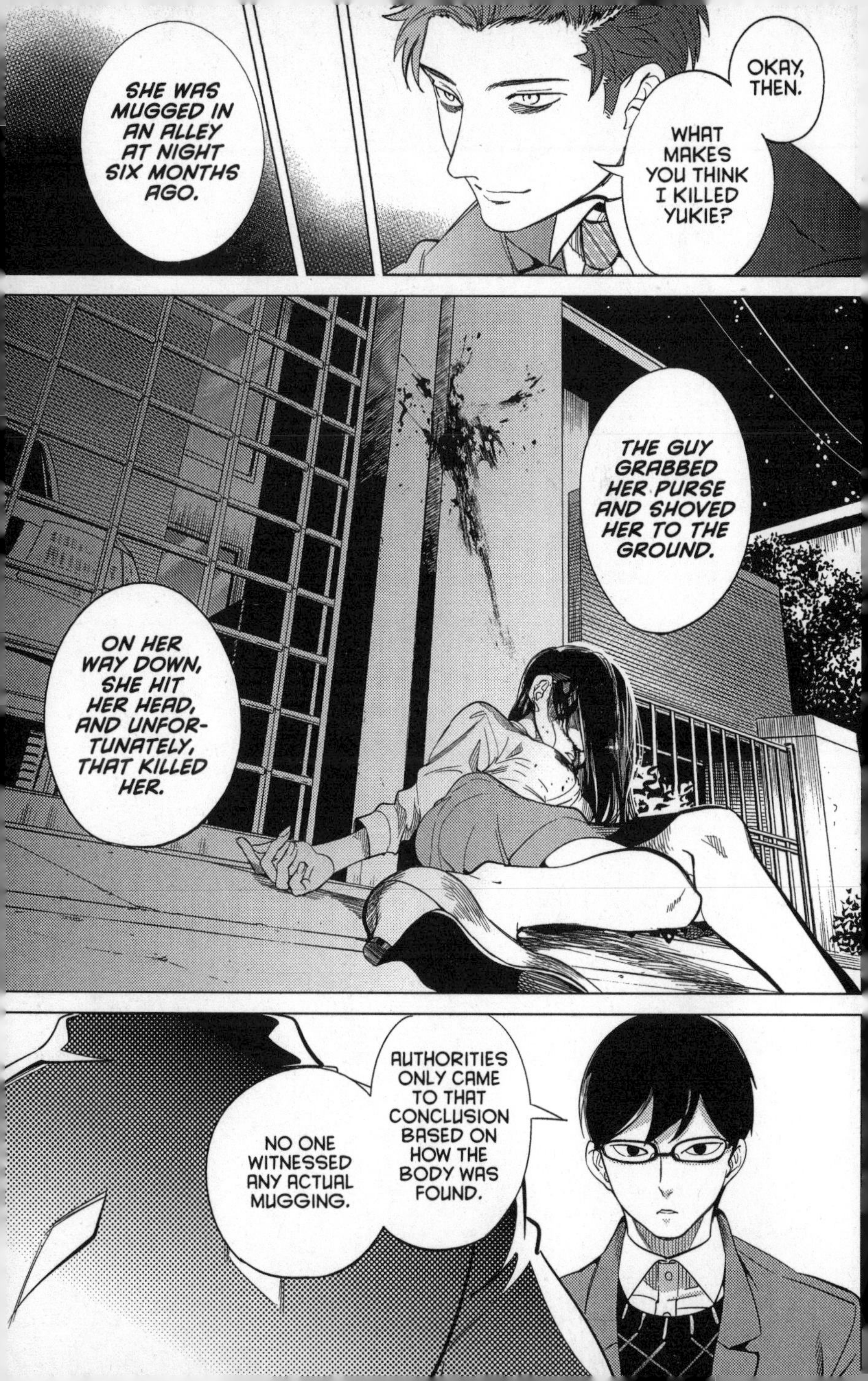
OKAY, THEN.
WHAT MAKES YOU THINK I KILLED YUKIE?
SHE WAS MUGGED IN AN ALLEY AT NIGHT SIX MONTHS AGO.
THE GUY GRABBED HER PURSE AND SHOVED HER TO THE GROUND.
ON HER WAY DOWN, SHE HIT HER HEAD, AND UNFOR-TUNATELY, THAT KILLED HER.
AUTHORITIES ONLY CAME TO THAT CONCLUSION BASED ON HOW THE BODY WAS FOUND.
NO ONE WITNESSED ANY ACTUAL MUGGING.

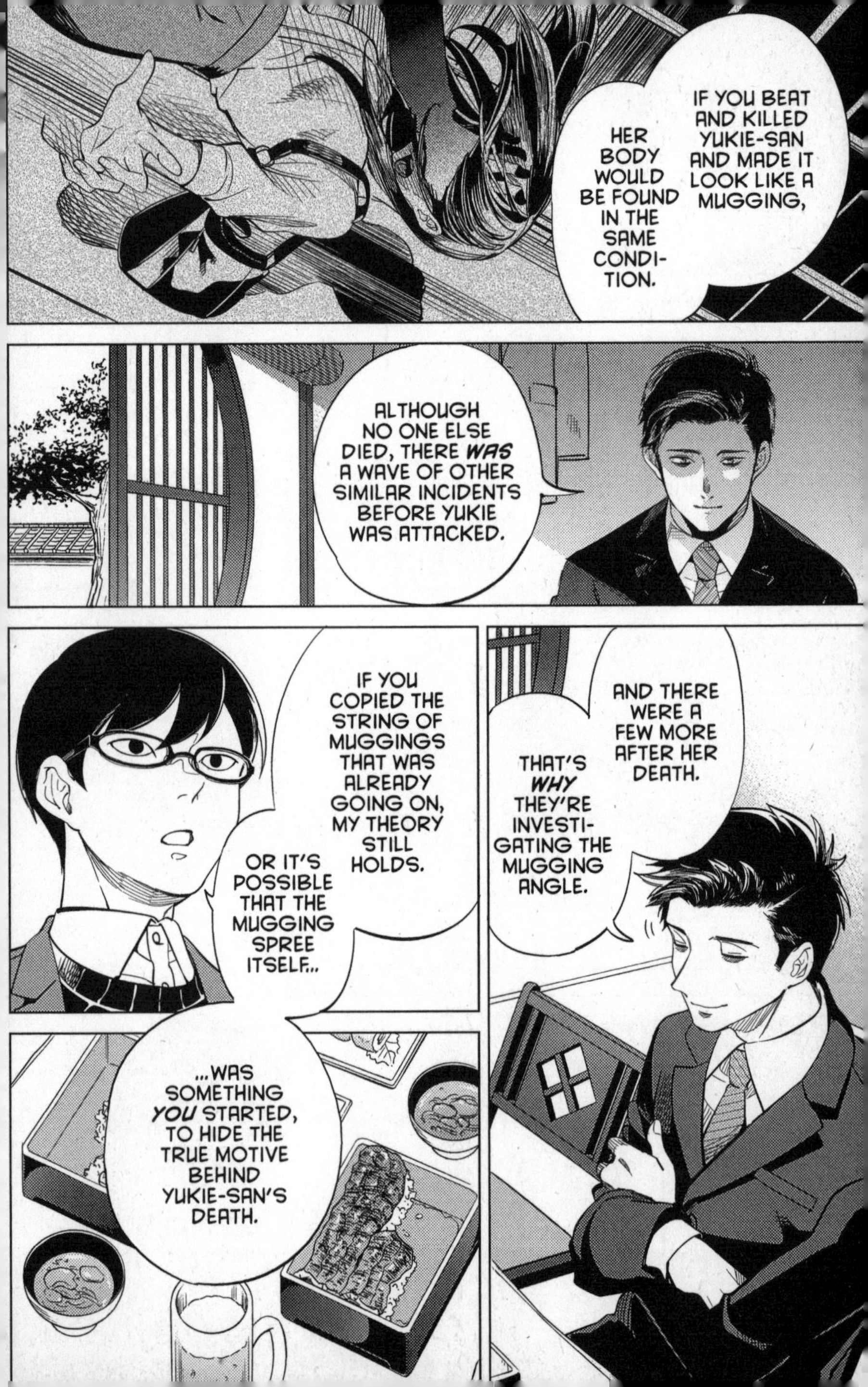
IF YOU BEAT AND KILLED YUKIE-SAN AND MADE IT LOOK LIKE A MUGGING,
HER BODY WOULD BE FOUND IN THE SAME CONDITION.
ALTHOUGH NO ONE ELSE DIED, THERE WAS A WAVE OF OTHER SIMILAR INCIDENTS BEFORE YUKIE WAS ATTACKED.
AND THERE WERE A FEW MORE AFTER HER DEATH.
THAT'S WHY THEY'RE INVESTIGATING THE MUGGING ANGLE.
IF YOU COPIED THE STRING OF MUGGINGS THAT WAS ALREADY GOING ON, MY THEORY STILL HOLDS.
OR IT'S POSSIBLE THAT THE MUGGING SPREE ITSELF...
...WAS SOMETHING YOU STARTED, TO HIDE THE TRUE MOTIVE BEHIND YUKIE-SAN'S DEATH.

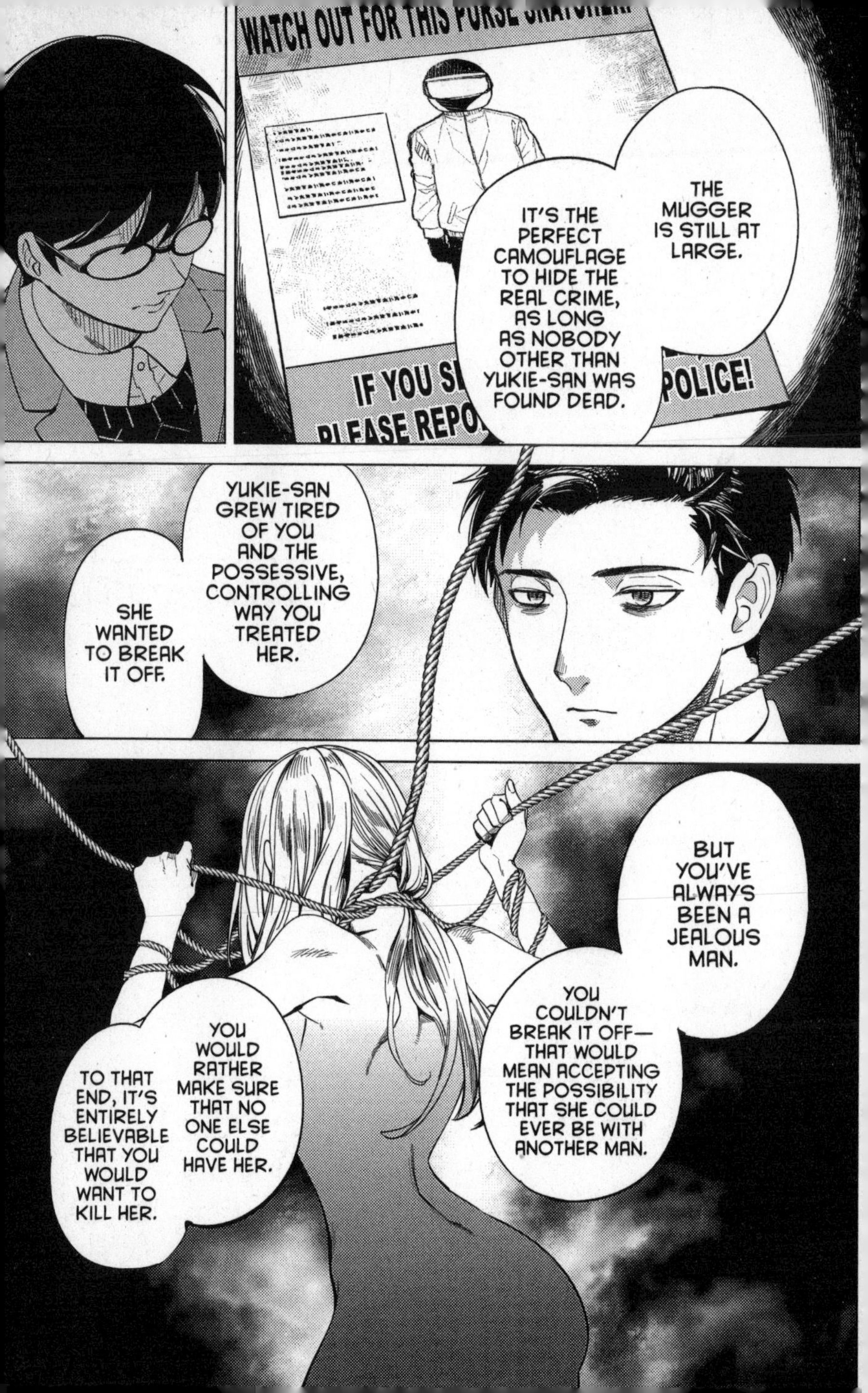
WATCH OUT FOR THIS PURSE SNATCHER!
THE MUGGER IS STILL AT LARGE.
IT'S THE PERFECT CAMOUFLAGE TO HIDE THE REAL CRIME, AS LONG AS NOBODY OTHER THAN YUKIE-SAN WAS FOUND DEAD.
YUKIE-SAN GREW TIRED OF YOU AND THE POSSESSIVE, CONTROLLING WAY YOU TREATED HER.
SHE WANTED TO BREAK IT OFF.
BUT YOU'VE ALWAYS BEEN A JEALOUS MAN.
YOU COULDN'T BREAK IT OFF— THAT WOULD MEAN ACCEPTING THE POSSIBILITY THAT SHE COULD EVER BE WITH ANOTHER MAN.
YOU WOULD RATHER MAKE SURE THAT NO ONE ELSE COULD HAVE HER.
TO THAT END, IT'S ENTIRELY BELIEVABLE THAT YOU WOULD WANT TO KILL HER.

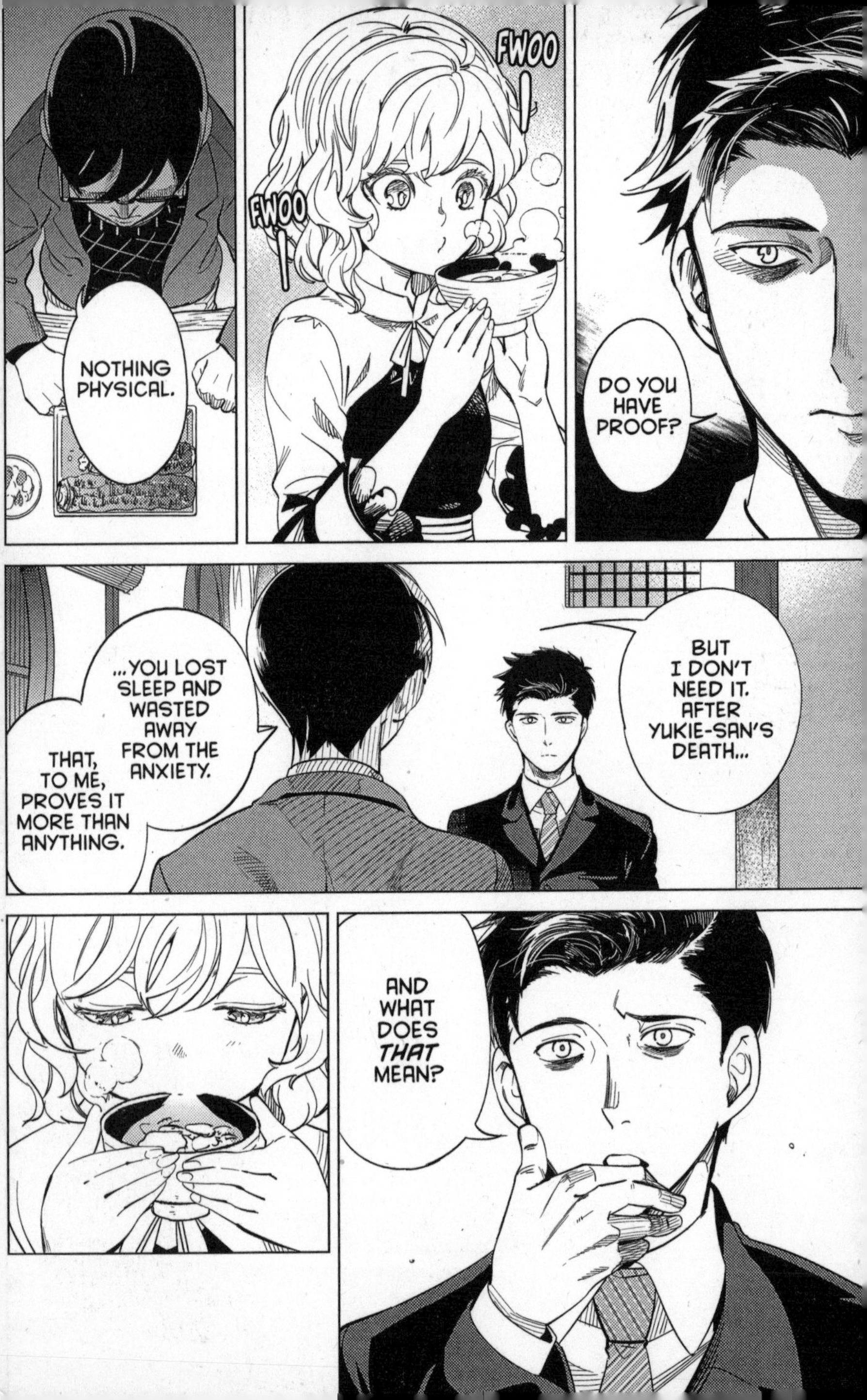
DO YOU HAVE PROOF?
FWOO
FWOO
NOTHING PHYSICAL.
BUT I DON'T NEED IT. AFTER YUKIE-SAN'S DEATH...
...YOU LOST SLEEP AND WASTED AWAY FROM THE ANXIETY.
THAT, TO ME, PROVES IT MORE THAN ANYTHING.
AND WHAT DOES *THAT* MEAN?

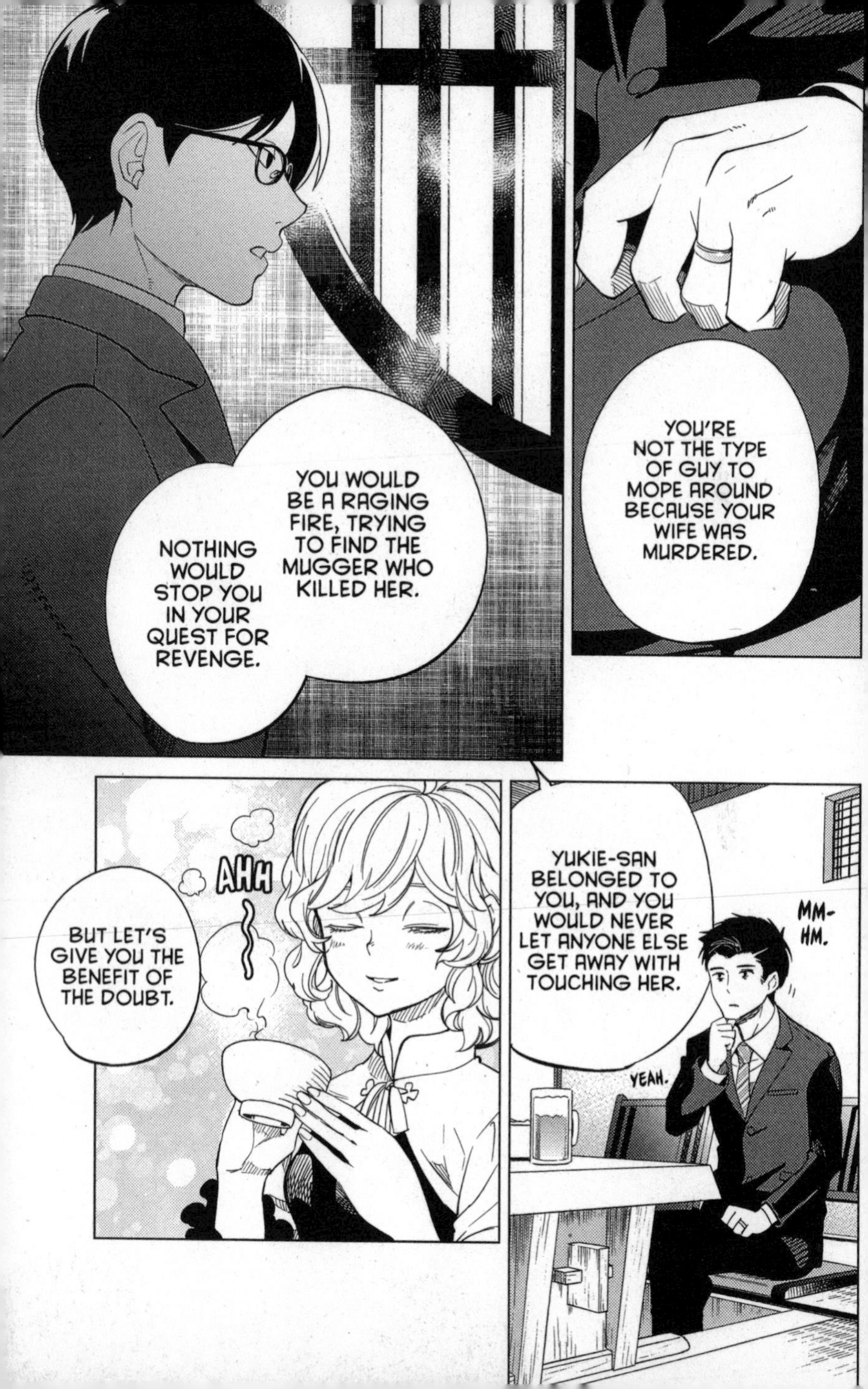
YOU'RE NOT THE TYPE OF GUY TO MOPE AROUND BECAUSE YOUR WIFE WAS MURDERED.
YOU WOULD BE A RAGING FIRE, TRYING TO FIND THE MUGGER WHO KILLED HER.
NOTHING WOULD STOP YOU IN YOUR QUEST FOR REVENGE.
YUKIE-SAN BELONGED TO YOU, AND YOU WOULD NEVER LET ANYONE ELSE GET AWAY WITH TOUCHING HER.
MM-HM.
YEAH.
AHH
BUT LET'S GIVE YOU THE BENEFIT OF THE DOUBT.

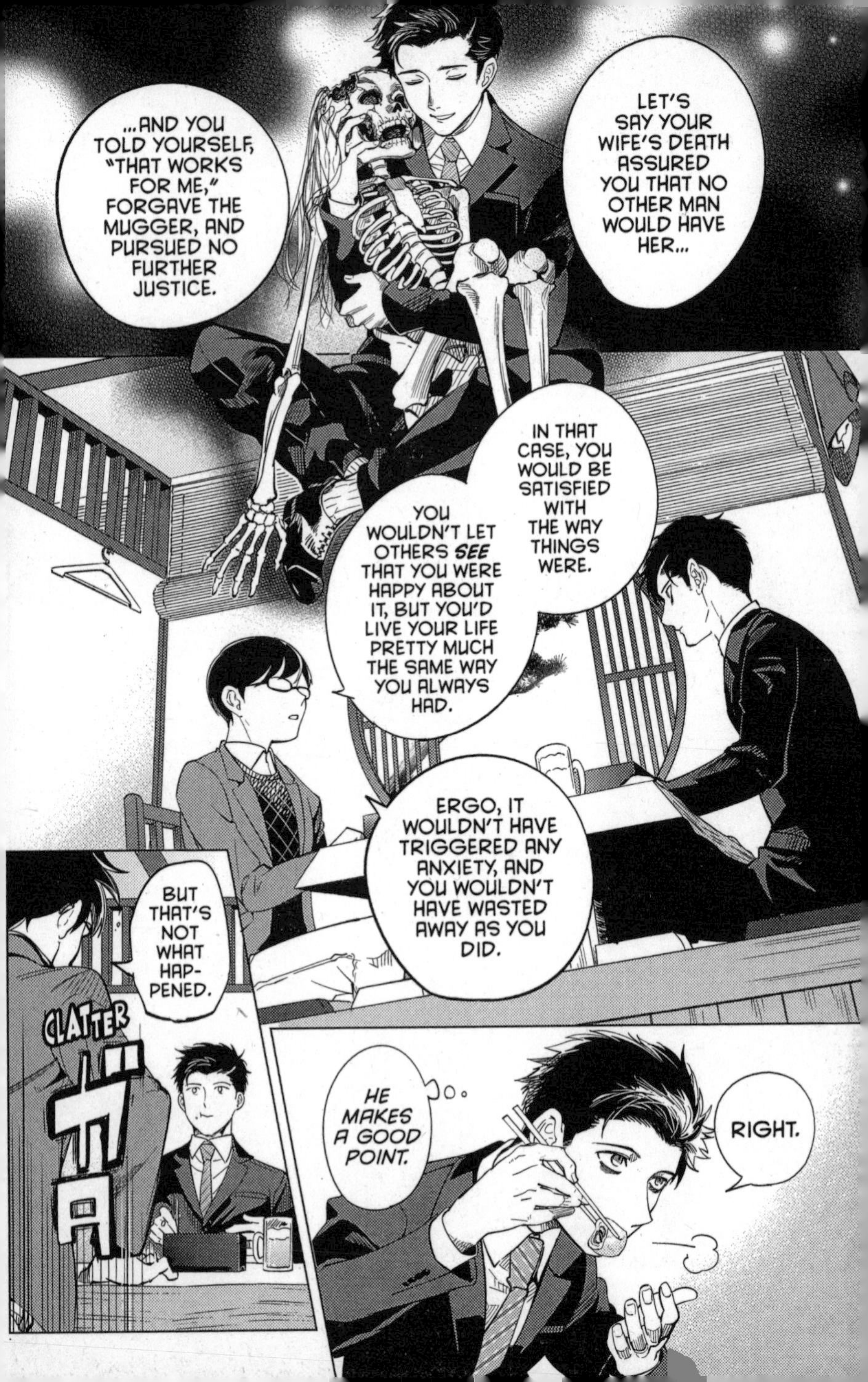
LET'S SAY YOUR WIFE'S DEATH ASSURED YOU THAT NO OTHER MAN WOULD HAVE HER...
...AND YOU TOLD YOURSELF, "THAT WORKS FOR ME," FORGAVE THE MUGGER, AND PURSUED NO FURTHER JUSTICE.
IN THAT CASE, YOU WOULD BE SATISFIED WITH THE WAY THINGS WERE.
YOU WOULDN'T LET OTHERS *SEE* THAT YOU WERE HAPPY ABOUT IT, BUT YOU'D LIVE YOUR LIFE PRETTY MUCH THE SAME WAY YOU ALWAYS HAD.
ERGO, IT WOULDN'T HAVE TRIGGERED ANY ANXIETY, AND YOU WOULDN'T HAVE WASTED AWAY AS YOU DID.
RIGHT.
HE MAKES A GOOD POINT.
BUT THAT'S NOT WHAT HAPPENED.
CLATTER
ガタ

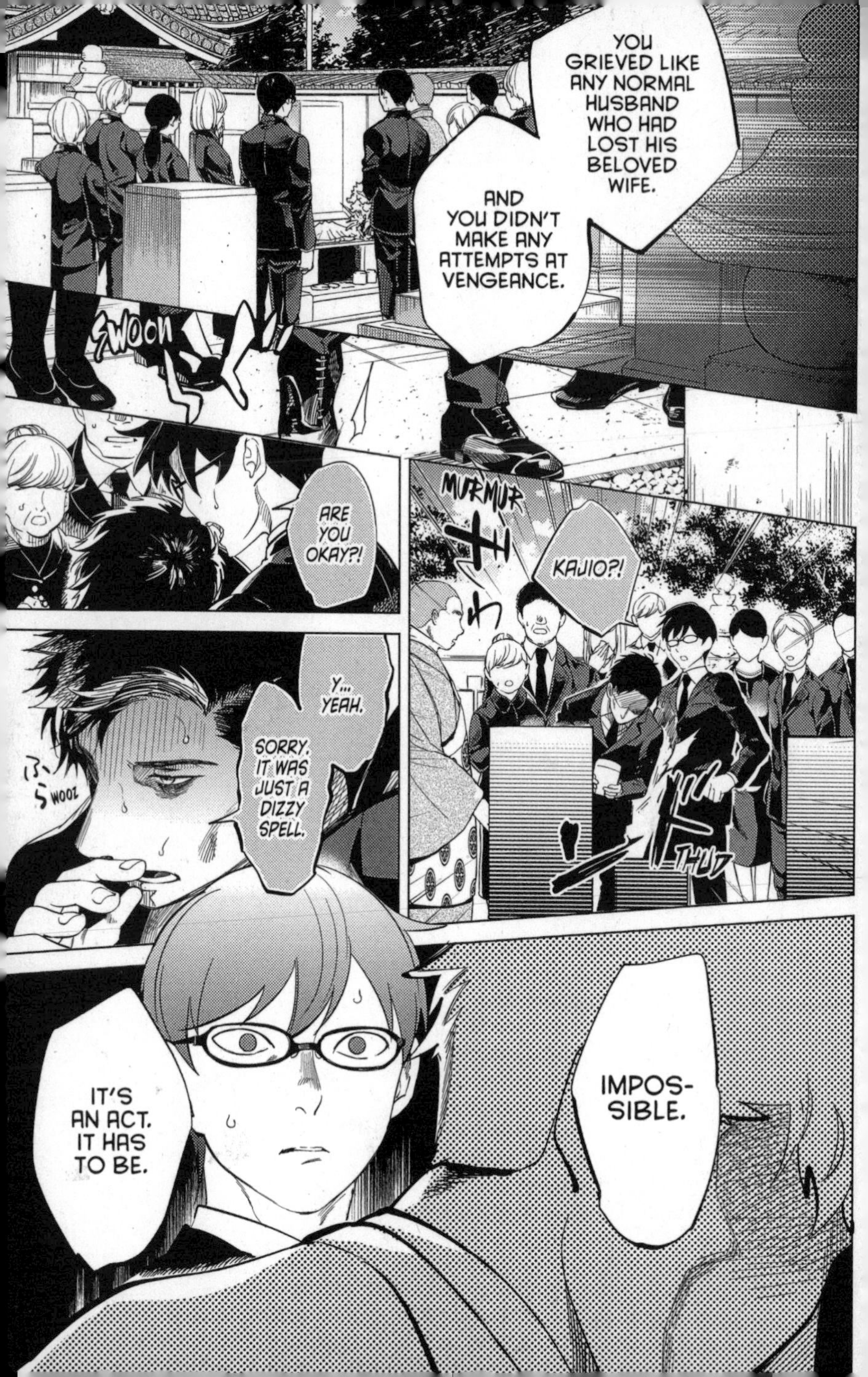
YOU GRIEVED LIKE ANY NORMAL HUSBAND WHO HAD LOST HIS BELOVED WIFE.
AND YOU DIDN'T MAKE ANY ATTEMPTS AT VENGEANCE.
SWOON
MURMUR
KAJIO?!
ARE YOU OKAY?!
THUD
Y... YEAH.
SORRY. IT WAS JUST A DIZZY SPELL.
WOOZ
IMPOSSIBLE.
IT'S AN ACT. IT HAS TO BE.

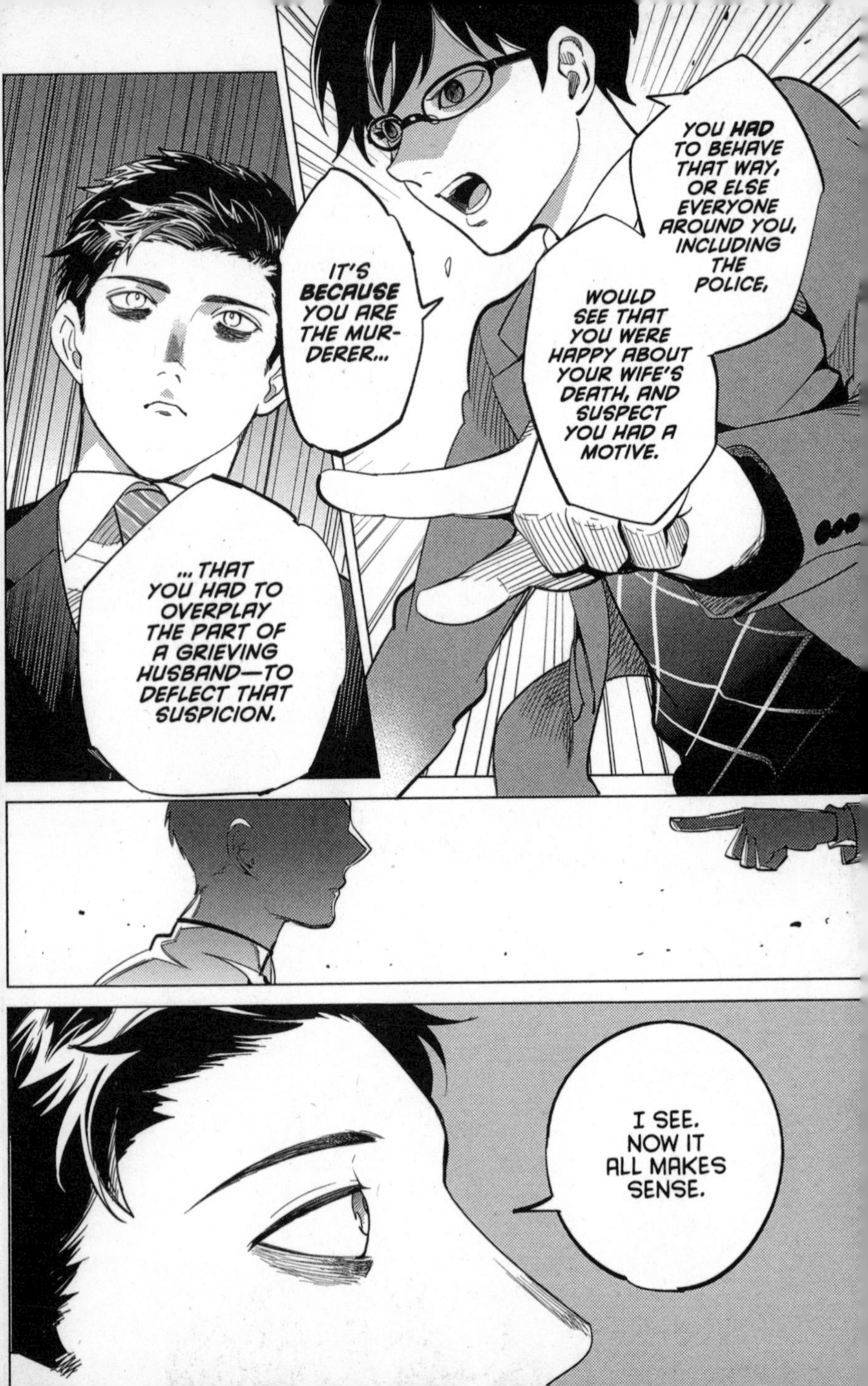
YOU HAD TO BEHAVE THAT WAY, OR ELSE EVERYONE AROUND YOU, INCLUDING THE POLICE,
WOULD SEE THAT YOU WERE HAPPY ABOUT YOUR WIFE'S DEATH, AND SUSPECT YOU HAD A MOTIVE.
IT'S BECAUSE YOU ARE THE MUR-DERER...
...THAT YOU HAD TO OVERPLAY THE PART OF A GRIEVING HUSBAND—TO DEFLECT THAT SUSPICION.
I SEE. NOW IT ALL MAKES SENSE.

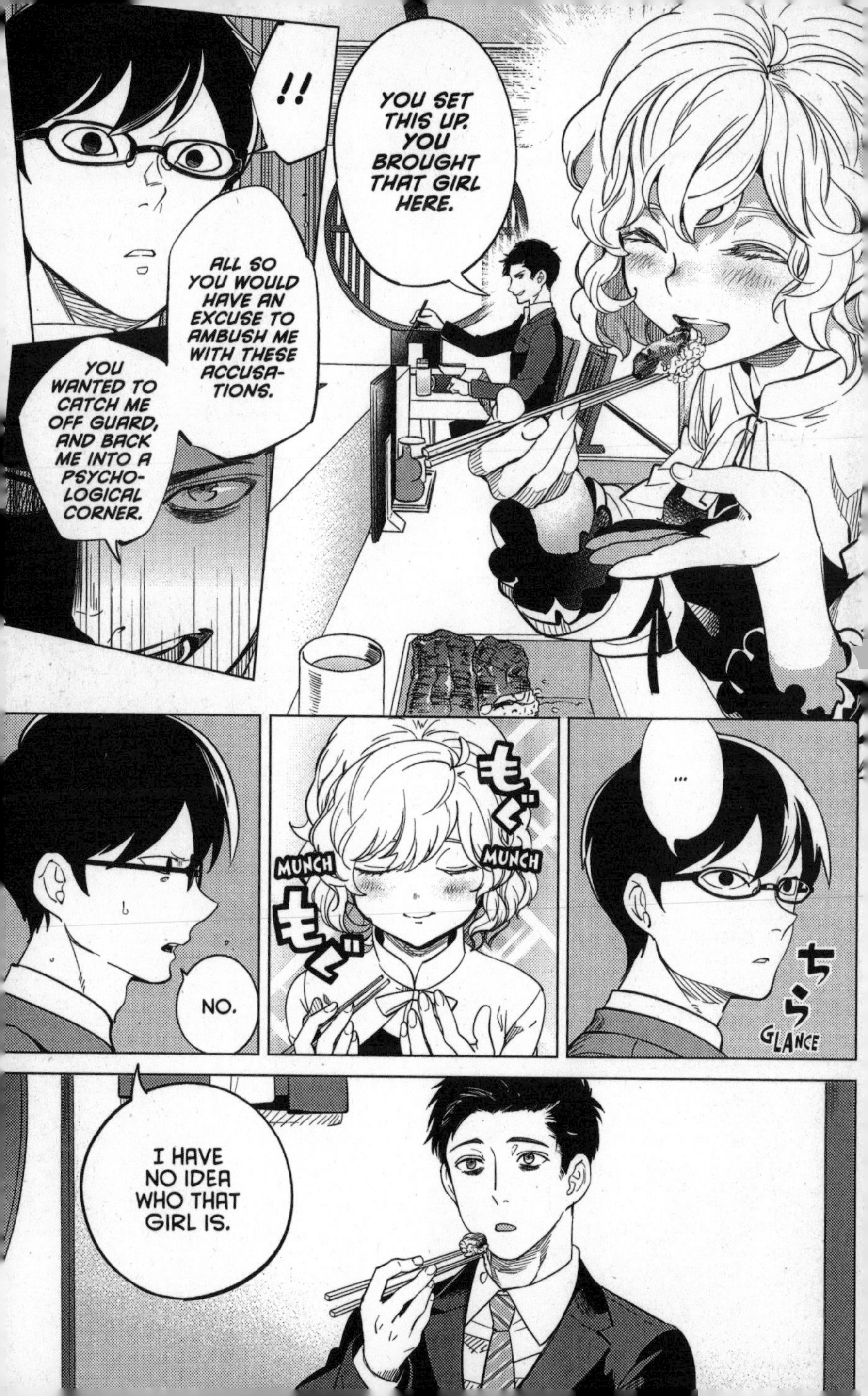
YOU SET THIS UP. YOU BROUGHT THAT GIRL HERE.
!!
ALL SO YOU WOULD HAVE AN EXCUSE TO AMBUSH ME WITH THESE ACCUSA-TIONS.
YOU WANTED TO CATCH ME OFF GUARD, AND BACK ME INTO A PSYCHO-LOGICAL CORNER.
...
ちら
GLANCE
もぐ
MUNCH
MUNCH
もぐ
NO.
I HAVE NO IDEA WHO THAT GIRL IS.

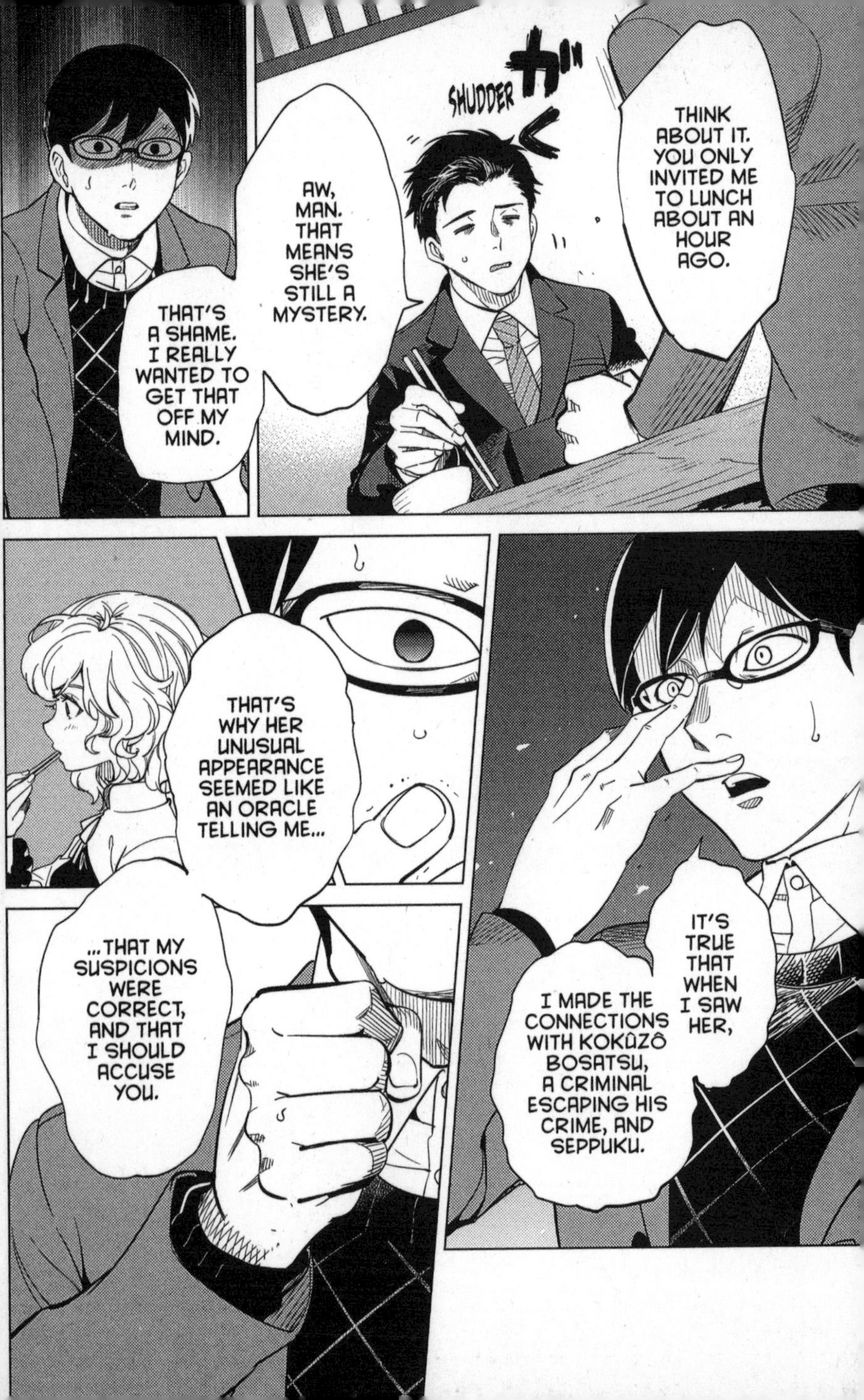
THINK ABOUT IT. YOU ONLY INVITED ME TO LUNCH ABOUT AN HOUR AGO.
SHUDDER
AW, MAN. THAT MEANS SHE'S STILL A MYSTERY.
THAT'S A SHAME. I REALLY WANTED TO GET THAT OFF MY MIND.
IT'S TRUE THAT WHEN I SAW HER,
I MADE THE CONNECTIONS WITH KOKÛZÔ BOSATSU, A CRIMINAL ESCAPING HIS CRIME, AND SEPPUKU.
THAT'S WHY HER UNUSUAL APPEARANCE SEEMED LIKE AN ORACLE TELLING ME...
...THAT MY SUSPICIONS WERE CORRECT, AND THAT I SHOULD ACCUSE YOU.

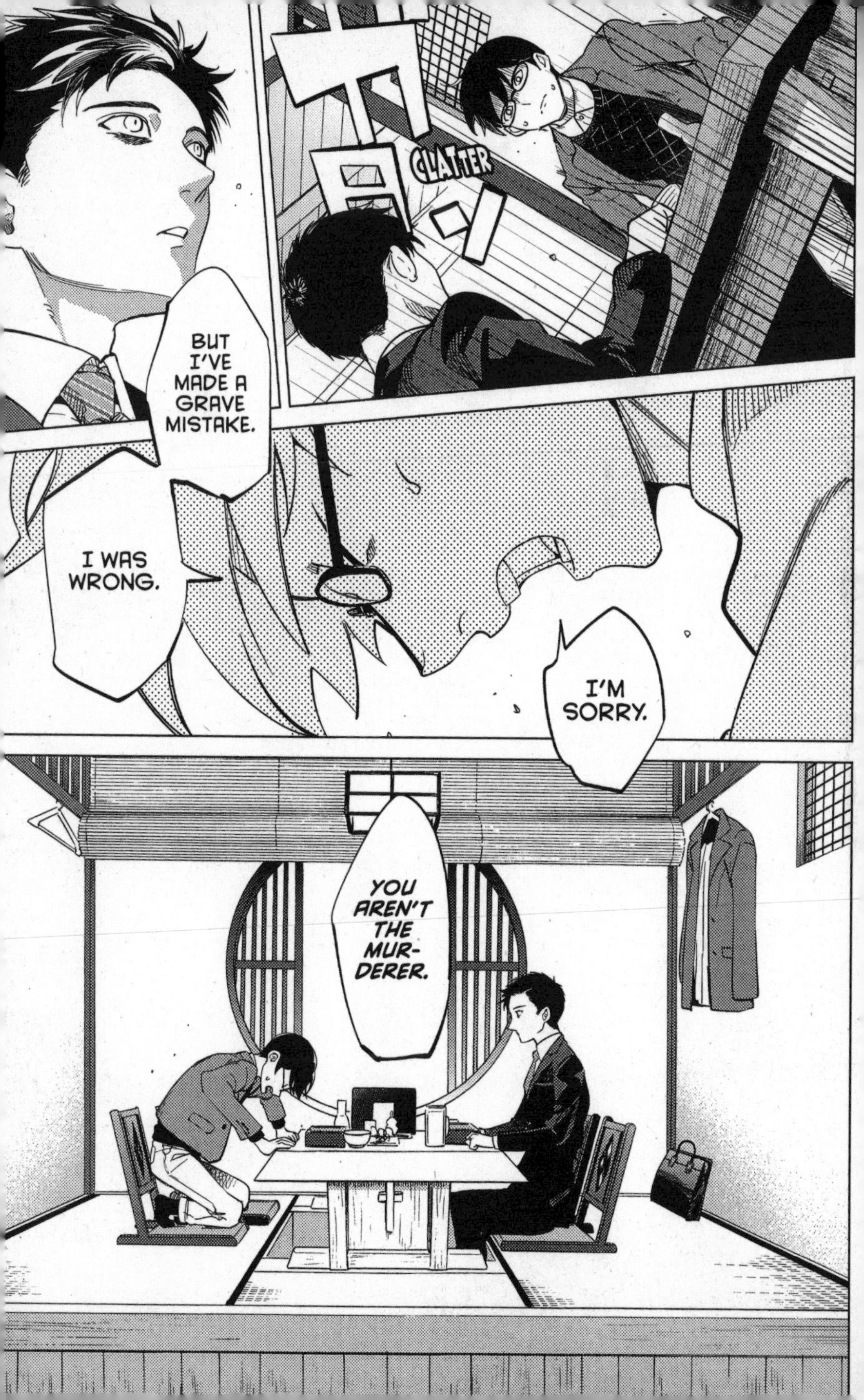
CLATTER
BUT I'VE MADE A GRAVE MISTAKE.
I WAS WRONG.
I'M SORRY.
YOU AREN'T THE MUR-DERER.

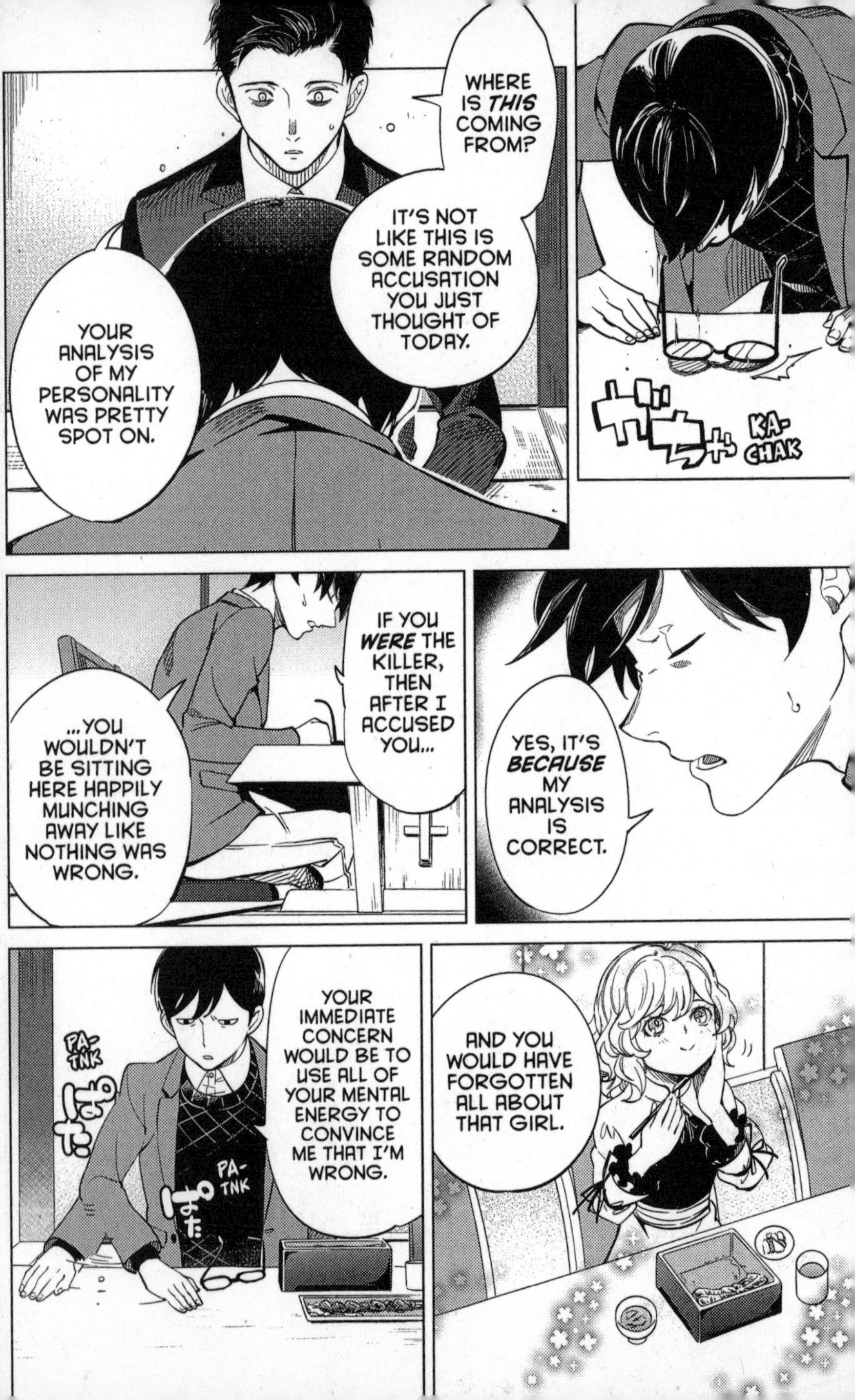
KA-CHAK
WHERE IS THIS COMING FROM?
IT'S NOT LIKE THIS IS SOME RANDOM ACCUSATION YOU JUST THOUGHT OF TODAY.
YOUR ANALYSIS OF MY PERSONALITY WAS PRETTY SPOT ON.
YES, IT'S BECAUSE MY ANALYSIS IS CORRECT.
IF YOU WERE THE KILLER, THEN AFTER I ACCUSED YOU...
...YOU WOULDN'T BE SITTING HERE HAPPILY MUNCHING AWAY LIKE NOTHING WAS WRONG.
AND YOU WOULD HAVE FORGOTTEN ALL ABOUT THAT GIRL.
YOUR IMMEDIATE CONCERN WOULD BE TO USE ALL OF YOUR MENTAL ENERGY TO CONVINCE ME THAT I'M WRONG.
PA-TNK
PA-TNK

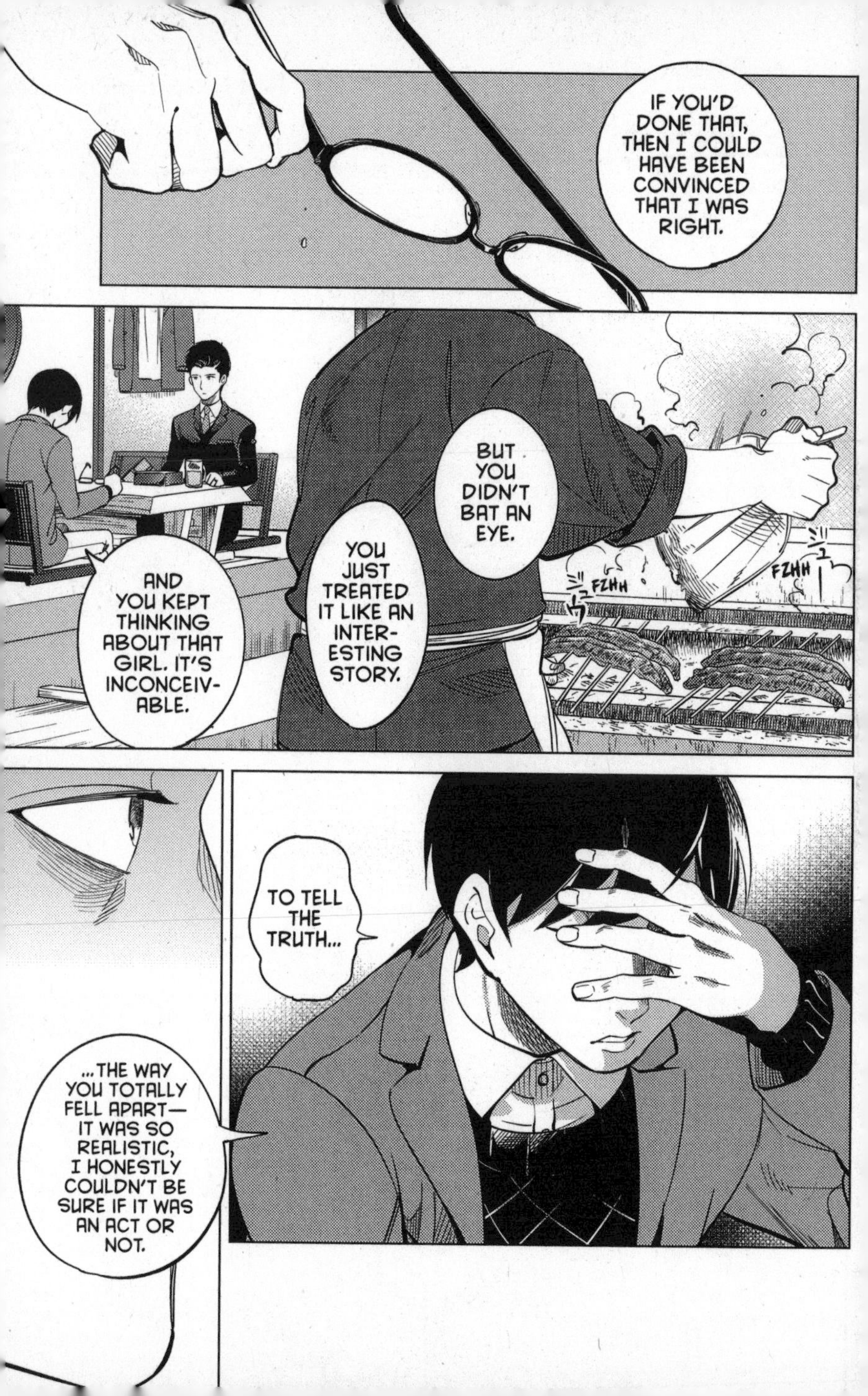
IF YOU'D DONE THAT, THEN I COULD HAVE BEEN CONVINCED THAT I WAS RIGHT.
BUT YOU DIDN'T BAT AN EYE.
YOU JUST TREATED IT LIKE AN INTER-ESTING STORY.
FZHH
FZHH
AND YOU KEPT THINKING ABOUT THAT GIRL. IT'S INCONCEIV-ABLE.
TO TELL THE TRUTH...
...THE WAY YOU TOTALLY FELL APART— IT WAS SO REALISTIC, I HONESTLY COULDN'T BE SURE IF IT WAS AN ACT OR NOT.

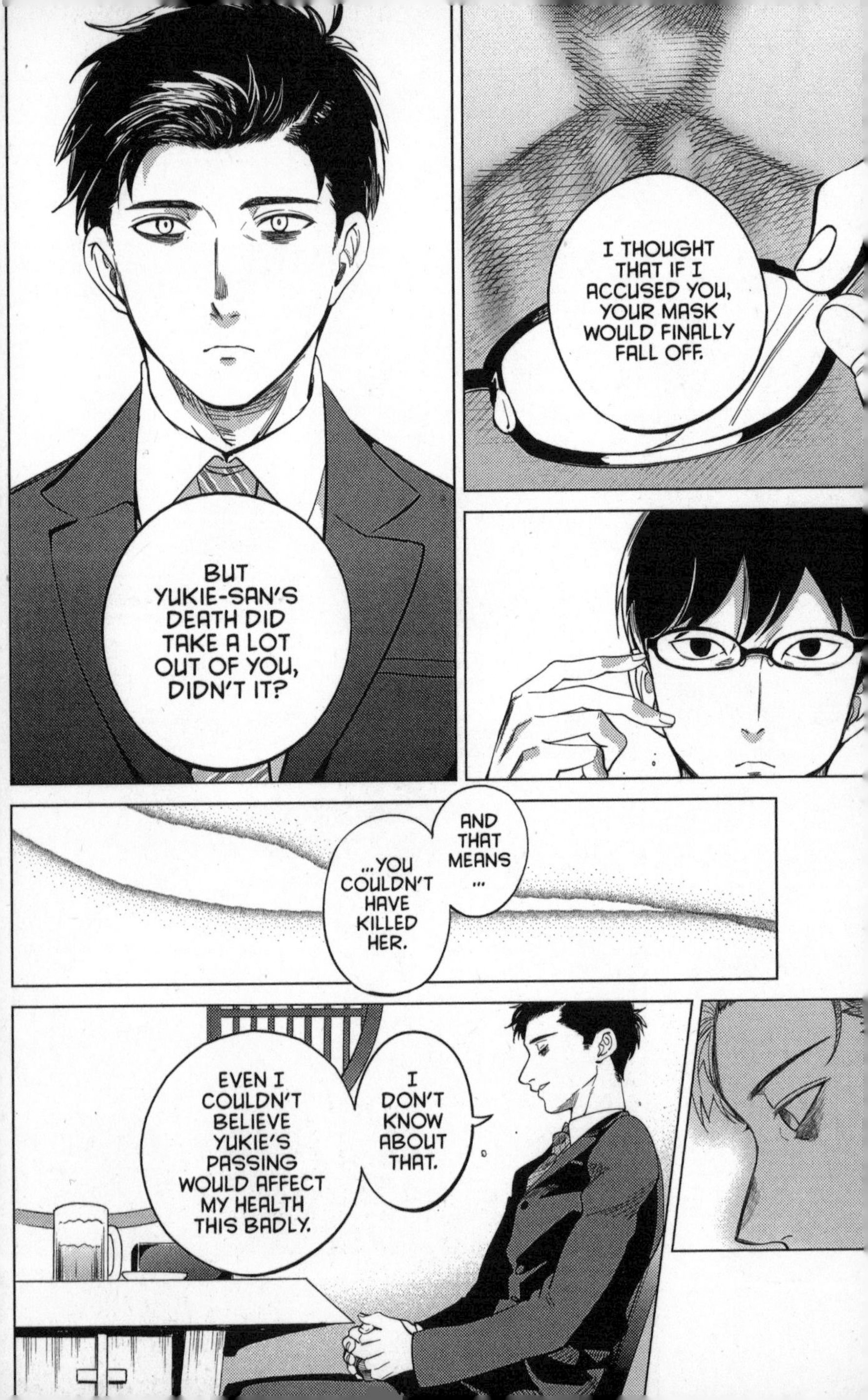
I THOUGHT THAT IF I ACCUSED YOU, YOUR MASK WOULD FINALLY FALL OFF.
BUT YUKIE-SAN'S DEATH DID TAKE A LOT OUT OF YOU, DIDN'T IT?
AND THAT MEANS ...
...YOU COULDN'T HAVE KILLED HER.
I DON'T KNOW ABOUT THAT.
EVEN I COULDN'T BELIEVE YUKIE'S PASSING WOULD AFFECT MY HEALTH THIS BADLY.

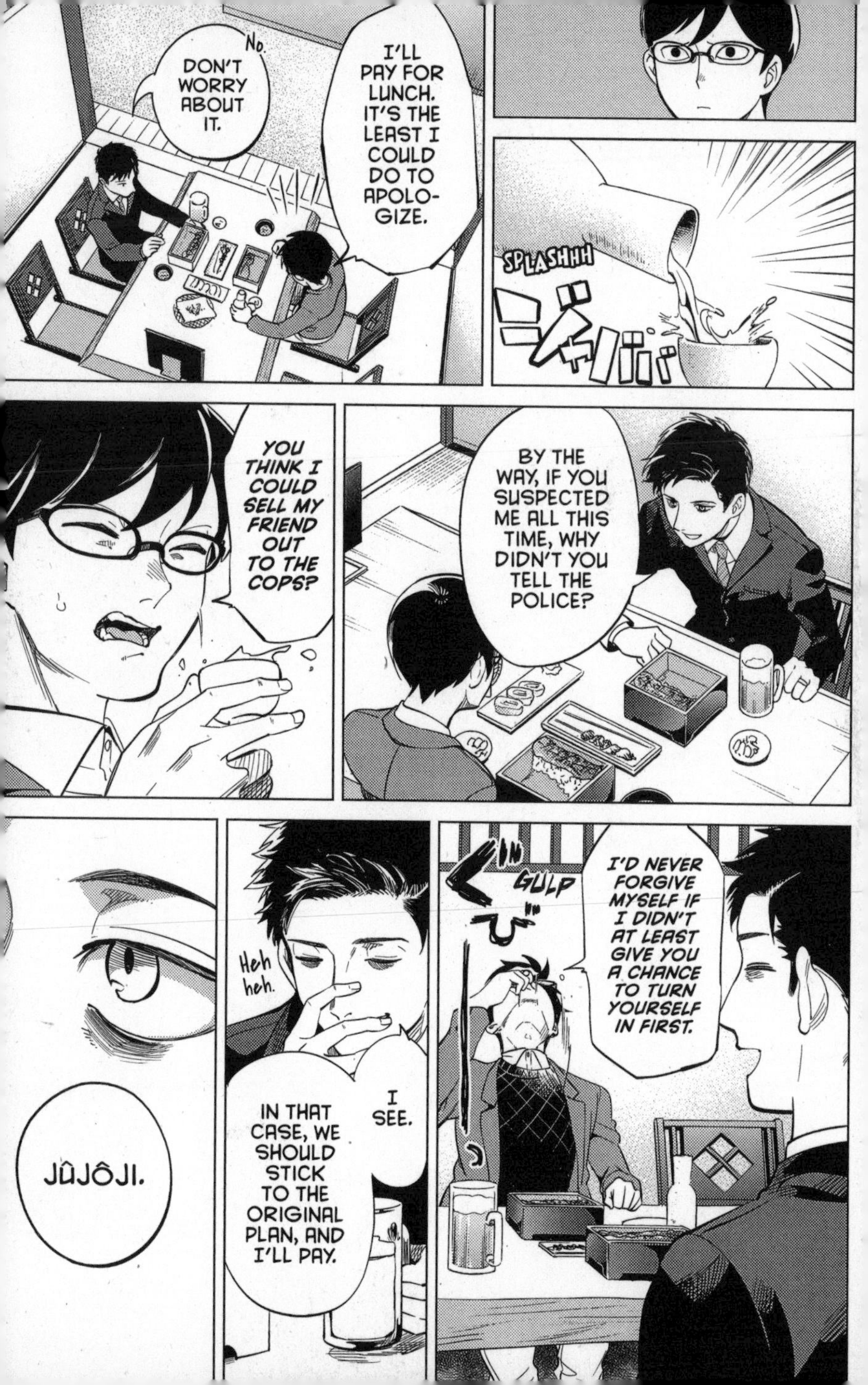
SPLASHHH
I'LL PAY FOR LUNCH. IT'S THE LEAST I COULD DO TO APOLOGIZE.
No.
DON'T WORRY ABOUT IT.
BY THE WAY, IF YOU SUSPECTED ME ALL THIS TIME, WHY DIDN'T YOU TELL THE POLICE?
YOU THINK I COULD SELL MY FRIEND OUT TO THE COPS?
I'D NEVER FORGIVE MYSELF IF I DIDN'T AT LEAST GIVE YOU A CHANCE TO TURN YOURSELF IN FIRST.
GULP
Heh heh.
I SEE.
IN THAT CASE, WE SHOULD STICK TO THE ORIGINAL PLAN, AND I'LL PAY.
JÛJÔJI.

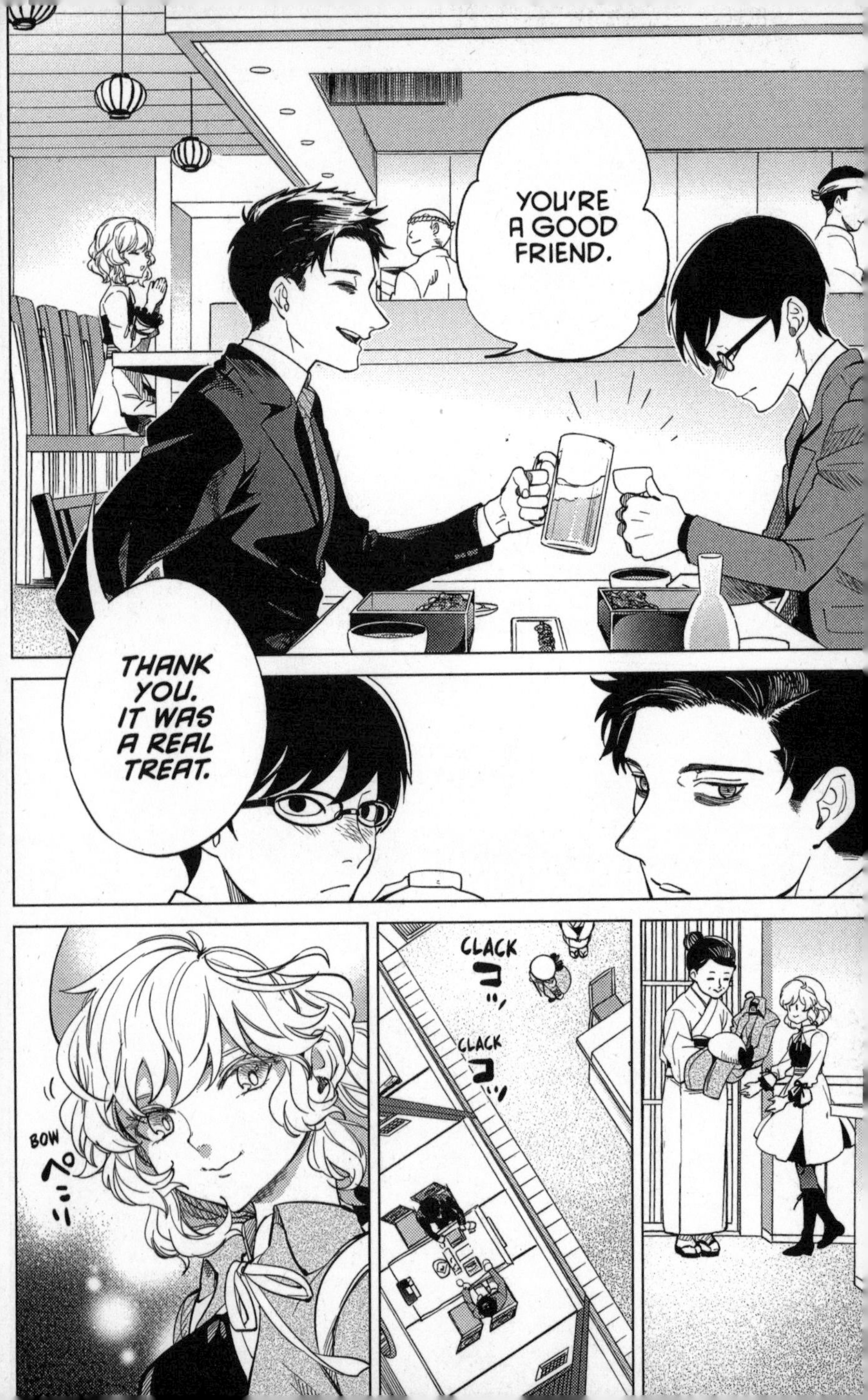
YOU'RE A GOOD FRIEND.
THANK YOU. IT WAS A REAL TREAT.
CLACK
コッ
CLACK
コッ
BOW
ペこ

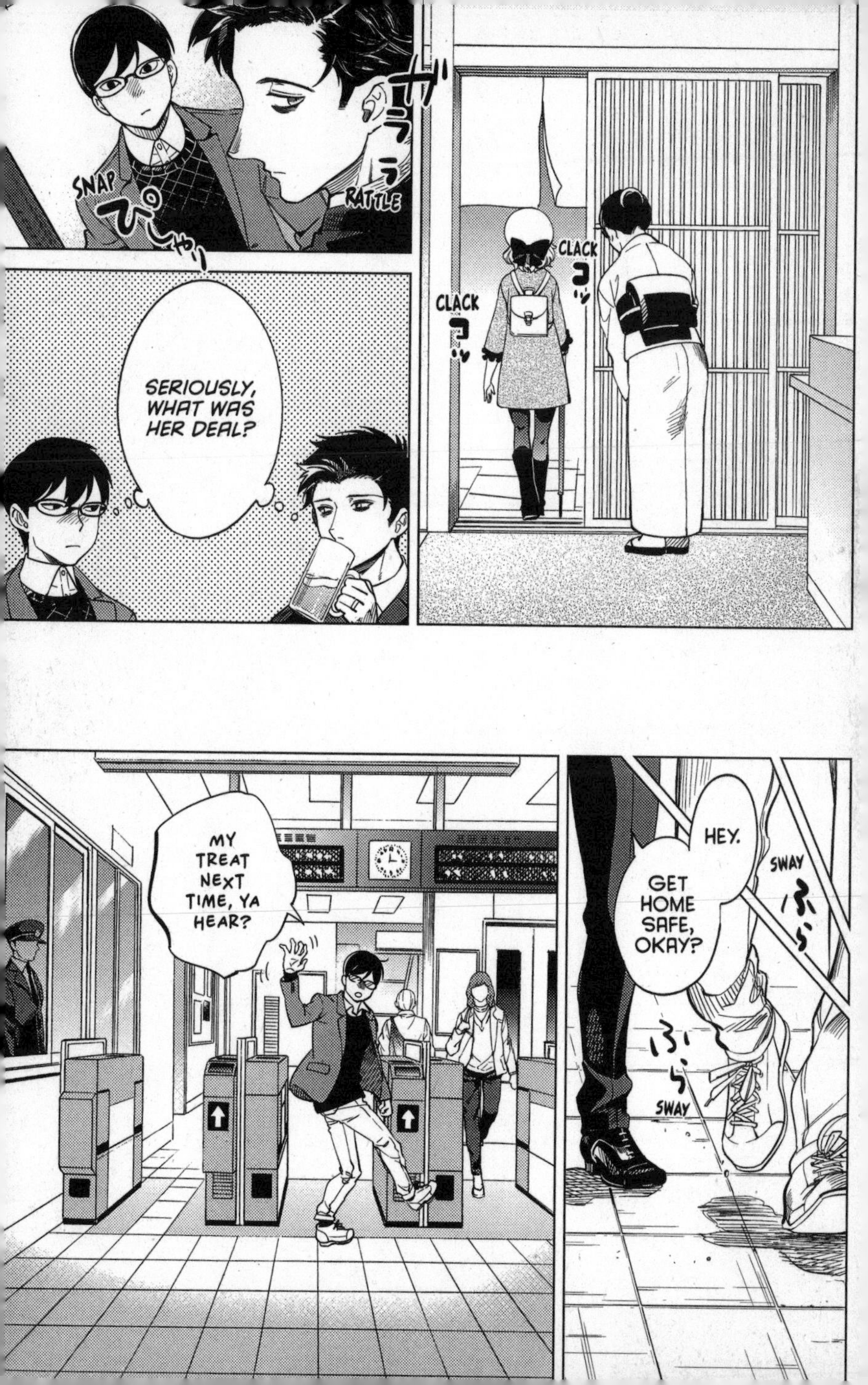
CLACK
コッ
CLACK
コッ
SNAP
RATTLE
SERIOUSLY, WHAT WAS HER DEAL?
HEY.
GET HOME SAFE, OKAY?
SWAY
ふら
SWAY
ふら
MY TREAT NEXT TIME, YA HEAR?

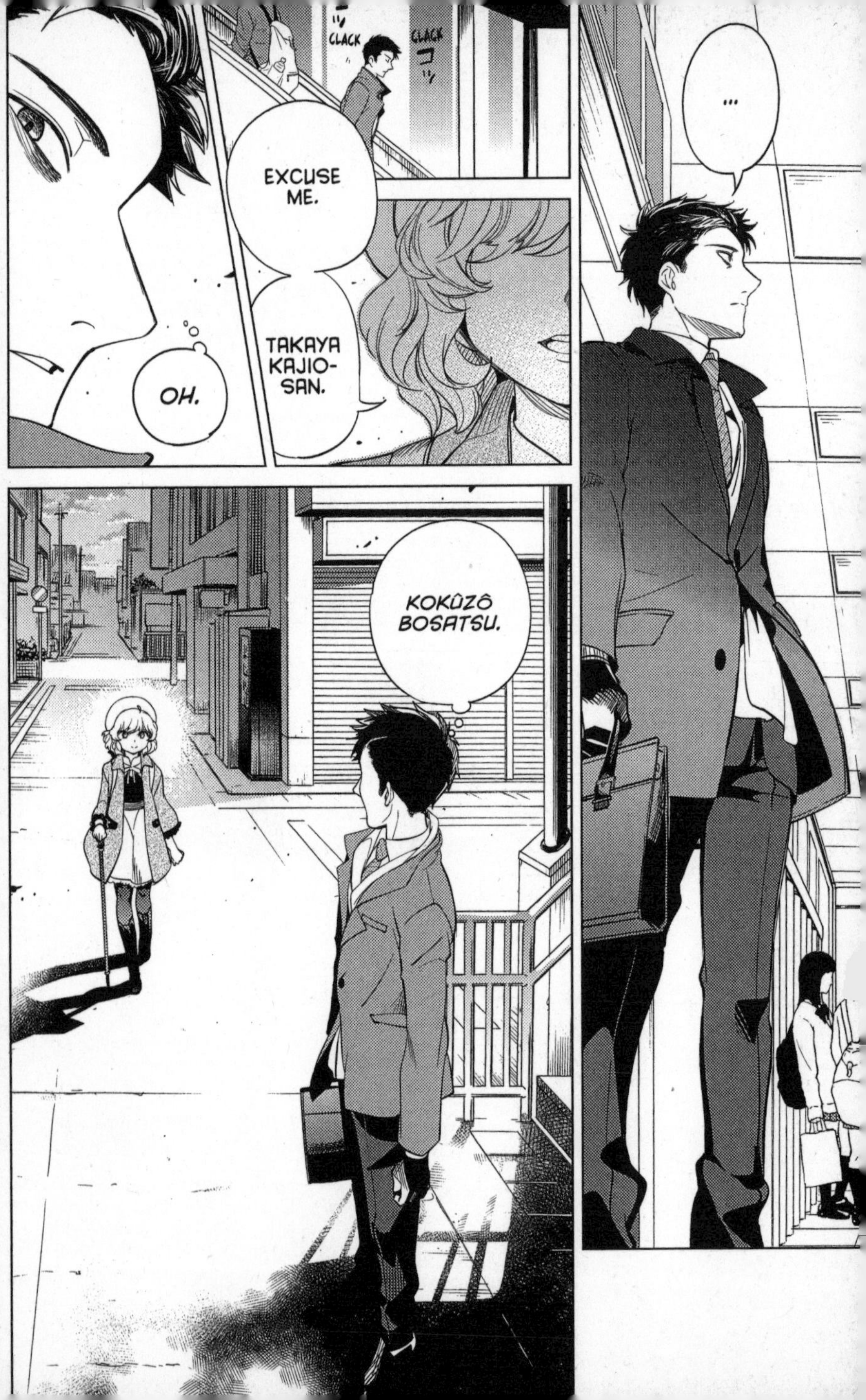
...
CLACK
CLACK
EXCUSE ME.
TAKAYA KAJIO-SAN.
OH.
KOKÛZÔ BOSATSU.

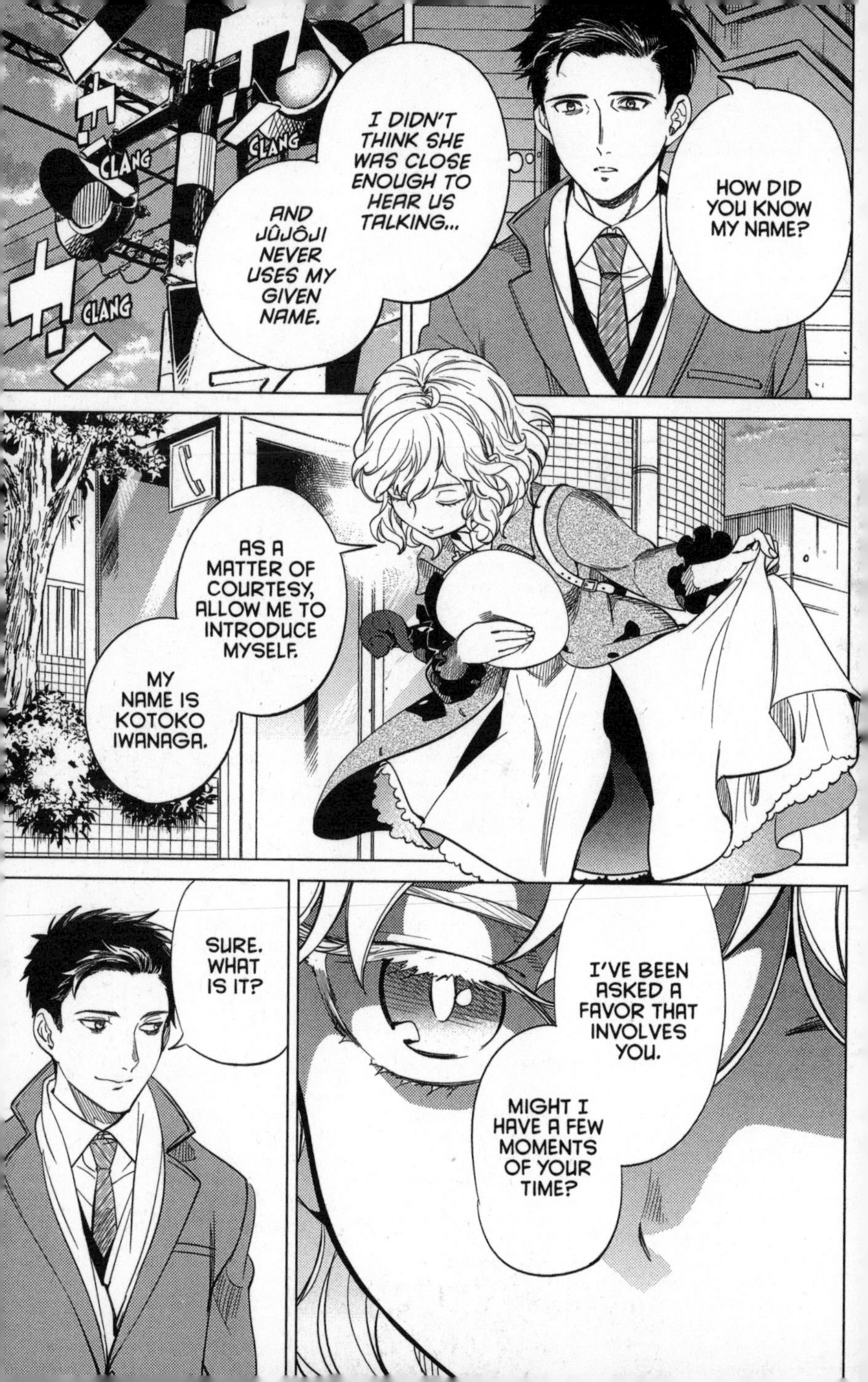
HOW DID YOU KNOW MY NAME?
I DIDN'T THINK SHE WAS CLOSE ENOUGH TO HEAR US TALKING...
CLANG
CLANG
AND JÛJÔJI NEVER USES MY GIVEN NAME.
CLANG
AS A MATTER OF COURTESY, ALLOW ME TO INTRODUCE MYSELF.
MY NAME IS KOTOKO IWANAGA.
I'VE BEEN ASKED A FAVOR THAT INVOLVES YOU.
MIGHT I HAVE A FEW MOMENTS OF YOUR TIME?
SURE. WHAT IS IT?

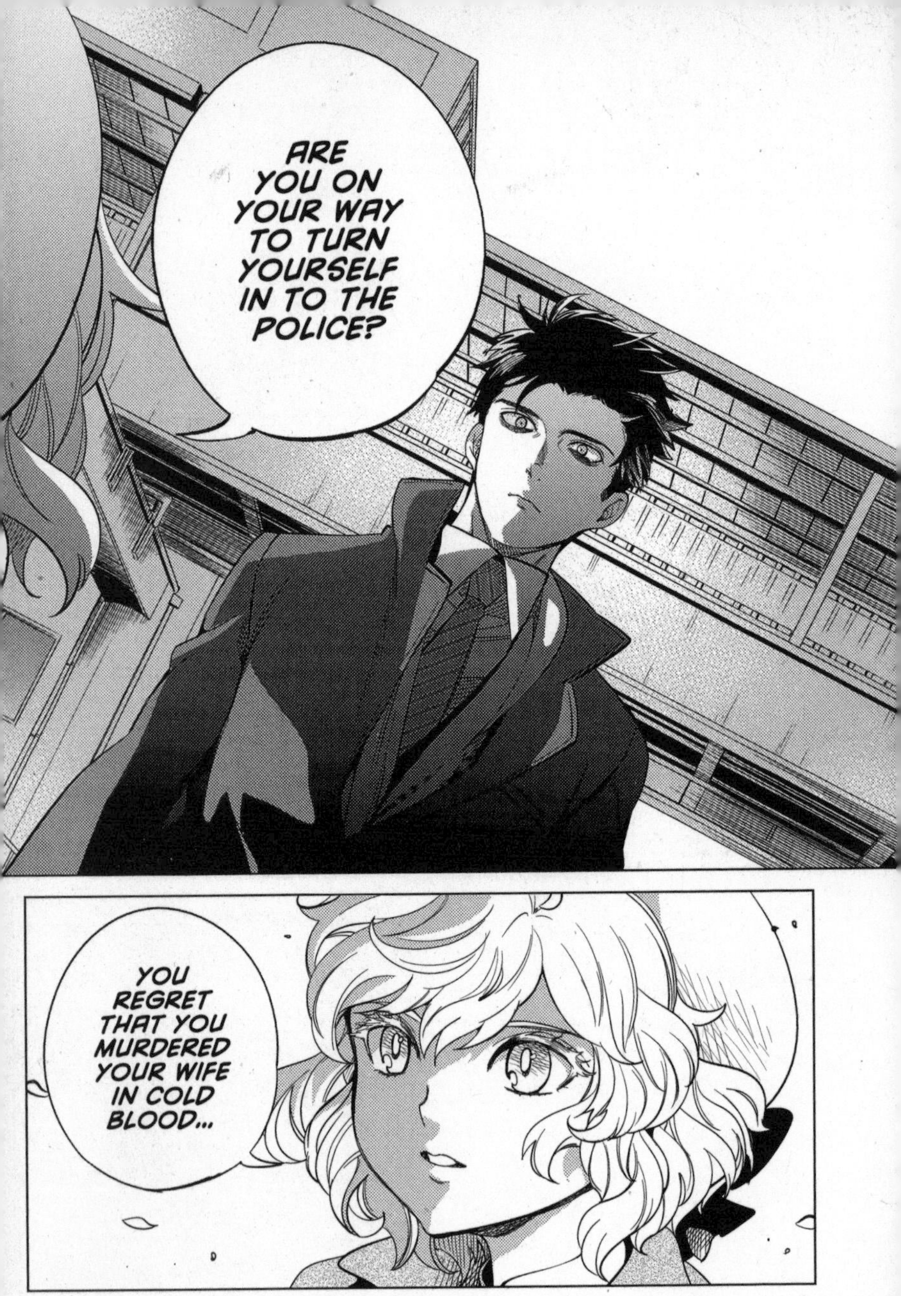
ARE YOU ON YOUR WAY TO TURN YOURSELF IN TO THE POLICE?
YOU REGRET THAT YOU MURDERED YOUR WIFE IN COLD BLOOD...

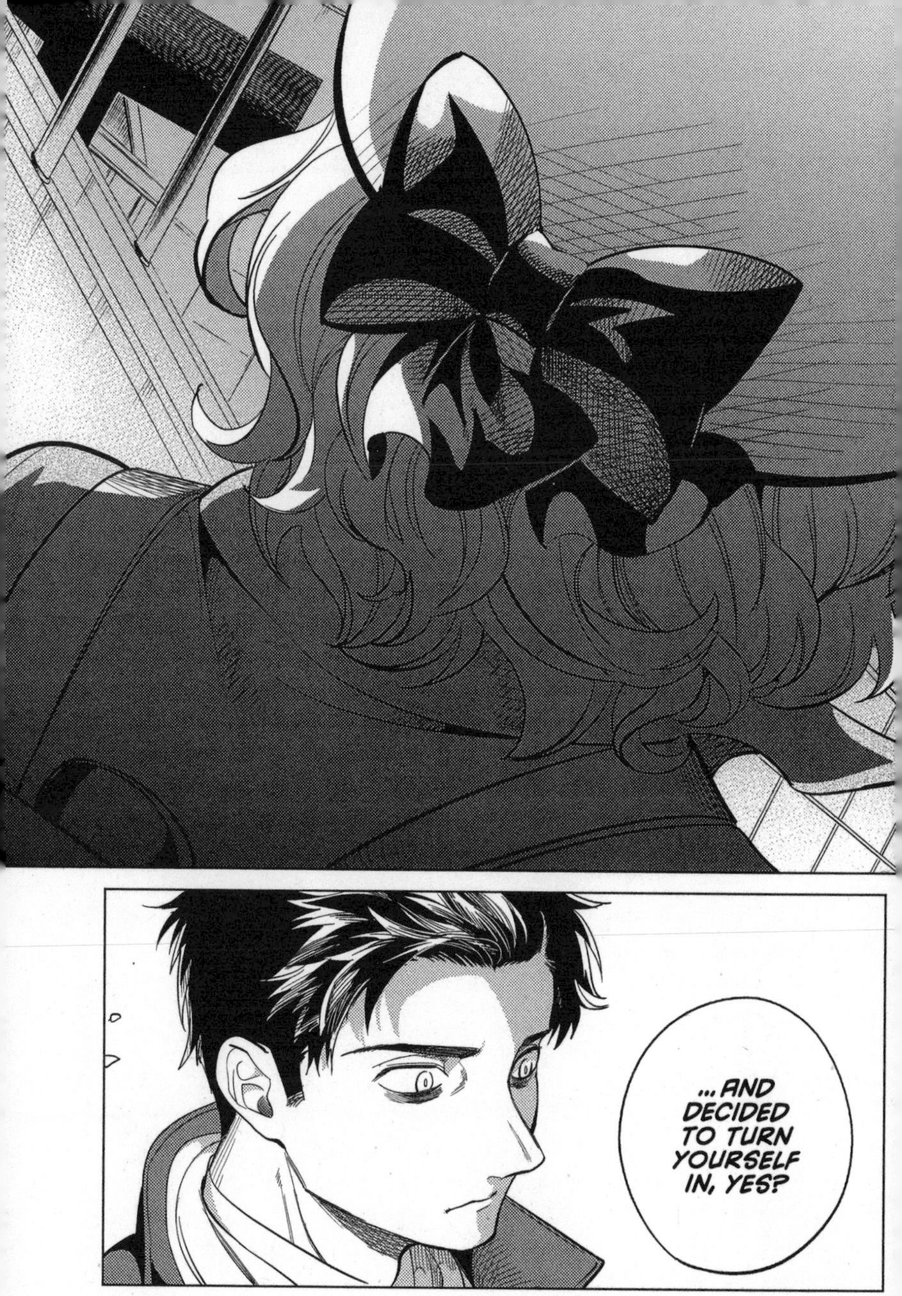
...AND DECIDED TO TURN YOURSELF IN, YES?

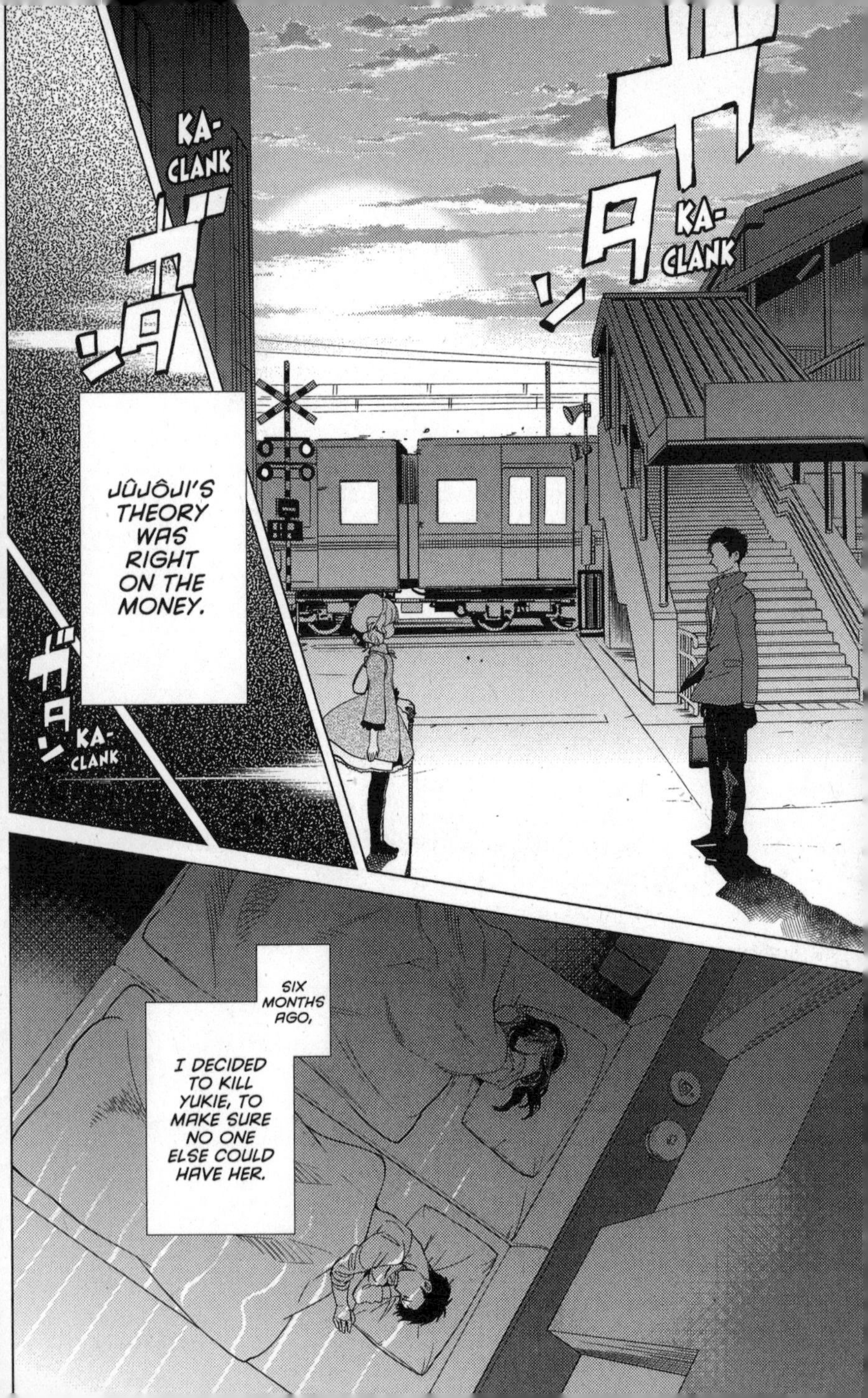
ガタン
KA-CLANK
JÛJÔJI'S THEORY WAS RIGHT ON THE MONEY.
KA-CLANK
ガタン
ガタン
KA-CLANK
SIX MONTHS AGO,
I DECIDED TO KILL YUKIE, TO MAKE SURE NO ONE ELSE COULD HAVE HER.

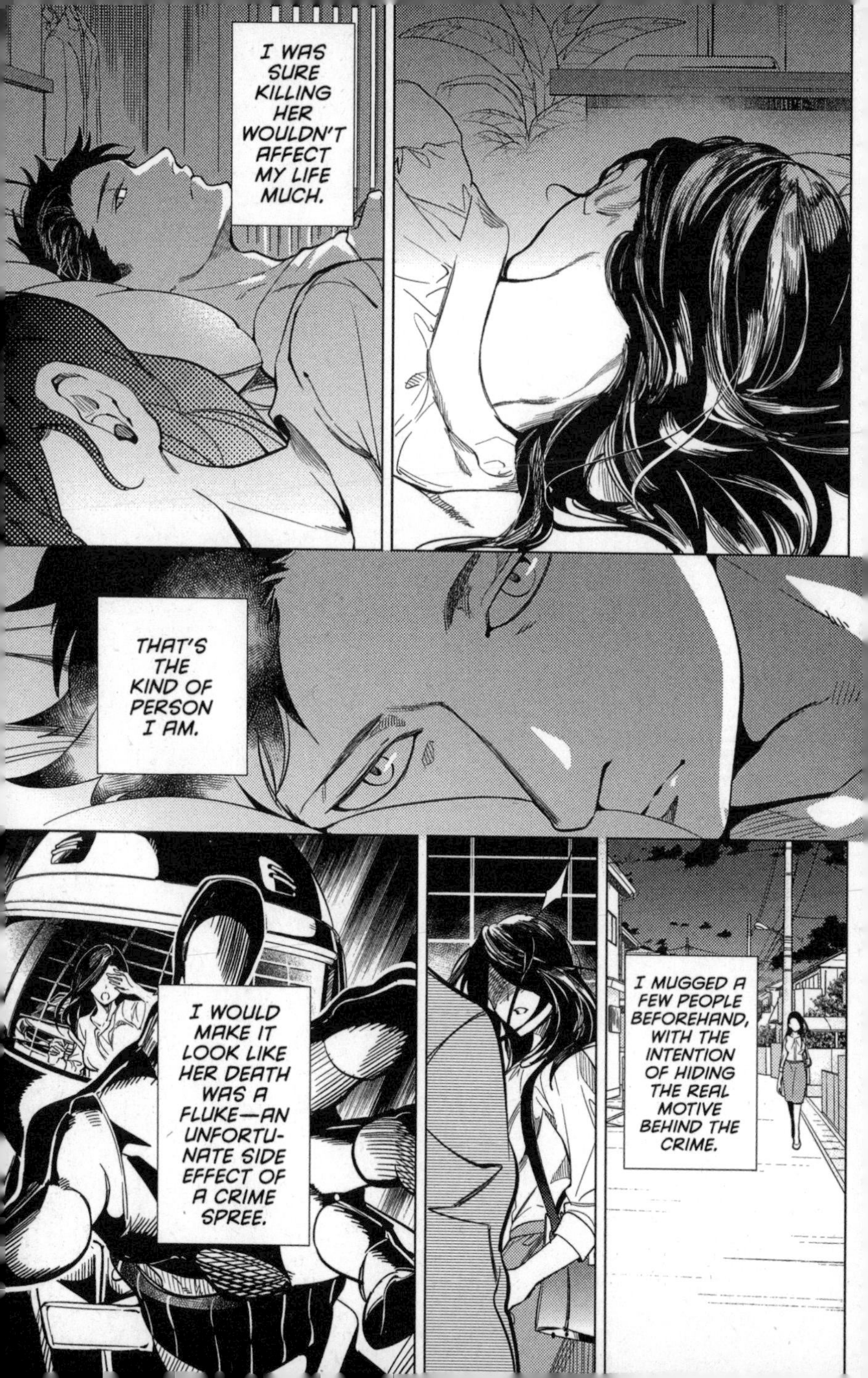
I WAS SURE KILLING HER WOULDN'T AFFECT MY LIFE MUCH.
THAT'S THE KIND OF PERSON I AM.
I MUGGED A FEW PEOPLE BEFOREHAND, WITH THE INTENTION OF HIDING THE REAL MOTIVE BEHIND THE CRIME.
I WOULD MAKE IT LOOK LIKE HER DEATH WAS A FLUKE—AN UNFORTU-NATE SIDE EFFECT OF A CRIME SPREE.

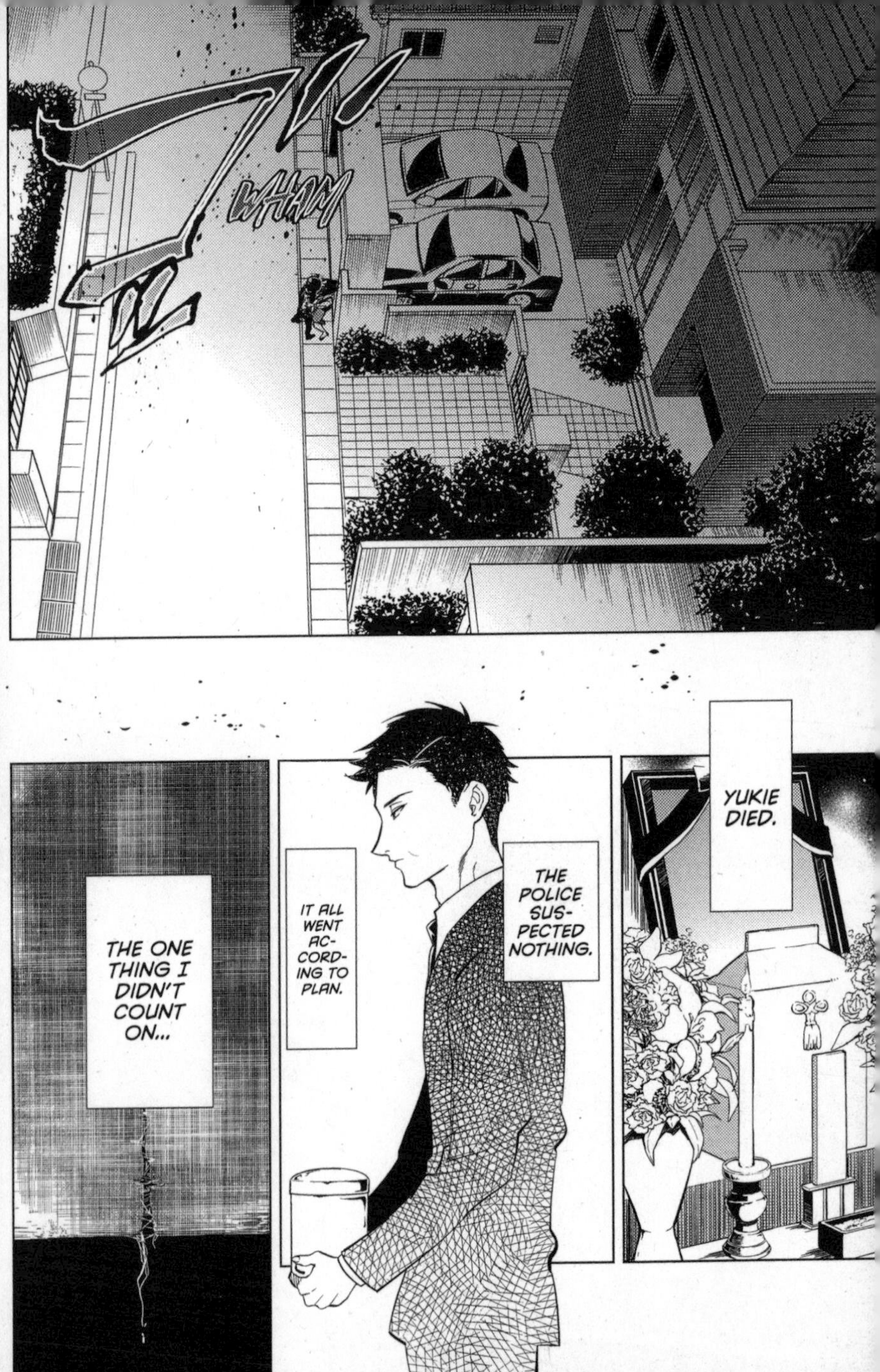
WHAM
YUKIE DIED.
THE POLICE SUSPECTED NOTHING.
IT ALL WENT ACCORDING TO PLAN.
THE ONE THING I DIDN'T COUNT ON...

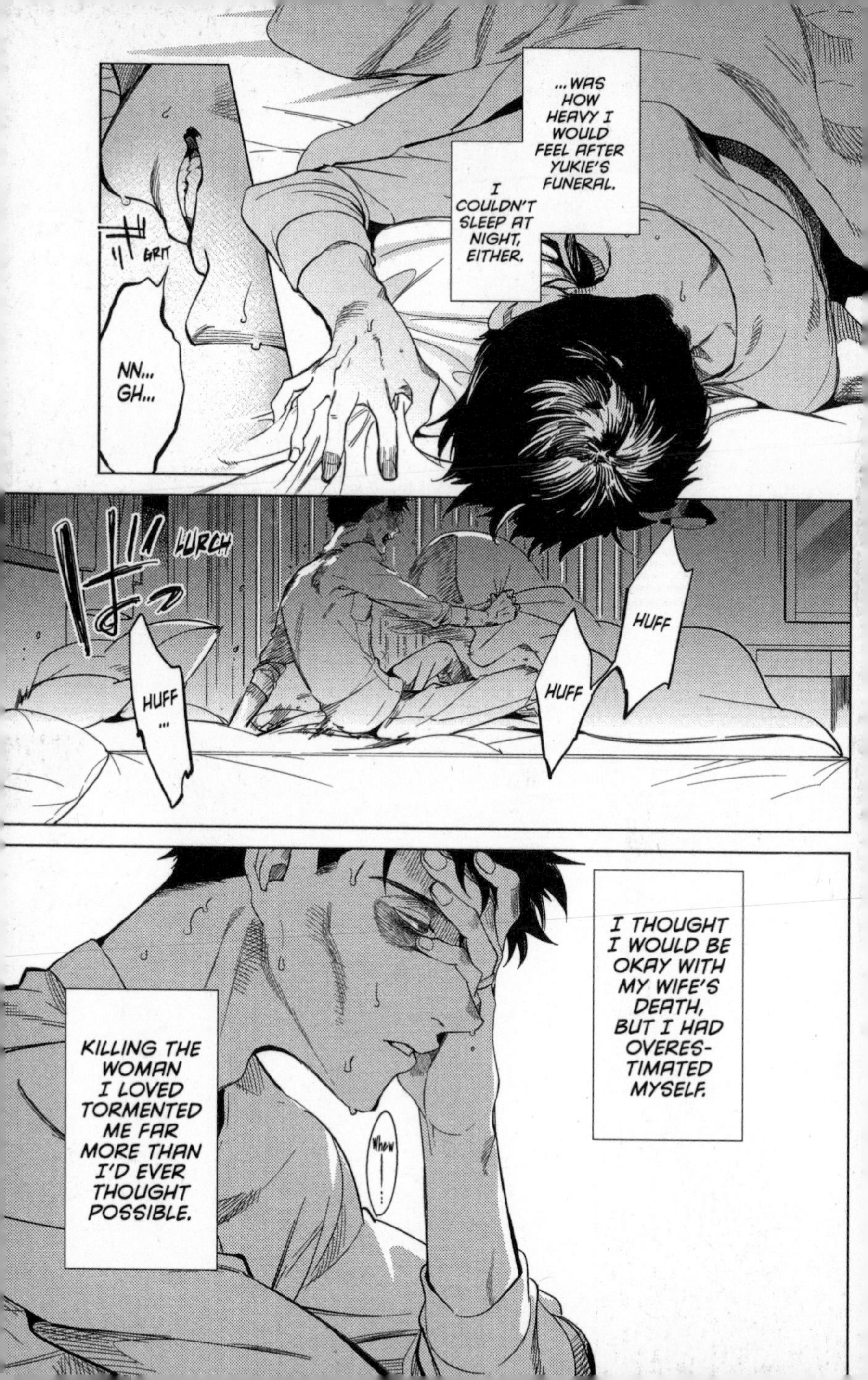
...WAS HOW HEAVY I WOULD FEEL AFTER YUKIE'S FUNERAL.
I COULDN'T SLEEP AT NIGHT, EITHER.
GRIT
NN... GH...
HUFF
HUFF
LURCH
HUFF...
I THOUGHT I WOULD BE OKAY WITH MY WIFE'S DEATH, BUT I HAD OVERES-TIMATED MYSELF.
Whew—...
KILLING THE WOMAN I LOVED TORMENTED ME FAR MORE THAN I'D EVER THOUGHT POSSIBLE.

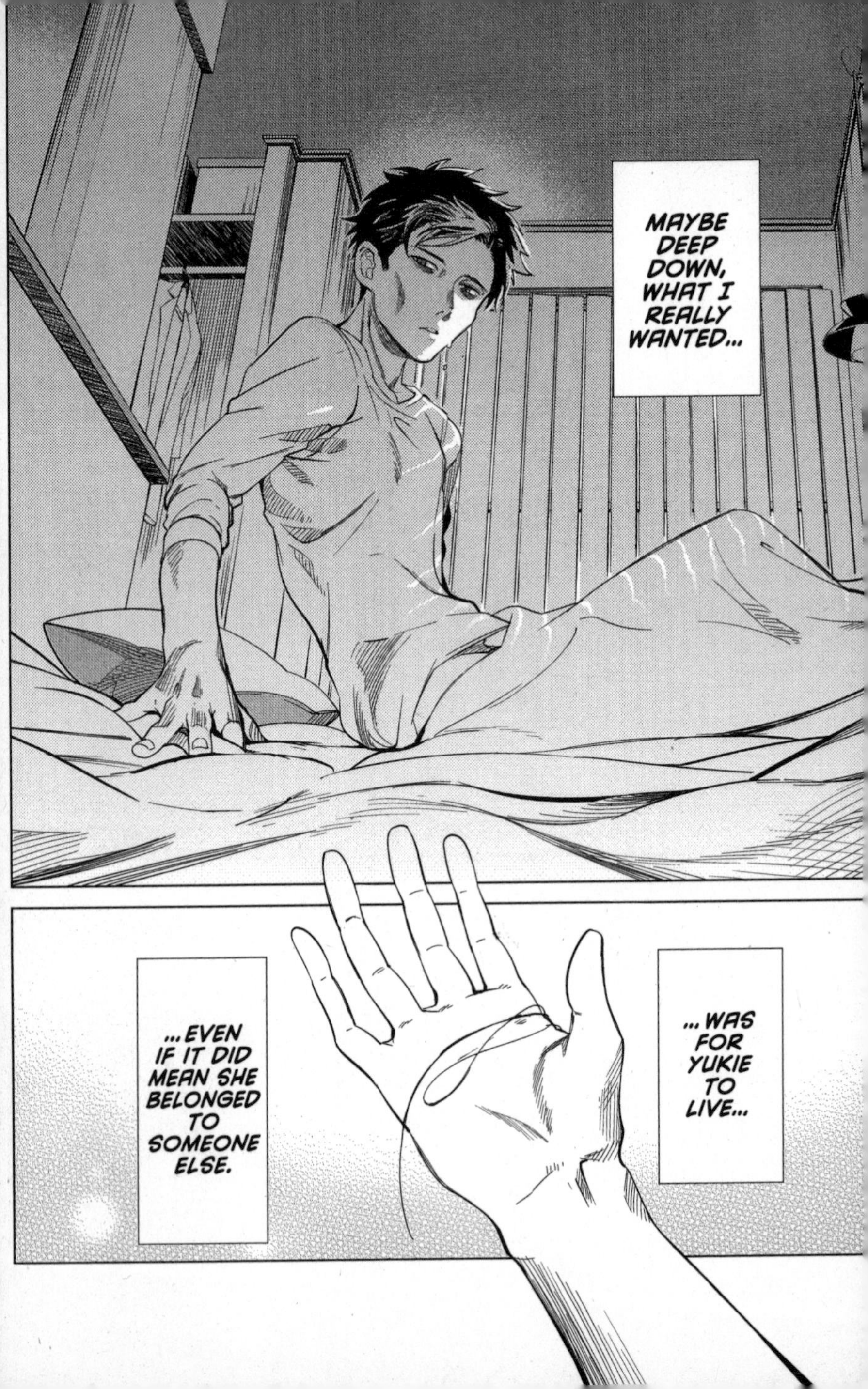
MAYBE DEEP DOWN, WHAT I REALLY WANTED...
...WAS FOR YUKIE TO LIVE...
...EVEN IF IT DID MEAN SHE BELONGED TO SOMEONE ELSE.

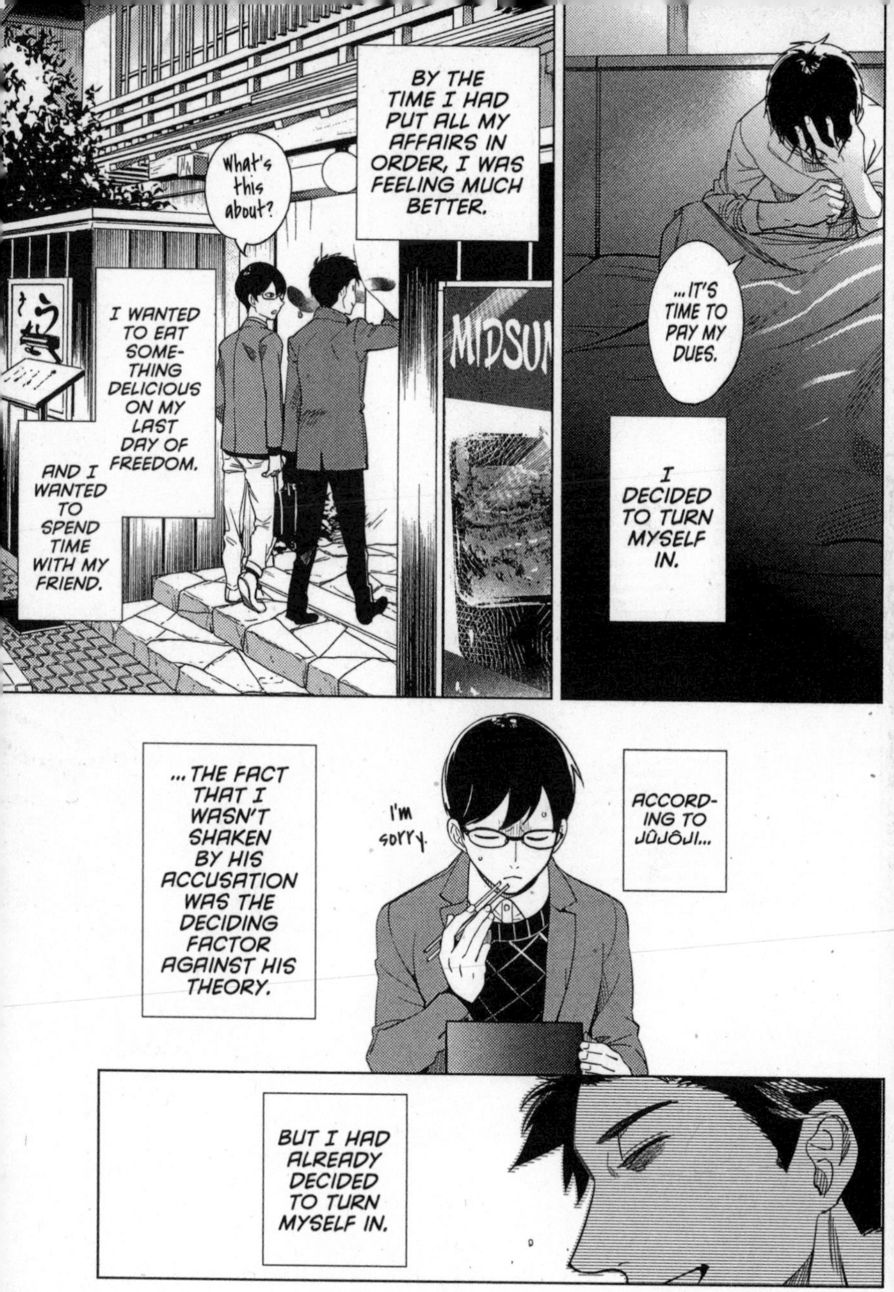
...IT'S TIME TO PAY MY DUES.
I DECIDED TO TURN MYSELF IN.
BY THE TIME I HAD PUT ALL MY AFFAIRS IN ORDER, I WAS FEELING MUCH BETTER.
MIDSUM
What's this about?
I WANTED TO EAT SOMETHING DELICIOUS ON MY LAST DAY OF FREEDOM.
AND I WANTED TO SPEND TIME WITH MY FRIEND.
ACCORDING TO JÛJÔJI...
I'm sorry.
...THE FACT THAT I WASN'T SHAKEN BY HIS ACCUSATION WAS THE DECIDING FACTOR AGAINST HIS THEORY.
BUT I HAD ALREADY DECIDED TO TURN MYSELF IN.

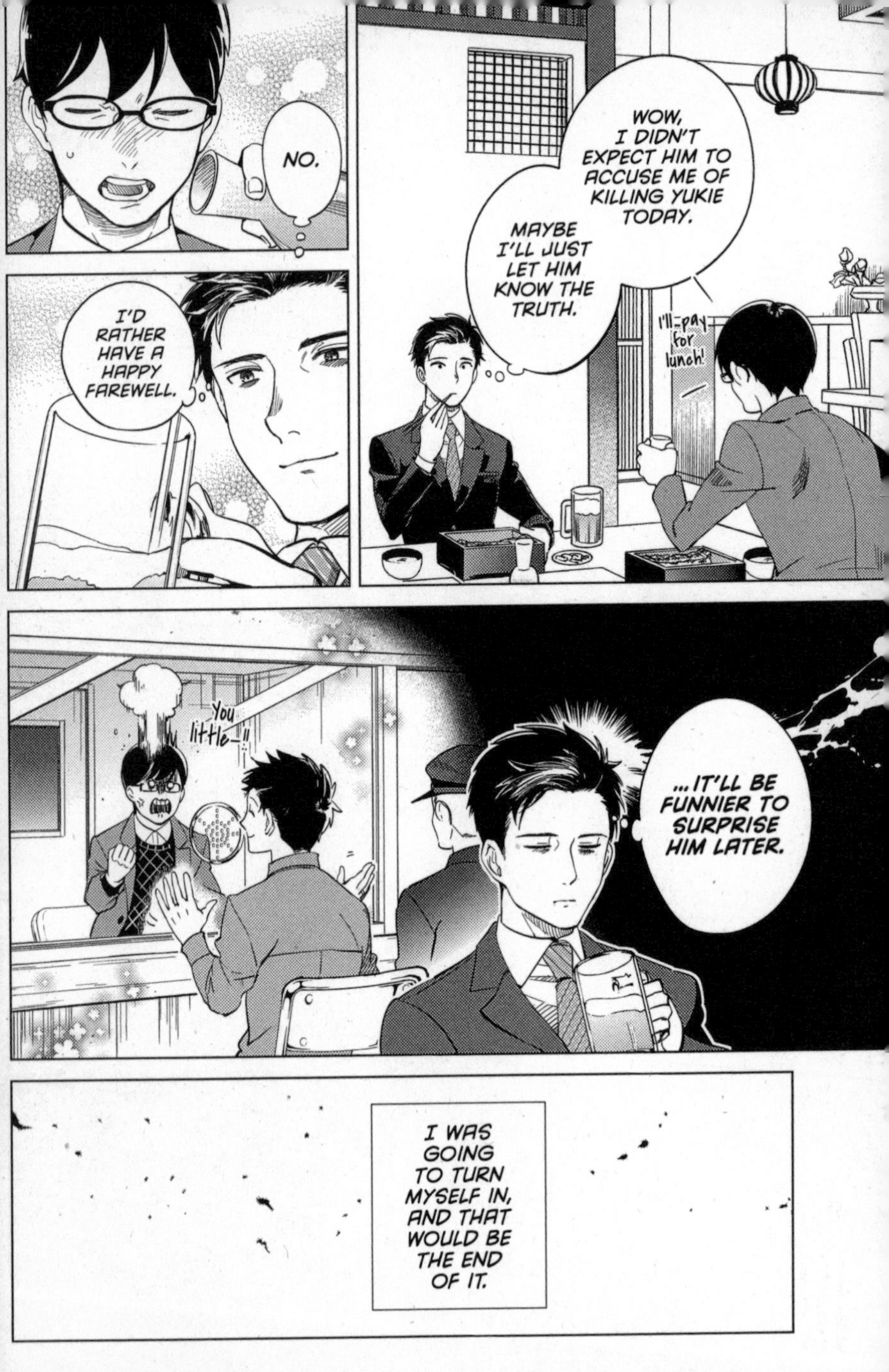
WOW, I DIDN'T EXPECT HIM TO ACCUSE ME OF KILLING YUKIE TODAY.
MAYBE I'LL JUST LET HIM KNOW THE TRUTH.
I'll pay for lunch!
NO.
I'D RATHER HAVE A HAPPY FAREWELL.
...IT'LL BE FUNNIER TO SURPRISE HIM LATER.
You little—!!
I WAS GOING TO TURN MYSELF IN, AND THAT WOULD BE THE END OF IT.

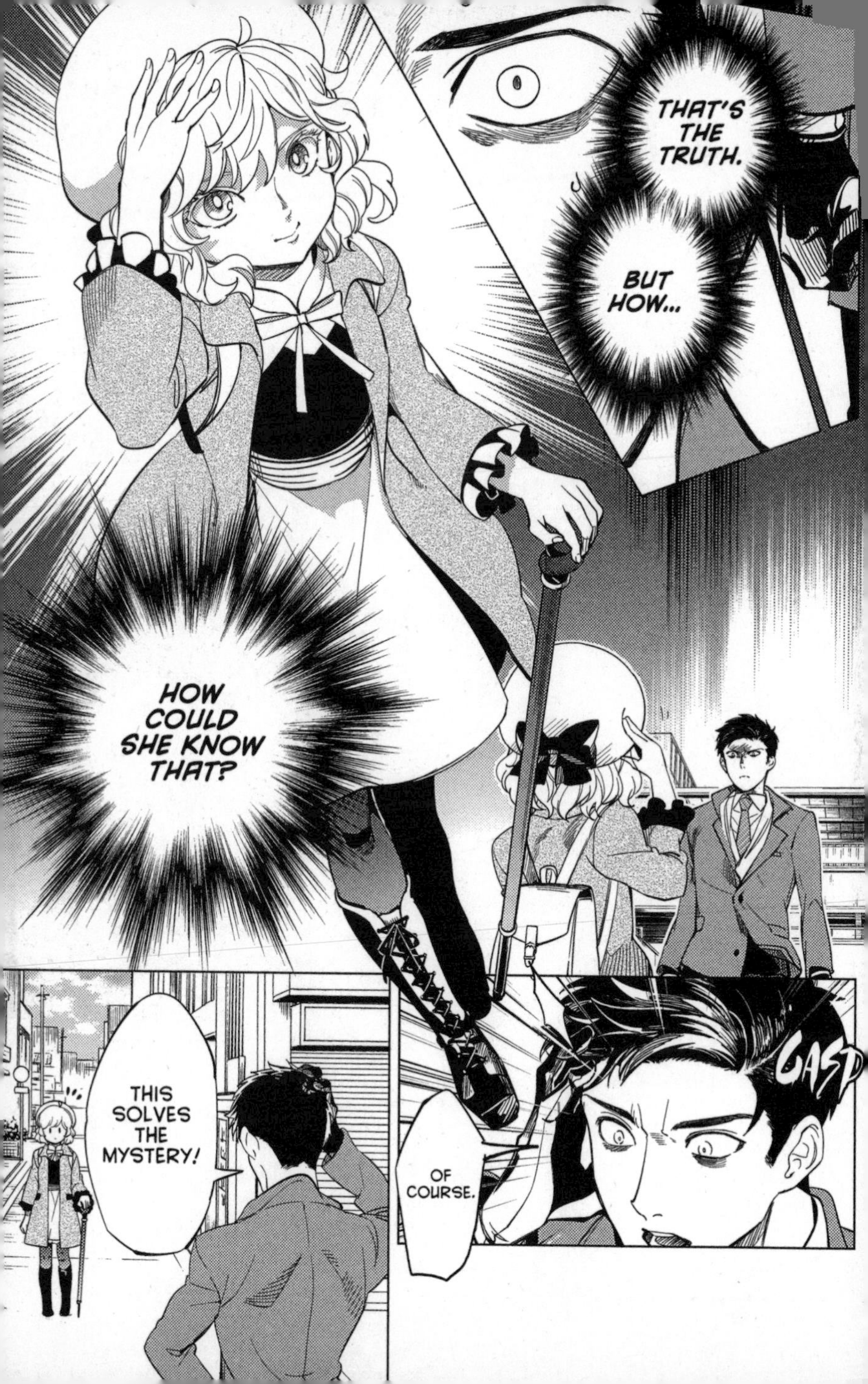
THAT'S THE TRUTH.
BUT HOW...
HOW COULD SHE KNOW THAT?
GASP
OF COURSE.
THIS SOLVES THE MYSTERY!

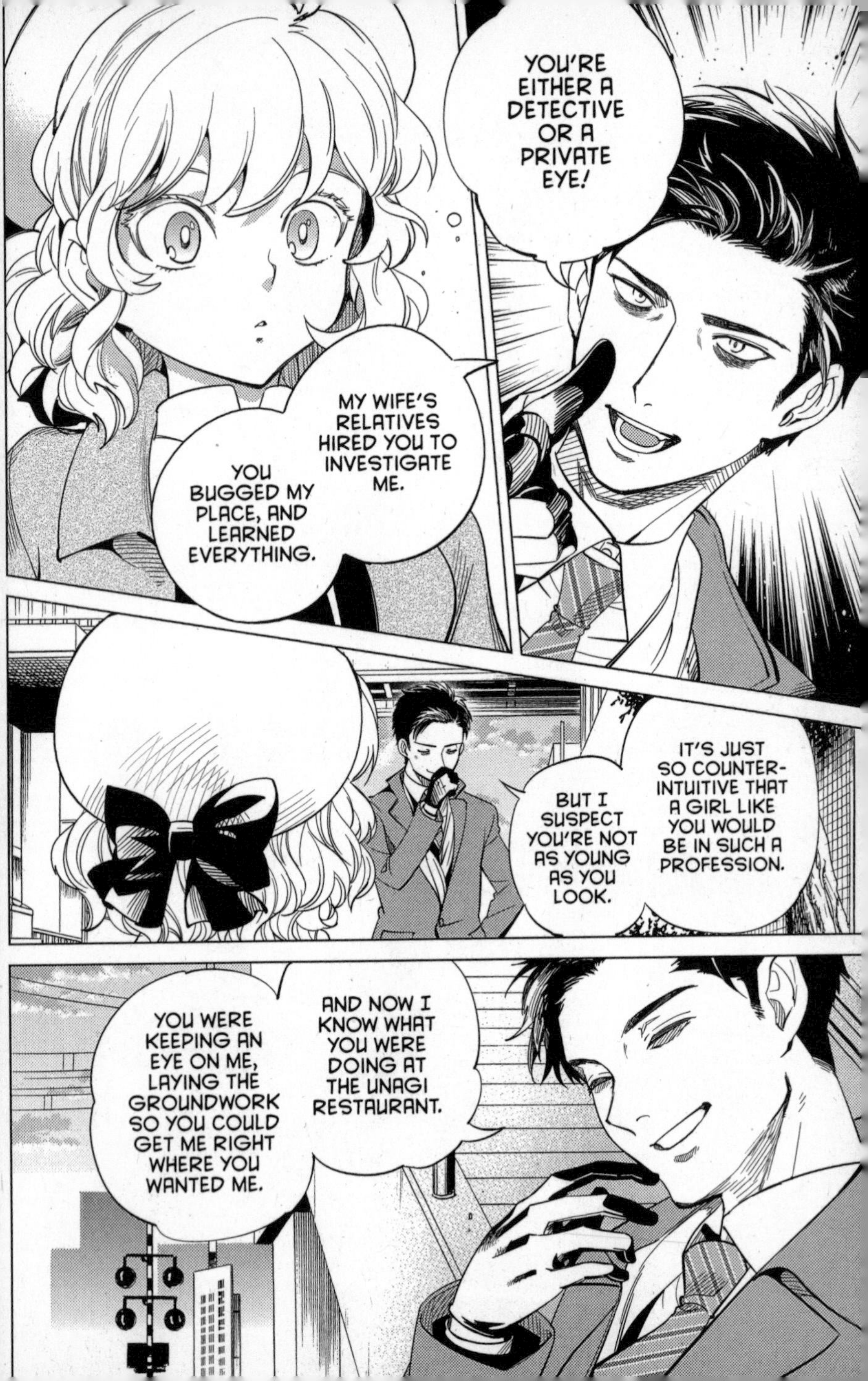
YOU'RE EITHER A DETECTIVE OR A PRIVATE EYE!
MY WIFE'S RELATIVES HIRED YOU TO INVESTIGATE ME.
YOU BUGGED MY PLACE, AND LEARNED EVERYTHING.
IT'S JUST SO COUNTER-INTUITIVE THAT A GIRL LIKE YOU WOULD BE IN SUCH A PROFESSION.
BUT I SUSPECT YOU'RE NOT AS YOUNG AS YOU LOOK.
AND NOW I KNOW WHAT YOU WERE DOING AT THE UNAGI RESTAURANT.
YOU WERE KEEPING AN EYE ON ME, LAYING THE GROUNDWORK SO YOU COULD GET ME RIGHT WHERE YOU WANTED ME.

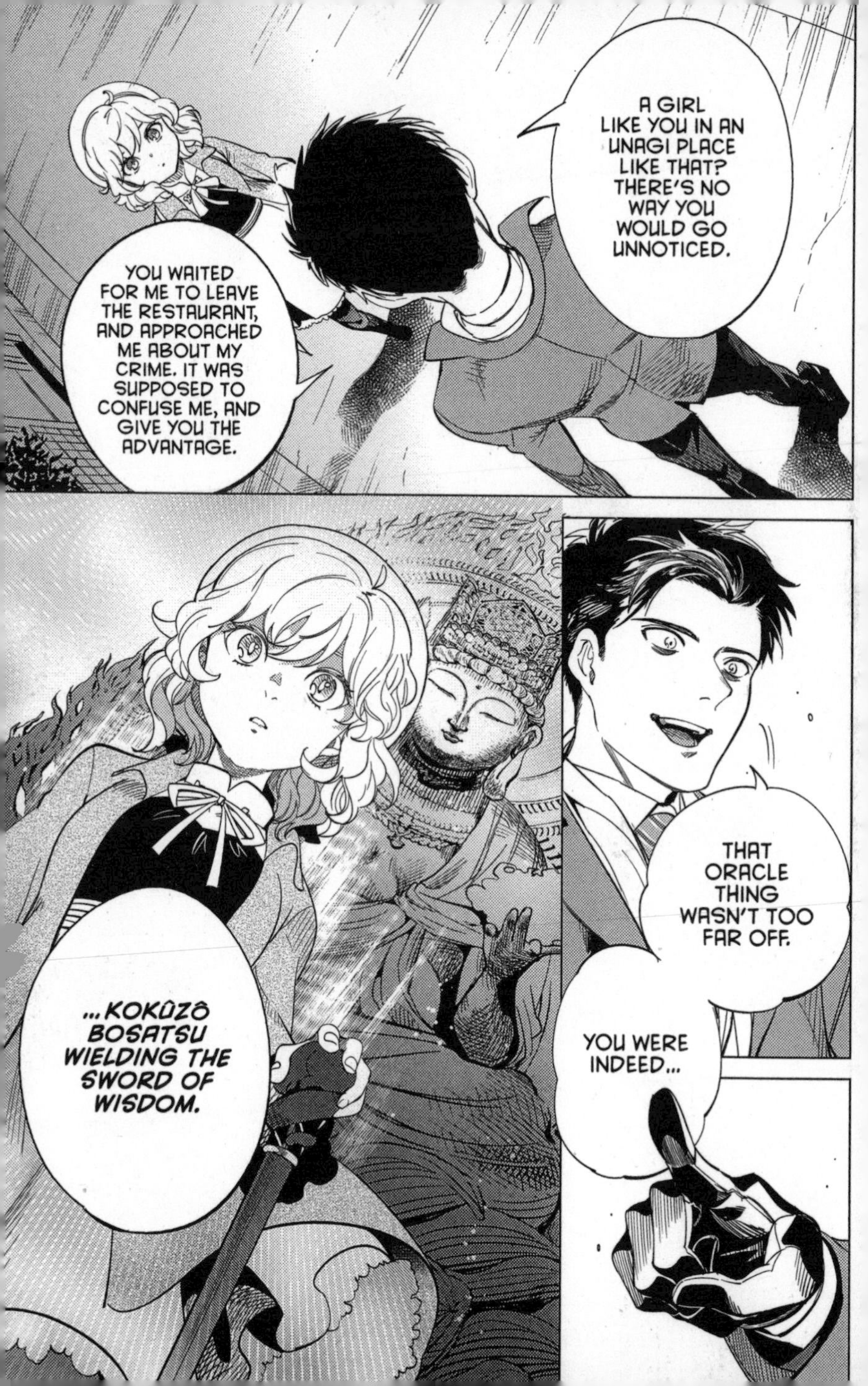
A GIRL LIKE YOU IN AN UNAGI PLACE LIKE THAT? THERE'S NO WAY YOU WOULD GO UNNOTICED.
YOU WAITED FOR ME TO LEAVE THE RESTAURANT, AND APPROACHED ME ABOUT MY CRIME. IT WAS SUPPOSED TO CONFUSE ME, AND GIVE YOU THE ADVANTAGE.
THAT ORACLE THING WASN'T TOO FAR OFF.
YOU WERE INDEED...
...KOKÛZÔ BOSATSU WIELDING THE SWORD OF WISDOM.

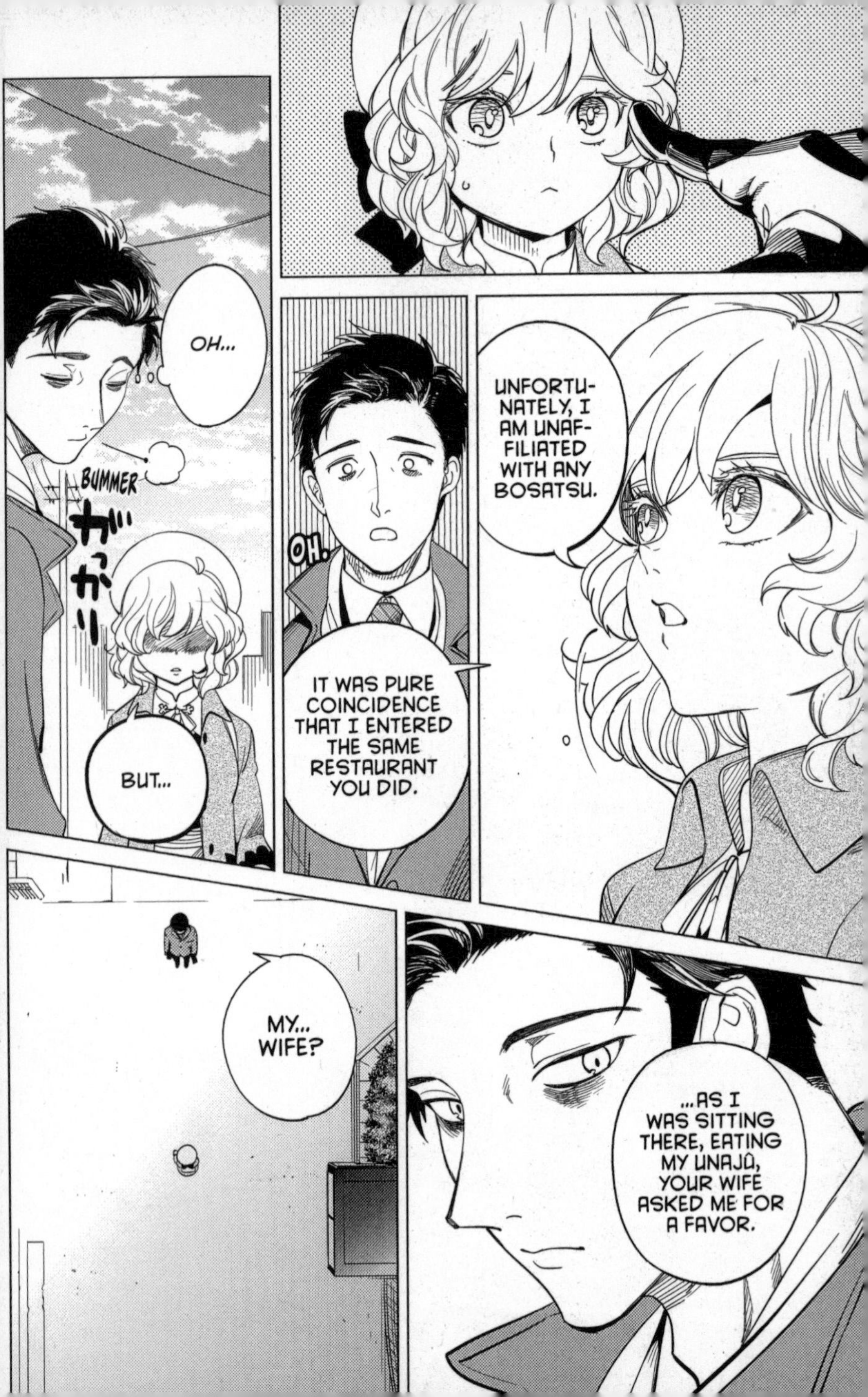
UNFORTUNATELY, I AM UNAFFILIATED WITH ANY BOSATSU.
OH.
IT WAS PURE COINCIDENCE THAT I ENTERED THE SAME RESTAURANT YOU DID.
OH...
BUMMER
がっかり
BUT...
...AS I WAS SITTING THERE, EATING MY UNAJŪ, YOUR WIFE ASKED ME FOR A FAVOR.
MY... WIFE?

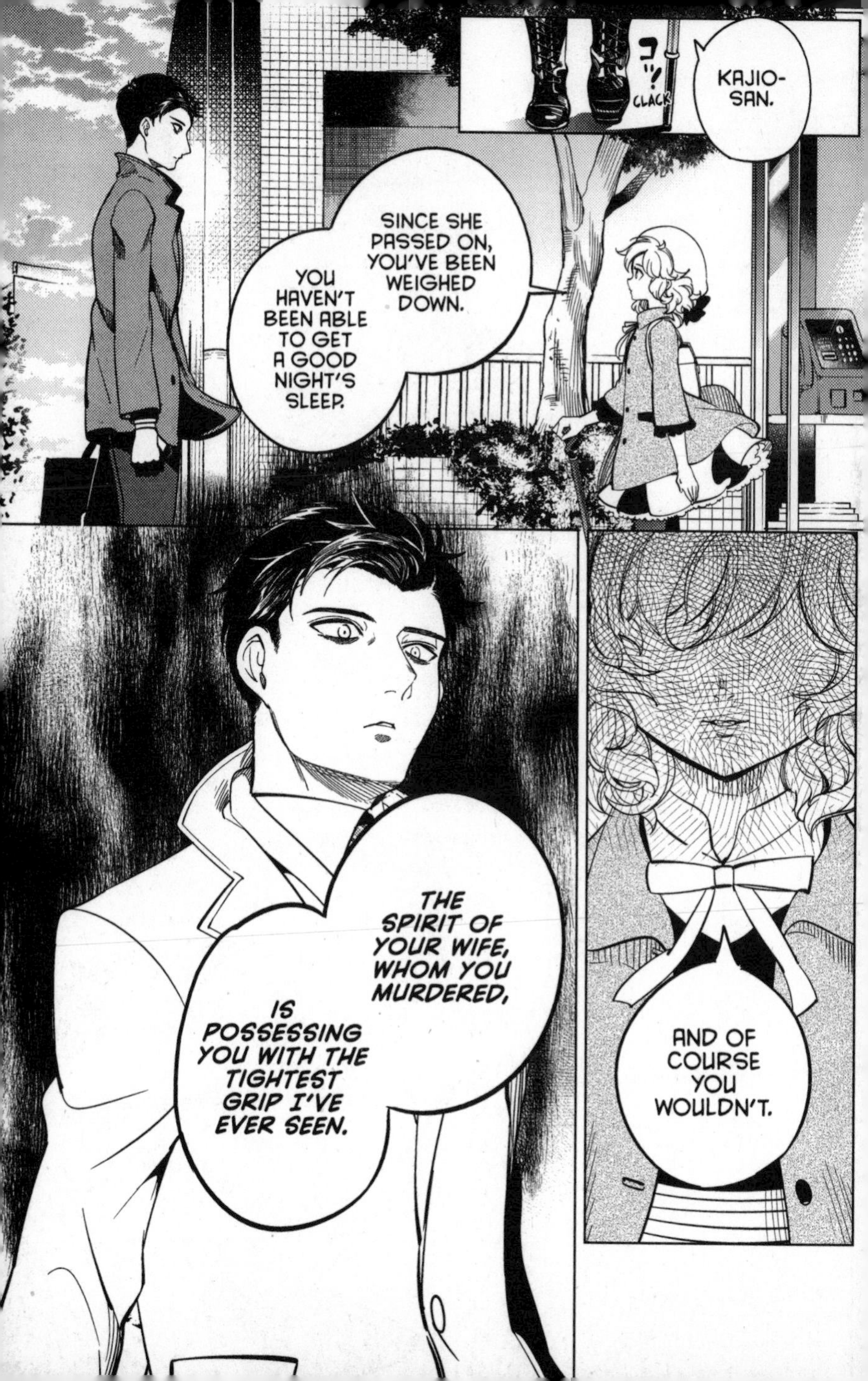
KAJIO-SAN.
コッ!
CLACK
SINCE SHE PASSED ON, YOU'VE BEEN WEIGHED DOWN.
YOU HAVEN'T BEEN ABLE TO GET A GOOD NIGHT'S SLEEP.
AND OF COURSE YOU WOULDN'T.
THE SPIRIT OF YOUR WIFE, WHOM YOU MURDERED,
IS POSSESSING YOU WITH THE TIGHTEST GRIP I'VE EVER SEEN.

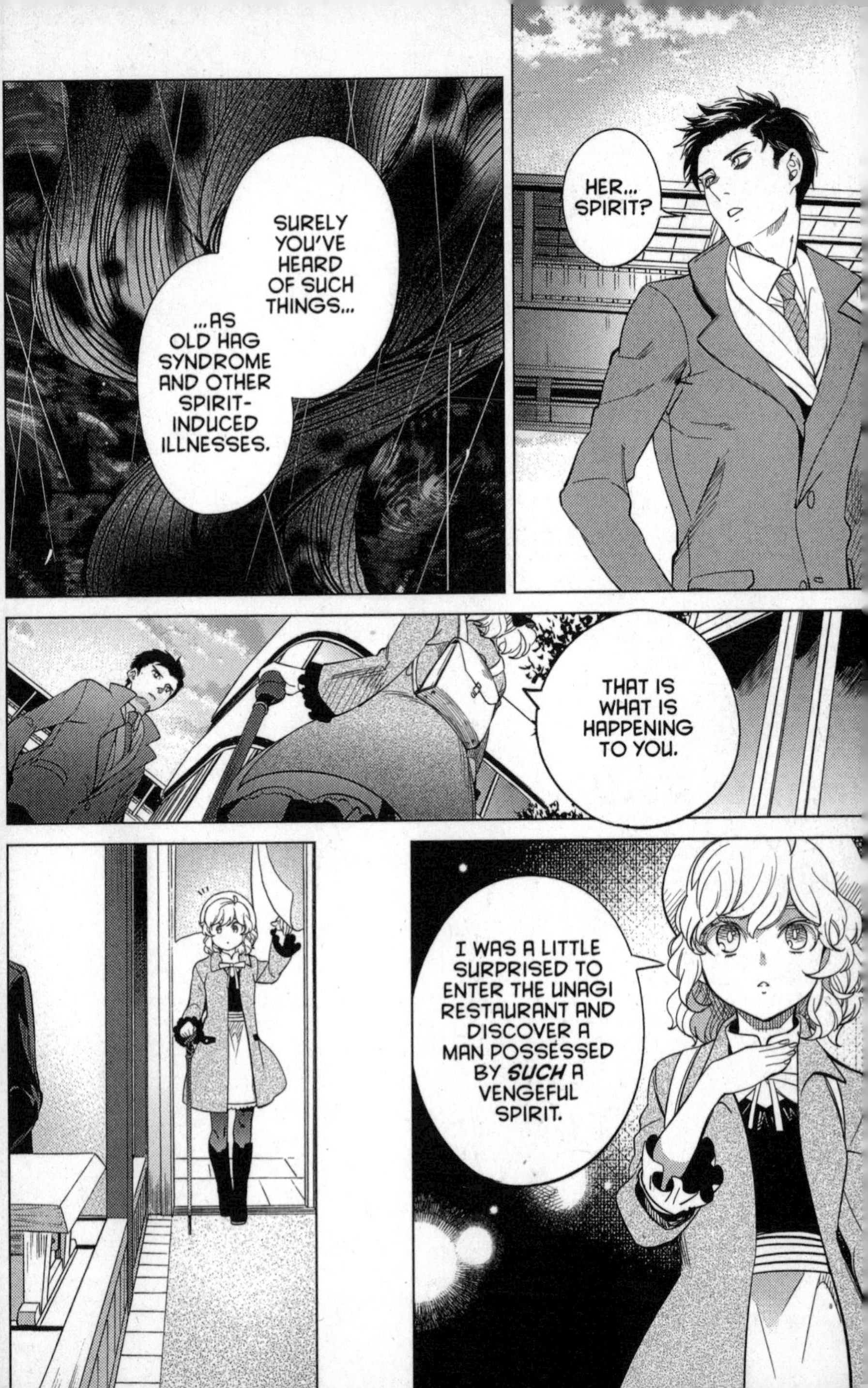
HER... SPIRIT?
SURELY YOU'VE HEARD OF SUCH THINGS...
...AS OLD HAG SYNDROME AND OTHER SPIRIT-INDUCED ILLNESSES.
THAT IS WHAT IS HAPPENING TO YOU.
I WAS A LITTLE SURPRISED TO ENTER THE UNAGI RESTAURANT AND DISCOVER A MAN POSSESSED BY *SUCH* A VENGEFUL SPIRIT.

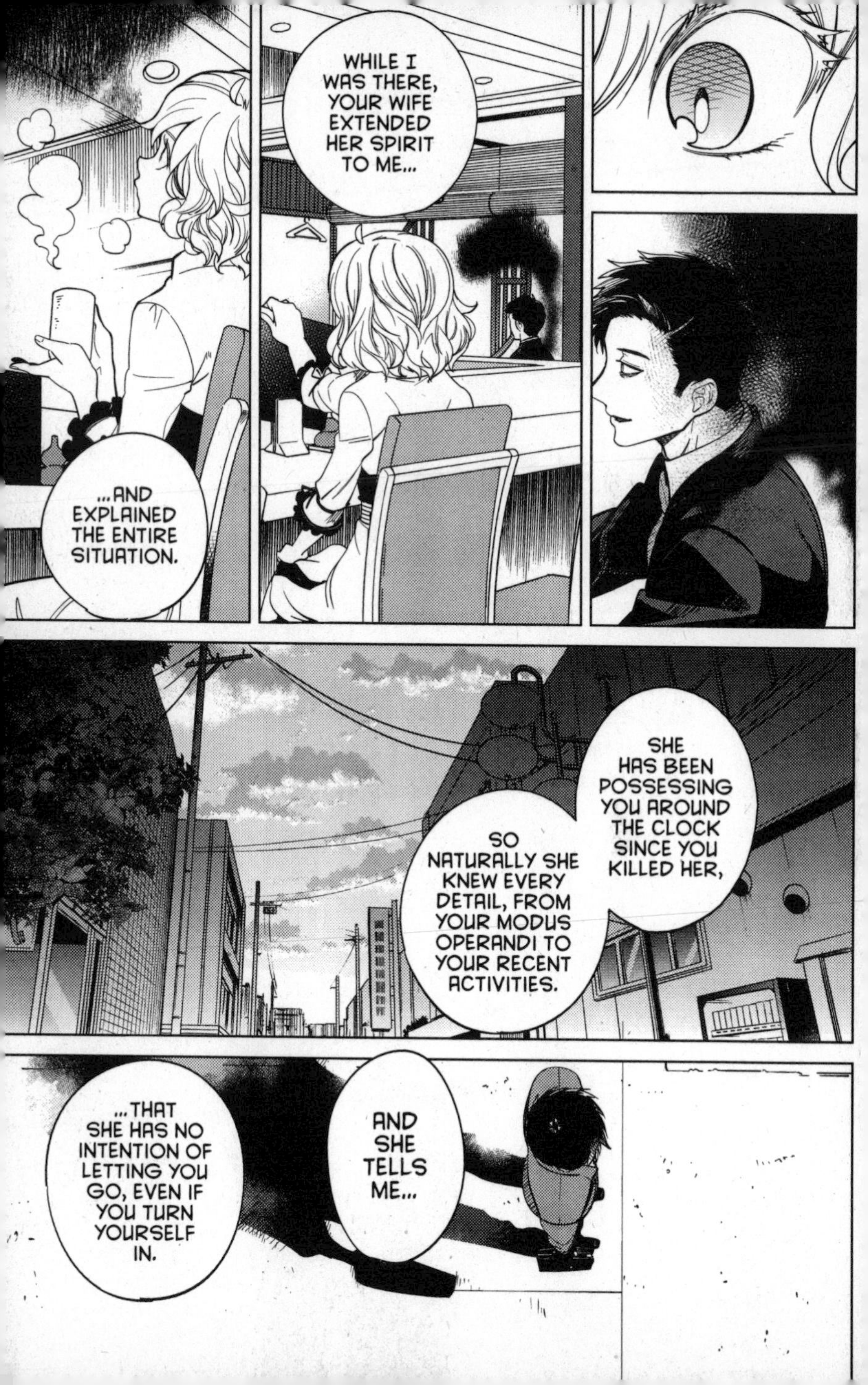
WHILE I WAS THERE, YOUR WIFE EXTENDED HER SPIRIT TO ME...
...AND EXPLAINED THE ENTIRE SITUATION.
SHE HAS BEEN POSSESSING YOU AROUND THE CLOCK SINCE YOU KILLED HER,
SO NATURALLY SHE KNEW EVERY DETAIL, FROM YOUR MODUS OPERANDI TO YOUR RECENT ACTIVITIES.
AND SHE TELLS ME...
...THAT SHE HAS NO INTENTION OF LETTING YOU GO, EVEN IF YOU TURN YOURSELF IN.

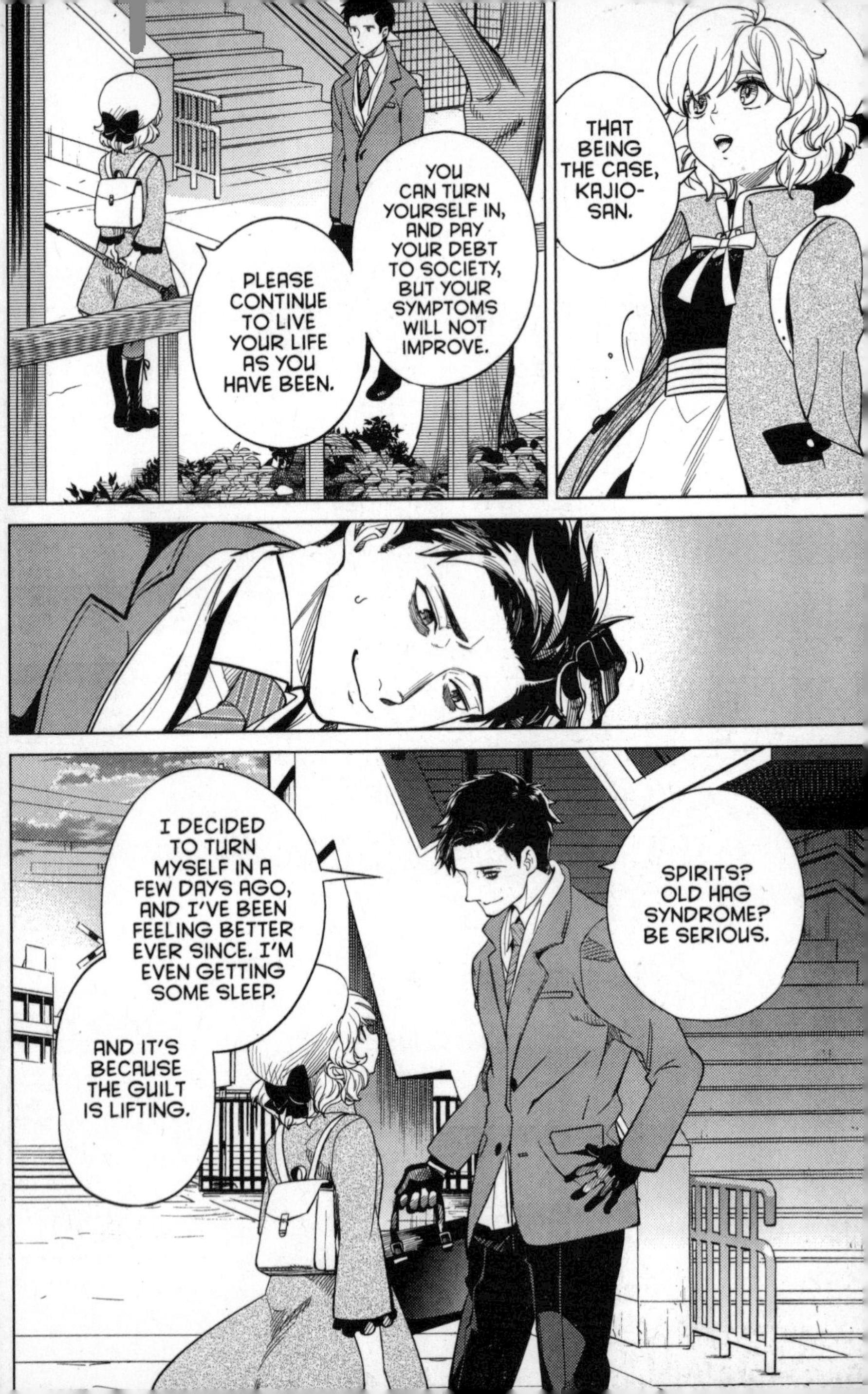
THAT BEING THE CASE, KAJIO-SAN.
YOU CAN TURN YOURSELF IN, AND PAY YOUR DEBT TO SOCIETY, BUT YOUR SYMPTOMS WILL NOT IMPROVE.
PLEASE CONTINUE TO LIVE YOUR LIFE AS YOU HAVE BEEN.
SPIRITS? OLD HAG SYNDROME? BE SERIOUS.
I DECIDED TO TURN MYSELF IN A FEW DAYS AGO, AND I'VE BEEN FEELING BETTER EVER SINCE. I'M EVEN GETTING SOME SLEEP.
AND IT'S BECAUSE THE GUILT IS LIFTING.

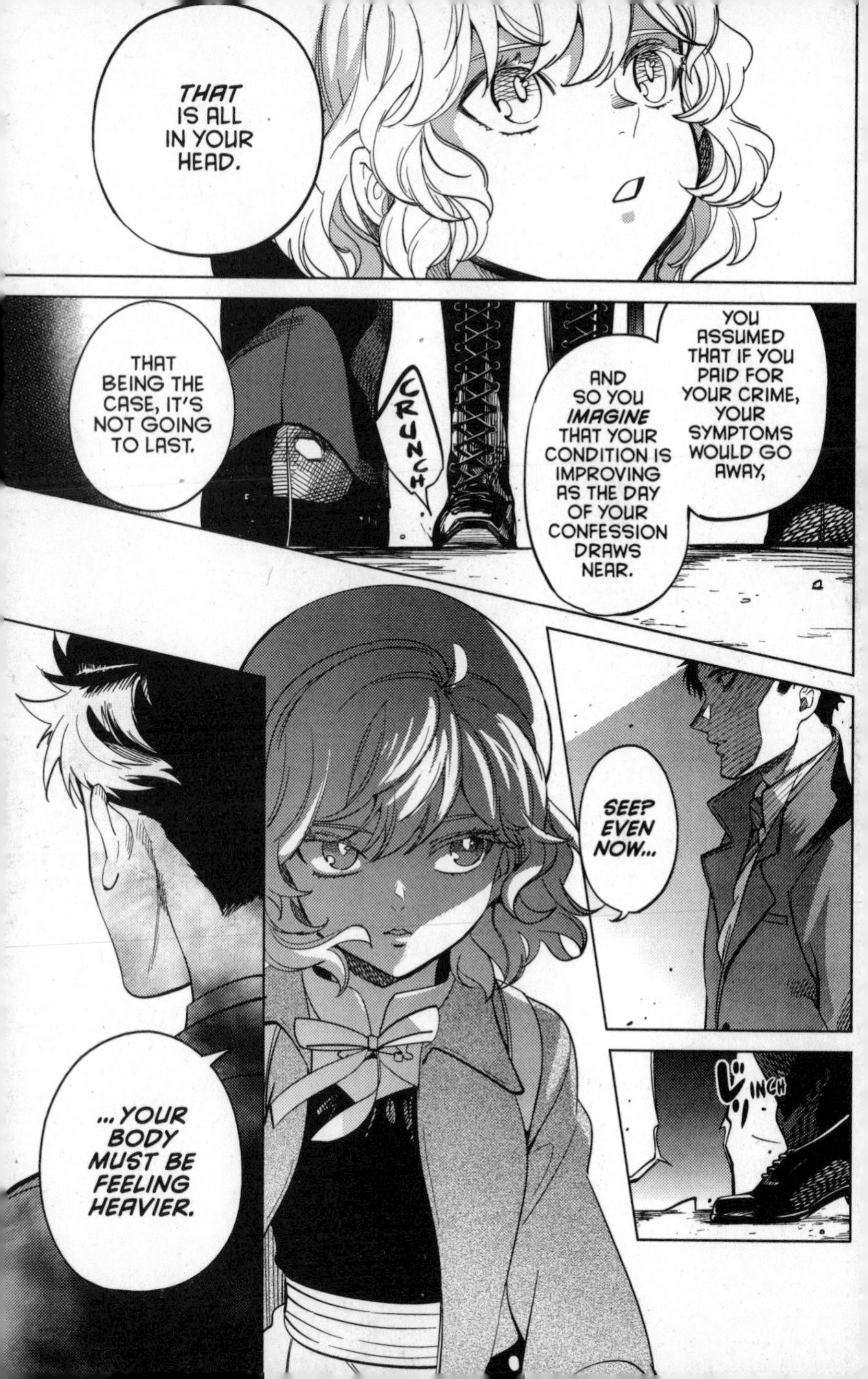
THAT IS ALL IN YOUR HEAD.
YOU ASSUMED THAT IF YOU PAID FOR YOUR CRIME, YOUR SYMPTOMS WOULD GO AWAY,
AND SO YOU IMAGINE THAT YOUR CONDITION IS IMPROVING AS THE DAY OF YOUR CONFESSION DRAWS NEAR.
CRUNCH
THAT BEING THE CASE, IT'S NOT GOING TO LAST.
SEE? EVEN NOW...
ジINCH
...YOUR BODY MUST BE FEELING HEAVIER.

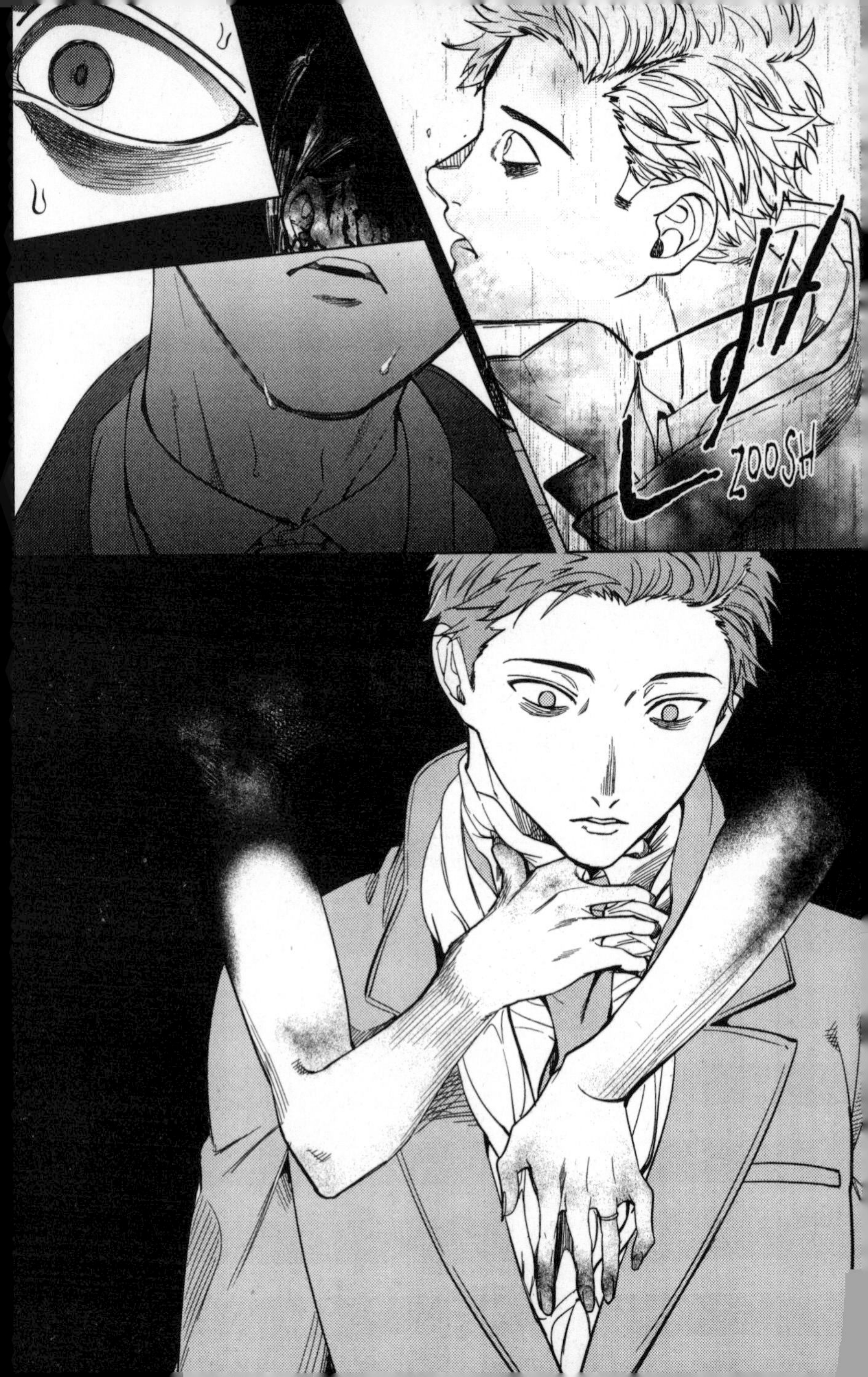
ZOOSH

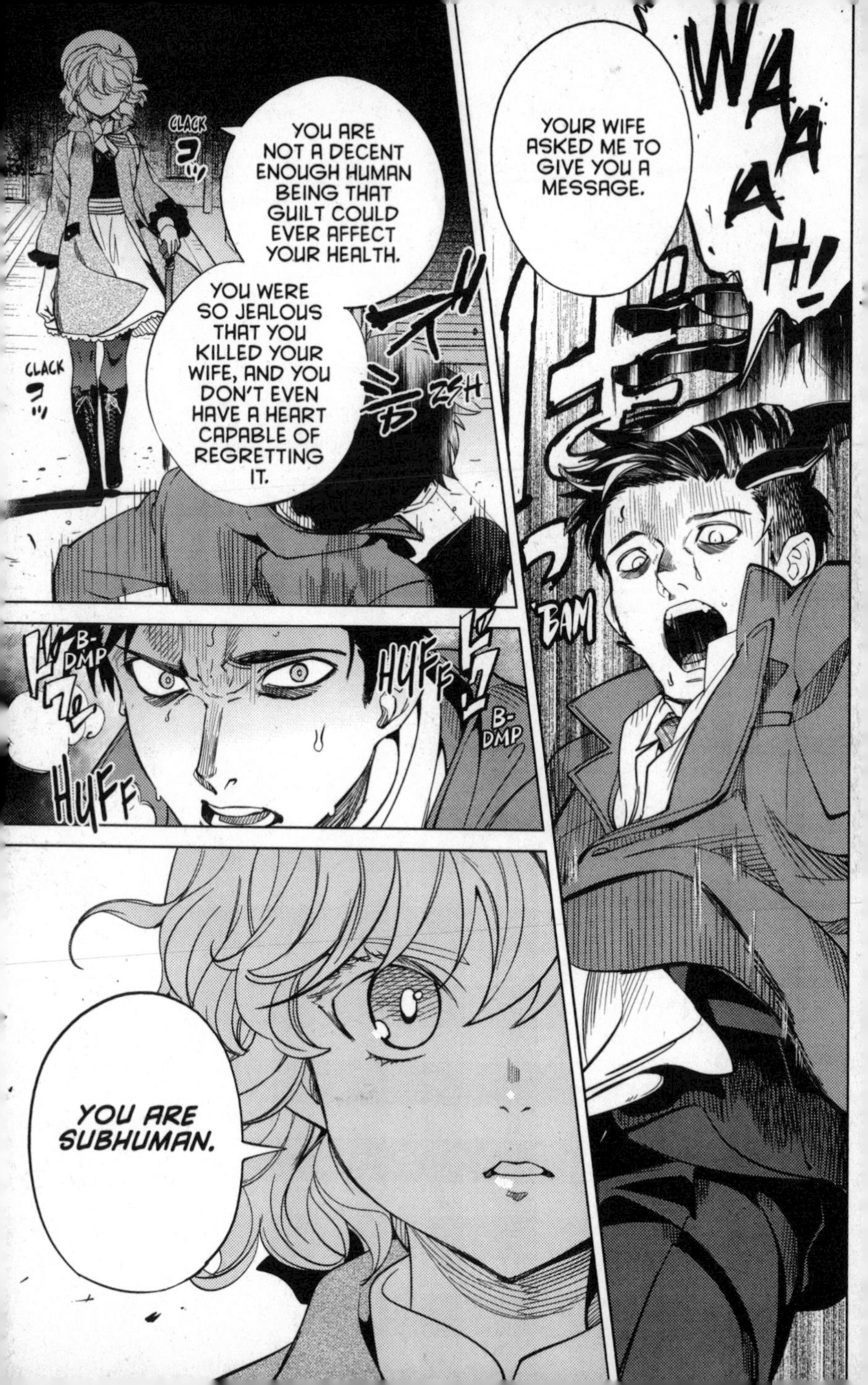
WAAAH!
YOUR WIFE ASKED ME TO GIVE YOU A MESSAGE.
BAM
CLACK
YOU ARE NOT A DECENT ENOUGH HUMAN BEING THAT GUILT COULD EVER AFFECT YOUR HEALTH.
YOU WERE SO JEALOUS THAT YOU KILLED YOUR WIFE, AND YOU DON'T EVEN HAVE A HEART CAPABLE OF REGRETTING IT.
ZSH
CLACK
HUFFF
B-DMP
B-DMP
HUFFF
YOU ARE SUBHUMAN.

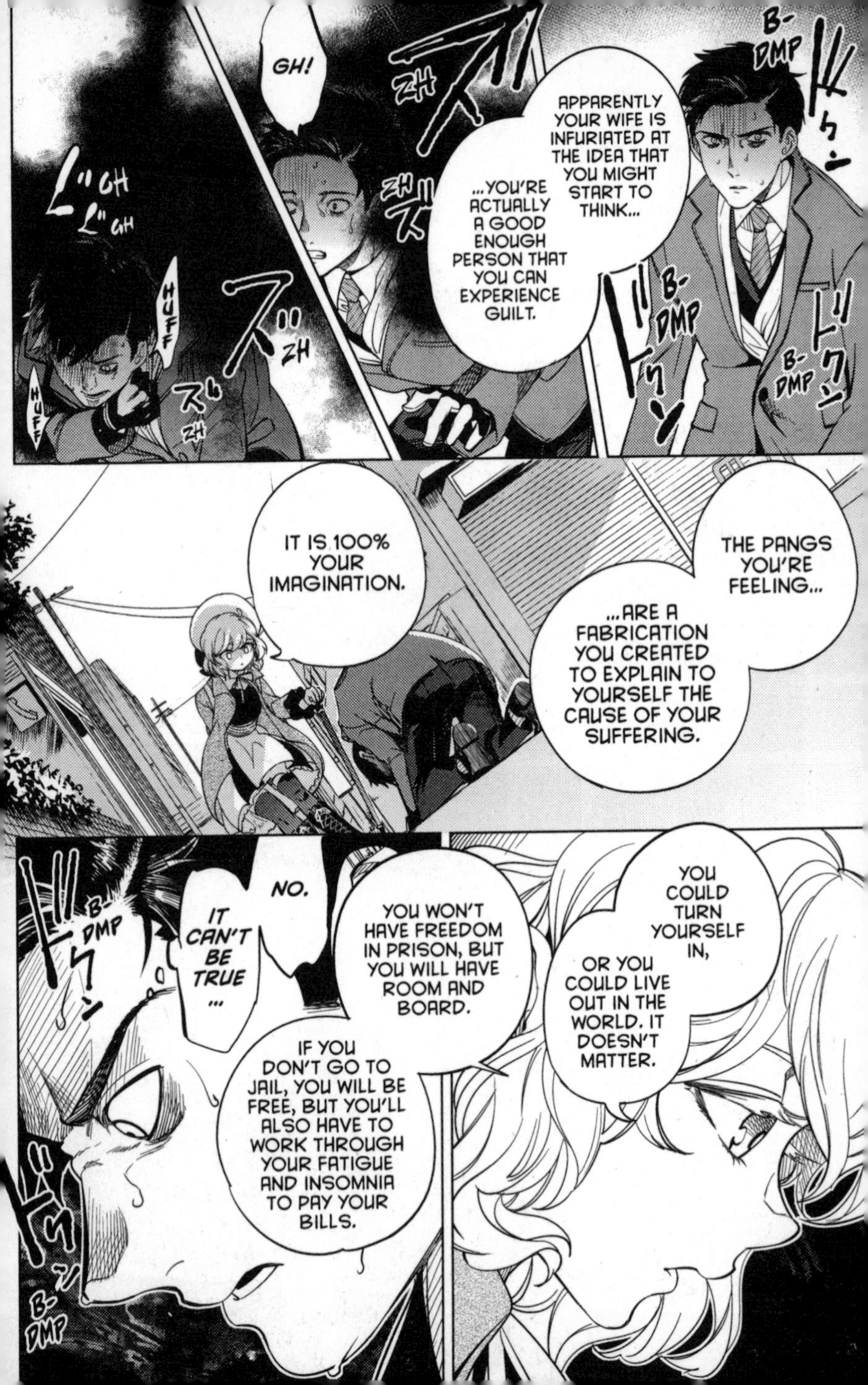
B-DMP
APPARENTLY YOUR WIFE IS INFURIATED AT THE IDEA THAT YOU MIGHT START TO THINK...
...YOU'RE ACTUALLY A GOOD ENOUGH PERSON THAT YOU CAN EXPERIENCE GUILT.
B-DMP
B-DMP
ZH
ZH
GH!
ZH
GH
GH
HUFF
HUFF
ZH
THE PANGS YOU'RE FEELING...
...ARE A FABRICATION YOU CREATED TO EXPLAIN TO YOURSELF THE CAUSE OF YOUR SUFFERING.
IT IS 100% YOUR IMAGINATION.
YOU COULD TURN YOURSELF IN,
OR YOU COULD LIVE OUT IN THE WORLD. IT DOESN'T MATTER.
YOU WON'T HAVE FREEDOM IN PRISON, BUT YOU WILL HAVE ROOM AND BOARD.
IF YOU DON'T GO TO JAIL, YOU WILL BE FREE, BUT YOU'LL ALSO HAVE TO WORK THROUGH YOUR FATIGUE AND INSOMNIA TO PAY YOUR BILLS.
NO.
IT CAN'T BE TRUE...
B-DMP
B-DMP

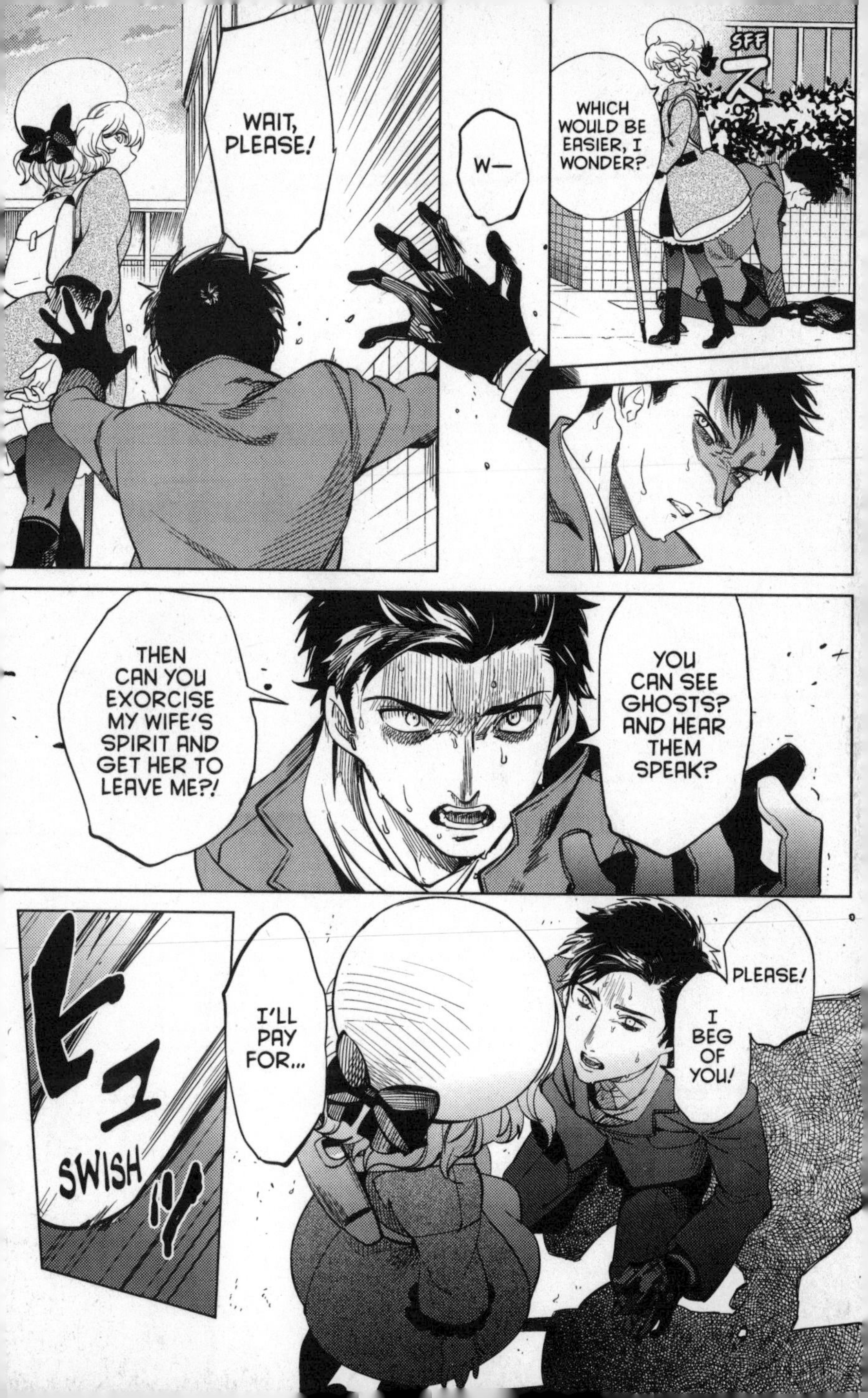
SFF
ス
WHICH WOULD BE EASIER, I WONDER?
W—
WAIT, PLEASE!
YOU CAN SEE GHOSTS? AND HEAR THEM SPEAK?
THEN CAN YOU EXORCISE MY WIFE'S SPIRIT AND GET HER TO LEAVE ME?!
PLEASE!
I BEG OF YOU!
I'LL PAY FOR...
ヒュ
SWISH

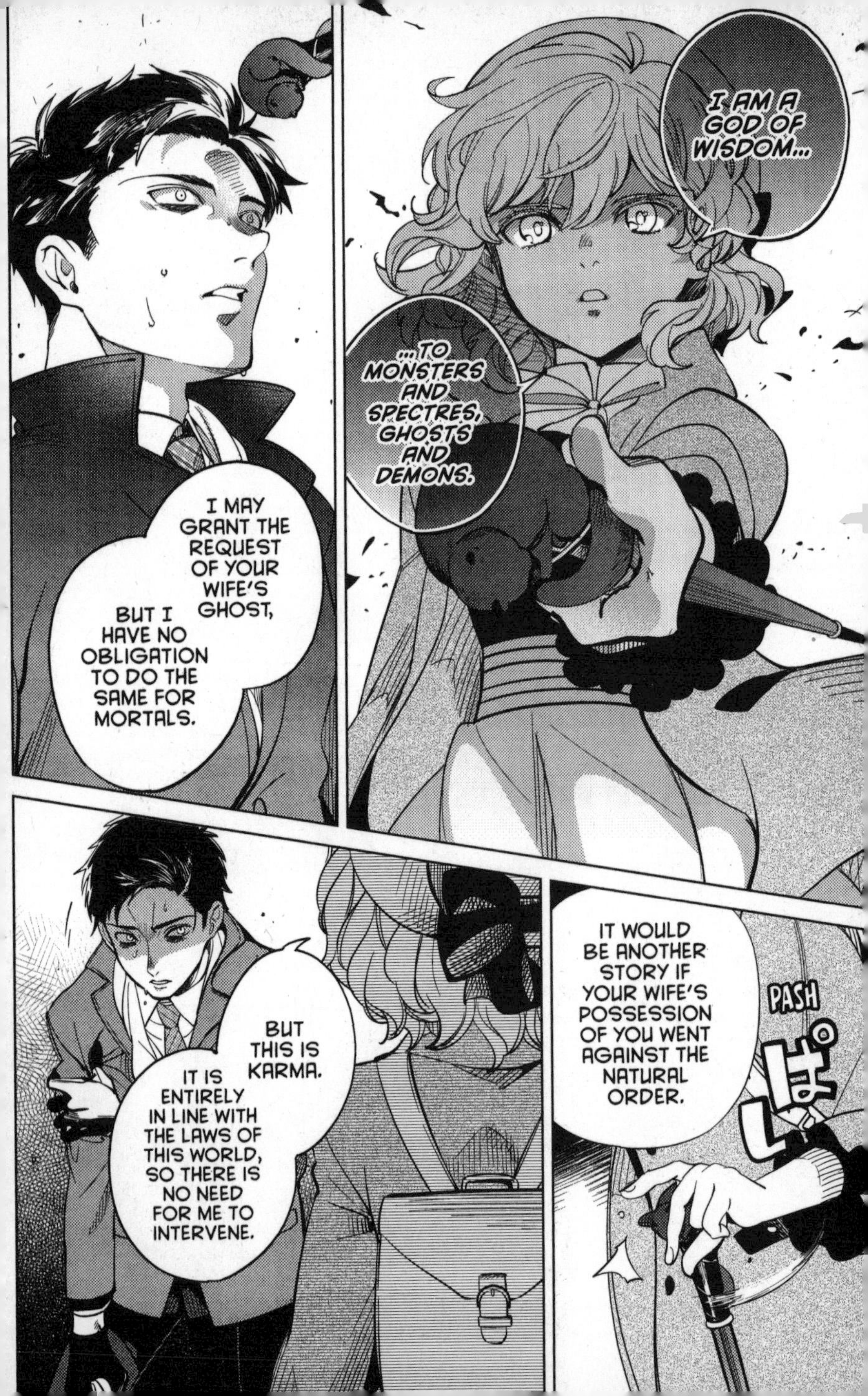
I AM A GOD OF WISDOM...
...TO MONSTERS AND SPECTRES, GHOSTS AND DEMONS.
I MAY GRANT THE REQUEST OF YOUR WIFE'S GHOST,
BUT I HAVE NO OBLIGATION TO DO THE SAME FOR MORTALS.
IT WOULD BE ANOTHER STORY IF YOUR WIFE'S POSSESSION OF YOU WENT AGAINST THE NATURAL ORDER.
PASH
ぱし
BUT THIS IS KARMA.
IT IS ENTIRELY IN LINE WITH THE LAWS OF THIS WORLD, SO THERE IS NO NEED FOR ME TO INTERVENE.

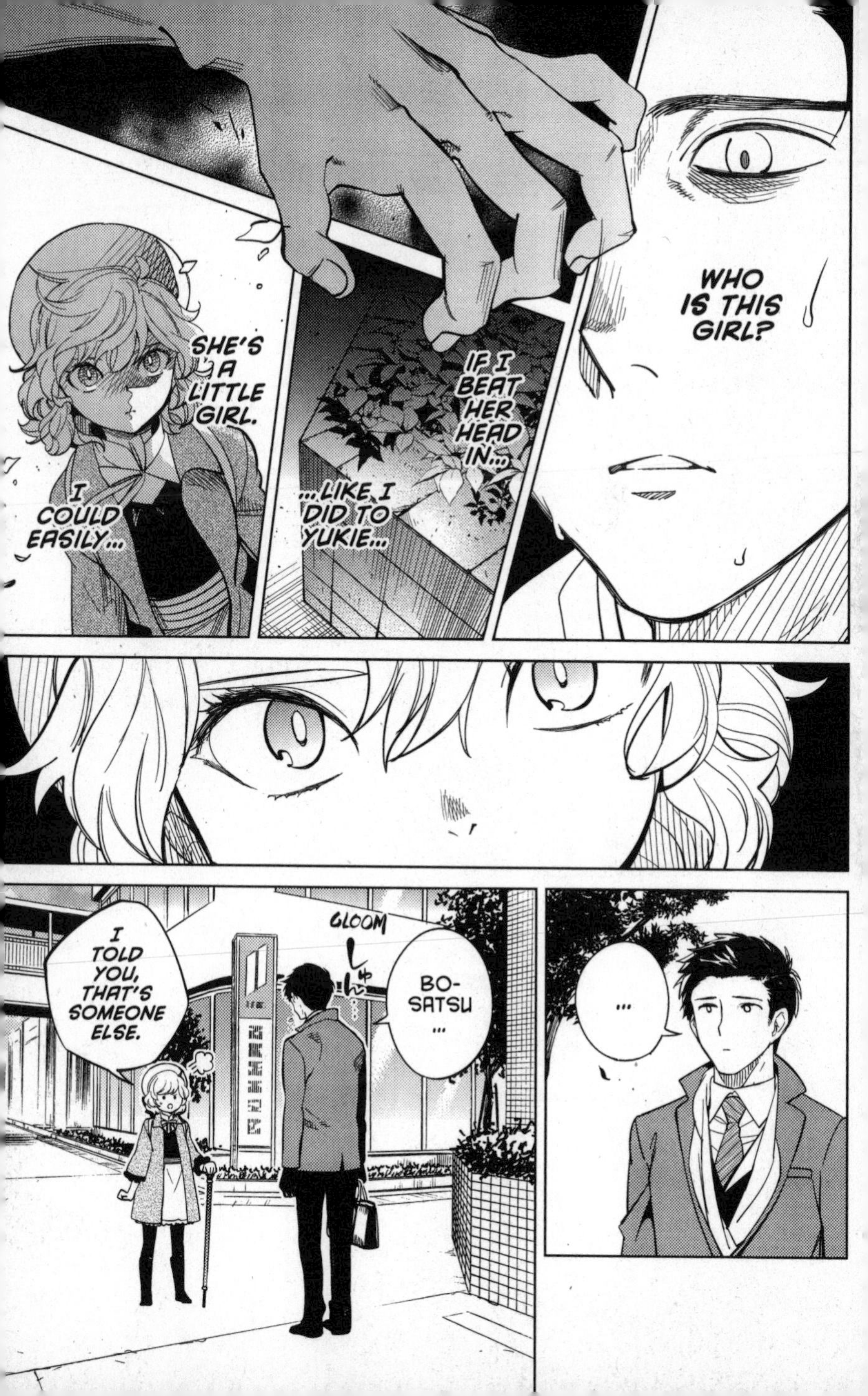

WHO IS THIS GIRL?
IF I BEAT HER HEAD IN...
...LIKE I DID TO YUKIE...
SHE'S A LITTLE GIRL.
I COULD EASILY...
...
BO-SATSU ...
GLOOM
I TOLD YOU, THAT'S SOMEONE ELSE.

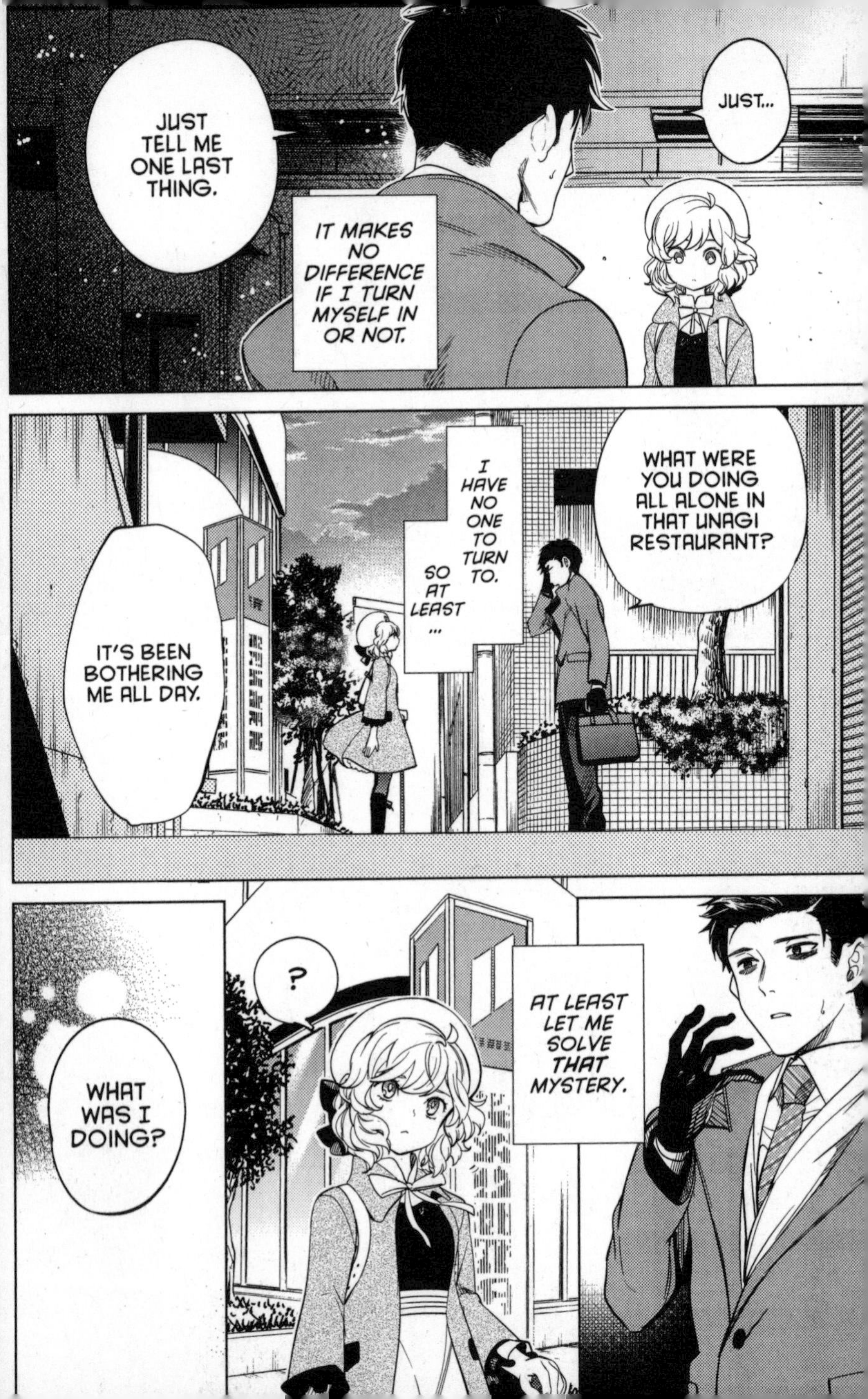
JUST...
JUST TELL ME ONE LAST THING.
IT MAKES NO DIFFERENCE IF I TURN MYSELF IN OR NOT.
WHAT WERE YOU DOING ALL ALONE IN THAT UNAGI RESTAURANT?
I HAVE NO ONE TO TURN TO.
SO AT LEAST ...
IT'S BEEN BOTHERING ME ALL DAY.
AT LEAST LET ME SOLVE THAT MYSTERY.
?
WHAT WAS I DOING?

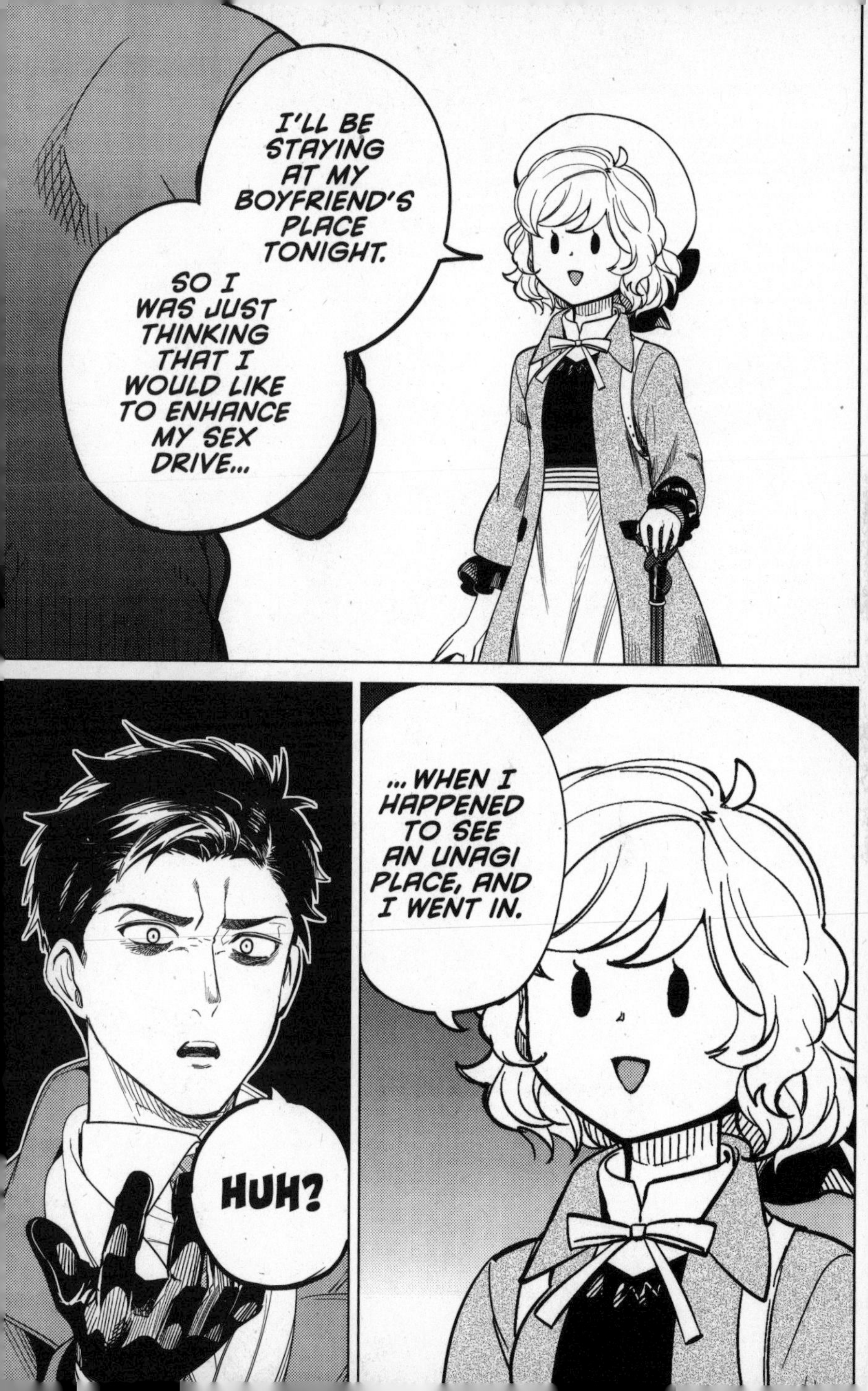
I'LL BE STAYING AT MY BOYFRIEND'S PLACE TONIGHT.
SO I WAS JUST THINKING THAT I WOULD LIKE TO ENHANCE MY SEX DRIVE...
...WHEN I HAPPENED TO SEE AN UNAGI PLACE, AND I WENT IN.
HUH?

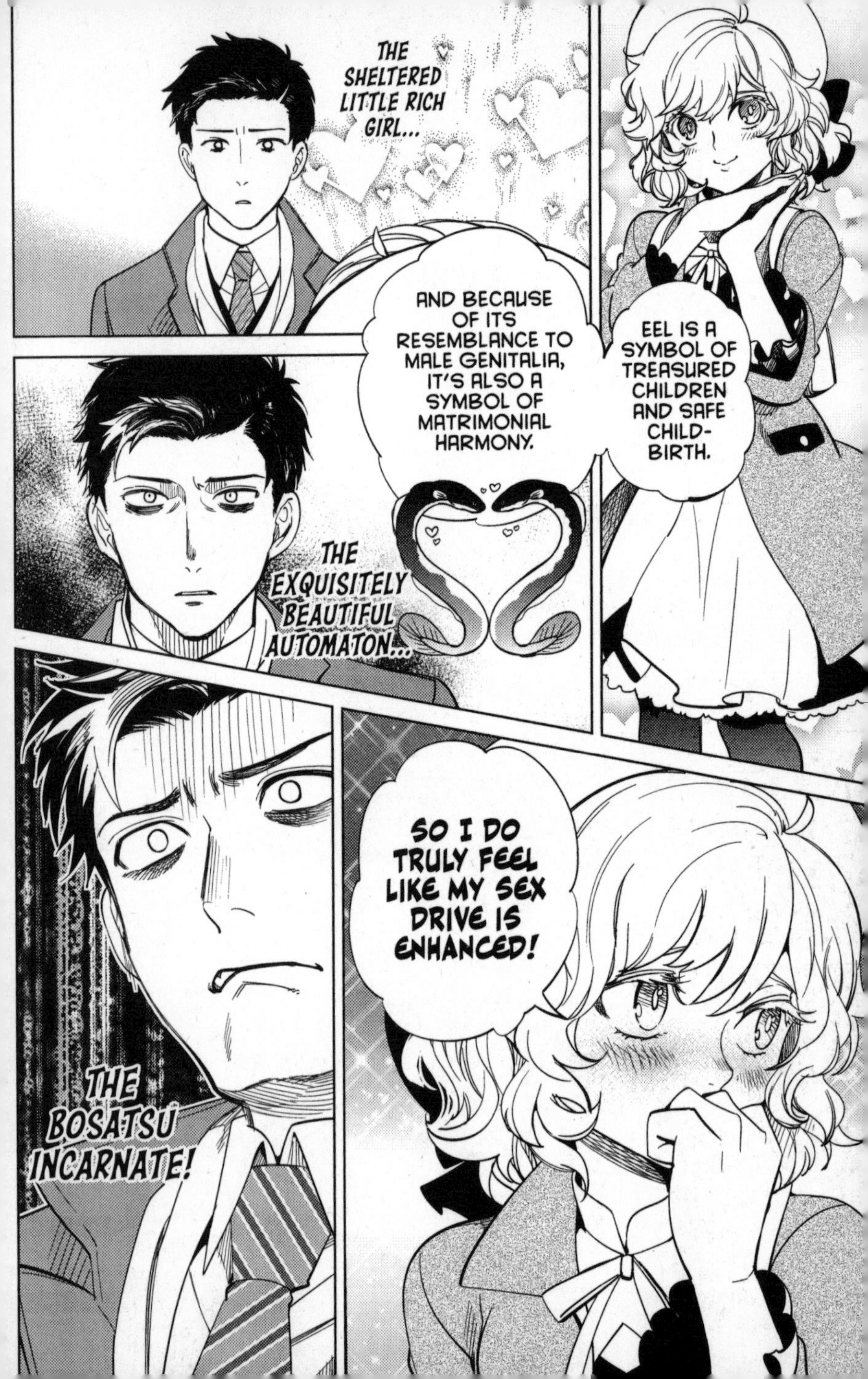
EEL IS A SYMBOL OF TREASURED CHILDREN AND SAFE CHILD-BIRTH.
AND BECAUSE OF ITS RESEMBLANCE TO MALE GENITALIA, IT'S ALSO A SYMBOL OF MATRIMONIAL HARMONY.
THE SHELTERED LITTLE RICH GIRL...
THE EXQUISITELY BEAUTIFUL AUTOMATON...
SO I DO TRULY FEEL LIKE MY SEX DRIVE IS ENHANCED!
THE BOSATSU INCARNATE!

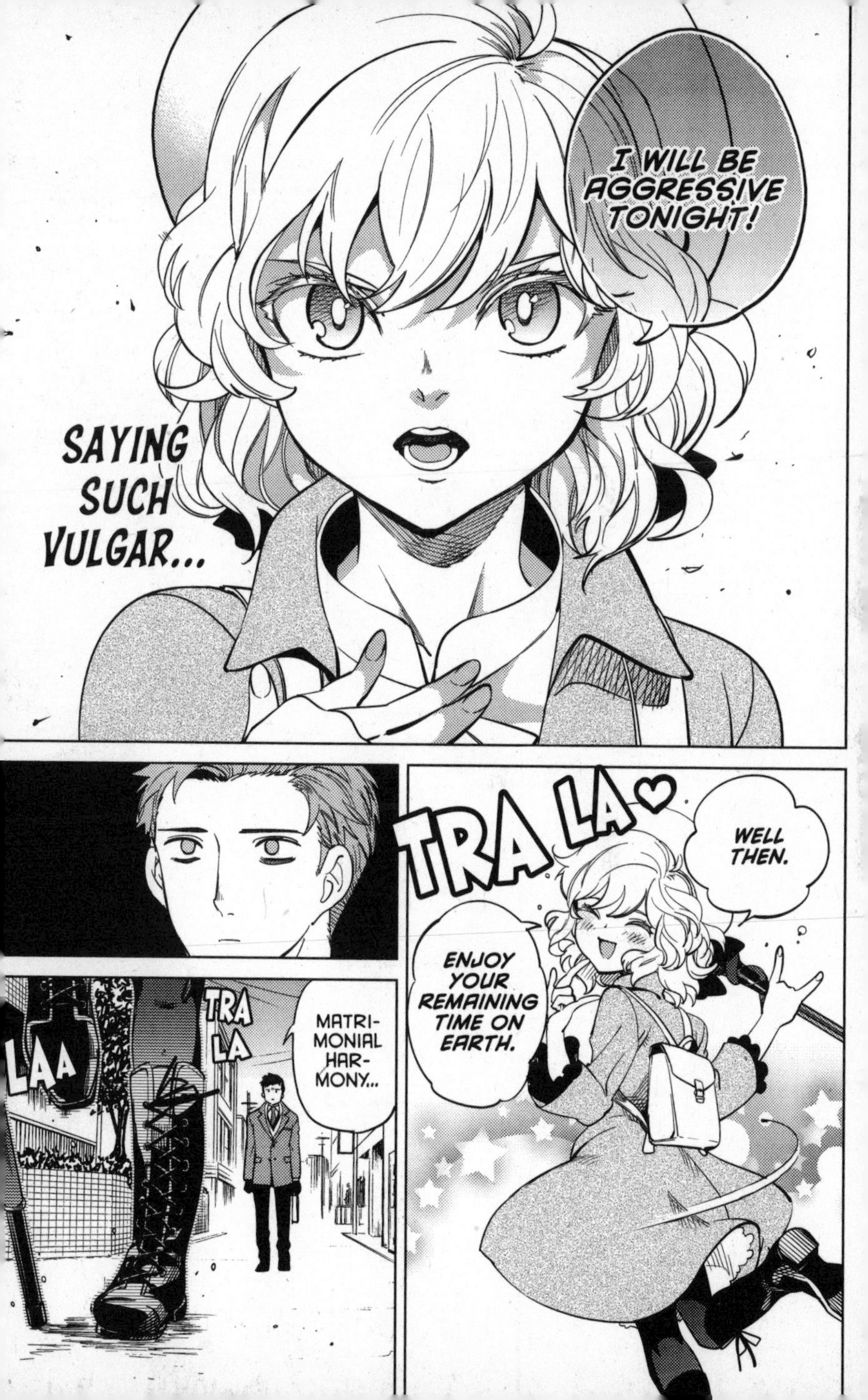
I WILL BE AGGRESSIVE TONIGHT!
SAYING SUCH VULGAR...
TRA LA♥
WELL THEN.
ENJOY YOUR REMAINING TIME ON EARTH.
TRA LA
MATRI-MONIAL HAR-MONY...
LAA

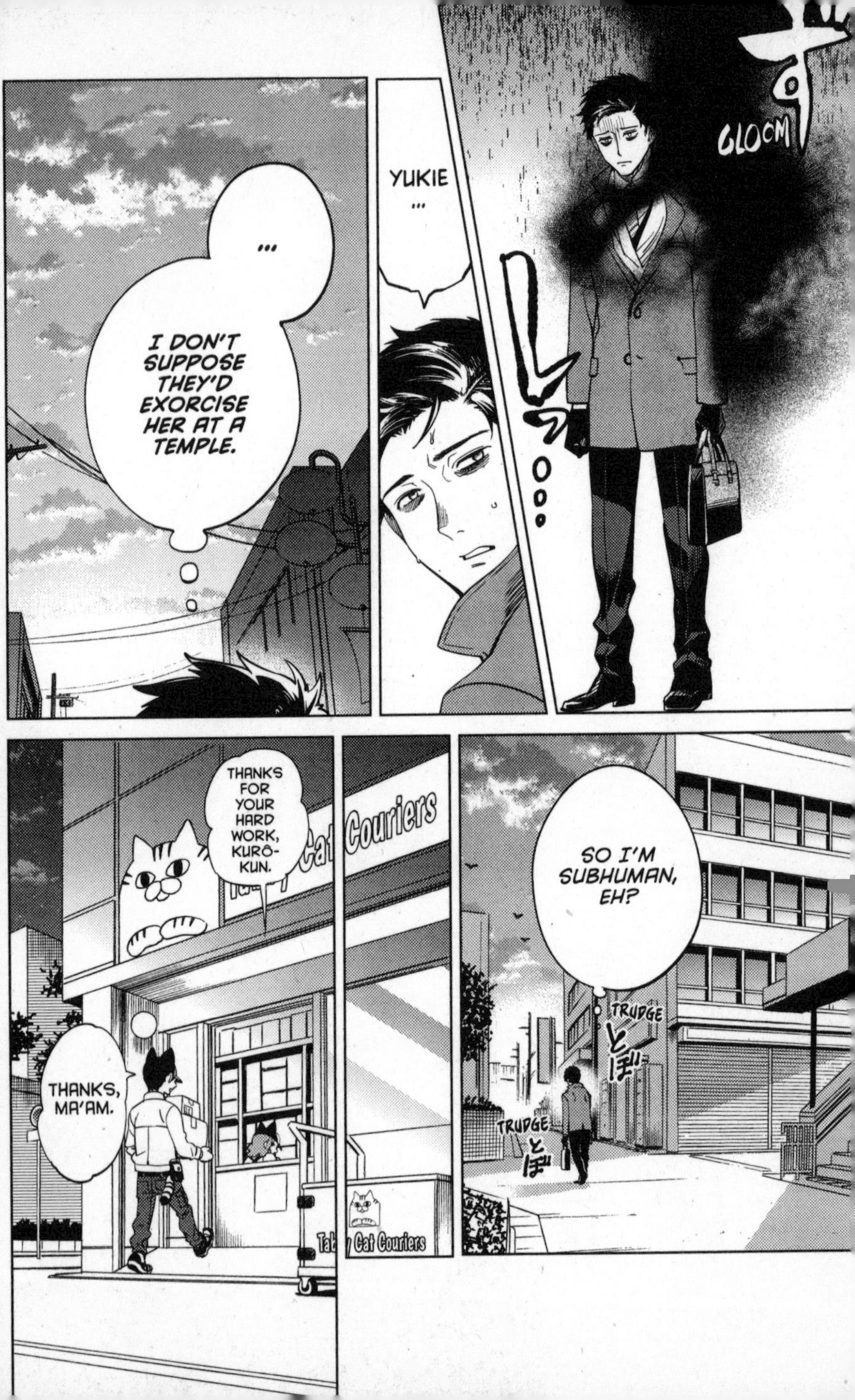
GLOOM
YUKIE ...
...
I DON'T SUPPOSE THEY'D EXORCISE HER AT A TEMPLE.
SO I'M SUBHUMAN, EH?
TRUDGE
とぼ
TRUDGE
とぼ
Cat Couriers
THANKS FOR YOUR HARD WORK, KURÔ-KUN.
THANKS, MA'AM.

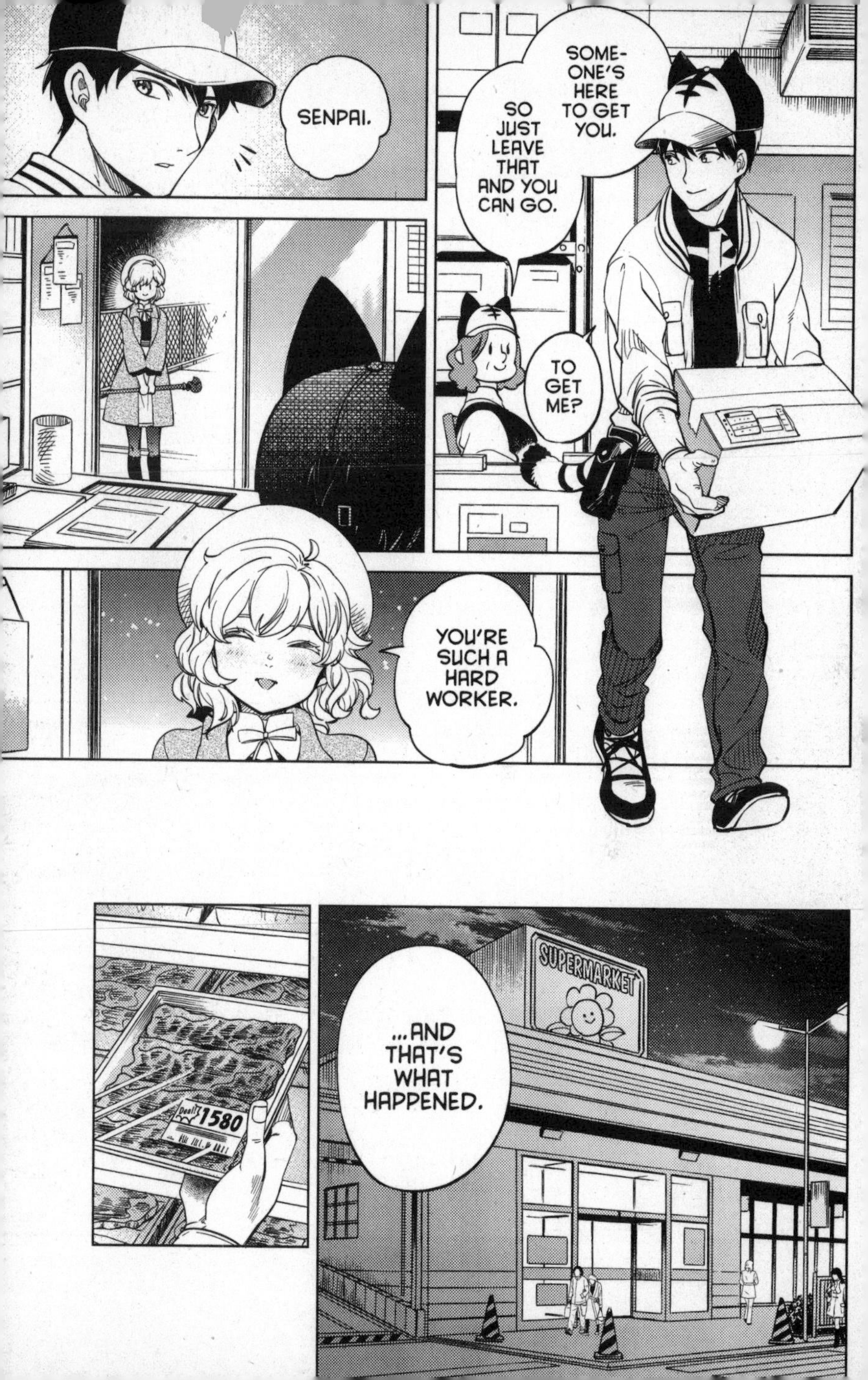
SOME-ONE'S HERE TO GET YOU.
SO JUST LEAVE THAT AND YOU CAN GO.
TO GET ME?
SENPAI.
YOU'RE SUCH A HARD WORKER.
SUPERMARKET
...AND THAT'S WHAT HAPPENED.
1580

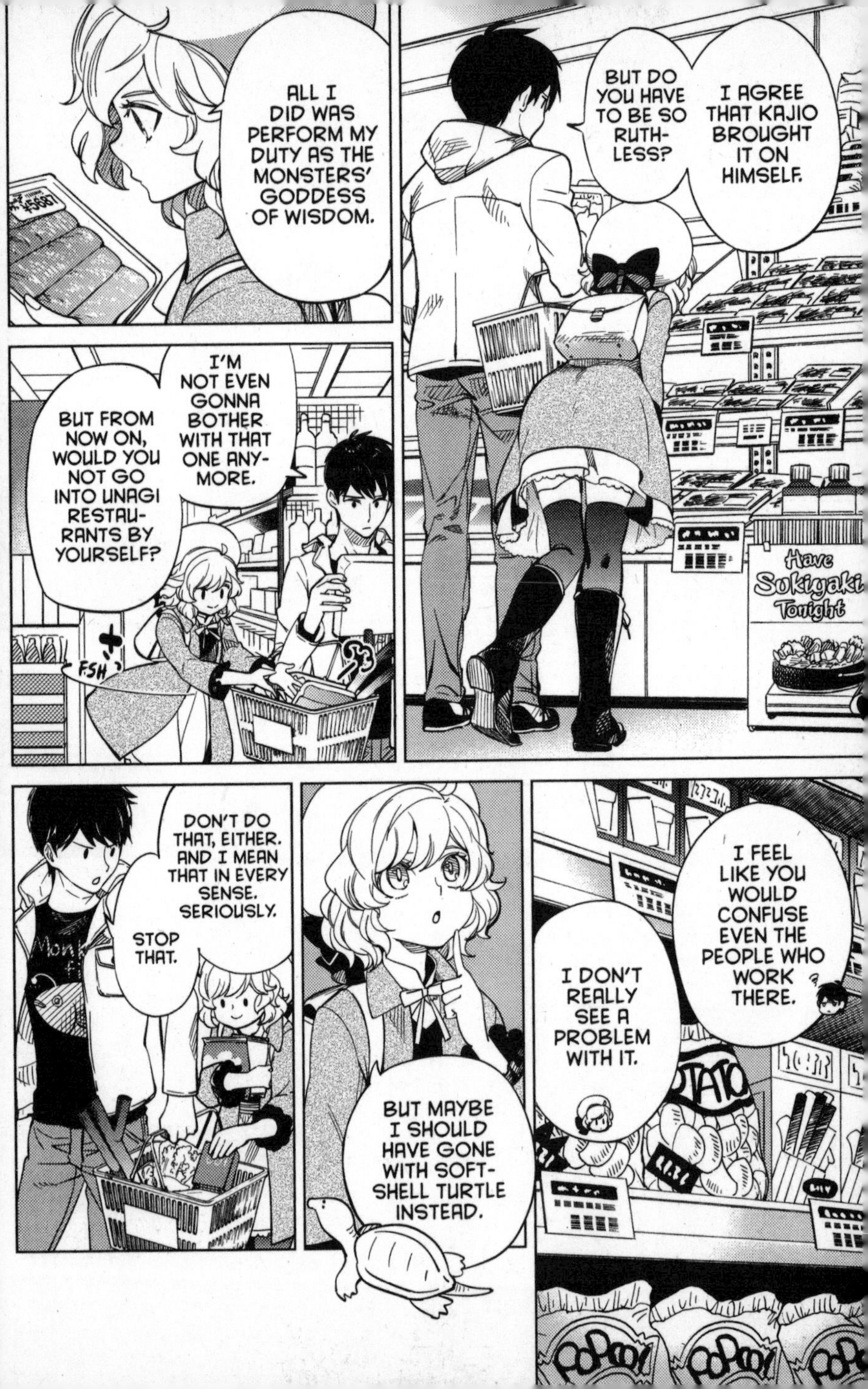
I AGREE THAT KAJIO BROUGHT IT ON HIMSELF.
BUT DO YOU HAVE TO BE SO RUTHLESS?
Have Sukiyaki Tonight
ALL I DID WAS PERFORM MY DUTY AS THE MONSTERS' GODDESS OF WISDOM.
I'M NOT EVEN GONNA BOTHER WITH THAT ONE ANYMORE.
BUT FROM NOW ON, WOULD YOU NOT GO INTO UNAGI RESTAURANTS BY YOURSELF?
FSH
I FEEL LIKE YOU WOULD CONFUSE EVEN THE PEOPLE WHO WORK THERE.
I DON'T REALLY SEE A PROBLEM WITH IT.
BUT MAYBE I SHOULD HAVE GONE WITH SOFT-SHELL TURTLE INSTEAD.
DON'T DO THAT, EITHER. AND I MEAN THAT IN EVERY SENSE. SERIOUSLY.
STOP THAT.

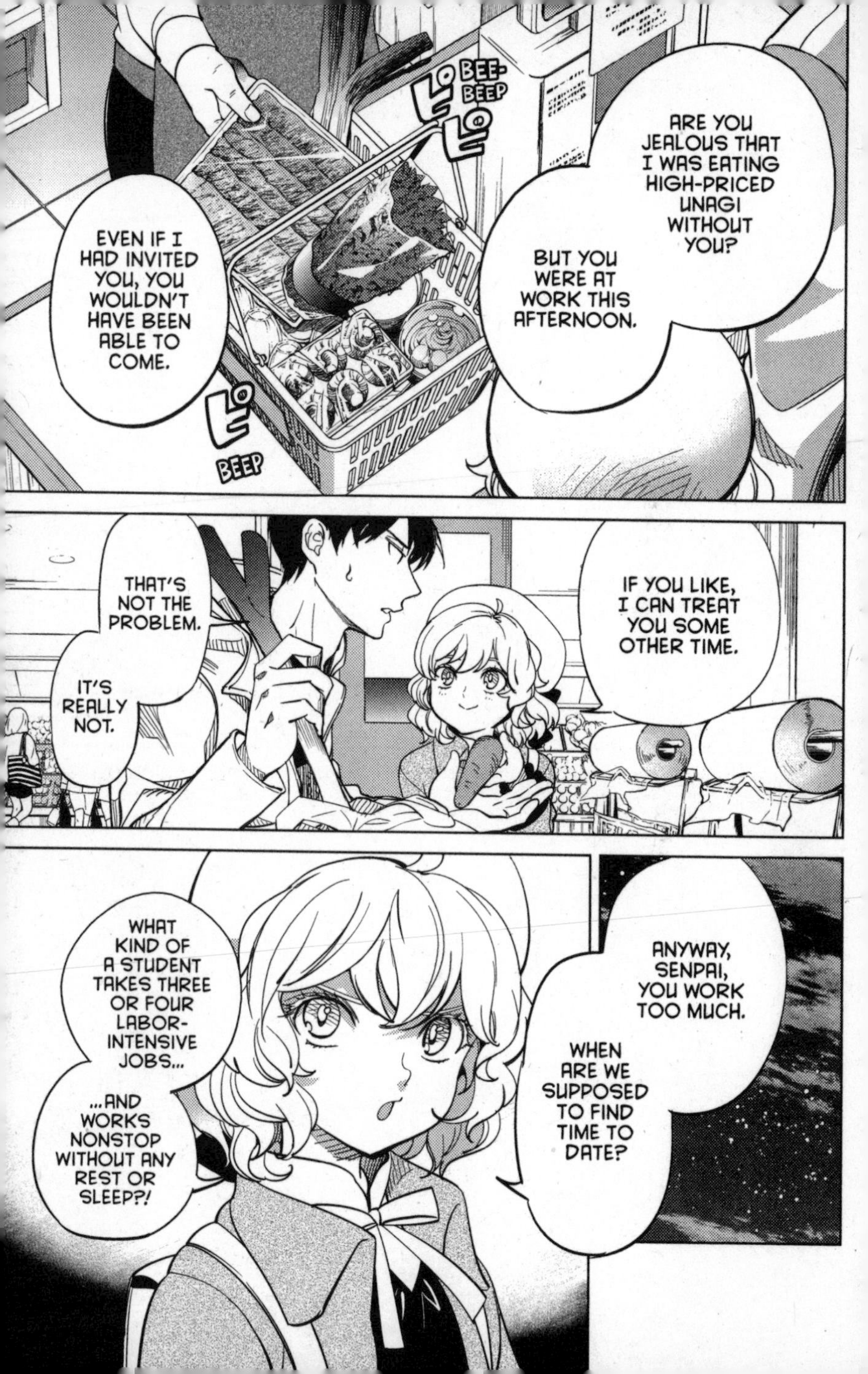
ARE YOU JEALOUS THAT I WAS EATING HIGH-PRICED UNAGI WITHOUT YOU?
BUT YOU WERE AT WORK THIS AFTERNOON.
BEE-BEEP
EVEN IF I HAD INVITED YOU, YOU WOULDN'T HAVE BEEN ABLE TO COME.
BEEP
IF YOU LIKE, I CAN TREAT YOU SOME OTHER TIME.
THAT'S NOT THE PROBLEM.
IT'S REALLY NOT.
ANYWAY, SENPAI, YOU WORK TOO MUCH.
WHEN ARE WE SUPPOSED TO FIND TIME TO DATE?
WHAT KIND OF A STUDENT TAKES THREE OR FOUR LABOR-INTENSIVE JOBS...
...AND WORKS NONSTOP WITHOUT ANY REST OR SLEEP?!

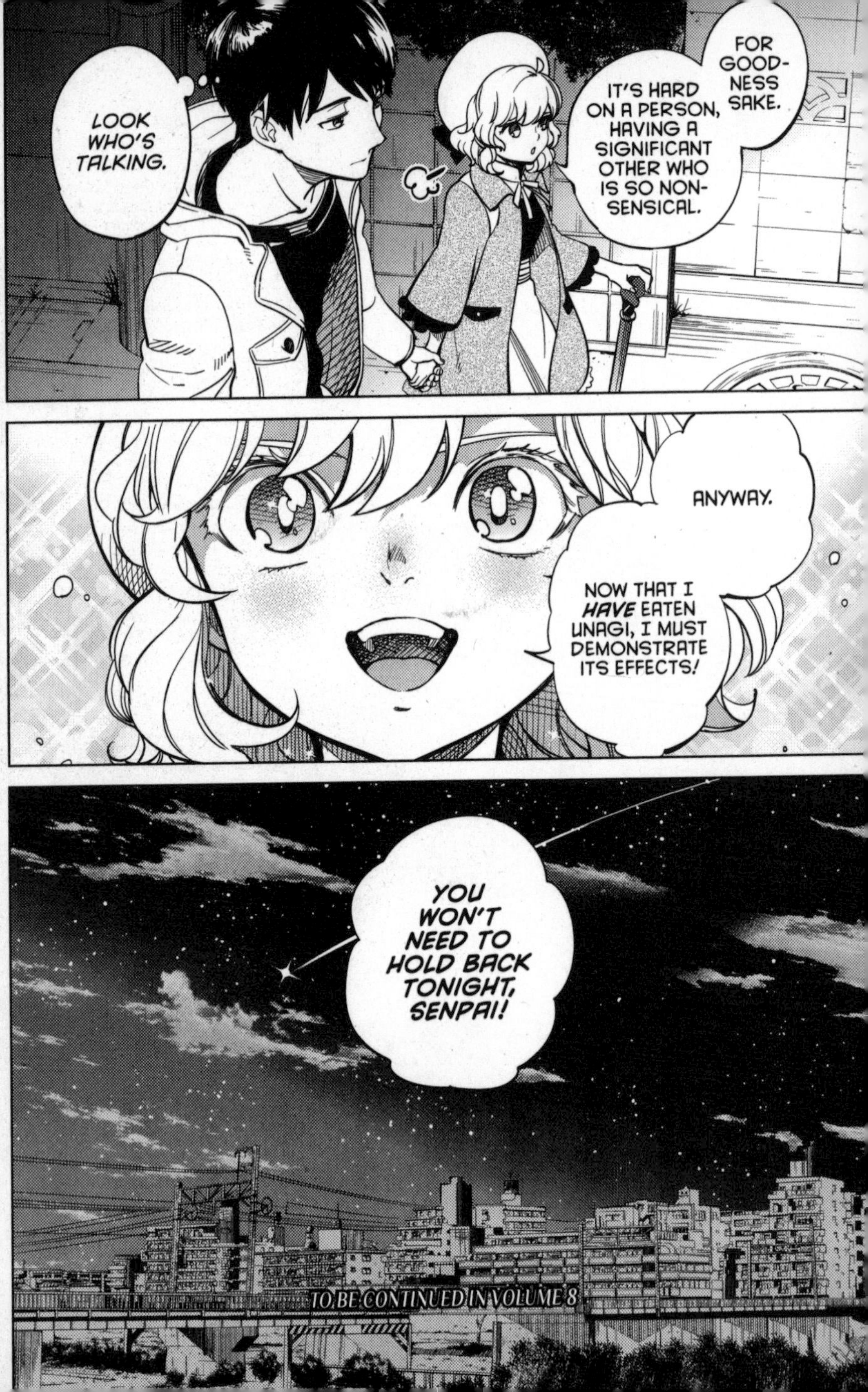
FOR GOODNESS SAKE.
IT'S HARD ON A PERSON, HAVING A SIGNIFICANT OTHER WHO IS SO NON-SENSICAL.
LOOK WHO'S TALKING.
ANYWAY.
NOW THAT I *HAVE* EATEN UNAGI, I MUST DEMONSTRATE ITS EFFECTS!
YOU WON'T NEED TO HOLD BACK TONIGHT, SENPAI!
TO BE CONTINUED IN VOLUME 8

KURÔ-SENPAI
MOURNS HIS
INABILITY TO
PARTICIPATE
IN CLINICAL
TRIALS AS
A VIABLE
SOURCE OF
INCOME,
WHILE
KOTOKO
IWANAGA
FEELS THE
EFFECTS OF
THE UNAGI.

Immortality
would
skew the
results...

Something Like a Real Afterword from the Author

I am the author, Kyo Shirodaira, and this is volume seven. The long arc has ended, and this volume is a new start.

And with this new beginning, I wrote each short story in this volume on the premise that it would then become a manga. They all have their differences; one has already been released as prose, one is going to be released in prose, and one won't be. Even so, they are all the same in that they were originally written as prose.

Some of you may be thinking that, if I know it's going to be made into a manga, I should just write it as a manga script to begin with, and it's true that there are several aspects to that method which would make things easier for me. When I write as a manga writer, that's usually what I do.

But *this* manga started out as the comic adaptation of a novel. And in that case, I felt that continuing in the same way would maintain the consistency in the series' mood and characters. It would more clearly reflect Katase-sensei's interpretation, concept, and composition, and it would give it more of the charm that can only be found in manga.

And in fact, the characters' personalities and actions do leave a different impression when compared to the novel. When the story was made into a manga, there were a few places where the scenes were abbreviated or embellished, or where the story composition was changed. Those changes affect the mood and implications of what happened. It's really quite fascinating.

From the perspective of the original author, there are some times where I think, "You took that out?" or,

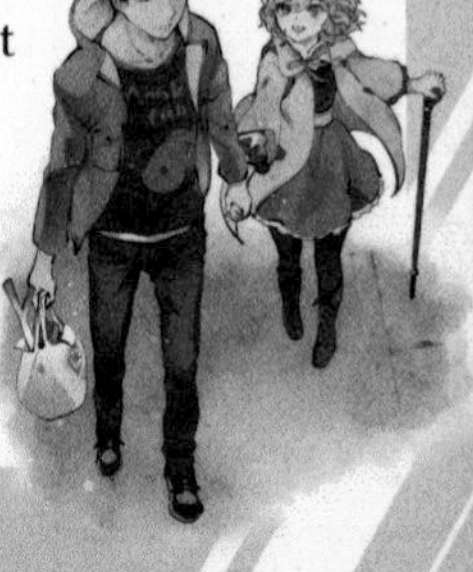

"That's not exactly what the original was going for," but on the other hand, there are other times when I feel, "Should I have expressed it that way in the novel, too?" or, "That may have actually been a more appropriate direction," or, "I could never have made it this entertaining."

I hope those differences will be one of this series' assets, which is why I make it a point to say as little as possible when it comes to the manga adaptation. But I am a little restless about the idea that the readers will tend to prefer the manga.

On the other hand, when I write the novel, part of me does pay a certain amount of attention to the fact that it will be made into a manga.

As I wrote the story about the café, I thought about how it's made up of several vignettes that might be vague in prose but will line up effectively in manga, and the story about the giant snake came from the idea that the contrast between Iwanaga and a giant snake would make a great visual (if it wasn't going to be a manga, I might have chosen a different monster). For the unagi story, I figured the concept that Iwanaga doesn't really have to do anything to make people well aware of her presence would come across better in a manga.

Also, I like to think that I'm writing each story based on mystery ideas and formulas, but I suspect some people will still think that they just don't qualify as mysteries. But there is such a thing as "occult detective fiction" in the world, so I hope you will put it into that category.

This volume was fairly simple, without a lot of action, but the next volume should be a little more spectacular.

So I hope you will read the next volume.

Kyo Shirodaira

"AFTER CHAPTER 15"

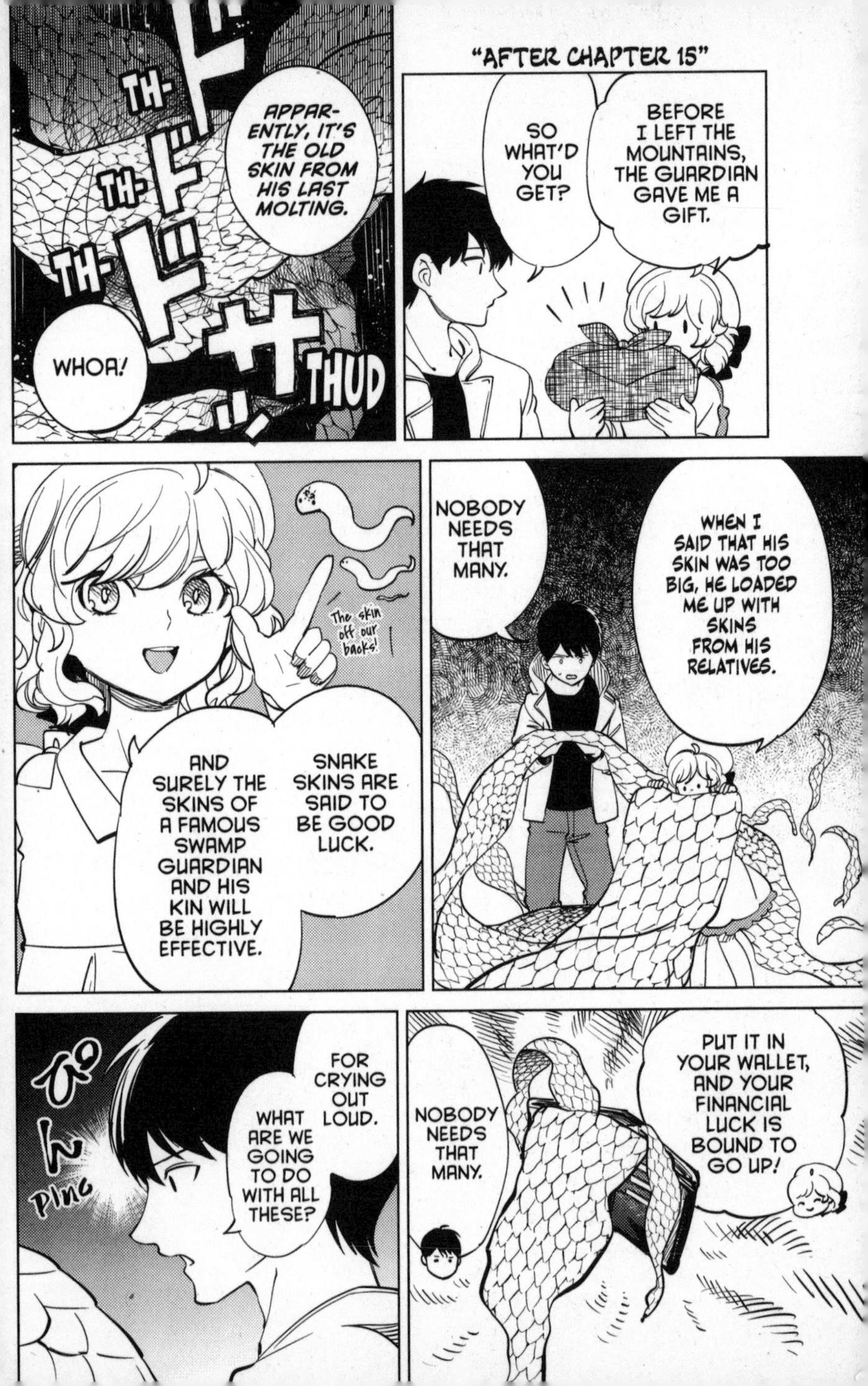
BEFORE I LEFT THE MOUNTAINS, THE GUARDIAN GAVE ME A GIFT.
SO WHAT'D YOU GET?
APPARENTLY, IT'S THE OLD SKIN FROM HIS LAST MOLTING.
TH-
TH-
TH-
THUD
WHOA!
WHEN I SAID THAT HIS SKIN WAS TOO BIG, HE LOADED ME UP WITH SKINS FROM HIS RELATIVES.
NOBODY NEEDS THAT MANY.
SNAKE SKINS ARE SAID TO BE GOOD LUCK.
AND SURELY THE SKINS OF A FAMOUS SWAMP GUARDIAN AND HIS KIN WILL BE HIGHLY EFFECTIVE.
The skin off our backs!
PUT IT IN YOUR WALLET, AND YOUR FINANCIAL LUCK IS BOUND TO GO UP!
NOBODY NEEDS THAT MANY.
FOR CRYING OUT LOUD.
WHAT ARE WE GOING TO DO WITH ALL THESE?
PING

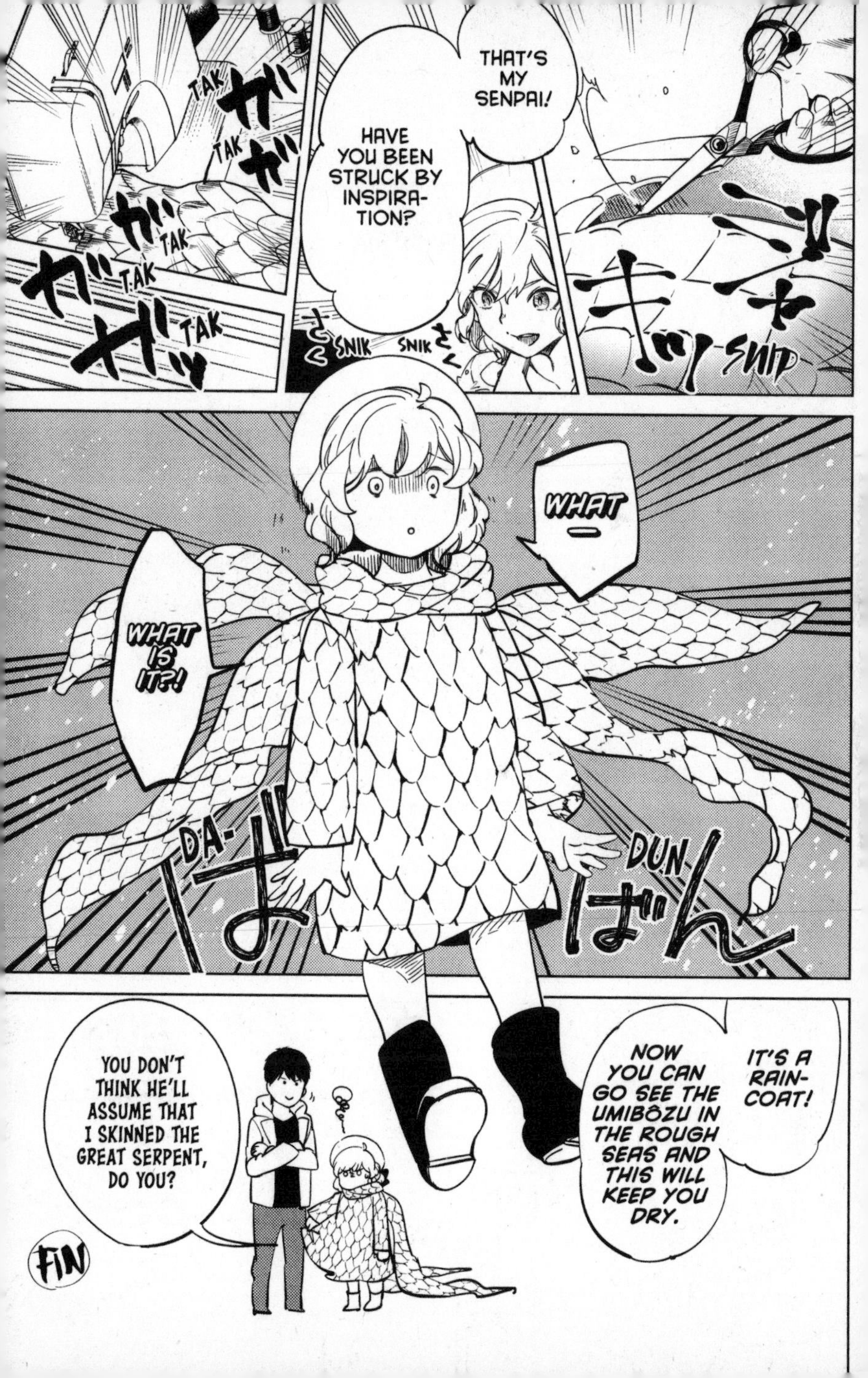
SNIP
THAT'S MY SENPAI!
HAVE YOU BEEN STRUCK BY INSPIRATION?
SNIK SNIK
TAK TAK TAK TAK TAK
WHAT—
WHAT IS IT?!
DA-DUN
IT'S A RAINCOAT!
NOW YOU CAN GO SEE THE UMIBÔZU IN THE ROUGH SEAS AND THIS WILL KEEP YOU DRY.
YOU DON'T THINK HE'LL ASSUME THAT I SKINNED THE GREAT SERPENT, DO YOU?
FIN

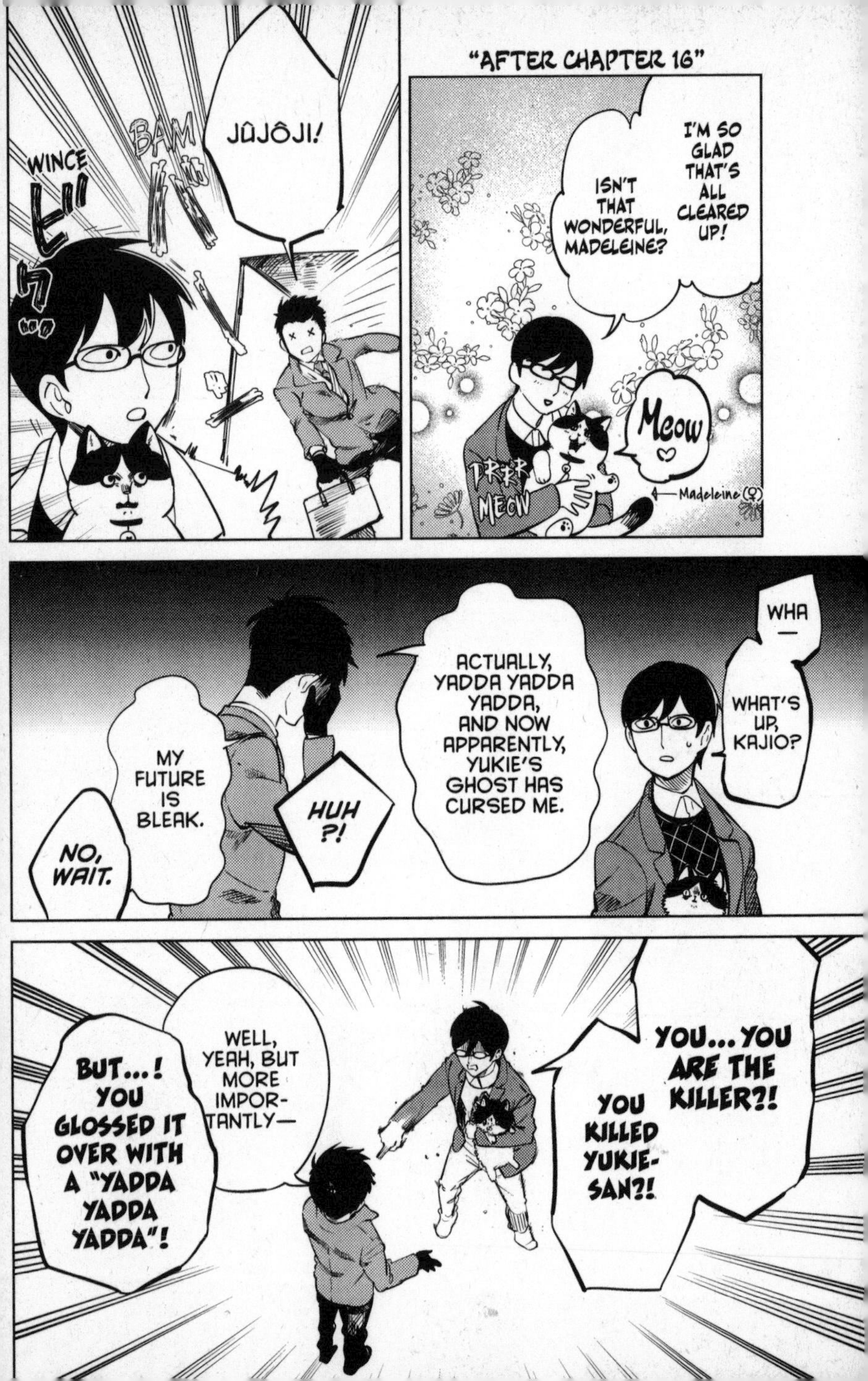
"AFTER CHAPTER 16"
I'M SO GLAD THAT'S ALL CLEARED UP!
ISN'T THAT WONDERFUL, MADELEINE?
Meow ♡
DRRR MEOW
Madeleine (♀)
JÛJÔJI!
BAM
WINCE
WHA— WHAT'S UP, KAJIO?
ACTUALLY, YADDA YADDA YADDA, AND NOW APPARENTLY, YUKIE'S GHOST HAS CURSED ME.
HUH?!
MY FUTURE IS BLEAK.
NO, WAIT.
YOU... YOU ARE THE KILLER?!
YOU KILLED YUKIE-SAN?!
WELL, YEAH, BUT MORE IMPORTANTLY—
BUT...! YOU GLOSSED IT OVER WITH A "YADDA YADDA YADDA"!

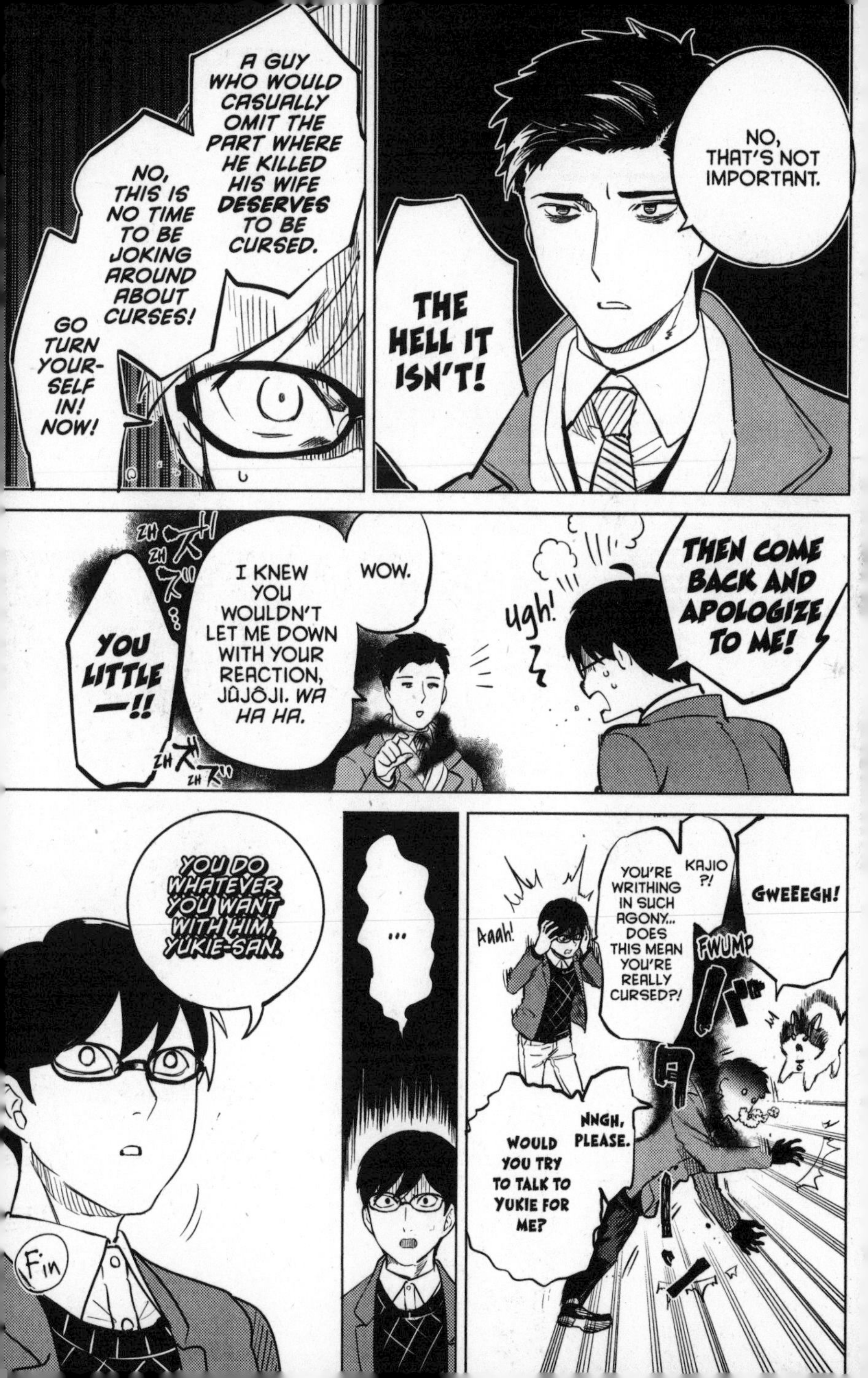
NO, THAT'S NOT IMPORTANT.
THE HELL IT ISN'T!
A GUY WHO WOULD CASUALLY OMIT THE PART WHERE HE KILLED HIS WIFE DESERVES TO BE CURSED.
NO, THIS IS NO TIME TO BE JOKING AROUND ABOUT CURSES!
GO TURN YOURSELF IN! NOW!
THEN COME BACK AND APOLOGIZE TO ME!
ugh!
WOW.
I KNEW YOU WOULDN'T LET ME DOWN WITH YOUR REACTION, JÛJÔJI. WA HA HA.
ZH ZH
YOU LITTLE—!!
ZH ZH
GWEEEGH!
KAJIO?!
YOU'RE WRITHING IN SUCH AGONY... DOES THIS MEAN YOU'RE REALLY CURSED?!
Aaah!
FWUMP
NNGH, PLEASE.
WOULD YOU TRY TO TALK TO YUKIE FOR ME?
...
YOU DO WHATEVER YOU WANT WITH HIM, YUKIE-SAN.
Fin

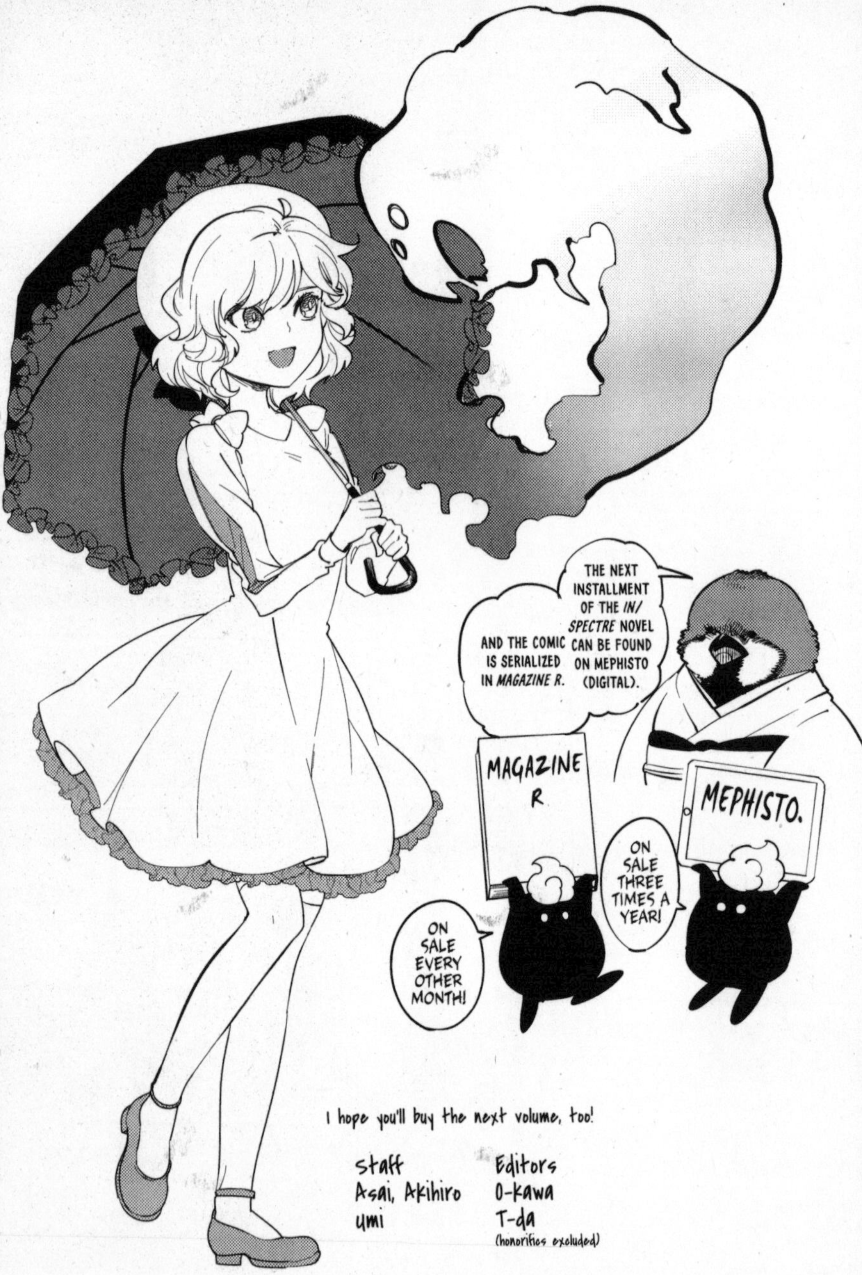
THE NEXT INSTALLMENT OF THE *IN/SPECTRE* NOVEL CAN BE FOUND ON MEPHISTO (DIGITAL).
AND THE COMIC IS SERIALIZED IN *MAGAZINE R*.
MEPHISTO.
ON SALE THREE TIMES A YEAR!
MAGAZINE R
ON SALE EVERY OTHER MONTH!

I hope you'll buy the next volume, too!

Staff
Asai, Akihiro
umi

Editors
O-kawa
T-da
(honorifics excluded)

TRANSLATION NOTES

The House of Hidden Treasures, page 10

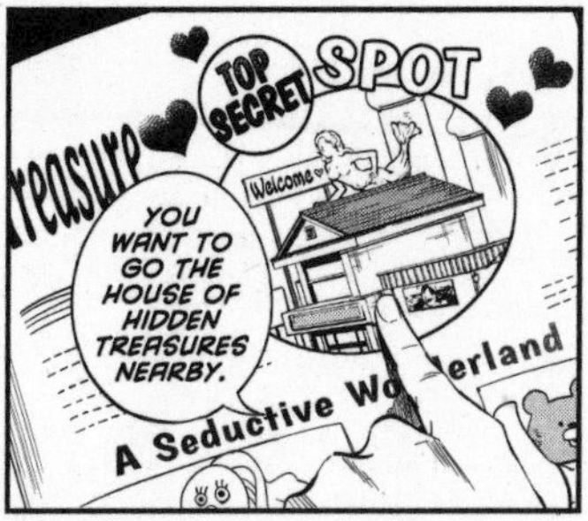
TOP SECRET
SPOT
Treasure
Welcome
YOU WANT TO GO THE HOUSE OF HIDDEN TREASURES NEARBY.
A Seductive Wo
erland

One thing Atami is famous for is its *Hihôkan*, or House of Hidden Treasures, which is the Japanese term for a sex museum. As Kotoko suggests, the idea for such museums may have been inspired by *Eisei Hakurankai*, or Health Expos, that came to Japan during the Meiji Era. These expos had displays and wax recreations of such health-related objects as the heart of someone who drank to much beer, a ruptured womb, and a small intestine with cholera. These exhibits tended toward the erotic as well as the grotesque.

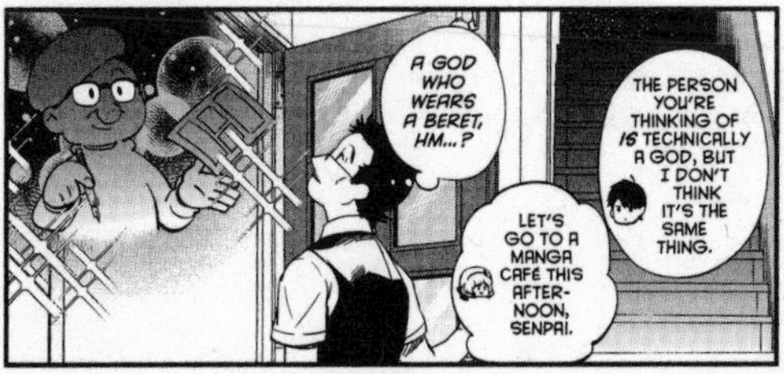
THE PERSON YOU'RE THINKING OF *IS* TECHNICALLY A GOD, BUT I DON'T THINK IT'S THE SAME THING.
A GOD WHO WEARS A BERET, HM...?
LET'S GO TO A MANGA CAFÉ THIS AFTERNOON, SENPAI.

The person you're thinking of, page 13

The person Kotoko is thinking of is Osamu Tezuka, the creator of *Astro Boy* and many other works that made manga what it is today. Because of his pioneering efforts in the field of manga, he is known as "the father of manga," as well as, "the god of manga." As you might imagine, he was in the habit of wearing a beret.

Yanari, page 26

Literally meaning "house cry," *yanari* is the name of the yôkai credited with causing inexplicable shaking of household objects and furniture. They appear in the form of miniature oni and love making noise.

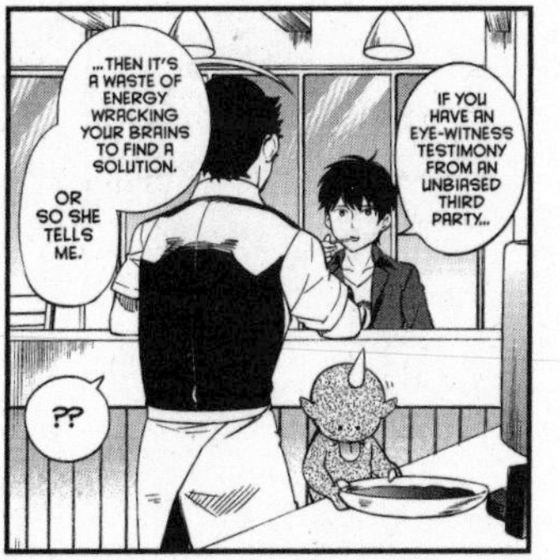
IF YOU HAVE AN EYE-WITNESS TESTIMONY FROM AN UNBIASED THIRD PARTY...
...THEN IT'S A WASTE OF ENERGY WRACKING YOUR BRAINS TO FIND A SOLUTION.
OR SO SHE TELLS ME.
??

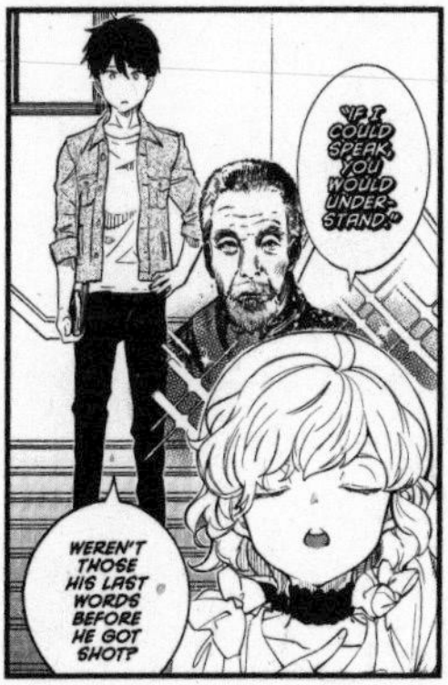
"IF I COULD SPEAK, YOU WOULD UNDER-STAND."
WEREN'T THOSE HIS LAST WORDS BEFORE HE GOT SHOT?

Great men from history, page 35

The reader will no doubt recognize the pictures of Mahatma Ghandi and Martin Luther King, Jr., but may be less familiar with Tsuyoshi Inukai. Inukai was a Japanese Prime Minister who was assassinated by the military for trying to limit their power before World War II.

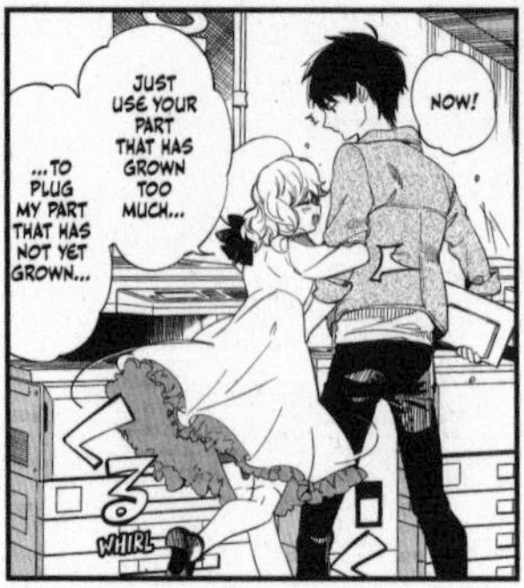
NOW!
JUST USE YOUR PART THAT HAS GROWN TOO MUCH...
...TO PLUG MY PART THAT HAS NOT YET GROWN...
WHIRL

Grown parts, page 37

This is a reference to the Japanese creation myth, where Izanagi and Izanami, the first man and woman, met and observed the differences in their bodies. They then suggested that they join together to procreate.

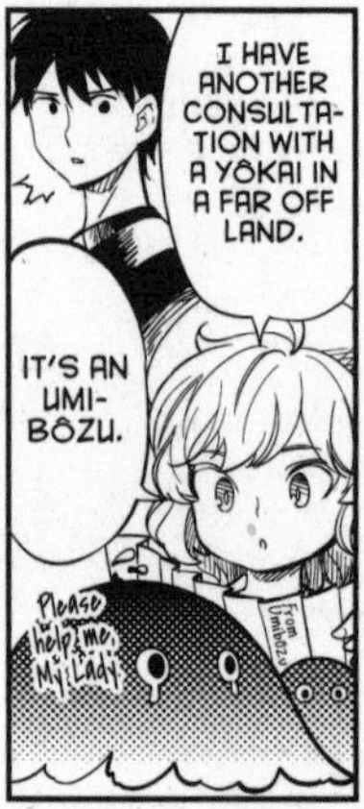
I HAVE ANOTHER CONSULTATION WITH A YÔKAI IN A FAR OFF LAND.
IT'S AN UMIBÔZU.
From Umibôzu
Please help me, My Lady

Umibôzu, page 123

Literally meaning "ocean priest," an *umibôzu* is a yôkai that lives by the sea. It has a round head, like the shaved head of a priest, and can be very dangerous to seafarers, as it is known for capsizing ships.

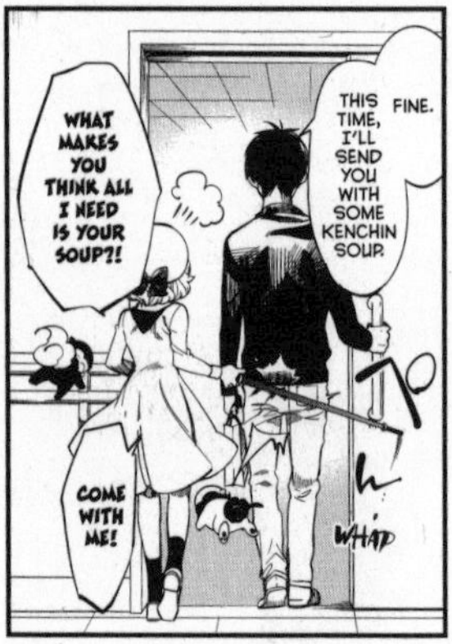
FINE.
THIS TIME, I'LL SEND YOU WITH SOME KENCHIN SOUP.
WHAT MAKES YOU THINK ALL I NEED IS YOUR SOUP?!
COME WITH ME!
WHAP

Kenchin soup, page 123

This is a type of vegetable soup using root vegetables and tofu.

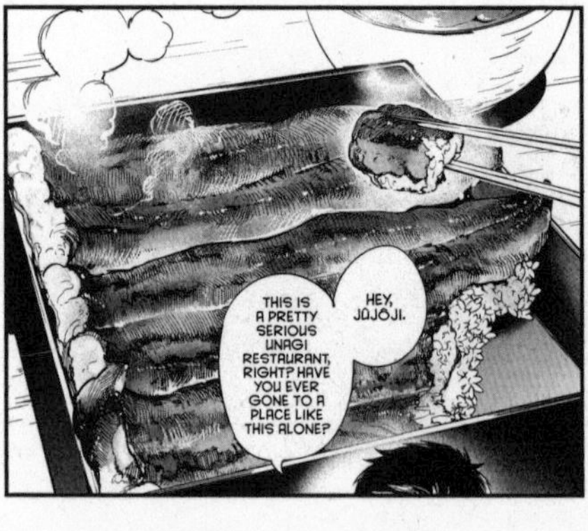
HEY, JÛJÔJI.
THIS IS A PRETTY SERIOUS UNAGI RESTAURANT, RIGHT? HAVE YOU EVER GONE TO A PLACE LIKE THIS ALONE?

Unagi, page 126

Unagi is a type of freshwater eel found in Japan, which is used in Japanese dishes. The dish shown here is *unajû*, grilled eel on top of rice, served in a lacquer box.